UNLOCKING THE IRON CAGE

UNLOCKING
THE IRON CAGE

THE MEN'S MOVEMENT, GENDER POLITICS, AND AMERICAN CULTURE

MICHAEL SCHWALBE

NEW YORK   OXFORD

OXFORD UNIVERSITY PRESS

1996

Oxford University Press

Oxford   New York
Athens   Aukland   Bangkok   Bombay
Calcutta   Cape Town   Dar es Salaam   Delhi
Florence   Hong Kong   Istanbul   Karachi
Kuala Lumpur   Madras   Madrid   Melbourne
Mexico City   Nairobi   Paris   Singapore
Taipei   Tokyo   Toronto

and associated companies in
Berlin   Ibadan

Copyright © 1996 by Michael Schwalbe

Published by Oxford University Press, Inc.,
198 Madison Avenue, New York, New York 10016

Oxford is a registered trademark of Oxford University Press

Library of Congress Cataloging-in-Publication Data
Schwalbe, Michael L., 1956–
Unlocking the iron cage : the men's movement, gender politics, and
American culture / Michael Schwalbe.
p. cm.   Includes bibliographical references and index.
ISBN 0-19-509229-5
1. Men's movement—United States.   2. Masculinity (Psychology)—
United States.   3. Sex role—Political aspects—United States.
I. Title.
HQ1090.3.S39   1996
305.32'0973–dc20   95-15348

1 3 5 7 9 8 6 4 2

Printed in the United States of America
on acid-free paper

ACKNOWLEDGMENTS

We talked about relationships with women, friendship, competition, fathers, work. Around 2:00 A.M. Cliff and I decided we ought to write a book about men. The need seemed urgent. Men were floundering in turbulent cultural waters, beweighted with guilt. If we could offer a guide to responsible manhood without guilt, we'd have a bestseller, we thought. Our ambitions outran us. After writing a chapter about the "current crisis of masculinity," we got stuck. There was too much we still had to figure out for ourselves before we could say anything useful to anyone else.

That was six years ago. Since then, some things have fallen into place. For me, this has happened in large part through researching and writing this book. It has been a liminal journey, one that is not over yet.

I've had a lot of help in getting this far. Much of it came from the men I studied, the men involved in mythopoetic activity. These men talked to me about their lives and about doing "men's work." They also accepted me as a participant and gave me the benefit of their support at gatherings. Without their sharing and acceptance, I couldn't have written this book. I know that some of them won't like what I've said here but, to put matters in terms they will recognize, my warrior and magician energies compelled me to say it.

More help than I could ever acknowledge has come to me via the work of other scholars who've written about gender, and about men and masculinity in particular. Their ideas are in my head and in these pages. Their names and works are in my bibliography. I offer this book and whatever insights it might contain as partial payment of my intellectual debt to this community.

I owe special thanks to friends and colleagues who read chapters, talked with me about my analysis as it developed, shared with me their own works in progress, or lent support in some other way. These people include Mike Messner, Barbara Risman, Cliff Staples, David L. Morgan, Gordon Murray, Viktor Gecas, Kevin Ryan, Scott Marlow, Scott Coltrane, Dwight Fee, Wayne Liebman, and Michael Kimmel. This list is incomplete; I know I am forgetting some of the people with whom I had helpful conversations about this project over the past few years. My apologies, then, to anyone I've left out.

Several years ago the research committee of North Carolina State University's College of Social Sciences and Humanities gave me a summer stipend to support work on this project. To you wise and anonymous folks, thanks. And thanks to the administrators of my department and college who also made the sound decision to grant me a semester's leave to write. It helped a great deal.

The best help I received was from my life partner, Sherryl Kleinman. She taught me how to do better interviews and fieldwork, and what a qualitative analysis should be. Our talks about gender, men, relationships, and spirituality were crucial to making whatever sense I have made here. My writing was also much improved by her generous and patient comments on my drafts. I feel blessed to have had the gifts of her intellect and spirit as I made the journey of this book. I could not have made it without her, and our love.

CONTENTS

UNLOCKING THE IRON CAGE

CHAPTER I

AN UNUSUAL MOVEMENT
OF ORDINARY MEN

Why do these middle-class white men gather at rustic camps to beat drums, dance wildly, make masks, invoke spirits, hug each other, hold sweat lodge rituals, tell poems, laugh and cry together, and listen to old myths and fairy tales? Because, they will say:

It feels great to be in the midst of all that male energy.

Just because I'm a man doesn't mean I'm secure in my masculinity. I need men's work to know who I am as a man.

The drumming does something for me that's hard to explain. It gets me out of myself and connects me to other men on a deep, nonrational level.

My father was absent when I was growing up, so I never learned what it meant to be a man. My mother couldn't teach me that. That's part of what I'm learning now, or maybe just figuring out, with the help of other men.

The fairy tales and myths help me to understand my life as a man. They help me see how the problems I'm facing aren't mine alone but are ones that men have faced for ages.

This is a way for me to discover things inside me that I never knew were there or that I was afraid to face. Men's work is teaching me to accept those things and find gold in them.

I knew that men had done bad things—started wars, polluted the environment, discriminated against women and all that. But I was tired of hearing from feminists that all men were rotten to the core. Men's work has helped me see that's not true. There's a lot of good in men.

For me this is like church. I had lost a connection to spirituality for many years. And now I'm finding it again by doing ritual work with other men.

I felt totally isolated from other men. I hadn't had any close male friends since college days. Through men's work I've met guys who want to talk about real stuff, not just sports or business. At gatherings I can drop the pretense that "everything's okay" and say what I really feel.

Every time I got together with men there was an undercurrent of competition. I got tired of it. This was why for years I didn't trust men and most of my friends were women. Now I'm seeing that we can create safe places where men can give each other support and not be judgmental or competitive. That's why I keep coming back. For me this is like having the kind of supportive family I never had.

Such are the accounts given by men involved in the so-called mythopoetic men's movement inspired by the poet Robert Bly, author of the 1991 bestseller *Iron John: A Book About Men*. Because of their curious activities and colorful, outspoken leader, this group of men drew heavy media attention in the early 1990s and—despite the existence of a much older, profeminist men's movement—became popularly known as *the* men's movement.

Much of what has been said about the men drawn to this movement has been based on contentious readings of Bly's *Iron John* and other movement texts without benefit of a close, sustained look at the men themselves. *Unlocking the Iron Cage* is the result of taking a close look at the men and their activities, from the inside, over a period of about three years. It is a book for anyone who wants to know who these "mythopoetic men" are, what they did, why they did it, and the likely consequences of it all.

Why are these guys important? Not because of their vast numbers. At the time when interest in mythopoetic activity seemed to reach its peak—about 10 years after Robert Bly held his first men's retreat at the Lama Commune in New Mexico in 1981—an oft-quoted, though unsubstantiated, estimate was that 100,000 men in the United States had participated in some kind of mythopoetic event.[1] The number of regular, dedicated participants was no doubt much smaller. But the importance of the mythopoetic movement is not a matter of its size alone.

The ideas that have come out of the mythopoetic movement—via the men who attended gatherings, via books such as Bly's *Iron John* and Moore and Gillette's *King, Warrior, Magician, Lover*, and via the media—have diffused through the culture. It's not only the mythopoetic men who believe that men suffer because they are cut off from their feelings and from the feelings of other men; that meeting work and family obligations is not enough to keep men spiritually alive; that men need a chance to play like male animals with other males; that feminist criticism of men and masculinity has caused many men to suffer a crisis of confidence; and that men need to be initiated into a secure sense of manhood. For a variety of reasons these ideas have gained currency with many more people—women and men—than have heard of Robert Bly or attended a men's gathering.[2]

Most of these ideas did not originate in the mythopoetic movement; some are ancient. Nonetheless, by reviving and injecting these ideas into the culture, the mythopoetic movement has altered the course of gender politics in the late twentieth-century. Even those vehemently opposed to ideas associated with the mythopoetic movement have had to respond to those ideas. It is the power of these ideas, in the cultural and economic context of late twentieth-century Western society, that makes the mythopoetic movement important.

By the same token, it's not just the mythopoetic men who are important to study; it's their thoughts and feelings in relation to the conditions of their lives as middle-class white men in late twentieth-century capitalist America. The psychic struggles faced by the mythopoetic men resulted from social forces felt by millions of other men living under similar cultural and economic conditions. Studying mythopoetic activity as one response to these conditions can thus provide insight into the lives of a much larger group of men.

The mythopoetic men and their movement are important, too, because of the issues they raise, either explicitly or implicitly. These issues have to do with gender, emotion, spirituality, power, inequality, and community. Studying the mythopoetic men is a way of exploring these issues as they bear on men's lives and on relationships between women and men. So again, the point is not simply to sketch the workings of a small, peculiar group and its world, but to see a larger world through the lens of a smaller one.

The mythopoetic men's movement was not what sociologists would normally call a social movement. It was not centrally coordinated, had no official leaders, did not proselytize for new members, imposed no doctrinal tests on participants, and was not aimed at changing public policy. And though it had an implicit politics, the mythopoetic movement did not have an overt political agenda. The men involved were not concerned with reforming society but with changing themselves. Mythopoetic leader Michael Meade thus disavowed the label "men's movement," preferring instead to speak of "men movements." Another mythopoetic leader put it more bluntly. "Whoever called this a 'movement' was an asshole," he said.

But there is a sense in which the movement label fits. Within a few years, thousands of men were drawn to mythopoetic activity, which looked much the same in hundreds of local manifestations around the country. Although these men were not being organized to influence public policy, nor were they being indoctrinated exactly, they were at least being *harmonized* by the writings and teachings of a small group of leaders who spread their ideas through articles, books, audio tapes, and talks at retreats. The men who got involved were thus led to share a view of men and their gender troubles. As a result, many men were, at once, moving in similar intellectual and spiritual directions. If this was not a social movement in the classic sense, it was at least a modern spiritual or therapeutic movement.

The men involved were ambivalent about seeing themselves as part of a movement. Like their leaders, the men disavowed the connotations of doctrine-mongering and politicality linked to *movement*. Yet the men liked feeling that they were part of something big, and so they did not always disparage the movement label; eventually most of the men came to accept it as a term they were stuck with. One label that some men preferred but which didn't stick was "inquiry"—as in, mythopoetic activity is an inquiry into the mysteries of the male soul and the nature of mature manhood. If that is the case, then this book is an inquiry into an inquiry.

So far I have not tried to define *mythopoetic*, allowing its meaning to emerge from my use of the term. Shepherd Bliss, a lesser-known mythopoetic leader, supposedly first applied this term to the therapeutic spiritual work being done with myth and poetry by Robert Bly and others.[3] There was, however, more to mythopoetic activity than myth and poetry. As I use it, the term refers to all the beliefs and practices associated with a particular group of leaders and men.

The principal leaders—or, as the men called them, teachers—were the poet Robert Bly, the Jungian psychologist James Hillman, and storyteller Michael Meade. The core beliefs, as I will discuss in chapter 2, derived largely from Jungian psychology. The practices included the use of myth and poetry as teaching tools, but also drumming, dancing, mask making, chanting, ritual, psychodrama, talking circles, and guided imagery. In the mythopoetic movement these activities were means to create and explore feelings, to achieve self-knowledge, to experience emotional communion, and to give new meaning to the identity 'man'.

Some of the men felt the same antipathy for *mythopoetic* as they did for *movement*. But again, it was a term they were stuck with. When they wanted to distinguish their activities from other kinds of group therapy or personal growth programs, the men accepted the adjective and spoke of "mythopoetic men's work" (a variation was "men's council" work). Other times, when context made clear what they meant, the men dropped the adjective and referred to their activity simply as "men's work." When I refer to "men's work," I mean activity that involved one or more of the elements of mythopoetic practice noted above.

This book is a critical analysis of mythopoetic men's work, not an exposé. Although there is material here that is likely to anger both the mythopoetic men and their feminist critics (for different reasons), I am not trying to blow the lid off the mythopoetic pot. My purpose is to make sense of what's been stirring inside it and inside the men who have been its rank and file. My hope is that the mythopoetic men will benefit from having a mirror held up to the shadow side of their activity. Other men, who perhaps share mythopoetic sentiments but have not attended gatherings, may also benefit from reflecting on what I have to say. I hope, too, that feminists, and anyone else interested in gender politics, will benefit from having a better view of this unusual movement of ordinary men.

THE STUDY

Getting Started

I began this study in September of 1990. Earlier that year I went to an informal seminar on "men's issues" organized by a professor (in another department) who was involved with a local men's center. Several men from the center attended. They talked about the troubles they faced, as men, and about helping each other deal with those troubles. I was impressed by their frankness and thought it would be interesting to find out more about who they were and what they were doing. My interest was further piqued when a colleague, who also attended the seminar, said, "These guys seem like a bunch of whiners. Why don't they just go have a beer and talk to each other if they need to talk?" Her unsympathetic response surprised me. So did my impulse to defend the men. All I can remember saying was, "I think it's more complicated than that."

Later I had lunch with the professor who organized the seminar and told him about my interests in gender. I asked if he thought the men involved with the men's center would talk to me about their lives. "A few might be reluctant," he said, "but I think most of them would be hard to shut up once they got going." He also said that if I wanted to meet some of the men and get a feel for what they were doing, I should attend an upcoming weekend workshop being led by Michael Meade and James Hillman. I decided to go, as a way to find out if this was a study I really wanted to do.

The morning of the first day of the workshop I was so anxious that I almost didn't go. I expected to be uneasy, since I was cynical about anything that involved public soul-baring or smacked of New Age mysticism. My anxiety rose when I arrived and saw a row of men thumping drums outside the building entrance. When I heard that we were supposed to *dance* our way into the main hall, while the men who were already inside chanted "go back, go back," I was ready to go home. But by the end of the day, which included much of the usual mythopoetic fare—poetry, storytelling, Jungian psychology, personal statements, dancing—I was hooked. I knew I wanted to tell a sociological story about these men and the unusual things they were doing.

At that first event I met several men from the men's center, told them of my interests, and arranged to call them later. That fall I also began to attend as many men's center events as I could. These included monthly discussion/workshop-type meetings, monthly drumming group meetings, and occasional retreats. In January of 1991 I joined a small support group organized under the auspices of the men's center. My involvement deepened over the next two years and, for a while, I attended as many as three different meetings a week. All told, between September 1990 and June 1993, I attended 128 different meetings, ranging in length from two hours to six days.

For the most part, I felt welcome from the start. I told the men (individually and through the men's center newsletter) that I was a sociologist interested in gender issues. I said I was especially interested in people's ideas about what it meant to be a woman or a man. The purpose of my study, I said, was not to test hypotheses, but to find out from men what was going on in their lives, how they were coping, and how their ideas about themselves as men were changing. A few men volunteered to be interviewed; most agreed when I asked; a few were suspicious.

The men's center leaders said I could not attend meetings just to observe. It was okay that I had "professional interests" in gender, men, and men's issues—this put me in the same camp as the therapists who were involved. But I also had to have "personal interests" that I was trying to satisfy through participation. In other words, I was welcome as long as I was present as a participant and not just an observer. I said that I had issues of my own to work on—sadness and anger left over from a previous relationship, grief over the impending death of a close uncle, silence between my father and me, fear of expressing emotion—and wanted to do so as part of my project.

This was not just an account I gave to gain entry. These were real issues in my life, and I hoped that participation in men's center activities would help me deal with them, if only by giving me a chance to talk to men in similar straits and by inducing self-reflection. I also wanted to get my research back in touch with matters that were important to me. For several years I'd felt that my research and writing had gotten more esoteric and distant from matters of concern to anyone outside a small group of academics. So I was very much looking for a way to bring my personal and professional interests together.

One reason some men were suspicious, and thus reluctant to be interviewed at first, was that around this time (1990–91) the media was beginning its lampoon blitz of the mythopoetic movement. Derisive stories were appearing in the Sunday supplements, in magazines, and on television. Some men feared that I too was interested in a quick or sensational story for the sake of an academic paper. "You can't get this stuff in a couple weeks, or even six weeks. I think it takes at least two years of personal involvement," one man told me as he refused to be interviewed. I was discouraged by this, because he was a key figure in the men's center and I wanted to get his story. I also didn't plan on collecting data for two years. But, as it turned out, when I asked him again for an interview, about two years later, he eagerly agreed.

Eventually the men stopped seeing me as a sociologist and saw me as just another participant—even a dedicated one—since I showed up at almost every event. On one occasion, when the topic of discussion was "workaholism," one man praised my willingness to attend events instead of staying home working. The irony was that, for me, attending events was fieldwork. Not all the men lost sight of my professional interests, however; over the years, the men I had interviewed occasionally asked how my book was coming.

As time went on and my analysis came together, it got harder to answer these questions. I could say, uneasily enough, that I had written a chapter on Jungian psychology or on emotional communion at gatherings, or that I had found a publisher. It was not easy to say that I was writing an analysis of why Jungian psychology appealed to the men, or of how they were doing identity work, or of their implicit gender politics. The rules of interaction at gatherings proscribed the kind of conversation that would have been necessary to explain what this analysis meant. I was also reluctant to go into the details of my analysis, especially the more political parts, because I didn't want to risk spoiling my acceptance in the group.

Even though I said repeatedly that my book was going to be an *analysis* of how and why men were doing men's work, not a how-to guide, I think some of the men did not understand what this meant. It may be that few lay people in any studied group really know what it means for their words and deeds to be treated as data. So I expect that some of the men I studied will be surprised, and perhaps unhappy, to see their accounts, experiences, and activities treated as grist for analysis. Some will be even less happy to see the conclusions I have arrived at, but that is another matter.

Data and Confidentiality

My data, created in the form of fieldnotes, came from being present as a participant-observer in a variety of settings. Sometimes I was able to write notes as a scene unfolded, sometimes not. If taking notes would have been obtrusive, I simply participated, listened, and wrote notes later. At some gatherings (the longer retreats) it was easy to take notes as things were said and done, since it was common to see men writing in their journals.

More data came from interviews with 21 of the 30 or so local men who were most heavily involved in mythopoetic activity. These hour-and-a-half to two-hour interviews generated over a thousand pages of transcripts. The interviews began by asking each man to tell the story of how he got involved in men's center activities. I also asked the men about their family backgrounds, relationships with women and men, work lives, joys and frustrations, and about their experiences at gatherings. The interviews were supplemented with occasional lunches and phone conversations. Over the course of the study I also had many informal conversations (mostly at gatherings) with these and other men.

Other sources of data included the books that constituted the movement's guiding literature; small mythopoetic publications (magazines, tabloids, newsletters) from around the country; and audio tapes (a popular form of movement "literature") of talks by mythopoetic leaders.

Throughout this study I struggled with issues of confidentiality. The easy part was assuring the men I interviewed that the interviews were confidential and that any identifying statements would be deleted or changed before appearing in print. Even my interview tapes and transcripts were coded so that they could not be associated (other than by me) with individuals. This is standard research practice by which I have abided here.

But much of my data comes from what men said and did at retreats and at other kinds of gatherings. Although I announced my identity as a researcher through the men's center newsletter, and in conversations with individual men, I did not re-announce my research interests at every gathering, since to do so would have been disruptive. At gatherings, things happened as they did because the men did not monitor their words and deeds with concern for how they would appear to a sociologist writing a book. Gatherings were supposed to be places where the men could speak openly and honestly.

At many gatherings I attended most of the men present knew—or had a fair chance to forget—that I was a sociologist doing a study. But since most of the men's center gatherings were open to any man who wanted to attend, there were always newcomers. Weekend and week-long events also drew larger numbers of men who were not affiliated with the men's center and thus would not have seen my notices in the newsletter. The tension I felt was between my desire to be open about my research interests, so that no one would feel his privacy had been violated, and my desire to avoid disrupting the natural flow of action.

The leaders of the men's center were comfortable with the fact that I was writing a book as long as I was also participating for myself. This helped me feel more comfortable about my dual role. I did indeed participate for myself, sharing my feelings and experiences with the other men, and giving support as the situation called for. But as the action was unfolding, I made mental notes, and later written notes, about what the men said and did. I was thus always torn between participating and observing. It bothered me sometimes that the other men didn't know how the analytic part of me was working, nor what that part of me was going to do with their words and deeds.

The truth is, I didn't know what I was going to do with their words and deeds. At the start of this project all I knew was that I wanted to tell a socio-logical story about who the men were, what they were doing, how they were doing it, and why. Everything I learned from what I heard, saw, and experi-enced went into the hopper. I didn't want to say or do anything that would keep me from learning as much as possible about and from the other men. So I tried to keep my identity as a researcher, which I think would have distanced me from some of the men, from being too prominent. On some occasions I simply didn't mention it to anyone who didn't already know.

None of the men in the small (four-man) support group to which I belonged for about a year and a half was heavily involved in mythopoetic activity. Yet these men faced many of the same issues that concerned those who were more deeply into mythopoetic activity. Being in the support group thus helped to flesh out my understanding of the thoughts and feelings of men drawn to men's work. Though I wrote extensive notes after each support group meeting, and though the men knew I was writing a book about men, I feel a special obliga-tion to preserve the privacy of this small group. And so while my experience in the support group and the insights gained from that experience inform my analysis, I have chosen not to include here, as data, any of the notes from those group meetings.

In writing this book I have chosen to report some incidents and conversa-tions in detail. Yet I have also taken pains to maintain confidentiality. No individuals are named or recognizably identified; only the men present on a given occasion would know who said or did what. The dates, times, and places of gatherings are generally omitted. I have even preserved the confidentiality of mythopoetic leaders, unless their remarks were made in a public forum or put into print or on tape for sale.

Reporting these matters in detail is necessary not only to establish the credibility of my analysis, but to enhance the possibility of dialogue between the mythopoetic men and their critics. Critics, most of whom have not ventured far from their armchairs, need to know what they're talking about, and the mythopoetic men need to give critics a fair shot at a clearly drawn target. Some of what's in this book will offer a target. On the other hand, the target isn't going to be the hairy monster that some critics have imagined it, or him, to be.

Focus on the Rank and File

My focus was primarily on the mythopoetic rank and file, not the celebrities. It was tempting at first to do what others had done and just critique Bly's *Iron John* and the other texts of the mythopoetic movement. Certainly that sort of thing would have been easier and safer than talking to real people. But it became apparent after a few months in the field that the mythopoetic men and their activity could not be understood via the analysis of texts or the personas of mythopoetic leaders. The men and their activities had to be understood directly, by being there as the men tried to figure out what they were doing together.

The beliefs and practices of the men I studied were typical. This was apparent from reading newsletters from around the country and from talking to men at regional and national gatherings. Although one man I talked to thought that mythopoetic men's groups in the upper Midwest included more men in blue-collar jobs, and another thought that groups in the Southwest included more men with experience in recovery programs, the overwhelming impression was of similarity between the local men and mythopoetic men elsewhere. When I asked men from elsewhere what their groups did, I learned that some did more or less drumming, told more or fewer stories and poems, and did more or fewer rituals—but the basic repertoire was the same. This wasn't surprising, since these men were reading the same books, listening to the same tapes, and going to gatherings led by the same people.

Without doubt, the character of the mythopoetic movement was strongly shaped by Bly's catalytic work and persona. But Bly was not, as many critics mistakenly presumed, the whole story. He was indeed the public icon and the easy target, but he was never an infallible guru to an army of slavish followers.

He was a model, an inspiration, and a delight (most of the time, anyway) to the men who were drawn to mythopoetic activity. I wanted to know why. I was interested in the men to whom Bly's message appealed and in how they put that message to use. To understand these men it was of course necessary to take Robert Bly, James Hillman, Michael Meade, Robert Moore, and other mythopoetic leaders into account. But the main story, as I try to tell it, is about the men.

A Sociological View

Readers will be better equipped to make sense of, and argue with, the rest of this book if I explain how members of my intellectual clan view the world. Explaining what it means to look at the world sociologically will also help to show the differences between my views of gender, masculinity, and mythopoetic activity, and the distinctly nonsociological ways the mythopoetic men looked at these things.

Sociologists presume that people often try to explain their actions in ways that have little to do with the truth. This is why we don't take at face value people's accounts of what they're doing and why. Instead, sociologists take people's accounts as *data*, not as explanations. This doesn't mean that people can never explain their own behavior; it just means that sociologists remain skeptical and want to make such determinations for themselves—after taking a bigger cultural picture into account and controlling for the self-justifying tendencies of the people under study.

Sociologists also try to see what kinds of assumptions people make as they carry out their daily activities. People may be unaware of these assumptions, simply because they've never had to reflect on them. Sociologists try to expose these implicit assumptions, hold them up for scrutiny, and figure out where they come from and whose interests they serve. This is why sociologists are often accused of "analyzing things to death" or "ignoring common sense." It is *our job* to doubt common sense and to examine the truth of all explicit and implicit claims about how the social world works.

Sociologists look at people's activities in historical, cultural, and economic context. This means trying to explain people's beliefs, feelings, and behaviors by reference to things outside of an everyday frame of reference. So, for example, in studying a group of people within a society, a sociologist looks at the group *and* its environment. The goal is to understand how the ideas and practices of the people in a group arise out of, or in reaction to, the surrounding culture and economy. A sociologist might also try to determine how the social class, gender, ethnicity, and other characteristics of a group's members lead them to react to the surrounding world in a particular way and to create certain beliefs and practices. This kind of analysis goes beyond what people in the group usually do by way of analyzing themselves.

Sociologists look at what people do and make happen by what they do. Often there is a huge gap between what people say they do and make happen, and what they actually do and make happen. People may give self-justifying or limited accounts of these matters. Sociologists try to make more thorough and impartial determinations. What's more, to a sociologist, people's intentions don't matter much—at least not as far as determining the consequences of their actions is concerned. People may intend to do one thing, yet make something very different happen. We say that action always has intended and unintended consequences. Sociologists look at both.

A sociological view sees masculinity, femininity, and gender itself as social constructions. This doesn't mean that biology is irrelevant, since gender is built on anatomy, and anatomy limits a few kinds of behaviors that are defined as gendered (e.g., men can't give birth). It means that sociologists see gender as a product of culture, not of biology. If gender were a product of biology, it would be invariant among all groups of Homo sapiens. But, in fact, masculinity and femininity vary greatly across cultures, time, and material conditions.[4] Gender, in this view, is not something people *have* but something they *do*— and do in various ways, based on learned notions of what's right.

By implication, sociologists don't see "maleness" as inherently good or bad— or as inherently anything. It is simply a biological category; what males and females become as types of people is a result of social experience.[5] To the extent that any given culture creates distinct patterns of experience for males and females, it is likely that males and females will become different kinds of people, or at least will learn different ways of conducting themselves in the world. Of course, people who are invested in seeing maleness or femaleness as indicating essential qualities of human beings will resist seeing gender as a social creation.

As will become apparent in the chapters that follow, the mythopoetic men largely rejected a sociological view of gender. They did this not for scientific reasons, but because seeing gender as socially constructed would have kept them from meeting some of the psychic needs they were trying to meet through mythopoetic activity. All this is understandable if we look at the men in context and at the social forces that impinged on them. That is the view of the men I have tried to take and to develop here. Sociologists do this sort of thing; we try to understand groups from the inside and from the outside.

The perspective I take on the men is not just analytic and sociological but also critical. I am trying—as the cultural studies people say—to document, interpret, and intervene. I want not only to show what was going on, to say how and why and what it meant, but also to influence its direction. I want the men to be affected by the criticism this book contains and calls down from others. I want the men to see the shadow side of their movement and, having seen it, to move a little differently.

My view is critical because I am also a feminist. That means I am a partisan of gender equality. It means that, having studied the world around me, I see nothing close to gender equality in this country or in most places.[6] But the version of feminism to which I subscribe is not the one that says women deserve a fair chance to compete with men for high places in a stratified society. My version of feminism calls for abolishing all race, class, and gender inequalities. I see these inequalities as intertwined and mutually reinforcing; we can't get rid of one without getting rid of the others. So I look at the mythopoetic men and ask how their activity grows out of, and serves to challenge, or reinforce, these systems of inequality.

This outlook sensitizes me to matters of power. In studying the mythopoetic men I was thus especially sensitive to their views of institutional power and how these views were linked to their gender politics. My views of these matters, as will also become apparent, are quite different from those of many of the mythopoetic men. This, too, was a source of tension for me as I did the study. But it was also an impetus for me to strive to understand where the men were coming from and my own position.

Some readers may want to discount my findings because of these avowed political values. That is any reader's prerogative. No doubt a sufficiently clever deconstruction of this text would find reasons for giving it no credence at all. Be that as it may, I hope readers will consider this possibility: because these matters of gender politics were so important to me, I wanted to be sure to get the story right. I believe that what is best for furthering feminist movement is speaking the truth about the lives of women and men. I have tried here to speak some sociological truths about the mythopoetic men. What I say is not the whole truth, nor without inadvertent error. But it is a good-faith start toward the kind of understanding that will ultimately benefit men who are not afraid of feminism, and also feminists who are not afraid to acknowledge the damage that capitalist patriarchy does to us all.

Terms and Conventions

I've already tried to give some meaning to "mythopoetic" and "mythopoetic men's work." It will help to keep things straight if I explain some other terms and matters of usage. First, there is the men's center to which I've already referred. This was the non-profit organization that sponsored the monthly discussion/workshop-type meetings, the drumming group meetings, and most of the other events I attended. The men's center also organized and provided start-up facilitators for the support groups.

The center wasn't much of a physical place; it had a phone and an answering machine in a small rented office in an older part of town (a medium-sized city in the Southeast). Almost all gatherings were held elsewhere—in rented spaces at churches, schools, parks, or camps. An elected, all-volunteer "leadership council" did whatever organizational work there was to do; there was no paid staff. Support for the center's operations came from the dues paid by the 150 or so men who were official members, and from passing the hat at gatherings.

The men's center was established in 1986. At that time only a few of the local men had heard of Robert Bly and knew of his workshops and conferences. According to founding members, the men who came to the earliest meetings of what became the men's center were interested primarily in forming support groups. It wasn't until a couple years later—after Bly, Meade, and other mythopoetic leaders had been brought in to do workshops—that mythopoetic activity became a staple part of what the men's center was about.

The mission statement of the men's center, reprinted in every issue of its newsletter, made no explicit reference to myth or poetry. According to this statement, the men's center was about

> men helping men become themselves by recognizing and promoting the wholeness and well-being of all men. We provide an opportunity for male self-awareness, fellowship, support, joyfulness and play, and enhancement of men's roles as friend, son, father, husband/partner and citizen. The Men's Center is committed to strengthening the individual, the family and the community.

Even though the men's center officially had a broader mission, mythopoetic activity came to be a mainstay of its programming. The center's major events were mythopoetic retreats; one of the most popular monthly activities was a drumming group meeting; and the monthly discussion/workshop meetings typically included ritual and were often devoted to themes associated with the mythopoetic view of men and their troubles. One reason things evolved in this way was that the center's most active members—the men who usually ended up on the leadership council—tended to be men who were enthusiastic about mythopoetic activity.

In addition to the center's 150 or so dues-paying members, there were another 100 to 150 men in the area who orbited at a greater distance, coming occasionally to gatherings or participating in support groups that were started through the men's center. Altogether this group of about 300 men constituted what I will call the Local Group. I did not have contact with all of these men.

But over the course of the study I did hear many of them make statements at gatherings of one kind or another. The Local Group included some men who didn't especially like mythopoetic activity, even though they might show up to hear Bly or Meade, or come to a discussion about a topic (e.g., relationships with fathers) that was given a mythopoetic twist.

Within the Local Group there was a core group of about 30 men who were the most enthusiastic and dedicated participants in mythopoetic activity. They showed up regularly for drumming group meetings; attended most of the mythopoetic retreats sponsored by the men's center; and were familiar with mythopoetic leaders, books and ideas. These were the men I interviewed and with whom I spent the most time. Sometimes I refer to them simply as the "mythopoetic men."

There is one other subgroup I need to distinguish. While *Local Group* is my term, invented for ease of reference, the Ritual Group was a real entity. This group was formed after a retreat in the spring of 1992. Some of the men who attended the retreat wanted to create rituals on their own, without going to expensive retreats run by mythopoetic leaders. By the second meeting of the Ritual Group, which met for a four-hour session every month, about 20 men had committed to participate; no new members were admitted after that. I belonged to the group for the first year of its existence.

So far I have used the terms *meeting*, *retreat*, and *gathering* synonymously. It may help to sort these out a bit. The men usually referred to any of their regular, monthly get-togethers as "meetings." The term "gathering" was reserved for special events. A few of the longer (several-day or week-long) gatherings were called "conferences." The men seldom used the term "retreat." My usage will differ, because I want to avoid conjuring the misleading images of professional conferences and business meetings. Unless it is important to note the type of meeting at which something was said or done, I will refer to all meetings by the generic term "gathering." If I use the term "retreat," it refers to a gathering that involved an overnight stay.

The gatherings I attended (not counting meetings of the four-man support group) varied in size. A few big events—talks by prominent mythopoetic leaders—drew hundreds, but most were much smaller. The attendance at the monthly drumming group meetings ranged from 15 to 40 men, averaging about 25. The discussion group meetings were about the same size. One week-long retreat I attended included over 100 men; one weekend retreat included only nine. Most retreats were kept to about 20 to 25 men. All but four of the gatherings and events I attended in three years were for men only.

So far I've referred to Bly and other key figures in the mythopoetic movement as leaders. Among the men, the term "teachers" was preferred. This was meant to avoid the connotation that Bly, and others, were in charge of an organized political movement or were dispensing dogma. "Teachers" was also meant to connote that the men were free-thinking seekers of wisdom rather than anyone's disciples. I adopt the men's term here and refer to mythopoetic teachers rather than leaders because I want to emphasize the role of Bly, Meade, Hillman, Moore, and the others as dispensers of ideas—and to indicate that not all the men embraced these ideas with fervor. "Teachers" is also more accurate in that it includes the less well-known men who traveled around the country leading mythopoetic workshops and retreats.

A term of which I will make frequent use is *traditional masculinity*. I realize that this is a problematic term, because what is understood to be traditional is always specific to a culture, may vary within a culture, is often subject to dispute, and changes over time. Yet I haven't found a better term for what I mean.[7] I use this term to refer to the way of enacting manhood that still commands the greatest respect in Western culture. To successfully enact traditional masculinity a man must show that he is rational, tough, indomitable, ambitious, competitive, in control, able to get a job done, and ardently heterosexual. He must also signify these qualities in a style befitting his ethnicity and social class.

This version of masculinity is a cultural ideal for men in our society; it is a prescription for what men should be if they want to be the best of men. It should also be apparent that traditional masculinity links masculinity to power and domination. Men who are emotional, submissive, unambitious, noncompetitive, dependent, or gay can't successfully enact traditional masculinity. Such men may enjoy residual male privileges, but they won't be respected as paragons of manhood.

To say that traditional masculinity is a cultural ideal in U.S. society is not to say that everyone explicitly endorses it as his or her ideal. It is to say only that many people share a sense that a man who approximates the ideal deserves more respect than one who falls far short. The concept of traditional masculinity is important here for precisely this reason: while it represented a widely shared cultural ideal, the mythopoetic men rejected parts of it. To understand these men it is necessary to understand their intense ambivalence about traditional (or what they sometimes called "1950s-style" or "Reagan-style") masculinity.

There are a number of other terms I use in later chapters: *communitas, identity work, false parity, therapeutic individualism*, and so on. These are analytic terms intended to provide a handle on some aspect of what the mythopoetic men believed or did. I'll explain these terms as they come up. Because Jungian psychology was such a central, if not always overt, part of mythopoetic activity, I devote a short chapter to laying out its basic concepts, and another to explaining why it appealed so strongly to the men.

PATTERNS IN THE LIVES OF THE MYTHOPOETIC MEN

It's easy to peg the mythopoetic men demographically. Nearly all of them were white, middle- or upper-middle class, between 35 and 60 years old, and self-identified as heterosexual.[8] But this sort of description isn't very informative; it doesn't tell us what it was in the lives of these men that brought them to mythopoetic activity. Nor does it tell us why Robert Bly enjoyed such credibility with them; why they had the psychic needs they did; or why they were so susceptible to feminist criticism of men. Some answers can be found by looking at common experiences in these men's lives.

Even if the men's life experiences at first seemed quite different, commonalities often became apparent. For example, some men said that as boys they were competitive and athletic. Other men said that they had always avoided sports and competition. From this it seems that these men came to mythopoetic activity from different backgrounds. Yet what eventually came out was that even the men who had been successful competitors in sports and other arenas really didn't enjoy competition—just like the men who had avoided it. Both kinds of men felt that competition had made them wary of other men, and thus both liked mythopoetic activity because competition was proscribed. This is what I mean by looking for what the men had in common. It is to describe them as a forest rather than as individual trees.

One thing that many of the men had in common were fathers they described as physically or emotionally "absent" (about a third of the men said that their fathers were also alcoholic or abusive in some way). Nearly all of the men I interviewed said their fathers gave them little emotional sustenance and nurturing as they were growing up. "He just wasn't there for me," was a common refrain. Many of the men felt that their father's absence had left them bereft of adequate tutoring in how to be a man. At least this is how many of the men came to interpret their pasts, through the mythopoetic lens.

But it was not just an experience of absence or abuse that many of the men had in common with regard to their fathers. It was a rejection of manhood as their fathers embodied it. Several men used the phrase "negative role model" to describe how they saw their fathers. Or, as one man put it, "I knew very early that I didn't want to be like him. For a time I even tried to be the opposite of what he was." In an interview, another man described his father and family life in a way that captured the experience of many of the men:

There is a tremendous amount of grief over the lack of connection that most of us had with our fathers. That comes up a lot. My experience along those lines was that my father was an alcoholic. He was out of the house a lot, worked a lot of overtime. He was a pretty good provider—not in terms of making a lot of money, but in terms of bringing home most of what he made. I was totally my mother's ally growing up and somehow really demonized him. Not to try to idealize him now; he really wasn't a very good father. He wasn't there physically as much as ideally he would have been, and when he was there, he was drunk or he was lying on the couch watching the football game on TV. Or he was out doing more work on the farm. We lived on a farm and he farmed as well as being a truck driver. So he was really absent physically, emotionally—every way you could imagine. I didn't have any sense of communication with him. I was afraid of him, and I didn't like or respect him very much.

I asked this man if there was any time when he was growing up that his relationship with his father had been different. He went on:

No, I can never remember a time when I felt close to my father. Never. Partly as a consequence of that, I tend to be a little distrustful of men and definitely ambivalent about my own masculinity. Early on in college, and shortly after college especially, that was very true and it played itself out in various ways. But there just wasn't this firm, kind of confident sense of "yeah, I'm a man and I'm glad to be a man and that means this and this." I didn't really want it to mean what my dad's life exhibited.

This rejection of the father's version of manhood occurred because the men, as boys, associated his absence or abuse with his being a man. Why did they make this link? Because, they said, their mothers had led them to believe that their fathers behaved badly *because they were men.* Early in their lives, then, these men were led to believe, or at least suspect, that there was something evil in men. Belonging to this category themselves, they became suspicious of their own moral character.

Many of the men said that while growing up they tried hard to be "nice boys" and to avoid making others angry. They tried especially hard to please their mothers. Some men said that they got caught up in trying to take care of their mothers because their fathers didn't seem to be doing a good job of it. One man said he felt that he had functioned as a surrogate husband to his mother. "I became her ally against him," was how another man put it. The man quoted above, who talked about having "demonized" his father, described how his thinking had changed, partly as a result of doing men's work:

It's not about somehow making Dad into a good guy at all. It's just about realizing that the problems weren't just because he was a man, which is what my mom
would say. Now I know that I'm not necessarily doomed to be a fuck-up just
because I also am a man. Seeing somebody fail, seeing them fail you, and then
generalizing from that that somehow your gender is not good enough—I mean,
that's a damaging thing. And a lot of mothers, like mine, actively encourage their
sons to feel exactly that. It's a way to claim their sons over again, because they
don't have a strong enough connection with their husbands.

These accounts of early family life were no doubt colored by the Jungian psychology the men imbibed, as adults, through mythopoetic literature. However much reinterpretation was going on here, it nonetheless seemed that many
of the men learned, as boys, that it was important to be nice and not make
their mothers feel bad—like their fathers did. It seems plausible that the men's
lack of assertiveness vis-à-vis women later in life was rooted in this sort of
childhood experience.

One reason for Bly's appeal is also evident here. Bly has written and talked
about how he too was forced into the repressed "nice boy" role in the family,
how his father was an emotionally absent alcoholic, and how this left him feeling, for a long time, angry at older men for what they failed to give him.[9] This
background gave Bly enormous credibility with the mythopoetic men. They
saw in him someone who had suffered much of what they had suffered; who
did not deny that the experience was painful; and who yet had found a way to
turn this experience into a resource for psychological and spiritual growth. This
commonality of experience allowed the men not only to viscerally understand
where Bly was coming from—in a way that outsiders often could not—but to
take hope from his example. Robert Bly gave the men reason to believe that
they too could turn their family-inflicted wounds into blessings.

It seemed that these family experiences also gave rise to a preference for
women as friends. Many of the men grew up seeing not only that women were
more available as emotional confidants and nurturers, but that men were scary
and untrustworthy. Perhaps, too, those men who formed alliances with their
mothers also learned to talk to women about feelings. This is how many of
the men accounted for their friendships with women. Women are "easier to
talk to," they said. Or, as one man put it, "it's the feminine side of me finding
a friend." At the same time, socialization to traditional manhood taught them
that men did not share feelings with each other. Many of the mythopoetic men
thus said that prior to getting involved in men's work, most of their friends
were women, and they had rarely shared their feelings with other men.

Several things combined here for many of the mythopoetic men: a sense

that men were not available for emotionally satisfying, noncompetitive relationships; a desire to be nice and to please others; vague doubts about their
own moral worth as men; and a kind of sensitivity to, or perhaps merely a
willingness to accommodate to, women's feelings. The result, as many of the
men saw it, was the kind of "softness" that Bly pointed to in his 1982 *New
Age Journal* interview with Keith Thompson.[10] These men felt that they had
long been too accommodating to others' emotional needs—and insufficiently
assertive of their own. For some of the men this was a general condition, a
way they related to most people. For others this softness was manifested primarily in relationships with women. These men felt, as one man put it, using
a phrase I heard several times, "overwhelmed by female energy."[11]

A substantial proportion of the men in the Local Group said they were sexually abused as children. Studies using nationally representative samples have
found that three to six percent of men in the United States report having been
sexually abused.[12] Based on what came out in interviews and a number of small
group discussions, the rate seemed to be much higher among the mythopoetic
men. At one gathering, three of seven men more or less randomly assigned to
a small discussion group spoke of being sexually abused as children. On a similar
occasion it was four of nine. Once when I remarked on this high proportion
to another man in the Local Group, he told me that four of the seven men in
his support group had been sexually abused. The men who I heard talk about
experiences of abuse cited mothers, fathers, and older male relatives as the
perpetrators.

While this is suggestive evidence that the rate of childhood sexual abuse
was higher among the men in the Local Group than among the population of
men in general, the proportions implied above must be viewed with caution,
since they do not derive from a survey of all the men in the Local Group.
Generalizing beyond the Local Group on this matter is even riskier. It would
take a separate study to determine the true prevalence of abuse experiences
among the mythopoetic men. I can say, however, that many of the men who
spoke of being abused cited this experience as a source of shame about their
sexuality, a source of compulsion to have (hetero)sex, a source of insecurity
about their masculinity, or of difficulty in setting "personal boundaries."

In light of the above, it is perhaps not surprising that a large proportion of
the mythopoetic men also had some involvement in the so-called recovery
movement, which included the legions of 12-step (or fewer) programs for
healing psychic wounds, gaining control over addictions, and achieving mental balance.[13] A few of the men in the Local Group had been in these programs because of problems with drugs or alcohol. But most of those who were
involved in some kind of recovery program were there as children of alcohol-

ics, as "sex addicts," as "co-dependents," or as survivors of abuse. They were recovering, in other words, as victims rather than perpetrators. My estimate is that about a third of the men in the Local Group were in or had been in a recovery program.

While experiences of abuse, addiction, and recovery were shared by large minorities of the mythopoetic men, all men of this generation encountered a generation of women emboldened by feminism. Even as these men grew up less assertive than they felt they should have been as men, they met women who voiced their grievances against sexism, demanded equal opportunity, and made their desires known. At first this created an affinity between pre-mythopoetic men, in the 1970s and early 1980s, and feminist women. Having learned—by observing their fathers and listening to their mothers—that men could be brutish and hurtful, these men were sympathetic to women's complaints about men and sexism. It also seemed to this generation of men that blame for violent resistance to the civil rights movement, for pollution of the earth, for political corruption, and for the deaths of over a million people in Vietnam could be laid at the feet of men. As one 45-year-old man said at a gathering:

> I came of age politically in the 60s, seeing the world as fucked up because of the actions of men. I couldn't help but accept the feminist analysis of men as villains. Because of this I wanted to see myself as human, not male.

And because these politically aware, premythopoetic men were "sensitive," willing to listen and to share feelings, they were also attractive to feminist women.

Yet as the 1970s became the 1980s, the affinity began to break down. One reason was that the men felt the sting of a radical feminist critique that saw men as morally irredeemable (this is what some of the mythopoetic men called the "all-men-are-rapists" school of feminist thought). Many feminist women, hitting middle age themselves, were also more willing to challenge the unconscious sexist behaviors of men who claimed to believe in gender equality. Stalled change on the political level also seemed to intensify gender politics on the personal level, and this put a lot of sensitive men on the spot. To these men, who saw themselves as nonsexist and supportive of women's rights, feminist criticism began to feel like a personal attack, even a betrayal: "Why are you nagging me? I'm not like those other guys. I'm considerate of women. I don't treat women as sex objects. I didn't start any wars. I'm on your side."

When conflicts over these and other matters brought relationships to an end, the mythopoetic men naturally sought sympathy and support.[14] But where to get it, if women had now become so damn critical? One place many of the men found it was in therapy. Another place was in men's support groups and mythopoetic gatherings (many of the men in the Local Group had in fact found their way to the men's center via the recommendation of a therapist). Thus in times of crisis, when the men found they could no longer rely on wives, lovers, and women friends for uncritical support, they turned to other men. The appeal of this was that if a man was willing to admit to other men that he felt weak, vulnerable, and confused, he could get from them not only sympathy and support, but help in repairing his identity as a man.

Despite their sensitivity and support for women's rights, the mythopoetic men were hardly radical feminists. They had been steeped in a male-supremacist culture and enjoyed many invisible privileges as educated, heterosexual white men.[15] They also didn't know what to do with feminist criticism of them *as men*. This criticism seemed unfair in light of the support the men had given to women's causes and to individual women in their lives. It also seemed unfair because, as the men saw it, they were not being appreciated as individuals, but being morally indicted for membership in a category to which they could not help but belong.

It might seem odd that any men were so affected by feminist criticism, especially since feminism seemed to lose its punch in the conservative political climate of the 1980s. But these men were uniquely vulnerable because of their biographies and circumstances. Doubts carried over from bad experiences with their fathers made these men especially sensitive to criticism of their moral character as men. Their closeness to feminist women, at work and in their private lives, also gave them front-row seats for taking an ear-beating about men's iniquities. And their liberal politics made them attentive to any underdog group's claims to victimization. So these were not men who could ignore feminist women or remain blissfully indifferent to the feminist critique of men.

These same experiences and circumstances made the men receptive to several key pieces of mythopoetic ideology: gender is rooted in biology and is nothing one has to apologize for; men are essentially good; and women are powerful enough to pursue their political goals without help from men. The appeal of these ideas also depended on other features of the context in which the men and these ideas came together. Later I'll discuss the cultural currents and social arrangements that shaped how the men felt about themselves as men, how they thought about gender, and how they acted on their political values. These are all pertinent to understanding why mythopoetic beliefs and practices appealed so strongly to the men. But for now I want to stay focused on the men themselves.

Although the men displayed a masculinized social presence—that is, they unambiguously presented themselves as men—in some ways they were, to use a term the men would not have applied to themselves, womanly. What I mean is that the men showed qualities conventionally associated with (not innate in) women: concern for feelings, desire to nurture, disdain for ruthless competition, gentleness, and some doubt about their right to personal agency.[16] In proper measure these qualities, which are usually defined as feminine, are desirable in any human being; in a sexist society, however, men who display them risk denigration. Many of the mythopoetic men indeed had been victimized for not being tough and aggressive enough. Growing up working class, as many of the men did (and about which more later), made the problem worse.

Again, this is why many of the men were sympathetic to women's criticisms of *other* men. Nonetheless, living in a male-supremacist society, the mythopoetic men still wanted to affirm their identities as men. Not only did manhood have its status advantages, but the men believed they had no choice but to be men; as they saw it, manhood was not a social veneer but part of the grain of their being. The problem remained, however, that these men had little sense of the worth of men, and no clear image of what a good man should be. Their fathers were not exemplars; nor did there seem to be any heroes who embodied and affirmed the value of being a man with feminine qualities—until Robert Bly came along.

What the men found in mythopoetic activity was the chance to be with men who would not shame each other in competition to see who could put on the best "manhood act," as John Stoltenberg calls it.[17] At mythopoetic gatherings the men could be emotional, noncompetitive, and nurturing, and still get their identities as men affirmed by other men—with no feminist criticism to spoil the celebration. What's more, Jungian psychology and the stirring persona of Robert Bly legitimated a version of assertive manhood free from the emotional repression that is part of traditional masculinity. The mythopoetic movement thus made it possible for the men to have it both ways: they could be feminine and still affirm their masculinity and manhood. As I'll show later, Jungian psychology aided this by allowing the men to redefine their feminine traits, especially their emotionality, as aspects of "deep masculinity."

Earlier I said that most of the mythopoetic men were middle or upper-middle class. Nearly all were college graduates; quite a few in the Local Group had advanced or professional degrees. Most had steady jobs, earned incomes above the national median, and owned homes. The jobs they held gave them much autonomy and control in their work. Among them were teachers, therapists, physician's assistants, engineers, commissioned salesmen, computer programmers, architects, consultants, editors, writers, social workers, and small business owners. I knew of three men in the Local Group who did blue-collar work for an hourly wage. They, too, had gone to college.

While the jobs the men held were, by usual standards, good ones, this did not mean that the men were happy in them. By middle age many of these men realized they had been working for 20 years and had done fair to middling well, but still felt vaguely dissatisfied, as if a piece were missing from their lives and there was no way it could be filled by success at work. These men came to see status, authority, and income as hollow pursuits, ones that caused emotional alienation and gave fleeting satisfaction when they were achieved.

Emotional alienation in their jobs was a common experience for the mythopoetic men who worked in corporations or large bureaucracies. A number of men told of incidents at work wherein it was made painfully clear to them that feelings were of secondary importance to profits and the preservation of managerial control. At least four men in the Local Group quit jobs in such places in part because of the distress they felt over these matters.[18] I heard several other men tell stories about being reprimanded, or at least teased, by their male bosses for worrying too much about others' feelings and for seeking cooperative, but less quick and efficient, solutions to workplace conflicts. In a small group discussion one man, a mid-level manager in a corporation, articulated the problem: "I think this [men's work] has been good for me. It's helped me learn to talk to my wife about my feelings. But I worry about it carrying over into my job. Sometimes I have to fire people, and I couldn't do that if I cared too much about how they felt."

Men who worked in large, profit-making corporations were a minority in the Local Group. Most of the men in the Local Group worked in smaller (sometimes nonprofit) organizations, or in public-service bureaucracies. These men had gravitated away from competitive, profit-making environments toward human-service fields: teaching, social work, counseling, health care, the ministry. Jobs in these fields called for and rewarded the nurturing the men were inclined to do.[19] In these occupations the men also had more chances to find meaning in their work by helping others.

While there was a better fit between the personalities of the mythopoetic men and work of this kind, there was one way in which it was still discrepant for them: It put them in workplaces that were numerically dominated by women. I heard several men—among them a nurse, a social worker, a therapist, an elementary school teacher, and a physician's assistant—refer at various times to the unease they felt being in the gender minority at work. One of these men also used that same phrase, "overwhelmed by female energy," to describe how he felt at work. For these men, mythopoetic gatherings were opportunities to experience the opposite, to bask in "male energy."

The lack of passion many of the men felt for their work seemed to spill over into the rest of their lives. Few of the men spoke of hobbies or other nonwork activities that deeply engaged and excited them. As a global assessment of their lives, some men spoke of being "numbed out." Others said they'd "gotten boring," and as one man put it, "I think that what a lot of these guys, myself included, have experienced is a kind of chronic, low-grade depression." Mythopoetic activity was a tonic for these men. "This [men's work] is the first thing I've been passionate about in years," one man said in an interview. Or as another man said offhandedly at a gathering, "Doing this stuff makes us special. If I didn't do men's work I'd be just a regular guy."

It would be wrong, however, to say that all the men were unhappy with their work or frustrated in their careers. Some were, some weren't. What many of the men shared—though I think the therapists were an exception—was a feeling that their work provided few, if any, opportunities for psychological and spiritual growth; that it didn't give them much sense of making a meaningful contribution to the larger community; and that it didn't really attest to their goodness as men. I'll say more about this—the problem of trying to stake a moral identity on work—in chapter 5.

It's useful to compare the mythopoetic men to the men of Robert Weiss's 1990 study, *Staying the Course: The Emotional and Social Lives of Men Who Do Well at Work*.[20] For Weiss's upper-middle-class achievers, work was central to their lives; everyone and everything else revolved around it. Weiss's men were virtuoso compartmentalizers; whatever else was happening in their lives, they could block it out and concentrate on getting a job done. Their friendships with other men were, as Weiss says, "more or less affectionate alliances" in which self-disclosure was carefully limited. Weiss concludes that these men did just fine to keep a lid on their feelings: "For most men, when contemplating a recommendation that they change their social styles so that they can have deeper, more meaningful, relationships with others, it may be best to adhere to the principle, 'if it's not broke, don't fix it.'"

The mythopoetic men differed from Weiss's men in at least two ways. For one, they questioned the centrality of work in their lives. Work was important to them, of course; but they did not believe that relationships, feelings, spirituality, and personal growth should be subjugated to it. Or if they had believed this, they were seeing that a lifetime of acting on this belief could cause a man to develop in a one-sided way and his spirit to wither. The mythopoetic men also differed in that they wanted closer, more emotionally honest and

expressive friendships with other men. They recognized that there was something broke in an enactment of manhood that kept men emotionally isolated
from each other. Mythopoetic activity was in part an attempt to fix it.

I've suggested that the mythopoetic men were spiritual seekers. Spiritual as
opposed to religious is an important distinction here. The men were not seeking a body of moral teachings to provide a guide to proper living, nor a philosophy to help them make sense of the universe. They did not want a church
in the usual sense. What they wanted was to transcend the mundane and experience a sense of mystery and wonderment about their connections to the
universe and to each other. The woolly terms *connection* and *sense of* must be
used here, for the men were indeed seeking something vague and perhaps
ineffable. Much mythopoetic activity was aimed at cultivating mystique and
"feelings of connection." It was also aimed at helping the men find for themselves a sense of purpose and meaning in life. Together these things constituted the spirituality the men were after.

Many of the men in the Local Group came from religious, or at least church-
going, families. Some of these men got a heavy dose of fundamentalist religion while growing up. What they had in common was not any specific
denominational training, but a dislike for moral dogma—all the "shoulds" that
they associated with church teachings. As one man put it, "I always liked the
ritual part of church when I was a kid. But as soon as the minister started with
all the 'shoulds,' I tuned out." Similar feelings led many of the men to reject
the churches and religions in which they were versed as children.

Yet these men often said they liked the ritual and feelings of communion
that were part of their church experiences. Longing for these experiences, but
having outgrown fundamentalism, they tried more liberal alternatives, such
as Quakerism, Unitarianism, Buddhism, and various forms of New Age mysticism. When mythopoetic men's work came along—with its rejection of fundamentalism in favor of finding one's personal truth, its gentle pantheism, its
Jungian-inspired theology of universal connection via the collective unconscious, and its use of ritual to create emotional communion—it gave the men
the wide, inclusive path to spirituality they wanted. As one man, the son of a
minister, put it, "This [men's work] is like all the good parts of church without the bad parts." Another man said the men's center was a "true church,"
because "it helps you do soul work and is accepting."

The move away from the fundamentalist religion of their childhoods re-
flects in part the upward mobility many of the men experienced. Many of the
mythopoetic men—about three-fourths of the men in the Local Group—came
from working-class backgrounds. Their fathers were farmers or blue-collar
wage earners. Most of the rest of the men came from middle- to lower-middle

class backgrounds. Their fathers were salesmen, insurance adjusters, and small business owners. Many of the men were the first in their families to get college degrees. In the Local Group, men whose fathers had college degrees and professional careers were in the minority.

I do not have the kind of detailed biographical data necessary to generalize about the causes and consequences of this upward mobility on the part of so many of the mythopoetic men. My sense, however, from interviews, conversations, and the men's personal statements is that it was in part the early rejection, or at least questioning, of their fathers' version of manhood that led many of them to seek ways to be different kinds of men, and education provided a path for doing so. School may also have been a safer place for boys inclined more to self-reflection than to displays of working-class masculine toughness. Education may then have further distanced the men from their fathers.

As these men moved away from their fathers into middle-class lives, they found that the images of working-class masculinity they acquired as boys did not fit the world they were in. This was perhaps one source of the confusion and anxiety the men felt about what it meant to be a man. For many working-class men, doing a rugged "man's job" is evidence of masculinity and an anchor for the identity 'man'. The mythopoetic men from working-class backgrounds probably learned this as boys. But the jobs they ended up in didn't attest to their ruggedness or masculinity. The large numbers of women in the same human-service occupations to which many of the mythopoetic men gravitated may have made it even harder to see these occupations—even success in these occupations—as signifying masculine prowess.

The story is more complicated, however, in that many of the men—despite believing that they had rejected their fathers' version of masculinity—nonetheless hungered for fatherly approval. In other words, these men still wanted their fathers to see them as men and to accept them for the men they had become. These men carried the weight of their fathers' evaluations of them upward across class lines, and in middle age they wanted relief from the burden.

Not all of the mythopoetic men had to cope with such discrepancies in images of manhood. The men from middle-class backgrounds didn't have quite the same problem. But they too had rejected a part of their fathers' version of masculinity and had tried to become different kinds of men. And like the men from working-class backgrounds, these men also wanted their fathers' blessings and a clearer sense of how to be a good man. Mythopoetic men's work was in large part a means for all these men to fashion a clearer image of respectable manhood, compatible with their womanliness. It was also a way to get the affirmation of manhood that many of the men felt they never got from their fathers or from other men who enforced the standards of traditional masculinity.

Although I previously dismissed demographic labels as uninformative, it is not irrelevant that the mythopoetic men were predominantly white, middle class, and heterosexual. Even if these men were not members of the power elite, they still belonged to privileged categories. As such, they had the psychic and economic resources—the literacy, self-confidence, time, and money—to create a powerful, collective response to their common problems. These were educated men used to solving problems and unused to being stigmatized and stereotyped. Once they got their backs up about feminist criticism of men, and found inspirational leaders, it's not surprising that they congealed into a movement of sorts. Nor is it surprising, considering their privileged statuses, that the movement they formed was primarily therapeutic rather than aimed at radical social change.

As I also noted earlier, it was via therapy that many of the men got involved in mythopoetic men's work. Quite a few of the men said it was a therapist who first recommended getting into a (leaderless) men's support group. This advice led them to contact the men's center and to sample various of its activities, including the mythopoetic. Other men said that they decided to try a drumming group meeting, weekend retreat, discussion group meeting, or public talk by a mythopoetic teacher, because their curiosity was aroused by reading a book or article. Few were brought in by friends. My sense (from watching men come and go over three years) was that only about a third of the men who came to an event to see what was going on stayed involved.

Some men in the Local Group had tried nearly every self-help and personal growth fad of the 1970s and 1980s; for others, men's work was the first such thing they'd gotten into. For all of them the mythopoetic men's movement was a place to satisfy a roughly similar set of psychic needs. Mythopoetic gatherings were, in the argot of the movement, safe places for sharing, tending wounds, and healing.

To say that the men's needs were psychic is not to say that these needs sprang into the men's heads from nowhere. As I've suggested here and will argue later, the men were receptive to mythopoetic ideas and practices because of experiences caused by social forces beyond their control. Certainly there is no shortage of reasons why, in this society, men and women might have to struggle for self-acceptance, freedom from emotional repression, valued identities, and spiritual communion. I would say that these needs marked the mythopoetic men as ordinary. What was special about mythopoetic activity, and what made it especially appealing, was the gender angle: the chance to bond around a common interest in redefining 'man' as an identity signifying moral goodness.

A final point about the men of the Local Group: these were not the men who attended "wildman weekends," as some critics wrongly labeled all mythopoetic retreats. There were indeed retreats, held elsewhere around the country, billed as wildman weekends; and these were part of the mythopoetic movement, broadly defined. But as men in the Local Group saw them, such events were likely to be the cheap stuff, led by self-proclaimed gurus of dubious merit, trying to cash in on the more serious work done by Bly, Hillman, and Meade. The men I studied objected to the idea, implied by the term wildman *weekend*, that a troubled man could get fixed in two days of sharing, drumming, sweat-lodging, or whatever. As the men in the Local Group saw it, mythopoetic men's work wasn't about getting fixed once and for all—in a weekend or a year; it was part of a long process, a journey, of psychological and spiritual growth. If they had thought the journey could be made in a weekend, this could have been a shorter book.

THE BOOK AHEAD

Much of the theory behind mythopoetic activity came from Jungian psychology and James Hillman's archetypal psychology. These psychologies provided a diagnosis of men's problems and a prescription for solving them. Jungian and archetypal psychologies also served as enabling theologies that gave quasi-religious significance to mythopoetic activity. Chapter 2 describes these psychologies and explains how they guided mythopoetic practice. In this chapter I also briefly discuss the influence of Sufism on the mythopoetic movement.

In chapter 3, I explain why the men found Jungian/archetypal psychology so appealing. I argue that this psychology gave the men a way to see innate goodness in themselves, to find self-acceptance and inner strength, and, most important, a way to redefine their feminine qualities as "deep masculine." What's more, Jungian/archetypal psychology required no guilt-inducing analysis of the structures of institutional power that benefited middle-class white men. In this chapter I also try to explain the appeal of Jungian/archetypal psychology by looking at the larger cultural context that shaped the men's beliefs about gender and their feelings about themselves as men.

More important than the theory upon which the men drew is what they actually did at gatherings. The popular image of a mythopoetic gathering included men drumming around a bonfire, telling tales of personal sorrow, and weeping in each other's arms. This image suggests that the men came to gatherings ready to unload a burden of emotions. While some men did bring strong feelings with them to gatherings, it is important to see that gatherings were about *creating* feelings. In chapter 4, I show how the men sought to create a special feeling of emotional communion—what the anthropologist Victor Turner calls *communitas*—through their poetry, storytelling, ritual, drumming, and forms of talk. The chance to experience the rare power and pleasure of communitas is what made gatherings so seductive and kept drawing the men back.

Mythopoetic teachers and men often denied that their activity was a backlash against the women's movement. While it was not a backlash in the sense of an attempt to rescind women's rights, it was indeed a reaction to what the men saw as feminism's blanket indictment of men. Many of the men drawn to mythopoetic activity felt that feminism had impugned the moral character of all men. In chapter 5, I argue that what mythopoetic activity offered—in addition to self-acceptance, feelings of inner strength, and communitas—was a chance to repair the psychic damage done by misunderstood feminist criticism. I show how a great deal of what the men did, in print and at gatherings, can be seen as a kind of identity work aimed at remaking the meaning of 'man' and investing it with new moral value.

Gender politics are a large and inescapable part of the story. While the men disavowed any political intent, their ideas and activities had definite political content and implications. I begin chapter 6 by considering why the men denied that their activity was political, and then I look at several pieces of gender ideology that the men embraced. I also show how all-male gatherings reproduced sexism, and critique the men's use of Jungian psychology as a basis for understanding matters of gender and power. Chapter 7 is also about gender politics. Here I explain the men's views of feminism, examine the androcentrism fostered by mythopoetic activity, consider the men's ambivalence about homosexuality, and give a brief account of their liberal politics.

The final chapter is titled "A Critical Appreciation." Here I examine the ideological shadows afflicting the mythopoetic movement and take issue with the men's strategic anti-intellectualism. A part of this chapter is devoted to my own account of the causes of trouble in men's lives—causes that have more to do with inequalities in economic and political power than with the psyche. The chapter is an appreciation because I also argue that there is value in mythopoetic activity and what it did for the men. I believe the mythopoetic movement has progressive potential, and one of my aims in this last chapter is to nudge the men toward realizing this potential by thinking more critically about what they're doing.

To return to the beginning: The title of this book predates my acquaintance with Bly's *Iron John*. At the first mythopoetic gathering I attended (in September of 1990, before *Iron John* was released), it occurred to me that one way to describe what the men were up to was as "trying to break out of the iron cage of rationality and re-enchant the world." This image came to me from the sociologist Max Weber (1864–1920), who described the master trend of Western history as the increasing rationalization and bureaucratization of social life.

It struck me, early on, that the mythopoetic men were reacting against the psychic fallout of Weber's master trend. Other social analysts have seen reactions manifested in various ways by other groups today. Michael McCallion, in reviewing a book on the satanism scare, comments:

> . . . the present historical moment is one in which people are yearning for some-
> thing beyond the self, something Max Weber has called a world of enchantment.
> . . . [S]ocial and physical scientists admit that the disenchanted, rational world
> of the Enlightenment period is fading in the wake of the rediscovery of the mys-
> teriousness and ambiguity of social life. The interest in satanism is simply one of
> the signs of the times that reveals a growing desire for enchantment, to dwell in
> something more than the rational self.[21]

Though mythopoetic activity has nothing to do with satanism, I see the same desire for enchantment as one of its driving forces. The mythopoetic men were seeking to dwell in something more than the rational self and its shrunken, bureaucratic niche. And so, in mind of Weber's metaphor, *Unlocking the Iron Cage* seemed a fitting title. When Bly's *Iron John* later became the bible of the mythopoetic movement, I thought the reference to·the iron cage was doubly fitting, in that it alluded to my ties and debts to two different worlds, one of the head and one of the heart.

Despite my sympathies for their project, no doubt some mythopoetic men will think that I've wounded them by writing a critical book. No doubt some feminists will think that I didn't go far enough—that I blew my chance to drive a stake through Robert Bly's heart. So be it. I think the mythopoetic men are resilient enough to bear my criticism and benefit from wrestling with it. I hope that feminist readers remember that the mythopoetic men are decent human beings trying to cope with gender troubles caused by social conditions not of their own choosing. As such, they deserve serious efforts to be understood— both for the sake of understanding them as human beings, and for the sake of understanding the social conditions that are a common source of gender troubles for women and men.

Finally, I should acknowledge the obvious: trying to capture the complexity and diversity of the mythopoetic men and their activities in a text has inevitably resulted in simplification. Men who have participated in mythopoetic activities will recognize this gap between text and lived experience. I certainly recognize it. One of the men in the Local Group made the point more vividly in an interview when he said, commenting on the mythopoetic literature, "You can't get it from books. No level of intellectual experience is enough. You've got to dance naked to grasp it." So it is with books about all things. The book is never the dance.

CHAPTER 2

THE THEORY BEHIND THE PRACTICE

In the early 1990s, journalists, television scriptwriters, playwrights, and cartoonists discovered that mythopoetic activity was ripe for lampooning. Scenes of middle-aged white men listening raptly to fairy tales, furiously beating drums, invoking spirits, cavorting about in masks, dancing like animals, and mimicking Native American chants while squatting naked in makeshift sweat lodges needed no commentary to evoke laughter. Such behavior on the part of adult men was seen as self-evidently funny, like Three Stooges-style slapstick.

The joke depended, of course, on allowing mythopoetic activity to appear absurd by ignoring the internal logic that gave it meaning. Even if it was said or implied that the men were trying to do something halfway sensible—such as heal old emotional wounds, engage in a new form of male bonding, or just escape the mid-life doldrums—the question of why the men were using these *particular* odd methods was not addressed.

This question can't be answered in a sound bite. It requires examining the psychological theory that underlies mythopoetic practice. This theory derives

principally from the writings of Swiss psychologist Carl Jung (1875–1961) and
his followers. To make sense of mythopoetic activity in its own terms, to fairly
criticize its gender politics, and to appreciate its religious aspect requires understanding the Jungian ideas behind it.

Feminist critics of mythopoetic activity have largely missed the significance
of its Jungian basis. This oversight stems from seeing mythopoetic activity only
in terms of its gender politics. In this view, the mythopoetic movement is about
men reproducing their power over women—if only by denying the power and
privileges they enjoy as men in favor of focusing on psychological pain. Mythopoetic activity of course has its gender politics, as I will discuss in chapters 6
and 7. But an analysis that begins and ends with gender politics misses much
of what mythopoetic activity meant to the men who engaged in it.

The Jungian basis of mythopoetic activity was no secret.[1] It was readily
apparent that the movement's most prominent teachers were steeped in Jungian
thought—James Hillman being one of the most famous living Jungian psychologists, and Robert Bly and Michael Meade, though not psychologists by
training, nonetheless drawing heavily on Jung to inform their work with poetry,
ritual, and myth. Many of the less prominent teachers in the movement were
also trained Jungians or self-taught users of Jungian theory.

Though he was ever present in one sense, Jung was usually kept in the background at mythopoetic gatherings. He was cited or quoted on occasion, but
seldom was there explicit discussion of his ideas. One reason for this is that
the men were allergic to doctrines, and keeping Jung out of sight helped preserve the appearance that mythopoetic activity had no doctrine. Another reason is that the men weren't interested in intellectual discussion, preferring
instead to seek emotional communion by speaking "from the heart."

James Hillman, on the other hand, couldn't be kept out of sight, since he
taught at mythopoetic gatherings. But even when Hillman lectured, offering
"archetypal" interpretations of all manner of things, his more abstract ideas
usually did not become the focus of discussion. The men simply did not go to
gatherings to engage in theory talk. Jungian ideas were thus put forth by
Hillman, Bly, Meade, and others, not for consideration of their possible value
for understanding men's lives, but for immediate use, preferably without dis-
sension. The Jungian perspective, in other words, was assumed, not examined,
at mythopoetic gatherings.

Nonetheless, knowledge of Jung and his ideas varied widely among the
mythopoetic men. Some were well versed in Jungian psychology; a few knew
little about it. Most knew something about Jungian psychology owing to prior
reading, experience in therapy, or to reading done after exposure to Jungian
ideas at a mythopoetic gathering. In addition to Jung, the men frequently

turned to other Jungian sources, such as Hillman's *A Blue Fire* (among his other books), Bly's *A Little Book on the Human Shadow*, Moore and Gillette's *King, Warrior, Magician, Lover*, Robert Johnson's *He: Understanding Masculine Psychology*, and Jean Shinoda Bolen's *Gods in Everyman*. Jungian ideas also came to the men by way of various newsletters, newspapers, and small magazines published by men's groups around the country.

While some of the men learned a lot of Jungian psychology, this wasn't necessary. A man could participate competently by following directions and taking cues from more experienced men. What men who knew less about Jungian psychology did not see was the extent to which mythopoetic practice derived from Jungian theory. I found that it was only after reading Jung and Hillman that I could see how mythopoetic activities in which I'd participated grew out of their thinking. Mythopoetic activity was also informed by ideas from Sufi theosophy, as I also came to see after the fact. This chapter puts the theory up front, so that the internal logic of mythopoetic activity will be clear from the start.

The Core of Jungian Psychology

In Jungian psychology the psyche is said to include the conscious ego and a vast unconscious consisting of both personal and collective elements.[2] The personal elements are the impulses and feelings each of us has repressed; this material becomes part of our shadow, which is the negative side of who we are—the side we prefer to deny exists. The collective unconscious consists of archetypes, which are inborn potentials for the patterning of psychic energy. By giving form to psychic energy, archetypes lead us to think, feel, and act in particular ways. Archetypes are products of species evolution. All humans naturally possess a complete set of them.

While these archetypes are inborn in all humans, certain archetypes tend to dominate in men, while others dominate in women. In men, the archetypes that give masculine form to psychic energy tend to dominate; in women, those that give feminine form to psychic energy tend to dominate. Women and men are thus predisposed to perceive, think, feel, and act differently because their psyches, like their bodies, are built differently. Men, by virtue of their masculine archetypes, are inclined to impose order on the world, defend territory, provide for others, give of themselves to others, and love women. Women are inclined by their feminine archetypes to perceive the connectedness of all things, establish intimate ties with others, nurture others, bear children, and love men.

Jungian psychology does not say that all men will act differently from all women by virtue of inherited traits. It says only that males and females inherit different potentials for their psychic energies to take shape in ways that are defined as masculine and feminine. It also grants that life experience affects the way these energies come to be expressed in the personalities of individual women and men. Jungian psychology can thus be described as loosely essentialist.[3] It recognizes that women and men can be very different or quite alike, depending on precisely how their archetypal potentials are activated by experience. As I will argue in the next chapter, part of the appeal of Jungian psychology stems from its being loosely rather than strictly essentialist.

Jungian psychology has more to say about gender. According to Jung, men possess a "contrasexual soul image," which is a man's inner woman, or what Jung called the anima. Similarly, women have in them an inner man, or what Jung called the animus. In Jung's view, the anima—which might be seen as the name given to the feminine archetypes as they operate in men—is associated with *eros*, that is, with feelings and with relatedness. The animus—which might be seen as the name given to the masculine archetypes as they operate in women—is associated with *logos*, that is, with logic, reason, and the kind of intelligence that gives order to the world. So while gender differences are conceived, abstractly, in terms of polarities, real men and women are seen as having both masculine and feminine sides.[4]

The goal for women and men is to integrate these sides, these masculine and feminine energies. When women integrate the animus, and men the anima, it expands and broadens their personalities; it gives them access to the qualities thought to belong to members of the other sex. For a man to access and integrate his anima he must first work through his shadow. And only then, after dealing with his inner femininity, can he become a Wise Old Man. The route to wholeness for each sex is thus via integration with the psychic energies conventionally associated with the other.

Jung called this process of psychic growth "individuation." This is a lifelong process whereby the parts of the psyche are integrated into a balanced, harmonious, unique whole. Individuation requires recognizing and accepting the archetypes at work within us. It also requires activating the archetypes that help us cope with the problems of life. Men whose feminine archetypes are not properly activated will have trouble dealing with problems involving emotions and relatedness. Women whose masculine archetypes are not properly activated will have trouble dealing with problems requiring discipline and assertiveness. Such troubles are thus seen, by Jungians, as signs of a psyche out of balance and of a need for special efforts to help individuation along.

The conscious ego cannot directly perceive the archetypes at work within us. But through the imagination we can perceive archetypes when they are manifested as images. Often these images take or can be encouraged to take personified forms; thus we may perceive gods or other characters—such as a king, warrior, magician, lover, or wild man—within us. The Jungian idea is that insight into the dynamics of the psyche can be attained by understanding the drama being acted out by these internal characters. The greatest insight can be achieved by entering into dialogue with these imaginal characters to find out what they have to tell us about who and what we are, about our troubles, and about what to do.

In the Jungian view it's crucial to recognize the archetypes that are operating within us. It is dangerous to fail to do this, because all archetypes are not benign in their effects. Moreover, every archetype has a dark side that can lead us to behave in ways harmful to ourselves and others. Knowing that we possess these tendencies is necessary to avoid the destructive paths on which they can put us. Likewise we must accept our shadow elements—those parts of ourselves that we would like to deny exist—lest we project these traits onto others. When we project our shadows onto others we react hurtfully toward them, because they remind us of what we most dislike about ourselves.

Because all archetypes have positive and negative sides, there is in us, for example, not just a king archetype, but also a good king that leads us to act wisely and generously, and a bad king that leads us to act like tyrants. The key to individuation is to recognize and accept the positive and negative within us and to strive for balance. Such balance and wholeness is, according to Jung, the telos of the psyche. There is supposedly within us an archetype of the Self, which is like a blueprint for the psyche's unification.[5] The psyche thus contains a pattern for health and wholeness, although the fulfillment of this pattern can be impeded by what happens to us in life.

The symptoms of distress that a person might present to a Jungian therapist are not seen as evidence of an irreparably damaged psyche; rather, symptoms are seen as a consequence of the psyche striving against resistance to achieve wholeness. Bad feelings are thus a good sign; if these feelings are not repressed they can aid individuation. Jungian therapy seeks to relieve distress by dealing with the problem that is impeding individuation.

This means helping people understand, first, the archetypal ordering principles that are part of the collective unconscious and which affect every psyche; and second, how psychic troubles may arise from complexes created by traumatic experience. Complexes are strong currents of emotion that swirl around particular ideas, images, or events.[6] The problem is that complexes and their emotional loadings can lead to bizarre, obsessive, or destructive behaviors that seem to arise out of nowhere and resist rational control. Individuals can sometimes seem to be possessed by these elements of the unconscious.

Jungian therapy therefore seeks access to the unconscious, where archetypes and complexes may be operating in ways that cause pain or lead to destructive behavior. But since archetypes and complexes are not directly accessible or visible, what must be sought are their manifestations in the form of images. Dream analysis is thus important in Jungian therapy because it is believed that in dreams archetypally-shaped energies appear as objects and characters. Jungian therapy may also use guided-imagery exercises, psychodrama, therapeutic touch, free form movement, and drawing or sculpting to create other routes to the unconscious. The idea is to bypass the ego, stir the imagination, and induce images to well up from the psyche.

When images appear, insight is gained by paying close attention to the type and intensity of the feelings they evoke. Images that evoke intense feelings indicate where complexes exist. What a Jungian therapist does is to provide symbolic interpretation of the images and the dramatic interplay between them, an interplay that typically reproduces a mythological motif.

The correspondence between the inner drama and a myth is not coincidence. Jung believed that myths are the articulated scripts of dramas that have been playing out in the psyche for millennia. These dramas and the forces at work within them are human universals arising out of the collective unconscious. So it often occurs that the drama being played out in an individual's psyche mirrors the plot of an ancient myth. Knowing how the mythical story unfolds can therefore offer insight into how things are unfolding in the inner drama. In therapy, then, myths might be invoked to give coherence to the otherwise confusing drama going on in the individual's psyche.

In this view myths are not fanciful explanations for natural phenomena; nor are they merely parables. Rather, myths are products of ordering principles at work in the psyche; the ego emerged as a result of these principles, it did not create them. Thus humans have consciously shaped only the surface content of myths, in the sense of using the words that cultures have provided. But the basic life struggles portrayed in myths, and the emotions they evoke, are not of our conscious creation, since these things are the products of evolutionary struggles that predated the ego. In a sense, then, we are more products of our myths than our myths are products of us.

Jungian psychology does not, however, give us over to fate or to primal forces. We can exert control, if we know what's going on. Myths can, in fact, be seen as warnings about what can happen when archetypal energies get out of control. Here is where the ego, which is also a product of evolution and an aid to survival, becomes important. It lets us make choices about using archetypally-shaped psychic energy in generative rather than destructive ways. Jungian psychology thus advocates a dual path of individual growth that involves both claiming the unconscious and the powerful energies it contains, yet also learning to separate ourselves from these energies so as to avoid being at their mercy.

Following this path of growth is made difficult by the ego's tendency to presume itself to be the whole of the psyche and to be in charge of what goes on there. Jungians believe this problem is especially severe in Western industrial societies, where the dominance of scientific rationality feeds the ego's illusion of preeminence. Progress toward individuation may thus be blocked (and other problems may persist) because the ego refuses to acknowledge the unruly forces that are also part of the psyche. The therapeutic response of Jungian psychology is to try to create access to the unconscious and understanding of the forces at work there. Once this is achieved, the ego assumes a new, less presumptuous role, which is to give meaning to, rather than to try to control, the archetypal dramas being played out in the psyche and in life.

Quick relief from psychic pain is thus not the avowed goal of therapy based on Jungian psychology. Therapy must also give meaning to suffering, for what is most unbearable, in the Jungian view, is meaningless suffering. Here again myths are important, because they can give meaning to suffering by providing a way to see it as part of an unfolding drama that is sensible and leading to a potentially fruitful conclusion. And because myths are said to be products of the collective unconscious, myth-based interpretations of personal suffering implicitly connect the individual to the entire human species and, moreover, to the creative power of the universe. Jungian psychology thus makes it possible to endow individual suffering with cosmic significance.

Jung recognized that his psychology and its therapeutic entailments held the greatest appeal for people in middle age. Before this, people are too busy establishing families and careers to have much time for deep introspection. But by mid-life, after families and careers are established, it is often the case that things repressed earlier come back to haunt. It is also the time when people begin to question the meaning of their work and accomplishments, and begin also to think of their own mortality. This is the time when a psychology that can help give meaning to one's life, one's past and present suffering, and one's impending death will be most compelling.

Hillman's Archetypal Psychology
James Hillman (b. 1926) began teaching at mythopoetic gatherings in the mid-1980s and, although he was not as publicly visible as Robert Bly, was arguably the movement's chief theorist. Most of the mythopoetic men had heard Hillman speak or had read some of his writings. His influence was also extended through Bly, Meade, Moore, and the host of second-tier teachers who drew on his work. Hillman was revered by some of the mythopoetic men, who expected posterity to place him alongside Freud and Jung in the pantheon of great depth psychologists.

The version of Jungian psychology with which Hillman is associated is called archetypal psychology, which is essentially Jungian in seeing the psyche as transpersonal and as patterned in form and function by archetypes.[7] It also accepts the Jungian view that archetypes are accessible only via their manifestation in images. But whereas Jung saw the set of archetypal images as limited to forms that were recognized across time and cultures as specially significant, Hillman says that anything can be an image. It takes some explaining to show how this move is more radical than just expanding the category of archetypal images.

Archetypal psychology is concerned with how we perceive and experience the world. It presumes that the archetypally patterned functioning of the psyche enables perception of both the mundane and the numinous.[8] It also proposes that even mundane things can have archetypal significance for the psyche—if we can learn to symbolically interpret these things as images. This requires an unusual perceptual stance. Instead of taking mundane things literally, as we ordinarily do, archetypal psychology would have us interpret them symbolically, as if they were objects in a fantasy or a dream. Archetypal psychology thus invites us to alter our ego-dominated, literal stance toward the world.

The problem that archetypal psychology addresses is our inability to see the archetypal significance or value of the images that fill the world. This problem arises in part because the conscious ego insists on taking things literally. Another source of the problem is that our culture, shaped by the rationalizing forces of science and bureaucracy, no longer encourages us to think symbolically, metaphorically, poetically. As Hillman says, we have lost our imaginal sense and can no longer see, borrowing the phrase from Wallace Stevens, that "there is always a poem at the heart of things."[9]

An image sometimes evokes such powerful emotional resonance in the psyche that its archetypal significance is plain. But to fully tap the power and significance of the image it must be "heard metaphorically," which is to say, again, that it must be given a symbolic rather than literal interpretation. Moreover, the message must be heard with the heart, since images are said to communicate via emotions and intuition rather than the intellect. Appreciating images in this way requires awakening the imagination and cultivating the ability to think metaphorically. These are the goals of therapy based on archetypal psychology.

Archetypal psychology does not use a fixed scheme to interpret images. Rather, an image must be "listened to" as a representative of a theme in the archetypal drama unfolding both within and around us. It is in dialoguing with the image, in imagination, that we receive its message. This is a matter of learning to see beyond the literal obviousness of things to the powers that are manifest in them, and thus to see the spiritual significance they may hold for us. Engaging the world in this way is what Hillman, taking the term from Keats, calls "soul making."[10]

In Jungian terms, soul making is a matter of enlivening more aspects of the psyche by learning to grasp the archetypal significance of images and by bringing those images to life in the imagination. In plainer terms, soul making is a matter of learning how to respond to things in the world in emotionally and aesthetically more complex, intense, and interesting ways by perceiving them as imagistic metaphors. This opens new possibilities for creating meaning and for experiencing more richly the world and one's self. Mythopoetic activity is sometimes described as dedicated to this sort of soul making, or "soul work."

In his talks at gatherings, Hillman (often teaming up with Michael Meade) distinguished between concrete, psychological, and mythological or "imaginal" thinking. Soul making through mythopoetic work requires imaginal thinking. This distinction between types of thinking—which has much earlier origins, as I will discuss in the next section—is an important piece of the theory behind mythopoetic practice.

Concrete thinking deals with things in the plainest possible terms. Thinking concretely, we might ask, Will this wood burn? Will this blade cut? Can I eat this? Such thinking is necessary for brute survival; it abhors ambiguity. Psychological thinking is necessary to deal with people and relationships. This type of thinking might lead us to ask, Who did what to me in childhood such that I turned out this way? or, How can this conflict be resolved? Although it may use abstract terms, refer to less tangible things, and tolerate more ambiguity, psychological thinking still aims at literal explanation. In thinking psychologically we are still in the common sense, everyday mode of perceiving what is real.

As this argument would have it, we are good at concrete thinking, since daily life demands a lot of it. Under the influence of modern social science we are also supposedly well versed in psychological thinking (sociology would be considered psychological in this sense). What's more, the ego prefers us to see the world only in concrete, rational, and scientific ways because this ensures the ego's dominance in the psyche. So it is imaginal thinking, which requires contact with the unconscious parts of the psyche, that we—as creatures of a scientific, rationalized world—have lost facility with. Recovering this facility, the argument goes, is necessary to be able to use myths, fairy tales, poetry, and ritual as means to find universal significance in our personal suffering.

If we can release our need for literal interpretations we might see, for example, that a dwarf in a fairy tale is not really a dwarf but an ugly truth that causes harm if ignored. Likewise we might see that a princess in a story is not a real woman but a symbol for beauty.[11] If this were all it proposed, archetypal psychology would appear to simply echo the lessons of basic literature courses: things aren't always what they seem; and any element of a story can function symbolically. But archetypal psychology is not about decoding literary symbolism. It is about using the metaphoric capacities of the imagination more generally to see the ordering principles that pervade and influence our lives. Thus to the extent that it is concerned with characters in fairy tales, myths, dreams, and fantasies, these are seen as playing archetypal roles, not as veiled or inverted representations of real people.

Imaginal thinking of the kind Hillman recommends is not intended to lead to correct metaphorical interpretations of things. It is intended, rather, to give things a presence in the imagination that opens possibilities for experiencing them in more intense and complex ways. In this sense imaginal thinking leads to mysteries rather than explanations. It is not a way to see things as they are, as if that were somehow possible; it is an attitude that encourages the creation of a world with multiple layers of meaning. Again this is soul making: deepening ourselves as persons by increasing our capacities to respond to life in richer ways aesthetically and emotionally.

In one illustration, Hillman goes so far as to call words "persons."[12] To do so is to highlight their character, their independent power, as ordering principles. In this view words are seen as paradigm incarnations of the spirit of logos acting on psychic energy. Words, in other words, have the power to shape raw experience. Like images, words are presences in the psyche with their own history and character (which can be fathomed by attention to etymology). An archetypal stance demands an appreciation of these powers on their own terms. It also suggests that we not mislead ourselves into thinking that the power of a word is a mere invention of the ego.

The powers represented by words and images, Hillman says, can even be thought of as gods within us, gods worthy of respect. In this view anything that is treated as an archetypal image is a theophanic presence—the face of a god. Imaginal thinking thus offers vision into an ordinarily unseen world of spirits, demons, angels, gods. Concrete and psychological thinking cannot penetrate this world and thus never let us see the connections, meanings, patterns, and powers at work that imaginal thought can. There is here a notion of mystical seeing that derives from Sufism and which has come into the mythopoetic movement in part via Hillman's archetypal psychology (more about this later).

Imaginal thinking is metaphorical thinking, by means of which concrete and psychological realities can be given new significance. For example, a heart attack stemming from the obsessive pursuit of careerist ambitions is, in concrete terms, a physiological problem. Thinking psychologically it could be seen as caused by stress and a lack of social support. In metaphorical terms, however, the heart attack might be seen as an *attack on the heart*. This metaphor suggests that a person's spirit or emotional core has been attacked by forces that imposed soul-killing demands and aroused one-sided ambitions. The metaphor thus gives a different insight into the problem, implying that its roots run deeper than a poor diet and lack of exercise.

Again, the core idea is Jungian: things, events, and emotions that have obvious literal meanings can also be symbolic of the archetypes that, at another level of reality, give form and meaning to life. To fathom such things, the argument goes, we must use a mythological or metaphorical schema to transcend our mundane worldview. Imaginal thinking is thus necessary not just for wringing symbolic meaning out of myths and fairy tales, but also for seeing and experiencing—for being fully alive to—the archetypal patterns that underlie every aspect of our spiritual and material existence.

One difference between Hillman and Jung is that whereas Jung wants individuation to yield a harmoniously integrated Self, which is also Jung's image for God, Hillman takes a polytheistic view and allows the psyche to be the place where many gods act, and not necessarily in harmony.[13] This difference is important in that Hillman's view normalizes tension in the psyche. Rather than resolving these tensions the goal is to "hold them" in a productive way, a way that keeps imagination and the soul alive and growing. Psychic tension and suffering are thus seen as essential to soul making and not necessarily to be avoided. Those who have never found tranquility through psychotherapy or other quests for personal growth might find this view appealing, since it implies that the persistence of psychic tension is not a mark of failure.

There is no denying the religious, even mystical, tones that ring through archetypal psychology.[14] But it is important to see that much of the language used by its practitioners, especially Hillman, is intended to illustrate the mode of thinking archetypal psychology prescribes. That is to say, the language is often metaphorical and playful. References to spirits and gods must be read in this light. As Hillman says, "The Gods of psychology are not believed in, not taken literally, not imagined theologically. . . . They are formulated ambiguously as metaphors for modes of experience . . . ."[15] This captures much of what Jungian and archetypal psychology are about: using metaphors to give a sense of coherence and purpose to an otherwise perplexing and absurd existence; and, especially in Hillman's case, enriching existence by making it more emotionally and aesthetically intense, complex, and provocatively mysterious.

So again, what archetypal psychology offers, in a way that seems strange if its terms are taken literally, is a method for seeing, hence experiencing, the world in an extraordinary way. Still, and despite the religious tone, archetypal psychology is fully concerned with the here and now of embodied human existence. One need not believe in nor speak of gods and angels to see the value in expanding our abilities to give meaning to experience and to respond to experience in more complex emotional ways. Poetry, literature, and other forms of art have provided this kind of therapy for millennia. Archetypal psychology is in this tradition rather than the tradition of scientific psychology.[16]

The Sufi Influence

The Sufis are a sect of Islamic mystics dating from the early seventh century A.D. Sometimes said to practice the "esoteric aspect of Islam," the Sufis, like the Christian Gnostics, seek to discover direct knowledge of the eternal and the divine. Sufis seek this knowledge through theophanic visions on the plane of imagination. One of the Sufi methods for inducing such visions, self-hypnotic chanting and dancing, has given the Western world its stereotypic image of the Sufi: the whirling dervish.

There is a great deal of overlap between Sufi theosophy and Jungian/archetypal psychology. One reason for this is that in developing his ideas Jung studied ancient Eastern religions and also the Christian Gnostics, both of which seem likely to have influenced the Sufis.[17] In the case of archetypal psychology the influence is more direct. Hillman cites the French scholar Henry Corbin (1903–1978) as archetypal psychology's "second immediate father," after Jung.[18] From Corbin's interpretations of the thought of the thirteenth-century Sufi master Ibn Arabi, archetypal psychology gets many of its ideas about images and imagination.

According to Corbin, Ibn Arabi conceived of a theophanic plane that was an intermediate world between body and spirit.[19] Arabi believed that it is possible to see on this plane divine thought manifested in image-symbols. The practice of active imagination that helps one gain access to this plane is called *ta'wil*, which means symbolic, mystical exegesis. This practice involves transmuting everything into an image-symbol; that is, interpreting all sensible objects as if they were dream images. This is essentially the same practice of metaphorical, imaginal seeing that Hillman prescribes.

Other of Arabi's teachings have become part of archetypal psychology. The distinction between concrete, psychological, and imaginal thought also seems to be an adaptation from Arabi, who referred to three corresponding forms of knowledge: intellectual, emotional or experiential, and real. The latter requires going beyond facts and feelings to perceive what is right and true. In Idries Shah's rendering of Arabi: "the people who attain to truth are those who know how to connect themselves with the reality that lies beyond [intellectualism and emotionalism]. These are the real Sufis, the Dervishes who have Attained."[20]

Some of this may indeed seem esoteric. But these Sufi teachings, echoed in Jungian and archetypal psychology, were part of the theory behind mythopoetic practice. Though few of the mythopoetic men would have recognized the names of Henry Corbin and Ibn Arabi, most would have been familiar with the ideas that came from these sources. The Sufi notions that the Divine is manifested in each of us; that truth is therefore to be found within; that there exists a world of unseen patterns that can be perceived only via the imagination; and that enlightenment comes not through the head but through the heart, were key pieces of mythopoetic philosophy.

Sufi ideas were also infused into the mythopoetic movement through poetry. One of the movement's most popular poets, Jalaluddin Rumi (1207–1273), was a great Sufi mystic. His poems were often read at mythopoetic gatherings, and many of the men bought books and tapes of his poetry.[21] Robert Bly, who has translated Rumi, was largely responsible for introducing him to the mythopoetic men. Another popular poet, whose ideas about ecstatic union with the Divine echo Rumi's, was the fifteenth-century Indian mystic Kabir (ca. 1440–1518). Bly also translated Kabir and brought his poetry to the mythopoetic men.

Reduced to literal terms, the idea conveyed by much of this poetry is this: Enlightenment, or Knowledge of the Real, requires cultivation of a love of God so intense that it overwhelms the self; only with such pure love does it become possible to achieve contact with the Divine. Many Sufi poems teach how such contact can be achieved. Those poems that are ecstatic paeans to the Divine, as manifested in the form of the Beloved, teach by showing the kind of emotional intensity needed to make contact with the Divine. Other poems seek to prepare the listener for contact with the Divine by arousing passionate longing for the Beloved.

Sufis try to produce perceptions of the Divine by getting the mind working on a higher level. This is what the *sema* (whirling) dance and the repeated chanting of a *zikr*—a remembrance, often in the form of "there is no god but God"—are supposed to do.[22] The poetry can also work in this way. In addition to praising the Divine and inciting passion, many Sufi poems are examples of *ta'wil* in brief, showing how ordinary experience can be metaphorically upended, thus revealing meanings and portents hidden from the literal minded.[23] Various Sufi sects are distinguished by the ways in which they use poems, dances, chants, and teaching stories to induce special perceptions or what is often called "seeing with the eyes of the heart."

As a form of religion Sufism is highly accommodating. Despite its connection to Islam, which is usually considered rigidly monotheistic, Sufism is essentially pantheistic. It teaches that the Divine is manifested in all things, and that the highest spiritual goal is the achievement of unity with the Divine through ecstatic love. Ego-dissolving ecstasy, induced by poetry, dancing, and chanting, is thus a path to God and divine wholeness. This can be translated into Jungian terms as the search for contact with the image of the Self, the God-image, via the unconscious.

The theme of love (or Eros) as a path to enlightenment resonates even more strongly in Hillman's archetypal psychology. For the Sufis, love is the way to discovering unity with God. For Hillman, love is the way to make soul. This means much the same thing, since to make soul is to use the imaginal sense to perceive and learn from images of the gods. Hillman says that therapy is "love of soul" and that love "leads the way as psychopompos and is, inherently, the 'way' itself."[24] Though he may not be committed to the same metaphysics as the Sufis, Hillman here sounds like a Sufi with a Jungian veneer.

Archetypal psychology and the poetry of Rumi (and, to a lesser extent, Kabir) were just the obvious paths whereby Sufi ideas entered the mythopoetic movement. Many of these same ideas (sometimes recognized as derived from Sufism, sometimes not) were part of the various New Age philosophies that many of the mythopoetic men imbibed in the 1970s and 1980s. Today the boundaries between these bodies of thought have largely dissolved, at least among New Age spiritualists in the United States.[25] Moreover, the ideas themselves have changed as a result of their travels and interactions with other ideas. It's thus difficult to trace any one piece of the theory behind mythopoetic practice to a single source.[26]

The theory behind mythopoetic practice was like a fuzzy ball of string. At its core were ideas from Jungian psychology, archetypal psychology, and Sufism. Though it looked as if the ball could grow by adding new things, what it picked up was more string: the same basic ideas with slight twists.[27] What held it all together was a belief that emotion, imagination, and metaphor were means to open doors to the unconscious and thereby to achieve not only insights into one's self, but transformative contact with powers and mysteries inaccessible to the purely rational mind. Mythopoetic activity involved just this kind of door opening. It wasn't that the men tried, as if they were devout Sufis, to achieve visions of or unity with God, although perhaps some men did. Most of the mythopoetic men were simply trying to explore more of themselves, and to wring more meaning and experience out of life, than they had been able to by use of ideas better suited to doing science or running a bureaucracy.

The Religious Attitude
The theory behind mythopoetic practice presumes invisible ordering principles at work in the universe and thus in every psyche. It also holds that we can learn to see these ordering principles, and that by doing so we can give meaning to

our lives by seeing how our existential struggles replay those faced by humans throughout time. The idea of a collective unconscious consisting of a common inheritance of archetypes implies that we are bound in this struggle both to our ancestors and to our contemporaries. And since these archetypes are said to be products of evolution, they are also therefore links between each of us and the mysterious, creative forces of the universe that engendered our being. In pointing to invisible forces that bind us to each other and to the universe, the theory behind mythopoetic practice evinces a definite religious quality.[28]

If these essentially Jungian ideas do not constitute a religion, they can certainly induce a religious attitude. By this I mean a sensitivity to the transcendent meanings of things, meanings that are supposed to help us find our place in the human community and in the universe. A religious attitude also implies reverence toward unknown powers greater than ourselves. To call archetypally shaped energies gods, if only metaphorically, indeed suggests they are powers worthy of respect and awe. For some people, then, Jungian psychology awakens a sense of the sacred—a sense of our universal, mysterious, and powerful connections to others and to the world. This religious attitude is what could make a spiritual community out of a mythopoetic gathering.

It is doubtful whether any other Western psychology could have done the same. Even Freudian psychology, which also posits a powerful and mysterious unconscious, offers no rewarding sense of connection to the human community, let alone to the cosmos. Most psychologies tend in fact to isolate the sufferer. The insights they offer into suffering must often be paid for with feelings of difference and separation. In contrast, Jungian psychology says that our psychic struggles are part of a drama that has been unfolding throughout the history of the species, and that, no matter how lonely we feel, our struggles are testimony to our bond with the rest of humanity. People hungry for community are likely to take heart in this way of seeing things.

To say that Jungian psychology induces a religious attitude is not to equate it with organized religion. Jungian psychology does not offer catechismic answers to questions about the purpose of human life or about rightful conduct. Nor does it impose a singular vision of the truth. In fact, Jungian psychology is anathema to organized religions that impose the truth from the top down. The doctrines imposed by organized religion are seen as stifling the imagination and impeding soul making. Instead of this, Jungian psychology urges discovery of one's personal truth by delving into the unconscious and relating what is found there to universal themes embodied in myths.

The religious comfort Jungian psychology offers thus comes not from doctrine but from its ability to foster a sense of connection and to help people create meaning in their lives.[29] In these respects Jungian psychology is compatible with most traditional religions. Since it offers no opposing doctrine, it can function as a kind of booster shot to intensify feelings of spirituality—whatever deity or doctrine a person might otherwise believe in. Even if one is not religious in a traditional Western way, it can still amplify generic inclinations to spirituality.

It might be objected that Jungian psychology contains a doctrine in the form of its presumptions about the existence of archetypes, the psyche, and so forth. This is true; belief in these things is foundational for Jungians. And certainly the belief in essential differences between men and women is a piece of doctrine. But the basic premise of the perspective is that there are ordering principles and energies at work in the universe and in the psyche that are ordinarily beyond our ken—a premise that most physicists would accept. This compatibility with other belief systems, be they religious or scientific, is part of what gave Jungian psychology its appeal.

DIAGNOSIS AND PRESCRIPTION

The Jungian theory behind mythopoetic practice informs a diagnosis of why men today are suffering. Briefly, the diagnosis is as follows: The demands of jobs and careers, and especially the expectations for success in jobs and careers, have caused men to develop in a one-sided way. Men's psyches are thus out of balance; the overvalued and overworked rational ego has crowded out those parts of the psyche oriented to eros, leaving men unable to feel as deeply and powerfully as possible. It's also a problem that certain archetypes haven't been activated, leaving men cut off from the full range of masculine energies that would otherwise be available to cope with life's problems and enjoy its pleasures.

A further problem is that many men have failed to accept these masculine energies as part of who they are. The archetypes that men are supposedly not adequately "in touch with" are those such as the king, the warrior, and the wild man. These are names for the archetypes that enliven men distinctly as men. If these archetypes are not activated in men, or if men deny that these archetypes are part of who they are, then they will be disempowered or lacking in life-giving force. They will be, as Bly said, "soft men."[30]

The diagnosis says that men got this way because they haven't had the experiences necessary to activate the positive sides of their masculine archetypes. What men have missed is initiation; they have missed out on a ritualized introduction to their "gender ground," and thus have never been shown how to safely activate the masculine energies that are their birthright. Part of the problem is that in modern industrial societies fathers aren't close enough to their sons to do the job. What's worse is that many men today, because they were raised by women and then told by feminism that maleness equals malevolence, have been made to feel ashamed of their masculine energies. Therefore many men in our society have never become mature men, in the Jungian sense, by claiming all their innate powers as men.

According to this diagnosis, the psychic problems many men begin to experience in mid-life—the feelings of emptiness, aimlessness, numbness—stem from the way corporations, government, and some women have conspired to keep them from becoming mature men, from developing deep or authentic masculinity. This Jungian notion of "deep masculinity" is not an exaggerated form of traditional masculinity. Rather, it is the secure, generative masculinity that develops after a man has accepted his feminine side. In Jungian terms, this is the development of the masculine personality into a fuller form, after union with its opposite.

The problem, then, is that the natural process of individuation, as it is supposed to occur in males, has been thwarted by a number of forces, and men are suffering as a result. Society is also suffering, in this view, because men who are not initiated, who are insecure in their masculinity, who have not accepted their feminine sides, and who are thus immature in the Jungian sense, may be unable to channel their masculine energies into anything but violent, domineering, or destructive behavior. While some men will behave in these ways, many others, because their masculine archetypes have barely been activated, will be flaccid conformists who don't fight to protect their communities and the environment. Again society suffers.

A prescription follows from this. If the problem is that men aren't in touch with the archetypes that are their birthright, then something must be done to put them in touch. What is necessary, first of all, is a conjuring of the archetypal images through which men can activate the various masculine energies potentially present within them. This is part of what mythopoetic activity aims to do: access the unconscious and call up images that give men a sense of their capacities to feel and act in archetypally masculine ways. In this way men are supposed to learn how their masculine energies can be tapped and integrated into a more balanced and powerful Self taking shape within them.

Storytelling, poetry reading and writing, ritual enactment, expressive movement, psychodrama, drumming, and dancing are supposed to help men bring their archetypal energies "on line," to feel those energies flowing through them, to connect with them more fully. Jungian psychology also prescribes this kind of activity as means of confronting the shadow, which is to say, as means of uncovering and dealing with repressed feelings which, if they remain repressed, lead to destructive behavior, ineffectuality, and stunted psychic growth.

The idea is to aid the psyche's natural movement toward individuation, but in a way that responds to the special needs of men in Western industrialized societies.

Earlier I said that to understand mythopoetic activity *in its own terms* it is necessary to understand its Jungian basis. But if the point were only to understand mythopoetic activity in its own terms, one might just as well read Jung, Hillman, Bly, Moore and Gillette, Meade, and a few others and be done with it. My purpose, however, is to tell a different kind of explanatory story about mythopoetic activity, one that goes beyond the terms its practitioners used to explain themselves. For this purpose Jungian psychology is only a starting point; it is part of the story, not all of it. Now the *appeal* of Jungian psychology to a particular group of men must be explained, so better to understand the men and their milieu.

CHAPTER 3

FEELING BETTER ABOUT BEING MEN

Why did the mythopoetic men find Jungian ideas so appealing? A big part of the answer is that Jungian psychology helped the men to feel better about themselves as men who did not live up to the standards of traditional masculinity. As I'll show, it did this by allowing the men to redefine their feminine traits as aspects of "deep masculinity." Another part of the answer is that Jungian psychology told the men that the power, wisdom, goodness, and joy they were seeking were all within reach, inside them. The idea that so much was already within them—in the form of psychic energies waiting to be discovered and tapped—appealed to educated men who were used to finding things out for themselves, who didn't want to believe they had been irreparably damaged by prior wounds, and who wanted to believe in their innate goodness as men.

As noted in chapter 1, almost all of the men in the Local Group were college graduates, some also having advanced degrees. By virtue of their schooling, the men appreciated science as a way to understand the world. But they had come to realize that science could not answer the questions of meaning to which they had turned in mid-life. Jungian psychology, in its mythopoetic form, seemed to be an effective alternative for dealing with problems that resisted other modes of thought. It was also a legitimate intellectual tradition. As one man in the Local Group said, "This isn't some kind of flaky, California New Age shit we're into."

Religion might have provided an alternative, but because of their education, autonomy in work, and social status, the men were not accustomed to being told what to think, and were thus resistant to doctrinaire answers to their questions about themselves and about life. Jungian psychology, rather than imposing an interpretation of experience on the men, gave them a method, and inspiration, to search for the truth within themselves, without having to rely on sacred texts or gurus. The mythopoetic teachers were not seen as leading the men toward the one true interpretation of their experiences. And rather than explaining away the men's experiences by neatly pinning them to a theoretical scheme, the Jungian approach kept those experiences alive in consciousness where they could be explored and given new meaning. It thus fostered the emotional and imaginative vitality many of the men felt they had lost by putting too much faith in scientific rationality and too little in intuition.

The Jungian idea that truth is to be found within also allowed the men to interpret the stories and poems told at mythopoetic gatherings however they chose. When a story or poem was told, the point was made that each man would find it spoke to him in a different way. It was often part of the instruction, either before a story was told or as it was about to be discussed, that each man should look for an image that evoked in him strong feelings. This image, it was said, would be his "doorway into the story." Again this allowed each man to see what he wanted in the story rather than having it predigested for him. Jungian psychology thus allowed the men to have as much autonomy in doing soul work as they had in their jobs.

Despite their relatively privileged statuses, many of the men said they felt their lives were out of control. For some men this was because the energy they had put into their careers had not paid off—materially, psychologically, or spiritually—as they had hoped. For others, a sense of powerlessness arose from failures in relationships. These men said that they felt unable to resist the demands of others. Sometimes these men described themselves as being unable to "defend their boundaries" and thus tending to let others abuse them. Whatever the source of these feelings of inefficacy, Jungian psychology told the men that the powers they desired were there inside them, waiting to be activated.

Jungian psychology said that the capacity to exercise these powers—to be a generous king, resolute warrior, wise magician, or passionate lover—was in every man by virtue of the archetypes wired into him. The power of this idea, like any good piece of ideology, did not depend on its literal truth but on the effects yielded by embracing it. Believing in these archetypal powers could inspire self-confidence and, as a result, more effective action, thus affirming the belief by creating a self-fulfilling prophecy.

To tap these powers, Jungian psychology prescribed a hero's journey into the psyche. This seemed doable to even the least stalwart of the men. It also helped that mythical heroes enjoyed a high rate of success. So even if men doubted their ability to resist demanding people in the outer world, Jungian psychology gave them a sense of power by turning them toward a more manageable inner world where, according to myth, things usually worked out in the end. If this sort of optative imagining gave some men a sense that they too could make things work out, it could again create a self-fulfilling prophecy whereby real gains in self-confidence resulted.

Men who felt plagued by uncertainty about how to be good men also found comfort in Jungian psychology. Many of the mythopoetic men said that their fathers had been emotionally distant, physically absent, or abusive. For a long time this left them, they said, without a positive image of masculinity and without guidance in how to be good men. Jungian psychology offered a solution by saying that the capacity to be good men was wired into them. Even if their fathers didn't do what was necessary to activate the best masculine archetypes, it was still possible, with a little work, to bring those archetypes on line and develop positive masculine traits.

Jungian psychology also allowed the men to own their troubles *safely*. It did this by portraying a man's troubles as part of a myth in which he was caught up, rather than as the result of his inadequacies. Whatever myth a man might be caught up in was said to represent a pattern of life struggle faced by men throughout time. Looking at troubles this way alleviated feelings of guilt and shame. If a man believed his problems were part of the grand scheme of life he could feel less at fault for creating them. Jungian psychology thus absolved the men of blame for creating their problems. But then—because it was said that with sufficient self-knowledge a man could find his way into a different myth—Jungian psychology also gave the men a chance to take credit for solving those problems.

By turning the men's attention toward the psyche and away from the outer world, Jungian psychology served their material interests. It did this by suggesting that the men could find the sources of and solutions to their problems inside them—and thus there was no need for critical analysis of or action to change the stratified, exploitive economic system in which they held comfortable positions. While the men were critical of corporations, government, and the media, Jungian psychology offered little insight into how these institutions caused trouble in men's lives. By promising the men that truth and power could be found within, Jungian psychology preempted the careful study of alienating political and economic (and, yes, male-dominated) institutions. It also allowed the men to avoid questioning the ways in which their own material ease depended on the very forms of social life that caused their psychic distress.

The Promise of Self-Acceptance

Shame is the opposite of healthy self-acceptance. Some of the men said they were troubled by feelings of shame, which they attributed to various sources: teasing about their bodies as they were growing up, personal failures, sexual abuse as children, and from diffuse messages about the depravity of men.[1] Feeling shame is not a problem unique to the mythopoetic men. Many of us are disciplined by messages from parents, teachers, bosses, ministers, and political enemies about our inadequacies, bad habits, and evil impulses. If such messages are received before adequate defenses are formed, psychic damage can result. Jungian psychology provides tools for repair.

It does this, first, by saying that it is in the nature of all things to contain good and evil. It is thus natural for the psyche to cause frightening, destructive, and nasty impulses to well up in the imagination. We can't help this, Jungian psychology says; it is part of what we are as humans. As long as we don't harm others by acting on these impulses, we have nothing to be ashamed of. No one then can be purely good, since to be human is to have a shadow side that is always a potential source of destructive behavior. What's bad, in this view, is not to *have* a shadow but to *deny* its existence. Jungian psychology thus allowed men to admit there was evil in them without feeling guilty about it.

This was a liberating message for some men. Those who had behaved themselves all their lives, who had been the "nice boys" their parents wanted them to be, but who felt guilty for wanting to raise hell and lash back at others, could rest their consciences. Even men who had acted badly to the point of hurting others could find solace in this way of thinking, since it allowed them to attribute their misbehavior to overwhelming archetypal forces. In either case, men who felt shame and guilt, deservedly or not, could, by thinking in Jungian terms, mitigate those debilitating feelings.

Jungian psychology also aided self-acceptance by naturalizing what had been defined as shameful or pathological. It thus helped men who suffered from views of themselves as weak or flawed. It also helped the men find value in their weaknesses and shadow sides. According to Jungian psychology, the shadow holds much psychic energy. To tap this energy for constructive purposes we must not only acknowledge our shadows but explore and integrate what is in them. The implication is that facing up to the shadow is what a good man must do. Jungian psychology thus allowed the men to turn their flaws and weaknesses into resources for feeling morally courageous.

In these ways, Jungian psychology helped the men reinterpret their troubles as potential sources of goodness, strength, and growth. In the language of the movement, a man discovered that "a wound can be a blessing." This might be because the wound, the trauma, the weak spot, taught a valuable lesson, or because it showed where a man's potential for growth was to be found. In this view, things previously felt to be sources of weakness or shame were redefined as offering chances to grow and develop a unique combination of strengths.

Jungian psychology also allowed the men to believe that if they were not as good or powerful as they wished, it was not because they were inherently bad or weak, but because certain positive archetypes had not been activated to balance the negative ones. It thus protected the men's sense of essential goodness by telling them that they were not irreparably damaged by prior abuse, and that there was much goodness in them naturally. All they had to do was to get the right archetypes on line.

The message here was not simply that the men were okay. In light of their feelings of shame or weakness—and their sense that *something* was wrong—such a message would have rung false and undermined the appeal of Jungian psychology. Its appeal depended precisely on its ability to acknowledge all kinds of bad feelings—of shame, fear, grief, sadness—and then to redefine these feelings as natural and as potential sources of growth and strength.

Although this has a New Age ring to it, the men, following Bly, rejected the idea, which they associated with New Age philosophy, that life can be all sunshine and harmony. Jungian psychology struck them as more realistic in its recognition of inner strife, destructive impulses, and bad feelings, and also more helpful for coming to terms with, rather than trying to deny, these psychic realities.

As discussed in chapter 1, many of the mythopoetic men, though conventionally masculine in appearance, were in other ways quite feminine. The men in the Local Group were gentle, expressive, affectionate, nurturant, and concerned with relationships. They rejected the model of traditional masculinity that demands competitive striving, heroic self-sufficiency, the ability to dominate, and the denial of tender feelings. For being this way—for not living up to the code of traditional masculinity—the men felt some of the devaluation that women typically experience in our society. Jungian psychology offered relief from the mild victimization they had experienced as gentle men.

Because it recognizes the masculine and feminine in us all, Jungian psychology allowed the men to accept in themselves traits that are devalued where the standards of traditional masculinity prevail. In the Jungian view, it is an important part of the individuation process for a man to "integrate his anima," that is, to activate and accept the feminine archetypes within him. As noted in the previous chapter, this is a necessary part of becoming a Wise Old Man who embodies radiant, solar masculinity.[2] So it is natural and good, according to Jungian psychology, for men to possess traits defined as feminine. Traits for which the men might have previously been victimized, or for which they felt shame, thus could be redefined as indicators of advanced progress on a journey toward wholeness.

There was, however, an even more compelling redefinitional move made possible by Jungian psychology. This was to redefine the feminine traits the men already possessed as aspects of the "deep," "authentic," or "mature" masculine. The best textual illustration of this can be found in Robert Moore and Douglas Gillette's *King, Warrior, Magician, Lover*, which many of the men saw as offering the most accessible and compelling account of the Jungian view of men and masculinity.[3]

In Moore and Gillette's account, mature masculinity combines and balances energies shaped by the four masculine archetypes of the king, warrior, magician, and lover. Ironically, these archetypes seem to produce some traditionally feminine kinds of behavior. King energy "seeks peace and stability, orderly growth and nurturing for all people. . . . The King cares for the whole realm and is the steward of nature as well as of human society" (pp. 62–63). Warrior energy is not just about discipline and resolve, but about being "warm, compassionate, appreciative, and generative" (p. 95). Magician energy "aims at fullness of being for all things, through the compassionate application of knowledge and technology" (p. 110). Lover energy makes a man feel "related, connected, alive, enthusiastic, compassionate, empathic, energized, and romantic" about his life, goals, work, and achievements (p. 140). It is Lover energy that is most clearly associated with eros and femininity. Under the sway of this archetype, a man "wants to touch and be touched . . . to touch everything physically and emotionally . . . to live out the connectedness he feels with the world inside, in the context of his powerful feelings, and outside, in the context of his relationships with other people" (p. 122).

Guided by this Jungian thinking, men who already had impulses to be peaceful, nurturant, warm, compassionate, empathic, sensual, and romantic—and had learned to devalue these impulses as feminine—could redefine them as aspects of deep masculinity. In this view, the men could see their gentle, tender, and emotional sides not as evidence of being failed men, but as evidence of progress toward mature masculinity. Traits that once aroused feelings of shame or inadequacy as a man now aroused feelings of pride in having attained a better, more complete kind of masculinity. Jungian psychology thus moved the mythopoetic men from the margin to the center of their gender category.

The Promise of Self-Knowledge and Authenticity

Though the mythopoetic men were "womanly" in some ways, they did not escape the socialization pressures men usually face. Like most men, they had to swallow a lot of hurt and, especially as boys, accept a great deal of domination at the hands of others. Some of the men believed that in being taught to be nice boys—to please their mothers or other powerful people in their lives—they were forced to stuff many masculine impulses into their shadows. Even in middle age many of the men felt as if they were still overly concerned with trying to please others. As a result they felt there was much about themselves that they did not know, since so much had been repressed.

Part of what Jungian psychology offered the men was encouragement and guidance in exploring these mysteries, which stood in enticing contrast to their often drab and predictable outer lives. The men were curious about what lurked in their shadows, wherein Jungian psychology said could be found the keys to self-knowledge and authenticity. And rather than offering bitter psychic medicine, Jungian psychology made this exploration sound like a great adventure into a complex, deep, and vast territory of the psyche.

To make a project of exploring an inner realm of psychic forces and emotion marked a departure from the path of traditional masculinity on which many of the men were set. Some said that an awareness of any feeling at all was a discovery, an awakening or, as one man put it, "a realization that I had been numb for years." A benumbed condition may be a predictable result of socialization into traditional masculinity, which requires denial of feelings that might interfere with getting a job done. Socialization, however, was not the only source of the problem for these men; another was the middle-class life path that led to absorption in work and family life. Such a path left little time, and offered little incentive, for self-reflective meditation or other spiritual pursuits.

Relationships with women were also cited as a source of self-repression. Some men blamed their mothers for causing this, either by abusing them sexually, by saying derogatory things about men, or by being overly protective. Some men blamed wives and lovers who, they said, stifled them by being domineering and relentlessly critical. The point is that many of the men believed their shadows were brimming with masculine impulses in part because some women in their lives insisted those impulses be put there. In some cases men saw, through the Jungian lens, that they were more tyrannized by a mother *complex*, with an *archetypal* mother at its core, than by their own flesh-and-blood mothers.[4]

The mythopoetic men believed that for many years they denied their own feelings, repressed their desires, ignored their emotional needs, and remained mysteries to themselves. Many also believed that this happened not only because of socialization into traditional masculinity but also because of wounds inflicted by others. The message taken from Jungian psychology was that self-blame was unwarranted if others had forced a man, as he was growing up, to create a huge shadow. Jungian psychology acknowledged that it was indeed a bad thing for a man to be cut off from part of his innate humanity. But it also said that recovery was possible. In fact, a man's distress at feeling numb was a good sign, because it showed that his one-sided psyche was striving for wholeness.

Jungian psychology was appealing because it promised that damage done earlier could be repaired. To do so, a wound or other painful act of self-repression had to be squarely faced, for only then could the energy surrounding it be used for therapeutic change. The objective, as Hillman put it, was to figuratively rewrite the traumatic experience and put a new, mythological frame of meaning around it. At mythopoetic gatherings men tried to do this by working with images in the imagination, by doing psychodrama, or by enacting rituals. In these ways the trauma or the wound could be dealt with in the company of supportive men and made into a kind of post-hoc initiation.[5]

For some men it was important to cope with feelings of shame and anger at themselves over not being assertive enough at other times in their lives. Assertiveness, or the ability to resist domination by others, is part of the ideal of traditional masculinity—a part the mythopoetic men still embraced. Under the force of this ideal, being unable to resist the domination of others can damage a man's masculine pride. He might thus feel ashamed and angry at himself for being so weak as to let others, especially women, "violate his boundaries."

Jungian psychology was helpful because it prescribed mythologizing, thus depersonalizing, the sources of men's wounds. In this view, a man could see his experience of hurt, betrayal, or abuse as part of a mythical drama, in which case it didn't make sense to stay angry at himself or anyone else. Feelings of anger and shame could be partly dissipated just by seeing things this way. Jungian psychology also allowed residual anger and bad feelings to be redefined. Instead of being seen as psychic dross to be discarded as quickly as possible, these feelings now could be seen as fuel for lighting a path to personal growth.

Being taught to be traditionally masculine makes it hard for men to explore, express, and cope with strong feelings. Traditional masculinity, especially in "WASP culture," even entails an attitude of scorn for feelings, since these are considered women's concerns. But for a variety of reasons the mythopoetic men rejected this aspect of traditional masculinity. They realized that they had strong feelings—sometimes churning beneath a numb exterior—that demanded attention. Pretending otherwise was seen as exacting too great a cost.

Awareness of the discrepancy between an "everything's-okay" persona and the troubled feelings it masked was a source of angst, or even existential crisis, for some of the men. They realized that it took enormous energy to maintain the usual masculine facade, and that doing so cut a man off not only from part of himself but also from others with whom connections might be made based on an honest sharing of feelings. What was worse than being depressed, some of the men said, was having to pretend otherwise and thus deny themselves needed emotional support. Jungian psychology spoke to this problem of inauthenticity by making *denial* pathological and legitimating the study of one's emotions.

Some of the men knew that denying their feelings had caused them trouble in the past. In addition to chronic inauthenticity, there was the episodic loss of control that came with failing to attend to and comprehend feelings. Some of the men believed that a lack of attention to their feelings had led them into addictive behaviors, bad relationships, or stifling jobs, perhaps repeatedly. These men sought self-knowledge not just to live more authentically, but to gain more control over the emotions that underlay destructive patterns of behavior. As some of the men saw it, it was their denial of feelings at odds with their "nice-boy" or "everything's-okay" personas that had caused them the most trouble.

Jungian psychology gave the men a way to talk about and understand what was going on inside them. It also legitimated the effort to find out. But it did not impose a diagnosis, pass judgment, or prescribe a specific remedy. It said simply that the root of the problem was to be found in the unconscious, and that strong emotions marked the path into this territory. This made sense to the men, especially those who had experienced uncontrollable, unpredictable, or frighteningly intense emotions as part of what was wrong. Rooting matters in the unconscious was also appealing. This allowed the men to face their problems in a way that preserved self-worth, since the conscious ego was let off the hook for creating the imbalanced psyche or the immense shadow from which a man's problems supposedly arose.

Jungian psychology was not merely comforting ideology for the mythopoetic men. It indeed comforted them by saying that the psyche is naturally a wellspring of unruly impulses; that strong, unpredictable feelings are a normal and fascinating part of every man, and thus no man need feel ashamed of being emotional. But it also implicitly demanded, less comfortingly, that a man who wished to become a whole person explore this part of himself, even if doing so was painful. Real and sometimes disruptive insights could thus be gained, if only by studying what was once ignored. If a man undertook this work, Jungian psychology promised relief from inauthenticity, relief from the loss of control to dark psychic forces, and the attainment of self-knowledge that was previously limited by the strictures of traditional masculinity.

The self-knowledge the men sought had to do only in part with liberation from feelings of anger and shame. It had to do also with liberating feelings of appreciation for beauty, affection for other men, and spontaneous joy. Many men came to the movement feeling that their lives were safe and bland. These men doubted their ability to feel, to experience life fully. And now, in middle age, they faced the depressing prospect of forty more years of the same. Jungian psychology offered hope by saying that no man lacked the capacity to feel, that an unlimited reservoir of emotional energy was there in the psyche, waiting to be tapped. This idea gave the men something to look forward to in the second half of their lives: the possibility of discovering new things about themselves and of experiencing life in new ways.

Hillman's archetypal psychology was especially appealing for this reason. Hillman advocated the use of the imagination, a heightened animal awareness of things in the world, as well as a cultivation of aesthetic sensibilities— a general enlivening of the mind and soul. This is exactly what many of the mythopoetic men were looking for. Hillman's talks at gatherings made it seem that this sort of enlivening was not only possible, but a noble goal that men were entitled to pursue without apology. This was the liberating message many of the men took from Hillman and for which they most revered him.

Much the same applies to the men's search for creative energy within themselves. As educated men who tended to have a great deal of autonomy in their jobs, the mythopoetics highly valued creativity. Yet at mid-life some of the men feared that their creative powers had waned, or that their jobs no longer provided the kind of challenges that stimulated creativity. Jungian psychology said that the potential was still there, perhaps in the shadow; the creative forces in the psyche just had to be tapped. This too opened up new prospects for the men to discover things about their capacities for creative work. It helped them believe that their best years were still ahead.

It might seem that the mythopoetic men were a group of dispirited, unassertive, middle-aged men who sought meaning and satisfaction outside their lackluster careers. While there is a grain of truth in this characterization, in that it fits some cases, on the whole it is a caricature. The picture must also include men who could be lively, bold, and intense, but who—no matter how successful they were in conventional terms—suffered deep dissatisfactions living under the demands of traditional masculinity. Such a life, as these men came to see it, entailed limited personal growth, a hollow search for wealth and status, emotional isolation from other men even while competing with them, and tiresome inauthenticity. Jungian psychology offered hope for change.

Pulling them together, the healing messages the men took from Jungian psychology were these: *The powers you feel you are lacking as a man are there inside you, waiting to be tapped. You need not be ashamed of your impulses, nor of your tender feelings, nor of the scars you've received from others; these do not make you immoral, flawed as a man, or eternally damaged. These are in fact important and valuable parts of who and what you are as a man. If you accept and integrate these parts of yourself—which is what your distress is a signal for you to do—then you will be on your way to wholeness. You will find that what you felt were wounds will become sources of insight and strength. If you are feeling uncreative, you can, via the unconscious, tap into the creative energies of the universe. And if you are feeling alone, realize that via the collective unconscious you are connected to all other human beings, past and present.*

Jungian psychology, as the men imbibed it in mythopoetic form, thus let them feel better about themselves right away by virtue of the comforting beliefs it offered rather than by virtue of its analytic power.[6] Ironically, part of the appeal of Jungian psychology was that it didn't seem to promise quick fixes. By saying that a man had to face and work through his shadow, then struggle to integrate various parts of his psyche and perhaps endure some anguish in the process, Jungian psychology dispelled the aura of frivolity associated with New Age navel-gazing. The men also wanted to feel masculine, yet many of them associated religious and spiritual pursuits with women and femininity. Jungian psychology, in contrast, made personal growth seem like an arduous process—a hero's journey requiring courage, intelligence, and resolve. It thus not only promised mature masculinity as the goal, but made the very attempt to get there seem like a manly thing to do.

The Appeal in Context

It may now seem obvious why Jungian psychology appealed to men who felt stuck, numb, isolated, disempowered, or unsure of their worth as men. But the appeal of Jungian psychology and its healing messages depended on more than the personalities of the mythopoetic men. The reasons for the appeal run deep into our culture, which I have so far let stand as a backdrop to my consideration of the men. Now I want to bring culture to the fore and look at how certain beliefs and values—ones the mythopoetic men breathed in like air as they were growing up—made Jungian psychology seem like a key to the iron cage.

In chapter 2, I said that Jungian psychology is loosely essentialist. Essentialism, in its extreme form, proposes a rigid, biological determination of differences between women and men. Jungian psychology is more flexible. It proposes that certain archetypes—those that shape psychic energies in masculine and feminine ways—operate more powerfully in women than in men, and vice versa. But since both sexes possess a full complement of archetypes, which must be activated by life experience, this leaves much room, in theory, for women and men to develop in various and perhaps quite similar ways. Hence there is an assumption of an essential, internal difference, yet it is nonspecific or "loose," with regard to claims about how this difference will be manifested in personality and behavior.

Any kind of essentialist view tends to see gender as a natural, rather than socially constructed, phenomenon. Despite much social scientific evidence to the contrary, belief in the naturalness of gender is still entrenched in our culture. This is the belief, to put it another way, that nature, not socialization and everyday social control, causes males and females to think, feel, and act differently.[7] The essentialism of Jungian psychology harmonizes with this current of belief, in which the mythopoetic men were swept up long before gender issues became salient for them. As a sociological view of gender would not have done, Jungian psychology affirmed what the men already believed.

The loose essentialism of Jungian psychology appealed to the mythopoetic men for other reasons. For one, it provided an ideological defense against feminist criticism of men. Such a defense was necessary precisely because the men saw gender as natural. The men were aware of generic feminist criticisms of men as brutish, insensitive, power hungry, and so on. However, the men did not see these criticisms as aimed at social arrangements that produced a lot of genuinely bad men. Rather, they interpreted these criticisms in light of a view of gender as natural, and hence saw them as criticisms of the essential nature of men. Feminist criticism of men was thus experienced as indicting the inherent morality of all men. A defense had to respond in kind; it had to somehow redeem the category.[8]

Jungian psychology did this in several ways. First, it said that the essential nature of men was much like the essential nature of women, since we are all endowed with the same archetypes. So if men have evil in them, well, so do women (many of the men felt that this corroborated their observations). Second, it said that just as the psyche naturally contains evil, it also contains good. Thus we are all, women and men, no more naturally evil than we are naturally good; we have the capacity for both, and the tension between them is ever with us. And third, it said that all of the archetypes at work within us evolved to aid survival and could, if properly balanced in the psyche, serve useful purposes. So even if we all possess energies that could produce evil results, those energies need not overwhelm us and might even lead to good results if they are properly integrated and balanced.

Jungian psychology thus also allowed the men to say, in response to feminist criticism (*as they experienced it*), "This is what I am as a man—take it or leave it. I won't feel guilty about it. I won't apologize for my gender." Since, as Jungian psychology saw it, gender is largely wired into us and then shaped in detail by forces beyond our control, there is nothing one can be expected to apologize for.

It is worth mentioning, in anticipation, that Jungian psychology provided another handy tool for defense against critics: the concept of projection. Outsider criticism of the men and their activities was often dismissed as a case of the critic projecting onto the men some aspect of his own shadow. The real problem, in other words, was said to be *with the critic*, whose troubled psyche was causing him to see in the mythopoetic men some disliked aspect of himself. The critic and his criticism were thus delegitimated. I use the masculine pronoun because this defense was used mostly against male critics. This was consistent with Jungian theory, which holds that we tend to project our shadows onto others of the same sex.

Part of the appeal of essentialism also derived from the cultural requirement for men to constantly prove their masculinity, usually by outperforming other men. For most men the important audience to satisfy—the audience that passes judgment on and validates masculinity—consists not of feminist critics but of other men. Despite the clear economic and political benefits of being a man, the need constantly to prove one's masculinity can make for an exhausting and insecure existence.[9] Jungian psychology relieved the insecurity that came from relentless testing by saying that masculinity was a natural quality of all males. This essentialist view was attractive to men who were tired of the testing and to those who, for whatever reasons, did not meet the standards of traditional masculinity.[10]

The reason *loose* essentialism was so appealing is that it left room for change. A stricter form of essentialism would have implied that a man's way of being a man was immutable—a matter of what the luck of the genetic draw had made him: very masculine, very feminine, or something in between. A man would thus have to bear either the emotional costs of living out traditional masculinity or the shame of being a feminine man. Loose essentialism, however, allowed the mythopoetic men to have it both ways. They got moral license for possessing the feminine and masculine traits they already had, and they got the theoretical possibility of changing what they wanted to change.

In a culture where masculinity and femininity are not seen as socially constructed, and where men feel attacked simply for being men, essentialist views of gender will be attractive. Such views provide more than a way to explain gender; they make it morally defensible, since only nature is held accountable for how we think, feel, and act as men and women.[11] For the mythopoetic men a loose version of essentialism was especially appealing because it allowed them to value and defend what they already were, to blame others for impeding development of their masculine potentials, and yet to believe in the possibility of change.

Yet the mythopoetic men were not oblivious to the role of culture in shaping men's lives. The men heard James Hillman criticize our culture for failing to cultivate soul in men; Robert Bly criticize it for separating fathers and sons and for putting immature men in positions of power; and Michael Meade criticize it for its lack of effective initiation rituals. The men themselves sometimes vaguely criticized the government, corporations, and the media for their homogenizing influences and demands for conformity. So it is not that the movement's philosophy totally naturalized or psychologized the reasons why men experience being men as they do.

For the most part, however, the men treated gender, masculinity, and the category 'men' as if they were primitive constituent elements of the universe. The unwillingness to see these things as social constructions stemmed in large part from a belief that our human worth depends on being self-determining, unique individuals. This kind of individualism creates resistance to analyses of how culture and social arrangements—through processes that often escape conscious awareness—make us what we are. Resistance to the constructionist view also came from the belief, shared by many of the mythopoetic teachers and men, that modern industrial culture is corrupt. Seeing the culture in this way, the men preferred not to see themselves as its products.

But if individualism insulated a bit of the men's self-worth from the alleged corruptions of "the culture," it also had a cost, because it led them to feel responsible for their circumstances and failures in the first place. Individualism, in other words, abetted both self-*worth* and self-*blame*. Jungian psychology let the men make the best of this situation. It let them selectively disparage "the culture" for impeding their development, yet believe that within them there remained a sacred, undamaged, unique Self striving toward wholeness. Feelings of self-worth were thus preserved, while self-blame was mitigated.

The Jungian emphasis on personal truth was appealing for similar reasons. Figuring out how the world works and how we fit into it is hard work, perhaps even unpleasant at times when arguments and evidence clash. Jungian psychology demanded no such struggle, only a sharing of feelings, which no man could contest unless the expression of those feelings seemed insincere. A man could thus say boldly what he felt, without fear of another man deflating him with a better argument. Talk of this kind, which occurred at mythopoetic gatherings, appealed to gentle men who disliked conflict. It also helped foster a sense of individual agency, since it let a man feel that he had independently discovered a bit of incontrovertible truth.

Another piece of the cultural backdrop to the mythopoetic movement is a loss of faith in science as a means to solve human problems. Since the bombing of Hiroshima and Nagasaki, it seems that science has caused as much harm as good. And while the physical sciences have at least given us technological benefits, the social sciences have given us no greater power to create a just and humane society. One result seems to be a widening recognition that our problems are not fundamentally technical ones, but are aesthetic, spiritual, and moral. If so, tough-minded and tough-hearted rationalism cannot save us. The need thus seems clear, by some accounts, for non-scientific means to cope with these kinds of problems.

Into this breach of faith have stepped fundamentalist religion and various New Age philosophies. Jungian psychology has also found a niche in the gap between science and religion.[12] It even explains the postmodern predicament by citing our natural tendency to be misled by the ego into believing that rational consciousness can solve all our problems. Jungian psychology sends us back to the unconscious, both personal and collective, to find out what's wrong and why we can't seem to get a handle on things. And where else to look for insights and solutions? If science has failed us, the reasoning goes, what comparably powerful tools do we have but myth and religion? New Age philosophies and Jungian psychology are logical alternatives for those who want spiritual growth and insight into themselves but who see the dangers of fundamentalist religion.

The mythopoetic men recognized that walking a path to spiritual growth was not a scientific problem. But the men were not irrational in their search for solutions, despite the disparagement of rationality sometimes heard at gatherings or found in mythopoetic writings. Jungian psychology provided a coherent set of ideas and a sane method for working on problems that were conceived as fundamentally spiritual and emotional. Together, what Jungian psychology and mythopoetic practice provided were rational paths to the mysterious and ineffable part of us that is beyond the ken and control of the conscious ego. If this is where spiritual and emotional problems are rooted and must be dealt with, then it made sense, the men reasoned, to use methods that gave access to this territory.

Dis-Spirituality and Male Supremacy

It can be said, without much exaggeration, that the mythopoetic movement arose amidst an epidemic of spiritual malaise among middle-class men in the United States.[13] For the mythopoetic men, who seemed to suffer from this malaise most acutely, the Jungian idea of a collective unconscious was appealing because it provided a sense of spiritual connection; it thus served as an ideological counterweight to the individualism that otherwise left them feeling isolated. But the suggestion was more than that men ought to feel connected because they belonged to the same sex or the same species. Jungian psychology implied something more profound.

Because the archetypes we all possess are supposedly products of evolution, we are linked to each other, to our ancestors, to the earth, and to the universe that spawned us, down to the roots of the psyche, which is to say, in Jungian psychology, down to the depths of our souls. Thus no man is really as isolated as he might sometimes feel. And since each Self is unique, every man can feel like an individual while also feeling deeply connected to others and to the cosmos. With these ideas Jungian psychology invites a religious experience of universal connection between all humans and between humans and nature, while also resonating with our cultural belief in individual specialness.

This was an alluring invitation for men who, in a secular age dominated by an ideology of individualism, longed for spiritual experience and communion, but who also rejected traditional religion as dogmatic, intolerant, and divisive. The men also longed to restore some sense of mystery, of unseen forces and greater powers—a sense of enchantment—to the rationalized, scientifically explained world in which they lived. With its premise of powerful, invisible archetypes, and its metaphoric language of gods and spirits, Jungian/archetypal psychology gave the men what they needed in this respect. It served to delightfully re-enchant the world without resurrecting a judgmental, lawgiving God such as the men had had their fill of as boys.

While the religious aspect of Jungian psychology provided a vague sense of connection with others, the mythopoetic men wanted more. They longed for spiritual connection *with other men*. Elsewhere in their lives their relationships with other men were bound by the rules of traditional masculinity. Those relationships were thus often tinged with competitiveness, concern for status, and distrust; there was also small space for the safe expression of emotion in those relationships. Even if all this wasn't acutely distressing, because the men were used to it, the difficulty of relating to other men spiritually and emotionally induced chronic low-level feelings of isolation, emptiness, and depression.

In our culture women have traditionally serviced the emotional needs that masculine existence left unfulfilled in men. But this has changed. More middle- and upper-middle class women today work in masculine environments and bring home their own emotional needs, which feminism has urged them to take seriously. Many women are thus less willing to put aside their own needs and tend uncritically to men's wounds.[14] This is one reason why some men have turned to other men for support. The mythopoetic men wanted some-thing more specific, however, from other men: affirmation of their identities as men. To see why this was so important it is necessary to recognize that ours is still a male-supremacist society.

To apply this label does not mean that every man in this society enjoys more status and power than every woman in every situation. Nor does it mean that men never feel powerless. It is simply a broad characterization of a society where a vastly greater share of political and economic power is in the hands of men. The term also describes a society in which greater value is given to things male and masculine. This is as would be expected in a society where men largely control the resources that are used to propagate cultural values, and where the chances of having a decent life depend on being man enough, regardless of one's genitalia, to successfully compete for power and status. Masculine energy, to use the Jungian term, is still what gets you taken seriously and wins the prize. Enacting masculinity is also what keeps men, as a group, on top.

Because Jungian psychology encouraged the men to recognize and accept the feminine sides of themselves, some, perhaps many, of the mythopoetic men would deny that the movement's implicit philosophy placed greater value on masculinity *per se*. They might say that while men naturally tend to place more value on masculinity, women do the same thing with regard to femininity. But neither tendency, they might add, establishes the inherently greater value of masculine or feminine energies or ways of being. Both are necessary and must achieve a sort of balanced tension in the psyche. One without the other is no good.

While this defense is correct in Jungian principle, it ignores the premise that masculinity is still held to be the true and best calling *for males*. Jungian psy-chology does not encourage men to pursue deep femininity; that is not the telos of the male psyche. So it is clear, as it seems to have been in Jung's mind, that men not only do but ought to value the masculine more highly than the feminine.[15] The whole ethos of the mythopoetic movement affirmed this. Despite the rhetorical homage the mythopoetics paid, in public, to gender equality, their search for and celebration of masculinity belied any disavowals about the greater value masculinity held *for them*.[16]

One of the things that Jungian psychology allowed the men to do was to redefine their feminine traits as aspects of mature masculinity. This redefin-ing made sense in a male-supremacist context because it raised the value of these traits. In a different kind of society, where maleness and masculinity were not the more highly valued attributes, the mythopoetic men might have said, "let's try to be better *people*." Or they might have said, "So what if we're femi-nine? Everyone should be." The importance of being better *men*—by getting

in touch with the archetypes of the mature *masculine*—stemmed from living
in a society where men and masculinity were valued above women and femininity. Male supremacy, in other words, was the key cultural fact that let the
men feel better about themselves as men by redefining masculinity, with the
help of Jungian ideas, to better fit what they already were.

Metaphorical Cages and Material Interests

The mythopoetic men were raised in a cage not of their own making. The
German sociologist Max Weber warned us about this cage long before Bly
found it in the Grimms' fairy tale "Iron Hans." Weber argued that rationalization was the master trend of history and that it would deaden the human
spirit in ever more areas of social life.[17] Weber's iron cage of rationality and
the cage that holds Bly's Iron John character are homologous metaphors for
the constraints imposed by a bureaucratic capitalist society. What the mythopoetic men discovered, like others before them, was that adapting to life in
the cage has high costs.

For these men, however, the cage was nicely gilded. The men wanted out
occasionally but still wanted the cage to come home to. Jungian psychology
let them have it this way. The men could use Jungian ideas to face the distress
caused by the emotional, aesthetic, and spiritual deprivations of traditional
masculinity and capitalist society. Yet Jungian thinking did not threaten their
material interests by insisting that their distress could be alleviated only by
abolishing the male-supremacist and capitalist social arrangements upon which
their material ease depended. Jungian psychology called for confronting the
shadow, not the ruling class.[18]

It makes sense, then, that Jungian psychology resonated so powerfully with
the mythopoetic men. The reasons for this were psychological, cultural, and
economic. Of course, the attraction of men to the movement wasn't just a
matter of what Jungian psychology did for them. It was a matter of what they
could do with Jungian psychology at mythopoetic gatherings. Mythopoetic
activity had its own appeal because it allowed the men to do things together
that they could not do on their own by reading all the psychology in the world.
The next two chapters will examine what the men accomplished and how they
did it.

CHAPTER 4

THE SEARCH FOR COMMUNITAS

At mythopoetic gatherings men greeted each other with hugs. In closing a meeting the men often held hands or locked arms in a circle. At other times the men massaged, lifted, or playfully wrestled one another. These were expressions of their desire for closeness with other men. Though the physical contact sometimes had an erotic edge to it, the men were not seeking sexual contacts. The communion they sought was emotional.

Sympathetic media portrayals of the mythopoetic men showed them getting together to share feelings of grief and pain. But mythopoetic men's work was not just about *sharing* feelings, as if the men knew what they were feeling and then met to talk about it. Often the work itself aroused feelings that surprised the men. And these feelings were not always pleasant. But even unpleasant feelings were resources for fashioning a special kind of collective experience that was rare and seductive for men in a highly bureaucratized society. Men who experienced it at a gathering kept coming back.

As noted earlier, most of the mythopoetic men were between the ages of 35 and 60. Nearly all were white, self-identified as heterosexual, and college educated. Most had good jobs, owned homes, and helped maintain families. They were, by and large, successful in middle-class terms. Yet the men said that living out this conventional script had left them, at mid-life, feeling empty and dissatisfied. They found that the external trappings of success were not spiritually fulfilling. What's more, many of the men felt isolated, cut off from other men, except for competitive contexts, such as the workplace. Hence many described mythopoetic activity as part of an effort to create a community where they could interact with other men in a supportive, noncompetitive way.

But it was not exactly community that these men created through mythopoetic work. Although they did sometimes establish serious friendships and networks of support, the men did not enter into relations of material dependence upon each other, live in close proximity to each other, work together, or interact on a daily basis. Usually the men who met at gatherings and in support groups went home to their separate lives. It was thus not a true community they created. What the mythopoetic men sought, and tried to create at their gatherings, was both more and less than community. It was communitas.

Victor Turner, an anthropologist who studied tribal rituals, describes communitas as both a shared feeling-state and a way of relating. To create communitas people must relate to each other outside the constraints of formally defined roles and statuses. As Turner describes it:

> Essentially, communitas is a relationship between concrete, historical, idiosyncratic individuals. These individuals are not segmentalized into roles and statuses but confront one another rather in the manner of Martin Buber's 'I and Thou'. Along with this direct, immediate, and total confirmation of human identities, there tends to go a model of society as a homogeneous, unstructured communitas, whose boundaries are ideally coterminous with those of the human species.[1]

Communitas, as Turner says, can happen when the force of roles and statuses is suspended; that is, when individuals in a group feel themselves to be equals and there are no other significant differences to impede feelings of communality. Although the mythopoetic men did not use the term communitas, they sought to relate to each other in the way that Turner describes as characteristic of communitas. At gatherings they tried to engage each other in a way that was unmediated by the roles they played in their everyday work lives.[2] The men tried to practice this kind of relating by talking about the feelings they had which they believed arose out of their experiences as men.

The mythopoetic men presumed it was possible to establish deep emotional connections with each other because they were all, at root, men. This presumption grew out of the Jungian psychology that informed mythopoetic activity. The idea was that all men possessed the same set of masculine archetypes that predisposed them to think, feel, and act in similar ways. In Jungian terms, these masculine archetypes are parts of the collective unconscious to which we are all linked by our common humanity. Thus all men, simply by virtue of being male, were presumed to possess similar masculine energies and masculine ways of feeling. Mythopoetic activities were aimed at tapping into these energies and feelings so that men could connect based on them and thereby mutually reinvigorate themselves.

Turner distinguishes three types of communitas: normative, ideological, and spontaneous or existential. Spontaneous communitas is that which happens in the settings and moments where people relate directly, as described above, outside the bounds of social structure. When this type of relating is organized into a system, Turner says, it becomes normative communitas, which is like planned spontaneity. Turner is echoing Max Weber's notion that charisma tends to destroy itself by becoming routinized. Ideological communitas is Turner's term for doctrine that describes how to create utopian communities in which communitas will flourish. The mythopoetic men wanted *spontaneous* communitas, which they did not want to see killed by too much organization of or theorization about their activities.

Turner says that spontaneous communitas is "richly charged with affects, mainly pleasurable ones," that it "has something 'magical' about it," and that in it there is "the feeling of endless power."[3] He compares hippies and tribesmen in a passage that also suits the mythopoetic men:

> The kind of communitas desired by tribesmen in their rites and by hippies in their 'happenings' is not the pleasurable and effortless comradeship that can arise between friends, coworkers, or professional colleagues any day. What they seek is a transformative experience that goes to the root of each person's being and finds in that root something profoundly communal and shared.[4]

The mythopoetic men indeed sought personal growth through their experiences of connection at mythopoetic gatherings. A "connection," in the sense the men used this term, was a feeling of emotional communion with another man or group of men. Such connections were made when a story, poem, dance, ritual, or psychodramatic enactment brought up strong feelings in one or more men, and this in turn induced strong feelings in others. In these moments the men learned about their complexity as emotional beings and about their similarity to others.

Turner's references to pleasurable affects and mysterious feelings of power are echoed in how the mythopoetic men described their experiences. Mythopoetic activity was enjoyable, the men said, because "It's just being with men in a way that's very deep and powerful"; "There's a tremendous energy that grows out of men getting together and connecting emotionally"; and "It just feels great to be there connecting with other men in a noncompetitive way." And indeed the feelings were often intense. As one man said during a talking circle at the end of a weekend retreat, "I feel there's so much love in this room right now it hurts."

Men also said that going back to their ordinary lives after a gathering meant "coming down from an emotional high." In an interview one man described his feelings about gatherings and about leaving them:

> I think what I get out of the gatherings is an assembly of people, not necessarily just male, but an assembly of people that is a family I never had. It's uncritical, it's supportive, and it's nurturing of the way I am. I'm not prone to anger. I'm not violent. I'm not mean. I'm kind to people. And all that is fine and accepted. They're not looking at whether I'm successful at work or a millionaire or brilliant or anything else that might be external to what's inside. I usually find myself driving home from a gathering and getting five miles down the road and just tearing up for no apparent reason except that I'm separating from that family I never had to begin with. The intensity of the feelings I get when I go to gatherings and leave have always been special to me. They touch that inner nature that there's no room for anywhere else.

I, too, experienced this transition from the warm, open, supportive, emotionally-charged atmosphere of a gathering to the relatively chilly atmosphere of a large research university.

The success of a gathering was measured by the intensity of the emotion it evoked and the connections thereby established. A less successful gathering was one where the emotional intensity was low and the men did not make strong connections. Near the end of a weekend retreat that had been cozy but not intense, one man said wistfully, "We've had some good sharing, but only once did I feel much happening in me. That was when B. was talking. I felt tears welling up. So there's a deeper level we could get to." This was said at the start of the final talking circle, in hopes of prompting a more emotional discussion before the retreat was over. In addition to showing the desire for communitas, this statement also shows that it took effort to achieve. Spontaneous communitas did not happen spontaneously.

CREATING SPONTANEOUS COMMUNITAS

Not all gatherings were aimed as intently at creating the same degree of communitas. Some gatherings were more "heady," in that they were devoted to discussion of a topic, such as fathering or men's health or men's friendships. Often there were moments of communitas at these kinds of meetings, as when a discussion exercise brought up some strong, shared feelings in the men. But it was at the retreats—those which had an explicit mythopoetic, ritual, or "inner work" theme—where the greatest efforts were made to create communitas. The methods used included telling stories and poems, enacting rituals, forming clans, chanting, and special forms of talk.

Forms of Talk
At mythopoetic gatherings men often made personal statements that revealed something shameful, tragic, or emotionally disturbing about their lives. Such statements might be made by each man in turn at the beginning of a retreat as part of saying why he was there, what he was feeling, and what he hoped to accomplish at the retreat. Before any statements were made, the leader of the retreat or gathering would remind the men of the rules to follow in making statements: speak briefly, speak for yourself, speak from the heart (i.e., focus on feelings), and speak to the other men—who were supposed to listen intently, make no judgments, and give no advice. The idea was that the statements should bring the unrehearsed truth up from a man's gut, since this would stir feelings in him and move other men to speak their "belly truth."

A great deal of feeling was stirred up as men talked about troubled relationships with fathers; being sexually abused as children; struggling to overcome addictions; repressed anger over past hurts and betrayals; grief and sadness over the deaths of loved ones; and love for their children. When men choked up, wept, shook with fear, or raged as they spoke it induced strong feelings in other men in the group. At one gathering a man, after hearing a number of personal statements, said to the group as a whole, "Your stories give me life. They make me feel more alive." And in an interview another man said:

> There was anxiety about doing that, about revealing personal stuff in a group of men. But I began to discover that it meant a lot to me personally, in terms of being able to do that and find the connection and the similarities and the support. But the thing I was most impressed with was how the group would happen once men got together and began to talk. The group would happen. It didn't

matter much what the topic was or what the content was, as long as somebody was willing to speak personally and honestly. Then other men would do that, too.

At gatherings no one was forced to speak, but the expectation was for every man to share something with the group. If a man's statement seemed inauthentic or insufficiently revealing it might evoke little or no reaction. The more disclosing, expressive, and moving a man's statement, the more likely it was to evoke from the other men heavy sighs, sympathetic "mmmms," or a loud chorus of "Ho!" (This was supposedly a Native American way of affirming that a man's statement has been heard and felt.) The men thus reinforced a norm of making risky, revealing, and evocative statements.

The sequence in which personal statements were made amplified this effect. Men would often begin their remarks by saying, "What that [the previous statement] brings up for me is . . . ," or "I really identify with what ___ said, because . . . ." As a result, personal statements that were similar in emotional tone often came one after another, building up a shared mood. Sufficiently intense moods, usually ones of sadness, were openly acknowledged. A series of especially sad or painful personal statements often led someone to say, "I think we should take a moment to honor the grief in the room." The men thereby brought themselves even more fully into the shared mood they had created.

The kind of connection that grew out of this form of talk is illustrated by an account one man gave in response to an interview question about the most powerful experience he'd had at a mythopoetic gathering. He talked about an occasion when three men told stories in sequence:

> It happened at the mythopoetic group meeting two weeks after my father died. I had never before said anything about myself. I had always read poetry. I had never spoken about myself personally, but I always wanted to say something. I felt like it was important to do that. Many of the men were doing that shamelessly, taking risks. At that meeting someone talked about how he had a hard time getting inside a building. No one would let him in. That reminded me of something that was very important to me, so I talked about it. It was a time my father and I were coming back from a motel to his house. He had forgotten his keys and couldn't get into his own house. We walked around the house trying to get in. And that was such a powerful metaphor—he couldn't get in touch with himself; he was never able to get in touch with his reality. He was locked out of his own house! Right after I talked about this, another man burst into tears. It wasn't because of what I said, but because of something it brought up for him. He talked about how his son was getting ready to leave the country. He was

sobbing and it was very moving and then another man asked what his son's name was. It was a wonderful question. He gave us the name "Jamie." In that moment I felt an incredible sense of what men can do to just feel their grief, which is a very male emotion. It seemed like a real sense of community, a communion then.

The men were thus not only sharing feelings but, by virtue of how they talked, knitting those feelings into a group mood. In this way they were also creating communitas.

Gatherings where these statements were made were explicitly defined as "safe," meaning that, by agreement, the men were not there to compete with or judge each other, but to listen and give support. Even so, there was an element of risk and some anxiety associated with making personal statements, since the mythopoetic men, like most men in American society, were unused to sharing feelings of hurt and vulnerability with other men. This anxiety helped create communitas because it allowed the men to identify with each other over being anxious. It also raised the general level of emotional arousal in the setting. As Turner likewise noted: "Danger is one of the chief ingredients in the production of spontaneous communitas."[5]

In making personal statements and in their conversations at gatherings, the men could not help but refer to people, events, and circumstances outside themselves that evoked the feelings they had. In doing this, the men were careful to add to their statements the disclaimer "for me," as in, "For *me*, the Gulf War was very depressing." This disclaimer signified that the man speaking was talking about *his* feelings based on *his* perceptions of things, and was making no presumptions about how other men should feel. The use of this disclaimer helped the men maintain the fellow-feeling they sought by avoiding arguments about what was true of the external world. The mythopoetic men wanted their feelings validated, not challenged. As long as each man spoke the truth from his heart, no one could say he was wrong.

At large gatherings men would usually stand and speak from the floor. At smaller gatherings the men often sat in a "talking circle." The same rules for speaking applied: speak briefly, for yourself, from the heart. Sometimes a specially designated object—it could literally be a stick, which was often decorated with string and feathers, or it might be a rattle or a piece of antler—was passed from man to man. Whoever held this "talking stick" was entitled to speak without interruption. The talking circle and the use of a talking stick were practices said to derive from tribal peoples.

This way of organizing talk helped to create communitas because it kept the men focused on feelings, encouraged them to make evocative statements, and discouraged them from intellectualizing. Since the men spoke one at a time, and were supposed to speak briefly, from the heart, there was no chance for the men to dissipate or escape their feelings by shifting into an analytic mode of conversation. In the talking circle feelings were piled on top of feelings, with the weight felt by every man in the group. In this way the circle worked just as the men intended: as a crucible for emotion.

It was not only the form but the content of the talk that mattered. At mythopoetic gatherings men often talked about their fathers (there was relatively little talk about mothers and wives). Because almost every man had a father to talk about, and those few who didn't could talk about not having fathers, every man could participate in the conversation. Father talk also brought up feelings of sadness and grief for many of the men, anger for some, and thus gave the conversation an emotional charge. And because many of the men experienced their fathers as physically or emotionally absent, or in some way abusive, the men could identify with each other based on these common experiences.

Talking about fathers also allowed the men to share strong feelings that arose out of situations where they were victims, or at least were not responsible for what happened to them. This had the effect of precluding judgments of each other and enhancing sympathy, since the men were talking about themselves as wounded, not as wounders. Father talk was unlikely to force the men to portray themselves in a bad light. Men sometimes expressed regret over not getting to know their fathers better, but I heard no man express guilt for not treating his father better after reaching adulthood. And sometimes in father talk the men cited the poor fathering they had received as the inspiration for trying to do a better job of it themselves. Father talk thus also provided opportunities for self-congratulation.

This is not to deny that genuine insights sometimes came out of such talk. In talking about their fathers in a way that tapped strong feelings, it seemed that many of the men came to deeper understandings of how their fathers had affected them. I believe I did. Men who were fathers themselves also said that such talk made them more reflective about how they were affecting their children. But father talk went on to the extent it did, and precluded other emotionally-loaded topics, because it was a safe and useful resource for creating communitas.

Although several times men were applauded for statements to the effect that they had "broken the spell" put on them by overbearing wives or mothers, talk about women didn't work as well as talk about fathers for creating communitas. For one thing, the men didn't want their talking circles to degenerate into gripe fests; nor did they want to see themselves as woman-bashers. The men also wanted to evoke and stay focused on feelings that fostered solidarity and reminded them that they were men (as in the previous quotation, "grief . . . is a very male emotion"). During an interview, one man, a therapist, speculated on why there was relatively little talk about women at gatherings:

> I think that within a group of men there is so much stuff going on—like what it means to be together, the feelings that stirs up, the fear, anxiety, and whatever— that the notion of bringing in our relationships with women who are not present in the group somehow makes the energy leave the group. Staying focused on what is happening in the moment, in the situation, keeps the energy there. I'm not sure, but I think that when we start talking about us and our partners, that takes away from the immediate experience in some way. I think it's preferable not to do that. In support groups we talk about the whole gamut. A lot of what we talk about is, you know, what's going on with our partners and how hard it is. In larger groups I think it's less safe to acknowledge that stuff—less safe to acknowledge how stymied and dependent we are on things like this.

Too much talk about women would thus have been distracting, possibly divisive, and reminded the men of their vulnerabilities vis-a-vis women. Talk about fathers, on the other hand, often brought up feelings of grief, which the men, doing a bit of identity work, defined as a male emotion. Grief was also more likely than anger or confusion to draw the men together.

The men used other forms of talk to make communitas more likely. One of these was the frequent reference to men or maleness in a way that reminded the men of their common identity. For example, a man who missed a meeting or two might show up again and proclaim, "It feels good to be back in a group of men," or "It's good to be back and feel this kind of male energy again." Often the reference to men was in the form of a sentence tag, as in, "This isn't the first time our society has considered absent fathers a problem, but now we're starting to think about what it means for us *as men*." Or, "Our culture has used fairy tales to some extent to teach children moral lessons, but now we're looking to see what they can say to us *as men*." In these statements there was both an idea being expressed—that men had a shared perspective or common circumstance—and a mood being subtly maintained.

Job talk was largely avoided at retreats because it would have threatened this sense of commonality. The men thus described their job-related troubles and triumphs in the most general terms. More specific talk might have raised status concerns and revealed differences among the men. By staying focused on feelings the men stayed on level ground with each other. As one man said in an interview, "When you begin speaking from your heart more than your head it's an equalizer; no one really cares how much money you have or what kind of car you pulled up in."

Occasionally the small talk at gatherings broached the stolid topics of sports and weather. But this sort of talk rarely went on for long. Several of the men told me that they cherished the chance to talk with other men about "real stuff." They said that in their everyday lives they had to present an "everything's-okay" front and not respond seriously when someone asked how they were doing. At mythopoetic gatherings, they said, they could be more honest and authentic. One time I asked a man how he was doing and, as a matter of habit, expected the usual robotic reply. I was surprised when he said, "I'm coming out of a depression that set in around the end of summer. I'm feeling better now but I think I need a good cry to get it all out."

"Brother" was another mood-inducing word that was occasionally used at gatherings. At the start of a talking circle the teacher or leader might encourage the men to "be present for your brothers." At other times, often when the men engaged in rituals or psychodramatic exercises, they were exhorted to "witness for your brothers," or to "support your brothers as they're doing a piece of work." One morning at a retreat, after leading a group of about 30 men through an hour-long set of stretching and breathing exercises that created a relaxed, tingly sensation, the teacher exhorted us to "stay in this place, stay connected to your brothers." Teachers or informal leaders used this talk of brothers and brotherhood more often than the men themselves. I rarely heard it outside of retreats.

Two other bits of language were used more widely. One of these was the talk of work, as in "doing a piece of work" or mythopoetic "men's work" itself. The men talked of what they were doing as work partly to make it seem serious. Cavorting in the woods with masks and drums could, on the surface, seem rather frivolous. To call this sort of activity men's *work*, gave it dignity and made clear that, if understood properly, it was not silly, easy, or without consequence. But the more subtle connotation when "work" was invoked, was that we are here together, as men, to do hard and important things, and we must support each other in this effort. A "piece of work" usually referred to a ritual or psychodramatic enactment in which a group of men collaborated. The further connotation was that men must pull together, as equals, to get this work done.

Talk of "connection" also enhanced as well as testified to communitas. The men often spoke of "making connections" with each other and with the movement's teachers. Any contact that yielded a moment of emotional communion, or a glimmer of mutual understanding, might be called a connection. These were rarely the beginnings of enduring friendships; usually the contacts were fleeting. Yet the talk of *connection* implied something deeper and more profound, like an intertwining of souls. Such talk gave weight to these moments of communitas. It also aroused expectations for men when they went on retreats, either as first-timers or repeaters. It was connection that the men spoke of seeking, that they knew was a possibility, and which they worked to create.

Ritual

Ritual is different from routine. Routine is the repetition of a behavioral pattern, like brushing one's teeth every night before bed. Ritual involves the symbolic enactment of values, beliefs, or feelings. It is a way of making external, visible, and public things that are normally internal, invisible, and private. By doing this, members of a community create a shared reality, reaffirm their common embrace of certain beliefs and values, and thereby keep the community alive. Ritual can also be a way of acknowledging changes in community members or of actually inducing such changes. The mythopoetic men used ritual for the same purposes: to call up, express, and share their otherwise private feelings, and to effect changes in themselves.[6]

Not all gatherings were ritual gatherings, though most included some ritual elements. For example, even discussion meetings usually began with a "naming ritual." For this the men stood in a circle, facing inward. Each man in turn would step forward into the circle and say, "My name is _____." The men would answer back in unison, "Welcome _____, _____, _____," repeating his name three times. Sometimes this was varied slightly; men might be asked to say their fathers' names or to introduce an adjacent man in the circle. But for the most part it was a static ritual, used in much the same form over and again. The men distinguished this kind of ritual from "radical ritual," which was intended to produce a change in the men involved.

Those gatherings where the men sought to create "ritual space" usually began with a symbolic act of separation from the ordinary world.[7] For example, the men might dip their hands into a large bowl of water to symbolize a washing off of concerns and distractions linked to the outside world. Or they might pass through a portal, such as a doorway or a gap between two trees, and receive a welcoming blessing from another man. At other times at the outset of gatherings the "spirits, powers, and guardians of the four directions" would be invoked and asked to bring the men strength and wisdom.[8] At still other times the men would dance their way into the space where the meeting was to be held, while the men already inside drummed and chanted.

While these acts were partly symbolic of separation from the outside world, they also signified the creation of a temporary world governed by special rules of interaction. By joining in the entry ritual it was as if the men tacitly agreed to suspend the usual rules of men's interaction. Under the new rules men were supposed to accept and support each other rather than judge and compete with each other. And rather than remaining unemotional, men were supposed to speak their heartfelt truth. Thus for some men, even the simple naming ritual at the start of a meeting was reassuring, because it marked the start of an encounter in which they could express their feelings without fear of ridicule.

The scene of a gathering also had to be set. Ritual gatherings were often held at rustic lodges and camps. To further evoke a sense of earthy spirituality, various objects—candles, feathers, masks, antlers, strangely shaped driftwood, animal skulls—would be placed around the main meeting area. Sage was often burned (a Native American practice called smudging) to make the air pungent and to "cleanse the ritual space." Usually the leader, or leaders, of the gathering made sure these things were done. Again, the idea was to heighten the sense of separation from ordinary reality, to make the gathering place seem special, and to draw the men together. This preparation was described in terms of "creating a container" that could safely hold the psychic energies about to be unleashed.

The separation from ordinary reality also helped the men let go of the concerns for status and power that shaped their interactions with other men in everyday life. In the ritual space the men were supposed to be "present for each other" in a direct and immediate way, as equals, as brothers, and not as inferiors and superiors. Defining the situation as one in which feelings and other psychic matters were the proper focus of attention and activity helped to create, and sustain, this sense of equality.

Two examples will help show how the mythopoetic men used ritual to create communitas. The first is from a six-day gathering of about 120 men in a remote rural setting. At this Big Remote Gathering, as I'll call it, the men were divided into three clans: Trout, Ravens, and Lions. During the week each clan worked with a dance teacher to develop a dance of its own, a dance that would symbolize the spirit of the men in the clan. At the carnivale on the last night of the gathering, each clan was to share its dance with the rest of the men. One clan would drum while another danced and the third clan "witnessed."

The carnivale was held in a large, dimly lit lodge built of rough-cut logs. Many of the men wore the wildly decorated masks they had made earlier in the week. When their turn came, the 40 men in the Trout clan moved to the center of the room and formed a circle. The men stood for a moment and then hunched down, extended their arms with their hands together in front of them, and began to dip and sway like fish swimming. Then half the men began moving to their right and half to their left, creating two flowing, interweaving circles. The Trout men also carried small stones, which they clicked together as they moved. About 30 men drummed as the Trout men danced. The rest of the men watched.

After a while the Trout men stopped and stood again, holding hands in a circle inside the larger circle of witnesses. They began a sweet and mournful African chant that they said was used to honor the passing away of loved ones. One by one each of the Trout men moved to the center of their circle and put down the stones he was carrying. As he did so, he called out the name of a person or people whose passing he wished to honor. Another of the Trout men walked along the row of men standing in the outer ring and said, "We invite you to join us by putting a stone in the center of the circle to honor your dead." The drumming and chanting continued all the while.

At first a few, then more and more of the Raven and Lion men stepped outside to get stones. Each man as he returned went to the center of the circle, called the name of the dead he was honoring, put down a stone, and then stepped back. There was sadness in the men's voices as they spoke. By now all the men had picked up the chant and joined hands in one large circle. The sound filled the lodge. After about 20 minutes the chanting reached a lull— and then one man began to sing "Amazing Grace." Soon all the men joined in and again their voices rose in chorus and filled the lodge. When we finished singing we stood silent, looking at all the stones between us.

This example shows how a great deal of work went into creating spontaneous communitas. The dance was carefully choreographed and the stage elaborately set. But later I talked to Trout men who said that they had planned the dance only up to the point of asking the other men to honor their dead. They were surprised by what happened next, by how quickly and powerfully the other men were drawn in.[9] No one had expected the surge of emotion and fellow-feeling that the ritual induced, especially when we began to sing "Amazing Grace." Several men I talked to later cited this ritual as one of the most moving experiences they had had at a mythopoetic gathering.

Another example comes from a sweat lodge ritual modeled on a traditional Native American practice.[10] In this case the lodge was a framework of saplings, held together with twine, covered with several layers of old blankets and tarps. Before the frame was built, a fire pit was dug in the center of the spot on which the lodge stood. Although sweat lodges could be made bigger, here it was about ten feet in diameter and four feet high—big enough for a dozen men to squeeze in. From the outside it looked like a miniature domed stadium.

It was a drizzly 45-degree morning on the second day of a teacher-led weekend retreat. I was in the second group of 12 men who would go into the lodge together. This was the first "sweat" for all of us. We bantered nervously as we walked from the cabins to the shore of a small lake where the sweat lodge had been built. When we got there the men from the previous group had just finished.

The scene froze us. Next to the lodge a large rock-rimmed fire was burning. A fierce, black-haired man with a beard stood by the fire, a five-foot staff in his hand. Some of the men who had just finished their sweat were standing waist-deep in the lake. Others were on shore hugging, their naked bodies still steaming in the cool air. Our moment of stunned silence ended when the leader of the retreat said to us, matter of factly, "Get undressed, stay quiet, keep your humility." We undressed and stashed our clothes under the nearby pine trees, out of the rain.

Before we entered the lodge the teacher urged us to reflect on the specialness of the occasion and to approach it with seriousness. Upon entering the lodge through a small entry flap each man was to say, "all my relations," to remind himself of his connections to the earth, to his ancestors, and to the other men. Once we were inside, the teacher asked the fire tender to bring us fresh, red-hot rocks. As each rock was placed by shovel into the fire pit, we said in unison, "Welcome Grandfather," again as symbolic acknowledgment of our connection to the earth. The teacher burned sage on the rocks to scent the air. When he poured water on the rocks the lodge became a sauna. The space was tightly packed, lit only by the glow of the rocks, and very hot. We were to do three sessions of ten to fifteen minutes each. Because of the intensity of the heat, a few men could not do all three sessions.

During one of the sessions the teacher urged us to call upon the spirits of our ancestors from whom we wanted blessings. In the cacophony of voices it was hard to tell what was being said. Some men were calling the names of people not present. A few were doing what sounded like a Native American chant learned from the movies. The man on my right was gobbling like a turkey. At first this all struck me as ridiculous. I looked around the lodge for signs of bemusement in other men's faces. Surely they couldn't be taking this seriously. But those whose faces I could see appeared absorbed in the experience. Some men seemed oddly distant, as if they were engaged in a conversation going on elsewhere.

Although I was still put off by the chanting and baffled by the gobbling, I too began to feel drawn in. I found myself wanting to suspend disbelief and find some meaning in the ritual, no matter how culturally foreign it was. In large part this was because the teacher and the other men seemed to be taking it seriously. I certainly didn't want to ruin the experience for them by showing any sign of cynicism. These were men who had taken my feelings seriously during the retreat. I felt I owed them the same consideration in the sweat lodge.

In both examples, a carefully crafted set of appearances made communitas likely to happen. The physical props, the words and actions of the ritual leaders, and the sincere words and actions of some men evoked real feelings in others and drew them in. Because it seemed that there were genuine emotions at stake, it would have taken a hard heart to show any sign of cynicism during the Trout dance or the sweat lodge. To do so would have risked hurting other men's feelings and dimming the glow of communitas.[11] It would also have cut the cynic himself off from the good feelings and mysterious power being generated by these occasions. Whether or not everyone really believed in what was happening didn't matter. Appearances made it seem real, and to achieve the communitas they desired, all the men needed to do was to act on these appearances.

Another dynamic was at work in the case of the sweat lodge. On the face of it, the idea of late twentieth-century white men enacting a Native American sweat lodge ritual was absurd. And for most of these men, the idea of squatting naked, haunch to haunch, with other men would have been—within an everyday frame of reference—embarrassing and threatening to their identities as heterosexuals. Thus to avoid feeling ridiculous, threatened, or embarrassed the men had to stay focused on the form of the ritual and show no sign of doubting its content or propriety. Because there was such a gap between their everyday frame of reference and the ritual, the men had to exaggerate their absorption in the ritual just to keep a grip on it. In so doing the men truly did create a common focus and, again, the appearance that a serious, collective spiritual activity was going on.

The sweat lodge example also illustrated how the creation of communitas was aided by literally stripping men of signs of their differences. In the sweat lodge, men were only men—as symbolized by their nakedness. They were thus also equals. When a small group of us spoke later about the experience, one man said, "The closeness and physicality, and especially being naked, are what make it work. Everyone is just a man in there. You can't wear any merit badges."

Teachers were important because they knew how to orchestrate appearances, how to script a retreat so that emotions would be evoked in the right way, and how to model appropriate emotional displays.[12] The men valued teachers who could do these things well. But they also felt that they could learn to do the same things on their own. And so, after one teacher-led weekend, several of the local men decided to form a group dedicated to doing ritual work. The men wanted to get better at "putting feeling into [ritual, symbolic, or metaphorical] form" and to have more frequent opportunities to create the experiences they had at teacher-led retreats.

The Ritual Group came to consist of about 20 men who met once a month for four hours at a retreat farm. I participated for the group's first year. Each month a different man or pair of men were the "ritual elders" who took responsibility for scripting the meeting. The meetings were usually organized around a theme, such as birth, renewal, creativity, community, connections with nature, fathers, using the senses. An entry ritual, a naming ritual, invoking the spirits of the directions, drumming, and dancing were regular parts of these meetings. Other ritual activities called for the men to explore and share their feelings about some personal issue and then devise a way to symbolically enact those feelings. These enactments often took the form of dance.

On several occasions the men devoted part of the meeting time to talking about how well the group was working. Some men felt it was disorganized. They wanted better planning so that more elaborate ritual work could be done with a clear intention of what it was supposed to symbolize and accomplish. Others liked it that on any given day there was room for adventure and everything was not planned by the leaders. There was indeed plenty of spontaneity. Whoever led the group on any given day usually needed only one or two exercises to get things going. Often the group then took off on its own until it was time to leave.

Although the men professed a principle of "radical freedom," which was each man's right to opt out of any activity he didn't like, there was rarely any objection to the activities proposed by the day's ritual elders. The men always went along good naturedly, in part because they didn't want to hurt the feelings of the man or men leading. It was also because, as in the sweat lodge, to imply that an activity was silly or threatening by refusing to participate might have called into question all the activities of the group, perhaps even its reason for being. This would have squelched any chance of achieving communitas. Instead, to achieve communitas, the men protected the feelings of the other men by suspending disbelief and playing along.

Taking ritual activity seriously did not mean that the men were relentlessly solemn. On the contrary, the men often teased and joked with each other, and the drumming, dancing, and "soul wrestling" were exuberantly playful. But the humor and play were almost always kept within the spaces between more serious pieces of work so that the collective mood was maintained. If a ritual elder or elders approached an activity with solemnity the men respected this and mirrored it. If an activity produced feelings of sadness, grief, or joy, the men likewise respected these feelings. The consistent feature of the interaction was not seriousness or silliness, but the men's emotional attunement to each other.

Most of the men in the Ritual Group were not friends who knew each other well. Yet the men took the group seriously and valued it because of the experiences it offered. This was true even if the men were dubious about the rituals themselves. In an interview a man in the group said, "The chanting and the stuff about spirits puts me off sometimes; that doesn't really appeal to me so much as the fellowship." Another man said he liked the group because "It's

like all the good parts of church without the bad parts." Most of the men felt
that the group and the ritual activity were indeed special. Speaking during one
of the group's meetings, a man said, "We're not just a bunch of guys. This
group *is* something. I feel connected to the men here and that's very important to me. We're a group of men who care for each other. That's rare in my
life. I don't get this anywhere else."

While most of the men seemed to like each other, or what they saw of each
other at meetings, it was the group experience that was most important. Putting it baldly, another man said to the group on one occasion, "I feel committed to the ritual process because it gets me into a different space—it makes me
be present in a way that I like. It opens up possibilities for connecting in different kinds of ways. I'm committed to the ritual process more so than to
individuals." Another man in the group said in an interview that ritual was
the most meaningful part of mythopoetic activity to him because "It's an
affirmation of the group. It's an affirmation of being there as an individual
with the group. The individual members make up the whole, the gestalt. It's
very important that that is bound together." These statements suggest how
ritual, even if it was disorganized, helped to create communitas: it allowed
the men to connect, to be together in what felt like an intimate way, without
having to get to know each other personally.

Drumming

Next to Bly, the most widely recognized icon of the mythopoetic movement
was the drum. Drumming was indeed an important part of mythopoetic
activity. Some mythopoetic groups held gatherings just to drum; the Local
Group usually mixed drumming with other activities. Not all of the men
drummed. A few didn't care for it; others preferred to use rattles or tambou-
rines during drumming sessions. The most enthusiastic men had congas, Af-
rican-styled djembes, or hand held shaman's drums, though all manner of large
and small folk drums appeared at gatherings. On one occasion a man used a
five-gallon plastic pail turned upside down.

Why did the mythopoetic men drum? Some of the men in the Local Group
said that they began drumming after a visit by Michael Meade, who was skilled
at using drumming to accompany his telling of folk tales. This is what inspired
one man I interviewed:

> Bly came and told his "Iron John" story and that was my first introduction to
> using stories as a way of illuminating dilemmas or emotional situations in your
> life. Michael Meade came the following year in the spring and introduced some
> drumming at that weekend. I just loved the energy of that right away. It just

really opened me up. After drumming I felt wonderful. I liked the feeling of it and felt a connection with the mythopoetic ever since then, more to the drumming than to anything else.

But on only a few occasions did any of the local men use drumming as accompaniment to story telling. Most of the drumming was done in groups, which varied in size from six to forty. And while the men who were better drummers might lead the group into a complex rhythm, often something samba-like, the drumming was usually free form, leaderless, and simple.

Although a few of the men took drumming lessons, the appeal of the activity was not in the achievement of virtuosity. The appeal stemmed, rather, from the fact that anyone who could bang a drum or make rhythmic noise could join in. One man, who said the drumming at first gave him headaches, later came to appreciate it for its ability to bring the men together: "We're looking for a common basis. Percussion, rhythm is universal. So we drum. Anyone can do that. You don't even *need* a drum. You can clap or you can use a rattle." Most importantly, then, drumming was another way to achieve communitas. Turner notes that simple musical instruments are often used this way: "It is . . . fascinating to consider how expressions of communitas are culturally linked with simple wind instruments (flutes and harmonicas). Perhaps, in addition to their ready portability, it is their capacity to convey in music the quality of spontaneous human communitas that is responsible for this."[13] This was equally true of drums, which were also readily portable and took even less skill to play.

What the mythopoetic men said about their experiences drumming tells much about not only drumming, but about the communitas it helped create and about the mythopoetic experience in general. In an interview another man spoke of drumming as both ordinary and special at the same time:

> You can kind of lose yourself in it. It's like any hobby—fishing or playing ball or whatever. There is something that happens. You go into an altered state almost, hearing that music. At this national meeting in Minnesota a month ago the common thing was the drums. You could hear the beating of that drum. At break people would drum and we would dance. So it's this common bond.

Put another way, drumming was an activity that gave men who were strangers a way to quickly feel comfortable and familiar with each other. Some of the mythopoetic men believed that men had a special facility for connecting with each other in nonverbal ways. The way that men were able to quickly bond via drumming was seen as evidence of this.

Although the men were aware that drumming was not an activity limited to men, some clearly felt that it held a special appeal for them. Another man said in an interview:

> Drumming does something—connects me with men in ways that I can't understand, in the same way I've observed women who have babies connecting with each other. There's something in it that I don't participate in emotionally. In the same way, the drumming—society with other men—is emotionally important to men in ways that women don't understand. They can't.

Some of the mythopoetic men's ideas about gender are evident in this statement. Many of them believed that women, no matter how empathic they might be, could not know what it was like to be a man, just as men could not know what it was like to be a woman. Hence men needed the understanding and support that could come only from other men, just as women needed the same things from other women.

It is revealing, too, that this man referred to drumming as "society with other men." On one level this can be taken to mean that drumming was simply an activity that held men together in a group. But it can also be taken to mean that, for at least some of the mythopoetic men, a drumming group represented an ideal form of society. This would be a society in which there were no inequalities or doctrines to divide men. It also would be a society in which men could enjoy emotional communion with each other through shared, noncompetitive activities. Thus for some of the mythopoetic men the drumming group was, in a sense, a briefly realizable utopia.

For other men, drumming was a communal, and sometimes personal, spiritual experience. In an interview one man told me:

> There was one point where I was really deeply entranced just drumming and then all of a sudden I had this real powerful experience where I felt like I was on a hill, on some mountainside or some mountaintop, in some land far far away, in some time that was all time. And I was in the middle of all my men, who were my brothers, who were all men. It was one of those powerful mystical experiences where all of a sudden I felt planted in the community of men. And that changed my life, because I felt like I was a man among men in the community of men and we were drumming and the drum was in my bones and it was in my heartbeat and it was good.

This statement captures in spirit, tone, and rhythm the experience that many of the men found in drumming. Even if they didn't report such flights of imagination, others said that drumming provided a similar sense of communality.

My own experience corroborates this. I found that when I could pick up a beat and help sustain it without thinking, the sense of being part of the group was strong. It was as if the sound testified to the reality of the group and the rhythm testified to our connection. By drumming in synch each man attached himself to the group and to the other men in it. The men valued this also because the attachment was created by physical action rather than by talk, and because it seemed to happen at a nonrational or primitive level. In an interview a man said, "When I'm in that setting with the drumming, and it's frenzied or passionate, I get into that body thing which is nonrational and I feel real connected to what we are doing right there in a kind of tribal, natural, preindustrial way. It's in my body. I feel it and I like it."

Other men said that the drumming caused emotions to well up mysteriously. As the men experienced it, this had to do with the way it affected the body and the psyche rather than the conscious ego. One man found that drumming stimulated his creativity. In an interview he said:

> For a long time I was thinking about how to write this story and one thing or another wasn't right. The plot just didn't move. I'm critical about what I do and this story just wasn't working. The drumming somehow put me in touch with another center. When I was drumming I felt inspired somehow. I could feel material that I wanted to write about. Afterwards I would often go home and write. The drumming would bring out emotions that I had not thought about that were related to what I was working on. So for me it's been a way to get in touch with the muse, with my creative energy. And also to get in touch with the body, which I'd not learned to appreciate much because I picked up from my mother that there's something wrong with male bodies. She didn't say that but she implied it in the way she was put off by men. So the drumming and dancing seem like a wonderful way to be totally into one's body and to be in it, and at the same time be outside yourself.

Drumming thus gave rise not only to communitas, but also, for some men, to uncommon emotional or psychic experiences. As mythopoetic philosophy called for, drumming helped the men to get out of their heads and into feeling their bodies; it was also a way to bypass the rational ego that kept a lid on the primordial, archetypal masculine energies the men sought to tap.

Poetry, Chanting, and Fairy Tales

Poems and fairy tales were also staple parts of mythopoetic activity.[14] Most of the time no commentary or discussion followed the reading of a poem. The men would just steep in the feelings the poems evoked. An especially stirring poem, like a moving personal statement, would elicit deep sighs, "mmmmm," "yeah," sometimes "Ho!" and often calls for the reader to "read it again!" And as with the personal statements, these responses, which were signs of shared feelings, served to turn the individual feelings into a collective mood, and thus served to create communitas.

While any poem that struck a common chord helped to create communitas, some poems amplified the effect by providing images of communitas. Some of these poems were written by the men themselves. This poem, written by one of the local men, was read at several gatherings and always evoked a strong response:

> This good man stands
>   on this selfsame ground,
>   well set,
>   his chest with breath
>   and arms unbound.
>
> He is a confirmation,
>   and full of himself.
>
> I will clap him to me tightly,
>   wrap his shoulders strongly,
>   feel his cheek against my cheek
>   and his heart beat in my chest.
>
> I will not bend slightly to him,
>   not lightly at the waist,
> I will not embrace him softly
>   without breathing.
>
> His body does not scare me,
>   and its parts do not scare me.
>
> And if we are cheek to cheek,
>   chest to chest,
>   stomach to stomach,
>   crotch to crotch,
>   that is so,
>   and that is right.
>
> My body is hungry for his body,
>   my mind searches for his mind,
>   my heart peals and rings,
>   and my soul flies out.

And do you know I love him
and delight in him,
at the joy in him.
I honor my breath;
I hold my blood dear
and I grip him close.

This good man stands
on this same ground,
and he is a consecration
and I am well blessed.[15]

In this case the poem evoked not just similar feelings in the men, but specifically feelings of brotherhood, of desire for direct man-to-man connection. The
image of the unabashed embrace captured the very feelings the men were
seeking.

By conjuring an image of connection at the boundary of the forbidden, this
poem, like the sweat lodge ritual, captured the men in a shared mood of fear
and desire. Despite their homophobia, the men savored the homoerotic
imagery in this poem because the conditions under which it was read made
it safe to do so. Since nearly all the mythopoetic men defined themselves
as straight, the poem was never taken as celebrating gay sexual desire, but
rather the kind of affection that straight men should be able to feel for each
other, fearlessly. When read with manly zest at a gathering, this poem, interpreted as a bold rejection of homophobia, powerfully aided the creation of
communitas.

Chanting was also done occasionally at mythopoetic gatherings. This too
had the power to create communitas. Sometimes the chanting was simply a
deep, elongated "aaaahhh" or "oooohhh" in tonal harmony. One man told me
in an interview how he experienced this kind of whole-note chanting: "It's a
way of expressing one's self in a group. You just flow to it and you flow with
the group. I think it's also recognizing the inclusive nature of mankind—that
masculine nature which is present in all societies." Even more masculine was
the leonine "group growl" the men often used to experience a final moment of
communion at the end of a gathering. The louder the better.

At some gatherings teachers would get a group of men chanting in unison,
either as part of a group dance or as an exercise in itself. At one gathering
I attended Bly did this with a Sufi chant, "la illaha illa'allah," which means
"there is no God but God." Sufis use this as a *zikr*, a repetition intended to
clear the mind to focus on Allah. Sometimes the local men learned chants from
audio tapes and introduced them at gatherings. On one occasion it was sup-

posedly a Lakota Sioux chant that honored "the power of the bear." On another occasion it was a Hindu chant to Shiva. A chant used on a number of
occasions was a thrice repetition of the lines: "We are an old people, we are a
new people, we are the same people, deeper than before."

The chants worked to create communitas much like the drumming did. In
chanting the men harmonized their voices to produce a song or just a resonant sound. In that moment there could be a merging with the group, a feeling of oneness. During interviews several men said they were not enthusiastic
about chanting because the chants were meaningless to them, and sometimes
hard to follow. But no one ever protested doing a chant when another man
proposed it. Most of the men didn't seem to care if the words made sense, since
the point was to enjoy the act of chanting. The point, in other words, was to
experience another moment of communitas, not to pay homage to the bear,
Allah, or Shiva.

When fairy tales were told communitas was created in another way. Before
starting, the storyteller would usually instruct the men to look for an image or
detail in the story that evoked strong feelings. That image, it was said, would
be a man's "doorway into the story"—his way of discovering what the story
could tell him about his life as a man.[16]

And so after a story or part of a story was told, men would talk about the
images that struck them and the feelings these images evoked. In a large group
of men many different images might be mentioned. Sometimes men reacted
strongly to the same image. Talking about the stories in this way created more
chances for men to express feelings and to find that they shared feelings and
experiences with other men. This was in part how feelings of isolation were
overcome and connections were made. Again, the stories may have helped the
men to better understand their lives. But it was *how* the stories were talked
about that helped the men to experience the good feelings and mysterious
power of communitas.

Focusing on individual reactions to images also precluded argument about
the meaning of a story. As long as a man spoke about how an image affected
him, there was nothing to argue about. If a man talked abstractly about a story,
the storyteller (or other men present) would press him to speak about himself,
to tell about a specific image or detail that struck him powerfully. If a man
questioned the larger meaning of a story—perhaps as conveyed by its imagery
of kings, warriors, violence, and male domination—he would be reminded that
stories had to be interpreted mythologically, not literally or psychologically.
In the Jungian view, the characters in the stories did not represent real men
and women, nor events in the real world, but psychic energies and psychic
processes. Men who questioned the political content and implications of the

images were not playing by the Jungian rules and thus impeded the creation of communitas.

The stories told at gatherings—Grimms' fairy tales, Arthurian or Greek legends, or Native American and African folk tales—typically featured male protagonists on a heroic quest. This made it easy for the men to identify with the characters. Teachers encouraged this by sometimes inviting the men to imagine what a character was seeing, thinking, and feeling, or how a character might resolve a dilemma he was facing. The men were thus led to project themselves into the same masculine position in a story. This did not ensure that all the men would feel the same things in response to a story. But it did make common responses more likely, in that the men were encouraged to approach the story from the standpoint of their shared identity as men.

The stories also portrayed gender roles and power relations between women and men in conventional ways. In the stories men were kings, princes, advisors to kings, warriors, hunters, and magicians. Women were queens, princesses, maids, and witches.[17] Kingdoms were ruled by kings. Any power a female character had was usually based on witchcraft, beauty, or deception. There was, in other words, little in the stories to disrupt the expectations about gender roles or gender inequality that the men brought with them from the literal world of late twentieth-century America (see chapter 6). Characters in the stories were also invariably heterosexual. This too made it easy for the predominantly heterosexual mythopoetic men to identify with the characters. And again this made it more likely that the men's responses to the stories would be similar enough to provide a basis for communitas.

Clan Formation

At gatherings men were often organized into clans. At smaller gatherings these usually consisted of five to seven men. At the retreat where the Trout dance occurred the clans were much larger, about forty men. But there the clans were subdivided into cabin groups of about eight men each. It was in these small groups that the most emotionally intense, face-to-face interaction occurred and the strongest connections were made. Communitas in the group as a whole was amplified by the strong feelings of connection created in the clans.

The ways in which clans were formed also enhanced feelings of commonality. One method called for men to identify with the spirit of an animal native to the place where a gathering was being held. Men who identified with the spirit of, say, the bear would then gather in one part of the room, while men who identified with the spirit of the eagle gathered in another. Presumably this meant that the men already had some feeling in common. At one retreat about half of the 24 men present at first identified with the bear. This caused an imbalance in clan sizes and prompted the teacher to ask the men to rethink their totemic affinities. After some reshuffling the clans settled down to six men each.

A more elaborate version of this method was used at the retreat where the Trout dance occurred. Here 120 men had to be organized into clans. The process began by asking each man to decide which of these three statements (tacked to a wall) they identified with most strongly:

> *Ravens catch the shadows of men*
> *And walk among the bones of the battlefields.*
> *They never neglect the darkness.*
> *Bearing hard, truthful messages from the invisible,*
> *They nourish the lonely soul with gifts of intuition.*
> *The wing of the raven brushes the air of memory;*
> *The eye of the raven sees through the bright reflections*
> *Of obvious life; and through their broken*
> *Cry speaks the sorrow of the world.*

> *Trout swim the deep waters of grief and suffer the*
> *Isolation of shallows.*
> *They see the world through tears and waves of emotion.*
> *Trout go unprotected through dark waters, hide their*
> *Hearts under rocks, and quietly carry wounds from*
> *Rapids, hooks, stones.*
> *Yet, the water sustains them, heals them, reveals*
> *The world above and parts open to allow a glittering leap.*

> *Lions rise proudly from the earth, drawing up the roar*
> *That carries their hunger, rage, fear, and fire.*
> *This roar from the heart's heat claims his wide territory;*
> *It tells of worldly facts and announces the royal presence.*
> *Shaking his mane, stretching his claws, he shows his power.*
> *The restrictions and shames of a life can close the throat,*
> *Blocking the sound of generosity, mercy, and fierceness.*

After indicating which statement he most strongly identified with, each man was directed to draw a slip of paper out of a bag. I chose to be a Raven and drew a slip of paper that said, "Drinkers of Darkness." This was my cabin assignment. It was also the archetypal role that my cabin group was supposed to play during the gathering.

In this case the men chose their clans based on the feelings evoked by the statements above. Assignment to cabin groups, however, was random, though it was not portrayed as such. During the first orientation session of the retreat, one of the teachers talked of the cabin groups as having "chosen us." The idea was that the mysterious power of the world-pervading psyche had brought each group of men together for a reason.[18] Often, the teacher said, men in a cabin group would find that they had something in common. He then encouraged each group to look for whatever this might be. But even if a group failed, as mine did, to find a significant commonality, the process of seeking it opened men up to each other and brought them together.

The idea that there was spiritual power or mysterious intention at work behind random assignments to clans was often reiterated at gatherings. It was a bit of magical thinking that aided communitas by attuning men to their commonalities and lending spiritual significance to their being together. The practical reason for forming clans was that men felt more comfortable talking in small groups. This was a recurrent concern in the Ritual Group, in which some men wanted to spend more time in clans of five or six. Proposals to do more "clan work" were buttressed with an argument that held a powerful appeal for the mythopoetic men: it's a more effective way to make connections.

FAILED COMMUNITAS

The mythopoetic men did not always succeed in creating communitas. Sometimes a man would read a poem that evoked no responses or felt inappropriate for the moment. Sometimes chants were proposed and begun but the words were so strange that the men could not catch on and join in. Sometimes personal statements, even sincere ones, didn't work. For example, at a one-day gathering led by Robert Bly and Robert Moore, men made statements after doing a one-on-one exercise in which they talked about "the power they needed or wanted to let into their lives." After the exercise men spoke from the floor. Many received applause. When one man said, "Part of what I learned from women was how to give up power," his statement was met with cold silence.

On another occasion a group discussion was devoted to "men's unfinished business." At the start of the meeting, at which about 20 men were present, the men did the naming ritual described earlier. My field notes describe an exchange that occurred shortly after the meeting began:

> A few minutes after we did the naming ritual a guy I'd never seen before straggled in. He said he'd gotten lost looking for the meeting. Mark, who was supposed to be leading the discussion, asked the guy his name. He said it was Tom. Then in unison we all said, "Welcome Tom, Tom, Tom." The guy seemed surprised

by this. He asked what this naming stuff was about. Mark explained, "We use ritual to create a container for our activity. Doing the naming ritual for late-comers is a way to bring them into the container." Bob added, "It's also great to hear your name said out loud by a group of men, and hearing it three times makes the bond stronger." Just then Ed, who had been to a few meetings before, walked in. Before he even sat down, Bob blurted out "Welcome John, John, John." Ed said, "Thanks for the welcome, but my name is *Ed*." Tom, the first-timer, turned to Bob and said, "It would probably be even more powerful to remember a man's name." Bob was clearly embarrassed by his gaffe. He just rolled his head sheepishly.[19]

The emotional tone of the meeting changed, at least for a while, after the pretense of brotherhood and the power of ritual were thus dented.

Things didn't always work in the Ritual Group, either. One time we were led on a guided meditation in which we were asked to imagine that our bodies had roots going down into the core of the earth and which brought energy back up through us. When this exercise ended we were kneeling in a circle waiting to see what would happen next. Now the man who had led the meditation began to lightly tap his shaman's drum and chant in an apparent Native American style, "hi-yah, hey-yah, hi-yah, hey-yah." He varied the pattern of syllables and his volume as he went along—for about ten minutes. During this time only one man joined in to any degree; the rest of us just listened.

The man who was chanting had done similar things before, going into trance-like states. When he did, the other men gathered closely around, trying to tap into the strange power of the moment. But in this instance there was awkwardness because it wasn't clear what, if anything, the rest of us could do to connect via the chanting. Later one of the other men said discreetly to the man, "It's really powerful when you get into chanting like that, but I never know if you're inviting the rest of us to join you or not." The chanting man said, "yes, of course, join in if it feels right." But this would have been difficult, since his chant was improvised.[20] Even if the men were willing to suspend disbelief and go along with almost anything, they still needed some opening to see how to do so, or else communitas was unlikely.

Another failure occurred at the Big Remote Gathering. A theme of this gathering was that men had to learn to "stand their ground," and so time was set aside for arguments and ritual insults. The arguments were staged during a "conflict hour." During this time the floor was open for men to speak their disagreements. The problem was that the disagreements were either trivial (e.g., over whether men should wash their hands after peeing) or contrived (e.g., over whether or not society was better off with rules). During the first conflict hour men took sides and shouted at each other from opposite sides of the big lodge. Only about half of the men said anything. And a number of men avoided subsequent conflict hours. I talked to a few of these men later and they said they found the conflict hour to be stupid and unproductive.

Learning to hurl ritual insults was also construed as part of learning to stand one's ground. The teacher who promoted this activity said that historically men had engaged in verbal dueling that included disparaging references to appearance, character, and lineage, and yet still loved and respected each other. By "ritualizing" this practice, the teacher said, it was kept within limits and could be a way for men to test their skills in a kind of mock combat. An example of this skill was displayed during a ritual insult contest. One man scored points against his opponent when, in a play on the storytelling style of Robert Bly, he drummed and said, "Once upon a time, before a time, and after a time, I fucked your momma."[21] This sort of thing went on for about an hour, by which time about half of the men had left the lodge. In talking to men later I found quite a few who thought the ritual insulting was an insult to their intelligence.

The importance of communitas was revealed on one occasion when I thought it had broken down. This occurred during a discussion of the Grimms' story "Faithful John," which was told at the Big Remote Gathering. At one point during the discussion I argued with two teachers about whether the story was written in a way that objectified women and assumed a patriarchal frame of reference (a full account of the exchange appears in chapter 6). I got into a shouting match with one of the teachers and worried that I'd blown my chances of completing this study, since a number of the local men witnessed the exchange. But later several men told me they agreed with what I'd said. Another man said he disagreed with me but respected my willingness to stand up and say it. One man hugged me and said that I had the admiration of all the men in the room for standing up to the teachers. To me this showed the strength of their desire for communitas. Even in disagreement the men found resources for creating it.

But such disagreements were rare. Communitas was seldom impeded by genuine or contrived conflicts of any kind. Considering the effort that went into making it happen, it's not surprising that the men usually succeeded in creating some degree of communitas. This is what made gatherings so alluring. They were even more alluring, however, precisely because communitas was not a sure thing and because it seemed to happen spontaneously and with unpredictable intensity. Rewards came, as a behaviorist would say, on an intermittent reinforcement schedule, which is the most powerful kind. Men kept coming back to gatherings and striving to achieve the good feelings and mysterious power of communitas, because they knew these things could happen and happen big at any time.

COMMUNITAS AND POLITICS

Mythopoetic men's work can be understood, in large part, as a search for communitas. This experience was rare in these men's lives and precious on the occasions when it occurred. Sometimes the men talked about the activities at their gatherings as "inviting the sacred to happen." Forms of talk, ritual, drumming, chanting, clan formation, poetry, and storytelling were means to this end. Because communitas was so valuable to the men, there were also things they avoided doing to make communitas more likely to happen. One thing they avoided was serious talk about politics.

It wasn't that the men were apolitical. Most of the men in the Local Group were informed on social issues and supported progressive causes. They were critical of the rapacious greed of big corporations, the duplicity and brutal militarism of Reagan and Bush, and the oppressiveness of large bureaucracies. But there were two revealing ironies in their politics. First, when they criticized the behavior of corporations and government, they avoided saying that these institutions were run by men. Usually it was an unspecified, genderless "they" who were said to be responsible for destroying the environment or for turning all culture into mass-marketable schlock. And second, while many of the men saw corporate power and greed as serious problems in U.S. society, they were uninterested in collective action to address these problems. This is as one might expect, since the white, middle-class mythopoetic men did not do badly in reaping the material benefits of the economic system they occasionally criticized.

In other words, the men were selectively apolitical because they did not want to risk losing their chances to experience communitas. To say that other *men* were responsible for many social problems in the world would have tarnished the image of universal brotherhood among men that helped sustain feelings of communitas. Talk about power, politics, and inequality in the external world was also incompatible with the search for communitas because it would have led to arguments, or at least to intellectual discussions, rather than to warm emotional communion. When discussions at mythopoetic gatherings inadvertently turned political and tensions arose, someone would usually say, "we're getting away from the important work here." Or as one man said in trying to stop a conversation that was getting acrimonious, "I think we're losing the power of the drums."

The mythopoetic men believed that engaging in political or sociological analysis would have led them away from their goals of self-acceptance, self-knowledge, emotional authenticity, and communitas. In an interview one man expressed his worry about the local organization taking a political turn:

If the men's center was to start supporting a certain political issue or action that
I disagreed with, then there would be a tension as to whether I could still be in
community with them or not. Does this mean I'd have to go find another community? The role that the men's center has played for me is the community, the
support, the personal affirmation. I'm not interested in losing that.

The men wanted to feel better about themselves as men, to learn about the
feelings and psychic energies that churned within them, to live fuller and more
authentic emotional lives, and to experience the pleasure and mysterious power
of communitas. They did not want to compete over whose interpretation
of social reality was correct or get into disputes over politics. They wanted
untroubled brotherhood in which their feelings were validated by other men,
and in which their identities as men could be infused with new value.

CHAPTER 5

MEN'S WORK AS IDENTITY WORK

My account of mythopoetic men's work has so far assumed the existence of creatures called men, who identify themselves as such. It seems odd to point this out, since we normally assume that men exist and that males will think of themselves as men. Yet what we take as normal is hardly natural. While biological maleness is a part of the natural world, manhood and the identity 'man' are not. The latter exist only because of meanings created by people.

The meanings we give to things, whether as solid as a drum or as abstract as soul, shape our feelings and behavior toward them. Meanings are thus important and are often fought over. These battles can be vicious when the meanings at stake are attached to groups of people. If members of one group can define members of another as savages, infidels, demons, or animals, the door is opened to exploitation and butchery. Great harm can also be done when people are told that, by virtue of the categories to which they belong, they are, in essence, worthless or evil and deserve to be treated as such.

Part of every struggle for freedom from oppression involves an attempt by the oppressed to redefine themselves in positive terms—as inherently good, capable, and worthy. This means changing both the ways a group is defined by the larger society, and the ways members of the oppressed group think of themselves. It involves a revaluation of the category and of the identity that stems from it. The best historical example in the United States is the effort by African-American liberationists in the 1960s to redefine black as beautiful and to make it the basis for a positively valued identity.

Mythopoetic men's work was, oddly enough, a similar kind of effort. It was, to a large extent, identity work, specifically, the remaking of 'man' as a moral identity. One reason this identity had to be remade was that the mythopoetic men felt it had been damaged by feminist criticism, some of which held that men were by nature brutish, insensitive, destructive, violent, competitive, untrustworthy, and emotionally inept. Feeling inseparable from this identity 'man', the mythopoetics felt that their moral worth had been impugned. Since the category itself had been condemned as corrupt, and the men were stuck in the category, they had no choice but to try to redeem it.

Identity work is usually done by using language to create and change meanings. So whenever the mythopoetic men talked or wrote about the meanings of manhood and masculinity, or about the good qualities of men, they were doing identity work. This was not a peripheral part of mythopoetic activity. Like the search for communitas, identity work was at the core of what mythopoetic activity was all about. The whole mythopoetic movement might even be described as a big identity reconstruction project.

Yet, unlike the creation of communitas, identity work could be done so subtly as to pass unnoticed. It might be done in the course of telling a poem or fairy tale, enacting a ritual, sharing a personal story, or in the act of one man touching another. Whenever the meaning of men or of 'man' was being made—through direct comment or subtle signification—a form of identity work was going on. In this chapter I'll try to explain why this identity work was so important to the men, what they aimed to accomplish by it, and how they did it.

Understanding Identity

Identities are labels we give to ourselves or that are given to us by others.[1] These labels can be based on category membership—sex, race, class, ethnicity, nationality; on individual qualities—appearance, age, skills, or temperament; and on things we do—our jobs, hobbies, sports, and sexual behavior. Each label has a meaning, which is to say it evokes a response in us and in others. Our feelings toward ourselves grow out of, and are in large part constituted by, the responses evoked by our identities. To put it another way, we *mean* something to ourselves—many things at once, actually; and how we feel about ourselves depends on these meanings.

Our inner life is greatly affected by social life because the meanings of the identities we possess are inherited from the culture. These meanings are always partly shaped by individual experience, but for the most part they are, like the meanings of words, collective creations that come to us ready-made. Indeed, we would have no meaningful identities if not for the language and culture of the community into which we are born. All this sounds innocuous until we consider that some of the identities imposed on us are worth more than others.

For example, in a society dominated by light-skinned people, being assigned to the category "white" allows you to claim an identity that is worth more than the identity "black." This greater worth can be measured in terms of what sociologists call prestige status. In everyday terms, having more prestige status means you are likely to be treated with more respect, listened to more seriously, and assumed to be competent and moral, unless you prove otherwise. Every culture instills in its members a shared sense of how various identities rank in terms of prestige status.[2]

Just belonging to higher-status categories, and thus being able to claim identities of greater worth in the culture as a whole, does not guarantee self-esteem, though it helps.[3] It makes a difference, too, that people who can claim higher-status identities are more likely to have access to jobs and other resources that boost feelings of competence. This is not to say that a person's position in a status hierarchy *determines* his or her feelings of worth and competence. It is to say that status inequalities based on ascribed characteristics create an unequal distribution of *chances* for developing self-esteem and self-confidence.

But if status hierarchies are based on meanings created by people, then they can be changed. A status hierarchy is not part of the natural order of the universe—as much as those at the top of it might like others to believe. Thus, as I noted earlier, those who are devalued by a status hierarchy, or whose competence and moral worth are impugned by the meanings of the identities imposed on them, may struggle to change the old meanings and to define themselves differently. They may also, as an attack on the status hierarchy itself, try to redefine members of the dominant group as incompetent or corrupt.[4]

Meanings can indeed be changed, but for good reasons people may resist changing the meanings of identities. To know what our identities are, and what those identities mean, is to know who and what we are, where we stand relative to others, and how to conduct ourselves in life. Even if they carry little prestige, our identities give us a sense of coherence and of place. Acquiring and discarding identities, or redefining them, is thus always disruptive. Since there's no guarantee that such disruption will lead to anything better, most people prefer to avoid it.

But if an identity becomes too costly we may try to disavow it, or simply no longer claim it. This is easier with some identities than with others; we can choose not to declare ourselves Republicans, Marxists, or gourd growers. But identities based on ascribed characteristics, such as race and sex, are stickier. We can't easily shuck them off if everyone else is attuned to them and uses them to define us. The only choices, then, may be to try to change what these identities mean in the larger culture, or to create a counterculture to sustain a different set of meanings.

How hard we try to manage the meanings of our identities depends on how important they are to us. Some identities are more central than others, meaning that we see them as more defining of who we are. In our culture, occupational identity is central for many people; in other cultures religious or ethnic identity is more important. Even if an identity is not centrally defining of who we are in the public sphere, it might be highly important to us because we value the relationships that are premised on it. This is often the case with identities such as father, mother, spouse, or partner.

Identity issues are often at the core of social conflicts. As suggested above, contention can arise over the value of an identity. Some people may try to claim a higher value for an identity than others are willing to grant. Or there can be conflict over who is entitled to claim an identity. We may want to claim an identity that others refuse to affirm, or we may want to resist an identity that others want to impose.[5] Conflicts can also arise over who has the right to bestow an identity and to say what it means. In this case, one often sees struggles enacted between different communities or segments of the same community. Each is competing for the right to make its meanings, its version of reality, stick.

These conflicts are often reproduced inside individuals. Each of us may sometimes doubt the value of our identities; doubt our right to claim an identity; wonder whether our reference groups are credible; or feel confused about the meaning of an identity; about what it implies about us; or about how to live it out. Or we might experience distress because we are tied to communities that give different meanings to our identities. Being a professor, for example, means one thing on campus and quite another at a family reunion. Ideally, we would live in communities that bestowed on us identities of high worth; that never let us doubt our right to these identities; that defined them unambiguously; and that reaffirmed these identities with powerful rituals.

Modern Western society is hardly like this. Because it is possible to mean so many things as a person; because these meanings are often in contention or subject to manipulation by more powerful others; and because there are so many audiences that seek to define us in different ways, identity work is a constant demand. When we're out in the world we must always be cognizant of, and strategic about, how we signify ourselves to others. We have to be careful to put the right spin on ourselves, lest we be interpreted in an undesirable way.

By identity work I mean anything we do, alone or with others, to establish, change, or lay claim to meanings as particular kinds of persons. As individuals, we must do some kind of identity work in every encounter. We do this when we give signs—through dress, speech, demeanor, posture—that tell others who and what we are, how we are likely to behave, and how we expect to be treated.[6] We do it also when we reflect on the meanings of our identities and try to reshape those meanings. This can be done alone, in thought or writing. Most identity work is interactive, however, since it is by engaging with others that we create and affirm the meanings that matter.

My concern here is with collective identity work. By this I mean to include all the acts of signification and interpretation used to shape the meaning of an identity shared by members of a group. In other words, when a group of people who share an identity collaborate to preserve or change the meaning of that identity, they are doing what I call collective identity work. This is different from the identity work done by a person to signify who and what she or he is as an individual. Collective identity work is done to affect the meaning, the signifying force, of the shared identity itself. In this way it redounds to the benefit of the identity holders who collaborate to help each other define what they are as a kind of people.

As noted earlier, members of oppressed groups sometimes organize to do collective identity work. What they are trying to do, perhaps as a matter of survival, is to redefine the devalued identity imposed on them by more powerful others. Often this identity work is the first step toward undertaking more far-reaching action in pursuit of justice. But identity needs are powerful motivators in their own right. It seems that many contemporary social movements, especially those made up of people from the middle- and upper-middle classes, are about meeting unmet identity needs—more so than about changing the culture or society in any profound way.[7]

In my view, this is what the mythopoetic movement was about. These men organized, if only loosely, to try to meet their unmet identity needs. Generally speaking, these needs were not unusual; like any other people, the men wanted valuable, meaningful, clearly defined identities which they could feel entitled to claim for themselves and bestow on each other. What was unusual was that the men's needs swirled around the identity 'man', which would seem to be an unlikely source of distress in a male-dominated society.

People in dominant groups don't usually have to do identity work consciously. Most of the work is a matter of habit and cultural prescription. As long as the dominant group's institutions and worldview hold sway, its members enjoy the luxury of not having to think much about how to maintain their own privileged identities. Most so-called white people, for example, are oblivious to the effort required to sustain the fantasy that humans fall naturally into distinct racial groups. In fact, most of the time "whites" don't even have to think of themselves as "having race" at all. White men long enjoyed a further privilege: unawareness of themselves as having gender. As the dominant group in U.S. society, white men could take themselves to be icons of humanity itself, and thus see themselves not as "white men," but as generic human beings. Feminism changed this. By making the identity 'man' problematic and forcing the mythopoetic men to reflect on its meaning, it was feminism that, in a sense, made them aware they *were* men.

I want to make clear that the men were by no means unsure that they were *male*; based on firsthand observation they had no doubt. And since they held an essentialist view of gender, they were equally sure that they were stuck with the identity 'man'. What they were unsure of were its moral implications. Did being a man imply good qualities or bad? If it implied good qualities, what were they? How could a man find these qualities in himself and put them into action? Jungian psychology, mythopoetic philosophy, and mythopoetic practice gave comforting answers to these questions. It was the collective search for these answers that defined the mythopoetic movement as a *movement*.

Gender Identities and Moral Identities

The most basic gender identity we have is our categorical one: 'woman' or 'man'. We can also give a host of other gender-related meanings to ourselves: male, female, masculine, feminine, father, mother, sister, brother, and so forth. This network of gender-related meanings tells us much about who and what we are in our culture. Abolishing gender is thus inconceivable to most people, since it so hard to imagine who or what we would be without it.

As natural as gender may seem to our way of life, we still must learn how to "do gender" in the right way for our place and time.[8] A large part of what we must learn is how to present ourselves as men or women. In this view, gender identities must be *accomplished* through acts of signification. The secondary sex characteristics of our bodies do much of this signifying for us; but we must do it also with clothes, speech, posture, gestures, and so on. To be recognized, unambiguously, as a man or a woman, requires that we learn how to do the right kind of identity work for our sex.

Because we learn to do this kind of identity work so well that it becomes second nature to us, it usually seems as if we're doing nothing at all. But with strange or suspicious audiences, we may feel the effort more clearly, especially when we must signify the *kind* of man or woman we are. Most men will remember, I presume, the intensely conscious identity work that, at some point in their lives, went into signifying manhood to their male peers. The point is that each of us must learn how to wield the signs that allow others to recognize us as belonging to one or the other of our culture's dichotomous gender categories. Refusing to signify our gender identities in the expected ways can create all kinds of havoc.

Though gender does not make us everything we are, it affects all the relationships that make us what we are. Every enduring relationship or brief encounter is partly shaped by our being men or women. This applies not only to men interacting with women, but to men interacting with men, and women interacting with women. Moreover, gender is not just a matter of signification; it is part of our inner lives as well, in that we learn to think and feel in ways defined as befitting our sex. So, as some sociologists say, gender is "omnirelevant."

This raises the question as to why, if they are so deeply ingrained, gender identities ever become problematic. Only in rare cases is the appropriateness of one's categorical gender identity likely to be doubted. Problems are more likely to arise over matters of meaning, clarity, and worth. As suggested earlier, such problems can arise when communities compete to define identities in ways that better serve their own interests. Or people may discover that old meanings don't suit new circumstances. As I'll discuss below, the mythopoetic men faced both kinds of problems.

One more identity concept is important here, that of a moral identity. A moral identity is one which implies unusual virtue or wickedness. For example, in our culture 'mother' and 'minister' are moral identities that, to most of us, imply goodness; 'convict' and 'mercenary' are moral identities at the other end of the continuum. Access to such identities is always restricted; certain criteria must be met before a moral identity can be claimed or imposed. Only women who bear children can become mothers. Only persons arrested, tried, and found guilty can become convicts.

Any identity can be made into a moral identity. What's necessary is a community to invest the identity with special significance and to define the criteria that must be met before it can be rightfully claimed or imposed. Status and privileges accrue to those whose claims to a positive moral identity are honored. Those upon whom negative moral identities are imposed will suffer the fate of Cain. In light of their damning or exalting consequences, it is not surprising that people seek to claim positive moral identities and avoid negative ones.

Part of what the mythopoetic men tried to do was to remake 'man' into a positive moral identity. 'Man' could be a moral identity because access to it was restricted by prevailing ideas about who was eligible to be a man. All one needed, to pass the first test, was a penis. The second test was a presentation of self signifying masculinity. To ensure that they passed this test, the mythopoetics redefined masculinity to fit them. In this way they could pass both tests and claim to be the males best qualified to claim the moral identity 'man'.

It is interesting to consider whether 'woman' is a corollary moral identity to 'man'. I would say it isn't. To say that a man is a "real man" is, or has been, high praise in our culture. Such a label normally means that a man is strong, capable, potent, and has integrity. The meaning of "real woman" is not as clear. When this is said of a woman, it usually connotes sexual prowess. My sense is that the corollary to 'man' for women is 'mother'. This is the identity to which women have restricted access and have sought to invest with special moral value.[9] Perhaps this is why many women have children even when they don't really want them; it is the only way to gain access to one of the few moral identities women are allowed in our society.[10]

To sum up, I have said that to obtain the benefits of a positive moral identity you must claim one to which you're allowed access. Males in our society are not only allowed access to the identity 'man', they *expect* each other to show their worthiness to make this identity claim stick, since this helps preserve the high status of the category 'men'. As males, the mythopoetics thus felt the imperative to claim the identity 'man' and to prove themselves worthy of it. To make this easier, the men redefined manhood and masculinity to fit themselves better. Then they did the identity work necessary to reinvest 'man' with new moral value.

THE NEED TO REMAKE 'MAN' AS A MORAL IDENTITY

For the mythopoetic men, the identity 'man' was problematic not because they doubted it was theirs to claim, but because they didn't like some of the meanings it had gathered. Even into the 1980s, the identity 'man' still implied qualities associated with the John Wayne/Rambo model of traditional masculinity. These qualities—stoicism, toughness, a capacity for violence, no need for others—fit with neither the personalities nor values of the mythopoetic men. They wanted to be men, not insensitive assholes. On the other hand, they didn't want to be sensitive New Age wimps, which seemed to them to be the alternative.

The men frequently bemoaned their lack of good models for manhood. According to the author of an article in a mythopoetic newspaper, the "primary images" of manhood in U.S. culture were, "Rambo and Oliver North, on one hand, or Fred Flintstone and PeeWee Herman on the other . . . ."[11] Men said similar things at gatherings, sometimes posing John Wayne and Alan Alda as the alternatives. The choices were usually portrayed as unacceptable extremes, or it was said that there were no alternatives to traditional masculinity. This dilemma came up in several interviews. As one man in his early 40s said:

> I internalized the message that there was something wrong with being with other men too much. But now [after doing men's work for a while] I'm more aware of what I need as a man. For a long time it was like my needs as a man were not legitimate because, you know, the only needs men have shown, historically, are like the needs to oppress and to be cruel. I mean like men were exclusively associated with oppression and greed and abuse. We [men who sympathized with feminist women] didn't want to be like that. But then, who were we gonna be like?

Some of the men were genuinely confused about who or what they should try to be like as men. But even while these men longed for a clearer image of authentic, righteous manhood, most of the men did not want more ideal images to feel bad about falling short of. They may have wanted more clarity and certainty about the moral qualities of a good man, but they did not want more "shoulds" hanging over their heads. What they wanted was a way to accept themselves as they already were, or were within reach of becoming. This was evident in the men's enthusiastic response, on several occasions, to the proposition that "there are as many ways to be a good man as there are individual men."

As noted in chapter 1, many of the men's biographies included abusive or absent fathers, mothers with whom they strongly sympathized, feminist women friends, and exposure to the civil rights and anti-war movements of the 1960s. The men were thus inclined to agree that there were things wrong in the world and that many of these things were indeed caused by selfish, unfeeling, violent men who abused their power. Feminist criticism resonated with the men, for a time anyway, because they shared women's concerns for equality and justice. And, as gentle men, many of the mythopoetics had also been the victims of macho bullies.

But at some point the men found themselves in a bind. They saw women's objections to machoism and male chauvinism as justified. Yet they were still men themselves, and at some point they began to feel a current of radical feminist criticism sweeping up every image of manhood and masculinity in its path. While the men were not devoted students of feminist theory, they were aware that some feminists had indicted all men as oppressors, plunderers, and rapists—making no exceptions for nice guys like them. The mythopoetic men understood the critique of machoism and old-fashioned male chauvinism. But the radical feminist critique of men and all forms of masculinity as morally corrupt was baffling. It felt like an indiscriminate and unfair attack.

All this produced a sense of being wounded. This is conveyed by a passage from a key piece of movement literature, Moore and Gillette's book *King, Warrior, Magician, Lover*:

> . . . the world is overpopulated with not only immature men but also tyrannical and abusive little girls pretending to be women. It is time for men—particularly men of Western civilization—to stop accepting the blame for everything that is wrong in the world. There has been a veritable blitzkrieg on the male gender, what amounts to an outright demonization of men and a slander against masculinity.[12]

Meade and Bly echoed this same theme—that men had been under attack for the last 30 years or so. The "tyrannical and abusive little girls" who are, by context in this passage, implied to be the attackers, were sometimes identified by mythopoetic men as "ideological," "separatist," or "anti-male" feminists.

The men felt another, less direct attack come from cultural feminists who vaunted women's moral superiority. According to this stream of thought (often linked to Carol Gilligan's work), women were naturally more caring, nurturing, empathic, and protective of life than men, because women bore and raised children. Since men couldn't bear children, and hence didn't have the same connection to life that women did, it was not surprising, in this view, that men were selfish, greedy, violent, and without tender emotions. Though these claims about women's morality were originally intended only to recognize the value of the sensitivities that supposedly came from intimate caretaking, men could see in these arguments the implication that, once again, men, because they were men, were morally corrupt.

Some of the men also had connections to a subculture of New Age spiritualism. Even here they felt denigrated when feminist spiritualists, building on the arguments of cultural feminists, vaunted women's *spiritual* superiority to men. Again, because women could bring new life into the world, they were said to be more adept at transcending themselves and connecting to the life-giving forces of the cosmos. Pertinent to this is an exchange I overheard at the Big Remote Gathering. The first man said, "Some of this [archetypal psychology] reminds me of the goddess stuff. My wife reads a lot of that." The second man said, "I don't read that shit." Replied the first, "Really, it's good stuff. But yeah, it can make you feel like the feminine is holy and the masculine is shit."

All this put many of the men in a position where they felt as if they had to apologize for being men, and could take no pride in any of the aspects of traditional masculinity that had been instilled in them. In an interview, one man, just under 50, talked about how he had come to feel, by the mid-80s, about being a man:

> I pretty much fit what Bly said about the soft male. My wife's a very strong feminist, and I'm very supportive of the women's movement and all. And what happened is—I don't think my wife meant this intentionally—that in working at the women's center my wife would see a lot of bad things men did to women. Abuse. Women abandoned with four kids to support. So she would come home and everyday it would be "goddamn men!" And I was like, well, "yeah, that's right!" But this gets to you after a while. At the time I didn't even know it was happening. After a while I found that I needed to sort of build back up the idea that, hey, men are basically good people, as men. Sure, there are a lot of bad things about the patriarchy and the system we have. But as men we're not bad people.

The conflict between political values, gender socialization, and identity needs was also reflected in this statement in an interview with a man just over 40:

> I jumped on the feminist movement and the civil rights movement. Those liberation movements told me that I didn't want to be that macho, socially constructed John Wayne American male. I knew that way back, in the late 60s, early 70s. But then a different confusion started with me because, and I have to give credit to Michael Meade for this, he told me something like "reclaim your maleness." It's like it's okay to be—I don't know what words to use—but like decisive, tough. I had tried to push those things away because I thought they were wrong. But now I think it's okay to be a little rougher and tougher or maler.

A younger man, just over 30, who had been active in working for abortion rights legislation, described how men's work had changed his thinking about men and masculinity:

It's legitimated things that I feel, things that I think feminists, maybe even women in general, want me to feel guilty about. But now it's like, I'm different from you and I'm gonna behave this way and even if you don't like it, that's okay, because that's me. You can accept it or we can talk about it, but I'm not going to let my boundaries be violated. What was not there before, in me, was a sense that, as a man I'm different and that's okay. It's true that it's very difficult to extricate the stuff that's okay—the energy, the wildness, the sensuality of being a man—from things that are considered negative—murder, violence, rape. The problem was that I couldn't talk to feminists about how I really felt because I always found myself in a position where they had all men categorized. All of men's energy was put in the same category they put violence, rape, and abuse.

These statements are representative of what other men said in interviews. The basic feeling the men shared was that, despite their sympathies for women, their support for the principle of gender equality, and their belief that male chauvinism was wrong, women—or some feminists—had made them feel morally tarnished just for being men. In response they sought a feeling that, *as men, we're not bad people.*

A sense of having been betrayed by women was sharpened by feminist criticism of "sensitive men" as fakers. Some radical feminists claimed that sensitive New Age guys had simply adopted a softer persona, behind which male privilege remained intact. This sort of criticism again made the men feel as if there was no way to win. Whereas previously the men felt appreciated by women for being softer and gentler than other men, now they felt as if there was nothing they could do to be good enough. Again, to be a man, no matter how nice and sensitive, was to be guilty.

It's not surprising, then, that the men became defensive. Seeing themselves as decent men, not as rapists, warmongers, pillaging capitalists, or even the emotionally distant men their fathers had been, the mythopoetic men felt stung by arguments implying that all men were moral or emotional cripples.[13] These arguments seemed to allow no room for men who, like them, were emotionally complex and could be nurturing, empathic, and gentle. The men also knew, based on experiences with mothers, lovers, and wives, that all women were not paragons of virtue. If feminist arguments said that all women were more kind, gentle, generous, empathic, and caring than all men, then the arguments were wrong and men were getting a bad rap.

Women, I want to reiterate, were not the only source of damage to the identity 'man'. In many cases it was the men's fathers who did the damage. In chapter 1, I noted that many of the men described their fathers as physically or emotionally absent, while about a third also said that their fathers were alcoholic or abusive in some way. As another man said in an interview, this made men of his generation doubly vulnerable to feminist criticism:

> I know a lot of men my age [late 30s] who weren't very involved with their fathers; we didn't have a strong connection there. So we didn't have very vital or strong models of what being an adult man was about. Then when feminism became a very vibrant movement we were presented by all these feelings, coming from strong women, that made men feel guilty for being the way men had traditionally been. A lot of the feminist critique of that was appropriate . . . but one of the thrusts of at least some feminists was to be anti-male. Maybe that was okay for some individual women as part of their personal evolution. But if you as a man took on that stance, it was very damaging—to think that there was something wrong with being a man or being in your gender. I certainly feel like I took on some of that, and was sort of contaminated by that attitude. I think the problem was compounded because of not having good images from our fathers.

Other men said in interviews that their fathers were "negative role models" for them, or that they had decided to be as different from their fathers as they could be. A few times at gatherings I heard men speculate on whether the tendencies to violence and sexual abuse that they had seen in their fathers would manifest in them. One man, whose father was an alcoholic, said that because of his father he'd grown up "hating all the male things in me." What these men saw, without needing their mothers to point it out, was that men could cause a great deal of pain. 'Man' was thus already tarnished, for some of the men, well before they encountered feminism.

Some of the men did speak, however, of how their mothers had exacerbated the negative labeling of men and masculinity. In Jungian-inspired mythopoetic lore, this supposedly occurs because the mother is trying to keep an unhealthy hold on her son, who is enlisted as an ally against the bad father. But in many cases it seemed as if a mother was simply venting a great deal of anger in what was arguably an unhealthy way. One man talked about how this affected his view of his father:

> He would come home and we [the children] would be wary of him, partly because of his behavior and partly because of the way Mom talked about him. She criticized him all day long. He wasn't home, but she was going around doing her housework and she had a non-stop torrent of rage against him coming out of her mouth: "God damn son-of-a-bitch motherfucker." This was day in, day out, year after year. Somehow I excused her behavior entirely. It seemed some-

how appropriate and natural because he was such a bad guy. I was so allied with her that there was just this incredible blind spot about her behavior, which was grossly dysfunctional. I find this is a fairly common experience talking to men. There's this strong alliance with the mother, and the father kind of gets demonized in certain ways, though not without some large basis very often.

The issue here is not the legitimacy of the mother's anger but its effect on the son. If the mother's anger is perceived as directed at the father *because he is a man*, and the son learns to associate the father's failings with manhood itself, then it seems likely that 'man' will be damaged as a moral identity in the son's mind.

What men's work did for the men was to counteract the negative messages about the meaning of 'man' that had come from all kinds of sources. It helped the men repair the damage done by childhood experiences and by later encounters with feminism. The man quoted earlier (whose wife worked at the women's center) talked about how men's work had helped him redefine masculinity:

> I think it's something I can be proud of now. Now I see that there are good things about it—the energy, the ability to get things done. You don't have to apologize because men get things done. That's good. There's nothing wrong with that. And again, we can overdo it—work all the time and dominate and all those bad things. But men can also nurture each other. That doesn't have to come just from women. So there's that feeling of being proud to be a man or proud of your masculinity. It feels good that you're not having to apologize for all the bad men of the world.

The man who spoke of fathers not providing good models also saw men's work as offering a remedy. His words from an interview capture the idea of men's work as identity work:

> It's a kind of counterweight to all that to get together with men in a sense that's not apologetic but just explores what it means to be a man and really looking for some value in there and a sense of empowerment and pride to be male. I think this is a real important and valuable corrective experience for the absence of clear role models and for the sense of being under attack. I guess I felt apologetic about being male for a long time and still feel that to a degree. The problem is the blurring between the reasonable criticism of patriarchy and being critical of men as a sex. When that line gets blurred and men start taking that as an attack on them, it becomes damaging and I think it needs to be countered in some way. I just have the sense now of feeling more secure and positive about being a man than I did a few years ago. Just doing things with other men and examining some of these issues has a lot to do with that. . . . For me the single most important

thing isn't what we would theoretically posit as being somehow the "essence of masculinity," but more just the sense of "let's face it, we're men, and wouldn't it be nice to feel positive about that?" So at a very basic level men's work doesn't presuppose any ideology about what being a man is at all. It's just a very basic and obvious statement of wanting to seek experiences that somehow validate a positive feeling about being a member of the sex that I happen to be a part of.

So it was for many of the men a combination of things—angry mothers, abusive fathers, and feminist criticism—that caused the men to doubt the moral value of 'man' as an identity.

Repairing or remaking the identity 'man' was not as simple, however, as the previous quote implies. Mythopoetic men's work involved a clear effort to redefine the essence of manhood and masculinity in particular ways. For the most part, as I'll show in the next section, this meant trying to foster belief in the innate goodness of men. But it also meant trying to "reclaim" certain traits associated with traditional masculinity, most notably assertiveness. In the following passage from an interview, a man in his early 40s talked about having "thrown away" his power and control, which men's work had given him license to reclaim:

> I'd thrown away those parts of myself. I then lied to myself about being a pacifist. You go through the peace movement and the civil rights movement and you see your heroes get killed, and so you say, "I'm a pacifist." But the truth is, I'm not. I think that in the recesses of my mind and body I knew that to claim I was an absolute pacifist was a lie. If you do this, you can end up not knowing who you are, because you're creating a persona and an identification, but deep inside you know you are capable of something else. I mean, if somebody tried to kill my sister or my mother, I would kill to protect them. I would kill before I would allow them to be killed. I am not a holy monk who would sit down to pray in that situation. That's bullshit. I would reclaim my, and I don't know if it's just maleness, but my aggression.

But as with most of the men, this reclaiming was complicated by commitment to values that did not permit an easy embrace of traditional masculinity. This same man talked about trying to identify what was good about "maleness" in light of his other values:

> I'm trying to fit these things together, where I can be on a personal level a male who can be receptive and sensitive and emotional and tribally peaceful, but at the same time would not deny the need to protect or to say no. I used the example of killing, but that's really hyperbole. It also has to be just saying, "No, I won't do that. I have limits." So I think it's about reclaiming this strength that I think

Meade was talking about. You know, that it's okay to have your limits and say
no and stand up and be direct and be strong without being a macho asshole. My
problem was that I threw out the baby with the bathwater. Now I'm trying to
reclaim the baby but make sure the dirty bathwater stays out. You don't have to
go on the football field and knock a guy's teeth out to prove you're a man. You
can show you're a man by defending your family or your tribe if someone threatens them. It's more defensive than offensive. Or if my wife wants to do something and I really don't want to, I say no. Which is maybe not a male thing, but
I'm a male, and I need to reclaim that.

After doing men's work, this man found

> I don't have to give myself up to a woman as much as I used to. I don't have to
> forget who I am. I don't have to give up my power, my control. It's partially
> therapy but also working in men's stuff, the mythopoetic stuff, that has made
> me feel more like a growler. The nonrational experience by the lake or in the
> sweat lodge also made me feel that if my life was threatened that I could prob-
> ably act like a beast. You know, I could be a beast and protect. I might die in the
> process, but I wouldn't shrink. I would be somehow, uh, animal-male.

Many of the men spoke of a desire to cultivate assertiveness, which was seen
as a piece of masculinity, or a quality of maleness. The desire for this kind of
assertiveness is what made the Jungian archetype of the warrior—the archetype of conviction, discipline, and resolve—so appealing to many of the men.
    For other men it was not so much ferocity as it was independence and auton-
omy that they were trying to reclaim. In an interview a man talked about how
he thought men's work had changed him:

> I think it's changed my feelings toward myself. It helped me find my masculin-
> ity. You know, we all have gender. The first thing you see from someone is if
> they are male or female. But I think I lost track of my own sense of masculinity
> and now it's coming back slowly. It was never really allowed to develop as a child.
> You do have to promote that with children. You want girls to be feminine and
> boys to be masculine. It is their nature and you should promote it. There were a
> lot of things in my family that squashed that, that sense of independence. I think
> I'm just finding it now. And it's not so much a change towards women as it is a
> change towards myself. Right now, after my last divorce, I feel very relieved and
> I feel comfortable getting into a new relationship with this new woman because
> I know within I just don't want to commit. I don't want to get married. I'll live
> here by myself and date who I want to date, have friends over when I want to.
> It's not going to be a couple here. It's going to be me. I had really lost my iden-
> tity in the couple. There was a marriage, but there was no me. I don't want to
> lose that again. I think that's what the men's movement is helping me find.

The key elements of masculinity for this man were autonomy, control over his domestic world, and freedom from commitment. This man, like a number of others, felt that he had denied his desires for these traditionally masculine things in an effort to please his ex-wife.

It's not just that these men were trying to boost their self-confidence, be more assertive, or live more authentically. More importantly, they were trying to feel okay about the traditionally masculine traits that had been instilled in them and which they felt expected to display as men. They also were trying to turn the feminist critique of men and masculinity on its head by saying that it was inherently *good* to be a man and to be masculine—in a properly deep, authentic, or mature way. Matters were complicated, however, because the men did not want to cast off the feminine traits they already possessed. As one of the leaders in the Local Group said in an interview, "Despite all that Robert Bly has said, I think that softening is a good thing for men to do. I think he's right, too, in that men soften sometimes in the wrong ways."

During the 1980s softness took a beating from another direction. The image of the sensitive man was buffeted by the same cultural currents that swept Ronald Reagan into office. Many Americans, men and women, longed to heal the damage to America's national pride caused by the debacle of Vietnam, the power of OPEC, and the seemingly interminable "hostage crisis" in Iran. Ronald Reagan's crafted image of tall-in-the-saddle traditional manhood answered to this longing. As this neo-traditional image of manhood was ascending, New Age spiritualism and male softness were mocked as vestiges of the 1960s—a time when Americans, and American men in particular, forgot that the world was a hard place and one had to be tough and competitive to survive.

The mythopoetic men thus faced blanket condemnation of men and masculinity on the one hand, and the resurgence of traditional masculine values, such as power and toughness, on the other. The men felt betrayed by feminists who said that all men were corrupt simply for being men; and they felt devalued—as they had been for a long time—by traditional masculinists who saw them as too soft, vulnerable, and nonaggressive. Caught between these two views, the mythopoetic men could have tried to give up their identities as men, or they could have embraced traditional masculinity. The former seemed impossible and the latter simply didn't fit with who the men were, how they felt, or what they believed.

This is why the creation of small, temporary communities of men with similar values and feelings was so important. In what seemed like a world turned mean, the men had to create safe places to do the identity work necessary to feel better about themselves as men. In describing how men's work had changed him, this man, also in his early 40s, reiterates what a number of other men said, but adds an important point:

I think I'm a lot less ashamed of being a man, a lot more accepting of the qualities in me. I've reinterpreted qualities that I always thought were, well, anything that smacked of machismo. I used to be sort of ashamed and self-effacing of my masculinity, and I'm not anymore. Another change is, I think, paradoxically, a renewed respect for women because I'm more comfortable with myself as a man. I don't react to women in a defensive way now. Women are not a threat to my masculinity because my masculine identity comes from a different place. It's nothing they can take from me.

What this man had found and helped create was a community of men within which a remade identity as a man could be anchored. In this "different place," the men could carry on their identity work safe from criticism by women and ridicule by traditionally masculine men.

The male-supremacist context in which this occurred also influenced the men's ideas about the kind of audience they needed to validate 'man' as a remade moral identity. By this I mean that men were considered more important sources of validation than women. The men often talked about this in terms of needing "affirmation" or "blessing" from other (usually older) men.[14] This was crucial also because the men had doubts about their masculinity stemming from their own feminine traits. The secure, remade identity they sought thus had to come from a community of men. Women couldn't do the job. In response to a question about why men's work excluded women, a man said:

> As far back as junior high school I picked up on the message that men should be sensitive and try to be the equals of women, not try to be above them. And I think being with men who can model showing the inside—the pain, the weakness—if they can do that and not be diminished in my mind, or if I can do that with them or other men and not feel diminished, then there is a certain validation of it, I guess. If I do those things with men and feel affirmed and validated that's one thing. But then if I do it with a woman, well, maybe I'm being too womanly or something. Do you follow me? In the past, before I got involved with the men's center, when I was attempting to be an equal with my wife or other women, I often on the one hand felt that was a noble, a good thing. But on the other hand I had a lot of doubts about, well, are you a wimp or a sissy? Probably there was some homophobia in there. What if this means I'm gay or something? Or I guess maybe the other thing was that I thought being this way meant not really being a man. Maybe there was some flaw or weakness that I was doing it with a woman—being open and sensitive with a woman. But to be able to do that with men, I don't get the same messages. I don't have the same fears and doubts. I am doing it with my own kind and I get validation from them. I guess I trust that more. Or at least I don't fall into those patterns of questioning my own manhood. There's a big difference between a man telling me it's okay to be a man this way and a woman telling me.

The goal, then, was to feel okay about being a man, even while being emotional and sensitive. The affirmation and validation necessary to uphold this sense of okay-ness had to come from other men, because, as the men saw it, women were not a sufficiently reliable or credible audience when it came to affirming manhood and masculinity as positive traits. Obviously, an audience of men steeped in traditional masculinity would not have worked, either; such men would have denigrated the "womanly" traits that the mythopoetic men had learned to value.

Since giving up the identity 'man' wasn't seen as an option, and since there were clear advantages to holding on to it, the men found a way out of the bind by redefining manhood and masculinity, among themselves, to fit what they already were. In chapters 2 and 3, I showed how Jungian psychology provided an ideological resource for doing this. It allowed the men to reinterpret their feminine traits as aspects of "deep masculinity." This tack also neatly exploited the resurgence in value attached to traditional masculinity. If masculinity was valuable, clearly it was better to have a deep rather than a shallow version.

Finally, another reason it was important to hold onto and revalue 'man' as a moral identity was that, for many of the men, it was all they had. Men of a previous generation had 'breadwinner' or 'provider' as moral identities to which they, as men, had nearly exclusive access. Things were different for the mythopoetic men, most of whose wives had careers of their own. And while most of the men had decent, middle-class jobs, the work these jobs entailed rarely provided much basis for feelings of moral worth.[15] Many of the men did not see their jobs as allowing them to be "who they really were" or to live out their most cherished values. Jobs were thus not a source of moral identity for many of the men. What the men discovered, after being spurred by feminist criticism, was that 'man', with some revamping, could fill the void.

IDENTITY WORK

The men called what they did "men's work." Yet the activities the men engaged in—talking about feelings, sometimes crying in each other's arms, hugging, reading poetry, same-sex dancing—are usually associated with women in our culture. Calling these activities men's work was partly a way to allow men to feel at ease doing them. But the term *men's work* connoted, and accomplished, much more. To call these activities *men's* work implied that those who gathered to perform them were indeed men; were deeply masculine if they did these activities well; and were not just chattering away their time, like women, because this was *work* going on. "Men's work" was thus more than a handy label. It was a way to build identity.

The term *men's work* was one of many rhetorical devices the men used to nudge the meaning of their identities in the direction they desired. It's not that the men did this consciously; they simply invented, or gravitated toward the use of, terms that felt right. Of course, terms "felt right" largely because of what they implied about mythopoetic activity and the identity 'man'. But I am less interested here in the men's intentions than in how they actually did collective identity work, consciously or not, through their words and deeds.

There were three things the men needed to accomplish through their identity work. First, they had to define themselves as men; that is, they had to assert and validate their own claims to being men. Second, they had to redefine 'man' in a way that raised its moral value; that is, they had to attribute positive moral qualities to all holders of this identity. Finally, because women had encroached upon men's prerogatives in this regard, the men had to reestablish themselves as having the exclusive right to define and bestow the revalorised identity 'man'. Once again Jungian psychology helped to get the golden ball rolling.

Jungian Psychology as a Resource
Jungian psychology held that positive masculine energies were innate in men. The inborn archetypes that gave form to men's psychic energy meant that all men had the capacity to be kings, warriors, magicians, lovers, and wild men. Also inborn was the archetype of the Self—a blueprint for the harmonious integration of the psyche—which was unfolding in all men, naturally impelling them toward a mature state of integrity, generativity, and enlightenment. In proffering these notions, which bespoke the natural goodness of men, the mythopoetic teachers used Jungian psychology to invest the identity 'man' with new moral value.

To speak of the innate goodness of men was not to deny men's shadows and capacities for evil. But in the Jungian view even the shadow held energies that were potentially useful if a man could integrate them properly. In recognizing the shadow as part of *every* psyche, and in seeing women and men as having the same capacities for good and evil, the Jungian view also deflated claims by cultural feminists that women were morally superior to men. And since accepting the shadow is a crucial step toward individuation, the Jungian view gave the men one up on cultural feminists. To exalt women's morality and ignore their capacities for evil, as cultural feminists seemed to do, showed that they were stuck at an immature stage that the mythopoetic men had the wisdom to go beyond.

The Jungian concept of the archetype gave the men another way to do identity work. Supposedly, according to Jung, the human psyche teemed with archetypes that were products of evolution. But since it was not possible to look into the psyche and see these archetypes directly, they had to be inferred from behavior and from reports of inner experience. So if some men did good things, *felt like* doing good things, or *dreamed about* doing good things, this could be seen as evidence for the existence of an archetype. Of course, this made it possible to see in men all manner of noble archetypes.

The best, and in some ways the silliest example of this, was the invention by mythopoetic writers of the "Green Man" archetype, which was supposedly the archetype that inclined men to respect and care for the earth.[16] Why suppose that concern for the earth was driven by an archetype rather than common decency or rational self-interest? Because proposing the existence of an archetype meant, again, that men were *innately* good, since they had these noble concerns wired into them. In this case it was the Jungian notion that thought, feeling, and behavior reflect the operation of innate dispositions that provided the ideological resource for doing identity work.

The other advantage of the Jungian perspective was that it was equalizing and universalizing. By this I mean that it helped to redeem the *category* men and didn't make anyone feel left out. So, for example, if one man didn't feel the same passion for the earth as the next man, it wasn't because he was ignorant or uncaring, it was only because he hadn't yet activated the Green Man archetype in his psyche. In other words, the goodness of a concern for the earth was part of all men, whether or not they had ever actually *done* anything to protect it. This way of thinking also avoided heaping shame on men who behaved ungreenly. So again, inventing or invoking an archetype was a form of identity work because it implied the innate goodness of all men, thus helping to remake 'man' as a moral identity.

The other place this archetypalizing of men's goodness went on was in the telling of fairy tales and myths. Many of the stories had a central heroic figure—Perseus, Sir Gawain, the boy who becomes a lord in "Iron John"—who symbolized some form of archetypal energy in men. The men were given to understand, in keeping with the Jungian approach to such stories, that these heroes represented capacities wired into them as men. Each telling of a story thus became an opportunity to do identity work via metaphor. Even without any sophisticated Jungian interpretations of the stories, the men could, by identifying with the archetypal male hero, feel that they shared in the power and virtue he represented on behalf of all men.

Identity Work in Print

Books by Jung-inspired mythopoetic teachers were extended attempts to show that men throb with noble impulses. In less prominent mythopoetic publications, identity work was done in articles with titles such as, "The Positive Attributes of Manhood" and "Uniquely Masculine Qualities."[17] Summing the adjectives used in articles of this kind shows the positive image of manhood that the mythopoetics sought to construct. Men were said to be wild, gentle, tough, loving, fierce, sensitive, pioneering, wise, vital, spontaneous, zany, forceful, and natural. A man was said to be one who speaks the truth, takes risks, shows feelings and affection for others, appreciates beauty, nurtures and protects, gets things done, provides for others, stands his ground, and dances when the spirit moves him.

An especially good example of identity work in print, in one of the smaller mythopoetic publications, was an article titled "It's Good To Be A Man!"[18] Several passages from this article are worth quoting, since they show how some men, outside the Local Group, experienced men's work as changing the meaning of 'man' for them. The first passage alludes to a turnaround in the meaning of 'man' as a moral identity:

> For me there is a strong sense of impending joy, as men, individually and collectively, begin to make startling discoveries about what it means to be a man. Some of our most important discoveries revolve around our incredible potential for goodness. Surprise! Things aren't always as they seem. Things aren't as we've been taught. We are finally discovering that it is good to be a man.

The author goes on to say that he'd been taught (although it's not clear by whom) to value the feminine sides of himself over the masculine:

> During my coming of age, there was a powerful societal emphasis on the development of my "feminine" side. It was encouraged, taught, reinforced, and rewarded and I worked very hard at it. The message about meeting this goal was loud and clear: If you succeed, you'll be a better person. You'll be happier, more content, and more well rounded. The more subtle message was even more powerful: The good aspects of my very being were feminine; the bad aspects—masculine.

Masculinity, this man learned, was morally inferior to femininity, which was the better quality of one's self to try to develop. Elsewhere in the article the author says that while developing his feminine side did make him happier, more content, and well rounded in some ways, it did not make him more complete, enthusiastic, energized, or connected with himself or others. Nonetheless, the consequences were ultimately good. "Ironically," the author says, "the journey toward my 'feminine side' brought me face to face with a much more powerful and more helpful discovery—true masculinity." Men's work was what led to this discovery. Other men doing men's work were benefiting similarly:

[Other men] are making the same discovery that I've made: The "good aspects" of our lives as men are not reflections of our feminine side but rather an expression that is simply and profoundly masculine. What's good about being a man is not our feminine side; it's the discovery of what Gillette and Moore have called our "mature masculine."

Under the influence of Jungian psychology, mythopoetic philosophy, and men's work, men were thus learning that they didn't have to be more like women to be good people. Goodness could be achieved by pursuing the right kind of masculinity. The tone of the author's words suggests this was not just a happy discovery but an epiphany:

Our quest for fulfillment, self-actualization and connectedness lies not, as we have been told, in our feminine side, but within, as we are learning, our "deep masculine." What a relief! It's good to be a man.

The author also notes that deep or mature masculinity is wired into every man. A man must work to explore and develop his ability to express it, but his goodness is innate. This is, as the author says, a relief. Doubt about the moral worth of men can be put to rest.

But then it was also necessary to give more specific content to 'man', to say more precisely what it meant and implied about the moral qualities of those who bore this identity. By filling in this content—by saying what deep masculinity entails—the author did a bit of identity work:

Within our "deep masculine" we will find the good things that we've been searching for. We will find our ability to be benevolent, courageous, decisive and appropriately aggressive. We will find enthusiasm, loyalty and energy. We will discover a spiritual dimension that gives our lives a sense of meaning. We will find that we are fully capable of nurturing, protecting, and grieving. We can feel joy, appreciate beauty, experience wonder and live our lives with spontaneity. We can experience these realities not by developing our feminine side but by acknowledging our deep, true, and undeniably masculine spirits.

Even more specifically, the author explains that a man who is in touch with his mature masculine is

a good friend and relies upon his friends to meet many of his needs for intimacy. He listens, he self-discloses, he teaches and he learns. . . . He has a full range of feelings and he can express them directly and honestly. He is gentle, vulnerable, and kind. He is tough and gutsy. He is a complete person—not because he has

learned to integrate his feminine side, but because he has uncovered the remark-
able gifts of true masculinity.

What this passage does is to redefine behaviors traditionally associated with
women—relying on friends for intimacy, listening, expressing feelings, being
gentle, vulnerable, and kind—as aspects of masculinity. It illustrates the chief
irony of mythopoetic men's work: it was in part a way for the men to redefine
as masculine the feminine traits they already possessed and valued.

Finally, in case there was any doubt about what all this means, the author
nails down his identity work with an ebullient conclusion:

> . . . this is an exciting time for men. Our minds and our hearts are opening and
> our search for our inherent goodness has ended. Finally, we have discovered a
> masculine spirit that simply and powerfully affirms that: Yes! It is good to be a
> man.

This article puts into plain language the ideas and feelings shared by many of
the men. How did they account for the appeal of mythopoetic literature and
activity? The commonest answer was that it "makes you feel good about being
a man." It did this, in large part, by doing what this author did: redefining
masculinity to fit what the men already were, defining this kind of masculinity as good, and saying that this good masculinity was innate in men.

Poetry
Poetry was another means for shaping the meaning of 'man'. In large part it
was the content of the poems that accomplished this, as I will discuss below.
But the very acts of reading, writing, and listening to poems accomplished it,
too, because to do these things signified another fine quality of men: sensitivity to beauty. And when poems evoked strong feelings in the men, this re-
futed the perceived feminist stereotype of men as shallow, simple, bland emotional creatures. Poetry was thus a subtle yet powerful means of doing identity
work, because it could affect the meaning of 'man' on several levels at once.

It wasn't the case that all the poems read or recited at gatherings venerated
men, although the poems usually addressed one of the main mythopoetic
themes: relationships between men, especially fathers and sons; how a man
ought to live or love; men's feelings of grief; and a man's connections to nature. Poems that were too obscure or that didn't speak to some common concern or experience fell flat. When a poem struck a chord it was obvious by the
men's reactions. The poems that resonated most powerfully with the men were
those that accomplished identity work.

To see how poetry helped the men do identity work, it isn't necessary to decode the poems to fathom what they "really say" about men, manhood, and masculinity. Besides, to focus solely on the words of the poems would be to miss the meaning of the poems *in context*. When read at gatherings these poems meant things that they could not mean in a classroom, in a coffeehouse, or in a book on one's lap. This is why I note the men's reactions to the poems, for therein lie the important meanings. When the men signified their liking for a poem this did not mean simply, "That was a fine poem," but rather, "That spoke to me. I can identify with that. It tells something about me." Thus to look at the poems to which the men responded most strongly is a way to understand how the men felt and what was important to them.

One special power of poems was that they could be used to repair 'man' precisely where the damage had been done. According to some feminist critics—or according to the men's perceptions of a vaguely identified body of feminist criticism (see chapters 6 and 7)—men were like sawdust inside, emotionally. Even though some men might admit to being numb, the men objected to the blanket claim that men had no complex emotions. Carl Sandburg's poem "Wilderness" offered a powerful counter-image:

> *There is a wolf in me . . . fangs pointed for tearing gashes*
> *. . . a red tongue for raw meat . . . and the hot lapping*
> *of blood—I keep the wolf because the wilderness gave it*
> *to me and the wilderness will not let it go.*
>
> *There is a fox in me . . . a silver-gray fox . . . I sniff and*
> *guess . . . I pick things out of the wind and air . . . I*
> *nose in the dark night . . . take sleepers and eat them and*
> *hide the feathers . . . I circle and loop and double-cross.*
>
> *There is a hog in me . . . a snout and belly . . . a machin-*
> *ery for eating and grunting . . . a machinery for sleeping*
> *satisfied in the sun—I got this from the wilderness and*
> *the wilderness will not let it go.*
>
> *There is a fish in me . . . I know I came from salt-blue water-*
> *gates . . . I scurried with shoals of herring . . . I blew*
> *waterspouts with porpoises . . . before land was . . . be-*
> *fore the water went down . . . before Noah . . . before*
> *the first chapter of Genesis.*
>
> *There is a baboon in me . . . clambering clawed . . . dog-*
> *faced . . . yawping a galoot's hunger . . . hairy under*
> *the armpits . . . here are the hawk-eyed hankering men*

. . . here are the blonde and blue-eyed women . . . here
they hide curled asleep waiting . . . ready to snarl and
kill . . . ready to sing and give milk . . . waiting—I keep
the baboon because the wilderness says so.

There is an eagle in me and a mockingbird . . . and the eagle
flies among the Rocky Mountains of my dreams and fights
among the Sierra crags of what I want . . . and the
mockingbird warbles in the early forenoon before the dew
is gone, warbles in the underbrush of my Chattanoogas of
hope, gushes over the blue Ozark foothills of my wishes
—And I got the eagle and the mockingbird from the
wilderness.

O, I got a zoo, I got a menagerie, inside my ribs, under my
bony head, under my red-valve heart—and I got some-
thing else: it is a man-child heart, a woman-child heart:
it is a father and mother and lover: it came from God-
Knows-Where: it is going to God-Knows-Where—For I
am the keeper of the zoo: I say yes and no: I sing and
kill and work: I am a pal of the world: I came from the
wilderness.[19]

I heard this poem read on several occasions; it always elicited enthusiastic applause and whoops of assent. The men loved it because it vividly celebrated the emotional complexity of men, a complexity imagined to stem from men's primordial connections to the wild and powerful and mysterious. This helped to repair the damage done to 'man' by claims that men were emotionally shallow or simple, or that men were disconnected from nature. And by evoking strong feelings in the men who heard it, the poem seemed to provide evidence of its own truth.

The men also felt that women often wrongly judged them to be emotionally inert or inept because men didn't talk about feelings the way women did. Although the men agreed that women were more adept at talking about feelings, they objected to seeing it as evidence that men had no understanding of feelings or of how they should be handled. On several occasions D. H. Lawrence's poem "To Women, As Far As I'm Concerned" was brought to the rescue:

The feelings I don't have, I don't have.
The feelings I don't have, I won't say I have.
The feelings you say you have, you don't have.
The feelings you would like us both to have, we neither of
us have.

The feelings people ought to have, they never have.
If people say they've got feelings, you may be pretty sure
    they haven't got them.

So if you want either of us to feel anything at all
you'd better abandon all idea of feelings altogether.[20]

The men took Lawrence to be saying that men can see something that women often don't: talk consists of ideas, and *ideas are not feelings*; moreover, *talk* about feelings can be dishonest. The implication was that men, in being less eager to effuse about their feelings—preferring to remain silent or to speak only briefly from the heart—perhaps understood emotion better, and dealt with it more authentically, than women. In light of this poem, 'man' no longer meant "emotional dolt."

By giving them a chance to identify with a statement written from a man's perspective, poems like Lawrence's also helped the mythopoetic men reaffirm their identities as men. When Lawrence's poem—to women from a man—was read and the men signified to each other their liking for the poem, this meant: We understand this poem, we understand what Lawrence is saying to women, because *we too are men*. This simple reaffirmation of shared identity was an essential part of the logic of men's work as identity work. The implicit syllogism was: men are good; we are men; therefore we are good.

Another frequently read poem was Rilke's "I Live My Life," which, like Sandburg's poem, offered an image of men as connected to the mysterious and powerful:

I live my life in growing orbits,
which I move out over the things of the world.
Perhaps I can never achieve the last,
but that will be my attempt.

I am circling around God, around the ancient tower,
and I have been circling for a thousand years,
and I still don't know if I am a falcon, or a storm,
or a great song.[21]

This poem didn't elicit whoops but rather loud mmmm's, deep sighs, and calls for it to be read again. One reason the men liked it was because they wanted to think of their lives as journeys in which facing challenges was more important than amassing victories. Another reason is that the poem attaches a sacred quality to a man's life thus lived. In this way it not only reconnects men to the ancient, mysterious, and powerful, it also remakes men—and particularly those who, like the mythopoetics, acknowledge their uncertainty in the face of life's mysteries—into questing, spiritual beings, thus opposing claims that all men are crass materialists bent only on acquisition.

A poem I heard only twice, but which drew raucous assent each time, was James Broughton's "I Am In Love With All Things Erect." It is an overt and unabashed paean to men and their phallic achievements:

> I am in love with all things erect
>
> I am in love with the erections of man
> steeples   derricks   pyramids
> pillars and pylons   towers and turrets
> totem poles   flagpoles   pole vaults
>
> I am in love with things firmly erected
> minarets   pagodas   campaniles
> all the monumentalities of man
>
> I am in love with all things erect
> particularly homo sapiens erectus
> the tower that lies down and can arise again
>
> man the phenomenal erection [22]

The plain message here is that men are marvelous creatures who build wondrous things. Celebrating men's creative powers and saying that men are themselves wonderful creations invests value in 'man'. What this poem also does, through its audacity, is to legitimate the love of men for being men. Reciting such a poem, with gusto, in a room full of men seemed to legitimate everything that was going on there. Poems like this not only did identity work directly, they helped the process along by allowing the men to feel that what they were doing was okay.

Not all of the poems the men recited were written by men about men. At various times I heard men read poems written by Sharon Olds, Marge Piercy, Denise Levertov, Nikki Giovanni, and others. One of Giovanni's better known poems, "Ego Tripping," worked like the Broughton poem to legitimate the practice of investing value in individual and collective identities:

> I was born in the congo
> I walked to the fertile crescent and built
>   the sphinx
> I designed a pyramid so tough that a star
>   that only glows every one hundred years falls
>   into the center giving divine perfect light
> I am bad

I sat on the throne
   drinking nectar with allah
I got hot and sent an ice age to europe
   to control my thirst
My oldest daughter is nefertiti
   the tears from my birth pains
   created the nile
I am a beautiful woman

I gazed on the forest and burned
   out the sahara desert
   with a packet of goat's meat
   and a change of clothes
I crossed it in two hours
I am a gazelle so swift
   so swift you can't catch me

   For a birthday present when he was three
I gave my son hannibal an elephant
   He gave me rome for mother's day
My strength flows ever on

My son noah built new/ark and
I stood proudly at the helm
   as we sailed on a soft summer day
I turned myself into myself and was
   jesus
   men intone my loving name
   All praises All praises
I am the one who would save

I sowed diamonds in my back yard
My bowels deliver uranium
   the filings from my fingernails are
   semi-precious jewels
   On a trip north
I caught a cold and blew
My nose giving oil to the arab world
I am so hip even my errors are correct
I sailed west to reach east and had to round off
   the earth as I went
   The hair from my head thinned and gold was laid
   across three continents

I am so perfect so divine so ethereal so surreal
I cannot be comprehended
*   except by my permission*

I mean . . . I . . . can fly
*   like a bird in the sky . . .* [23]

This was another poem that elicited whoops and applause. Again, the language is audacious; but in this case it is inflated to mythic proportions. When Michael Meade read this poem at gatherings he said it was in the "I-am" tradition. Poems in this tradition worked, he said, to help people define their "gender ground" and to boost self-esteem. For the mythopoetic men this poem served to legitimate their efforts to "reclaim their grandiosity," as it was sometimes put in Jungian terms, and as I am describing in terms of identity work.

Giovanni's poem helped the mythopoetic men in other ways. For one, it suggested to them that attempts by feminists to define women as morally superior to men could be seen as mythic exaggerations. In other words, exaltations of women by cultural and spiritual feminists could be seen, like Giovanni's poem, as patent exaggerations women used to boost their self-esteem. Men thus didn't have to take literally, or feel shamed by, women's claims to superiority, since such claims were in the mythical order of things. What's more, seeing things this way suggested that men also needed esteem-boosting poems. If women had poems like Giovanni's in their bag, then it was okay for men to put a few like this in their bag, too.

Jalaluddin Rumi, the thirteenth-century Sufi mystic, was the poet most often quoted by men in the Local Group. His poems did identity work by portraying men as full of intense passion and spiritual longing. The pantheism that infused Rumi's poetry also did identity work by portraying men as manifestations of the Divine and thus possessing innate goodness (though not only goodness). But Rumi's poems fed into another kind of identity work the men did. This was not so much revaluing 'man' as a moral identity, but making sure that none of the value that derived from its association with heterosexuality was lost. A Rumi poem that gave the men a chance to reaffirm their identities as heterosexuals was this:

When I am with you, we stay up all night.
When you're not here, I can't go to sleep.

Praise God for these two insomnias!
And the difference between them. [24]

As comprehension sunk in, this poem, which was read or recited on numerous occasions, elicited more-guttural-than-usual mmmms, yeahs, and a few nudge-winks among the men. The poem reminded the men, in the midst of much male bonding, of their true desire for women.

It was important for the men to reaffirm their identities as heterosexuals, since they were doing things that, from the perspective of traditional masculinity, could be seen as evidence of homoerotic desire. Even Broughton's poem, for all its manly brass, contained a suspicious amount of attraction to "things erect." Etheridge Knight's poem, "Feeling Fucked Up," in contrast to Rumi's subtlety and ambiguity, gave the men a chance to identify as heterosexual in no uncertain way:

> *Lord she's gone done left me done packed/up and split*
> *and I with no way to make her*
> *come back and everywhere the world is bare*
> *bright bone white crystal sand glistens*
> *dope death dead dying and jiving drove*
> *her away made her take her laughter and her smiles*
> *and her softness and her midnight sighs—*
>
> *Fuck Coltrane and music and clouds drifting in the sky*
> *fuck the sea and trees and the sky and birds*
> *and alligators and all the animals that roam the earth*
> *fuck marx and mao fuck fidel and nkrumah and*
> *democracy and communism fuck smack and pot*
> *and red ripe tomatoes fuck joseph fuck mary fuck*
> *god jesus and all the disciples fuck fanon nixon*
> *and malcolm fuck the revolution fuck freedom fuck*
> *the whole muthafucking thing*
> *all i want now is my woman back*
> *so my soul can sing* [25]

The image of a man alone, bleached out emotionally and ornery after ruining a relationship, struck a chord with the men. This poem always elicited whoops, loud yeahs, and crackling applause—a response which seemed odd, given the image of despair the poem contains. What the men liked was the tough, masculine street language and the final image of longing for a woman. The other thing this poem did, like Rumi's love poems, was to give the men, most of them anyway, a chance to remind themselves that they were heterosexual. It thus helped to do a subsidiary bit of identity work: ensuring the value of 'man' by keeping it linked to the society's privileged form of sexual practice.[26]

The men didn't think of poetry as a way to do identity work. It was, in their account, a means to awaken feelings or discover images that evoked deep feelings; it was a means to self-creation and a path to self-knowledge. I don't deny that poetry did these things for some of the men. But what I've been concerned with is how poetry functioned to meet the identity needs that drew the men to mythopoetic activity in the first place. Given the shared needs of the men to feel better about themselves as men, to repair the damage done to 'man' by feminist criticism, and the desire to have their identities as men affirmed by other men, it is not surprising that they gravitated, consciously and unconsciously, toward poems that helped them do these things. Poems that worked well in these ways were read over and again. None of this is to say that the poetry was not enjoyed for other reasons, or that identity work was all that it accomplished.

Other Forms of Identity Work

In chapter 4, I quoted a man as saying that grief is a "very male emotion." The man who said this was echoing Robert Bly's claim that grief is an emotion found naturally and abundantly in men. This claim was part of the larger mythopoetic argument that emotionality in men is natural and good. But it was also a piece of identity work because it turned a common emotion, one not ordinarily thought of as gendered, into a sign of manhood. So if men felt grief and showed it (perhaps by crying), they were not doing a womanly thing but were bearing an emotion that attested to their maleness. Defining grief as naturally linked to maleness thus did more than legitimate emotionality in men; it turned a universal human emotion into a resource for affirming the men's identities as men.

Some of the forms of talk the men used to foster communitas also accomplished identity work. I've already noted use of the term *men's work* as one example. Another example is the use of the tag phrase, "as men." Just as this helped the men feel like brothers, and so fostered communitas, it also affirmed their shared identity as men. To say in a gathering of men, "we're here to try to figure out what we need to do for ourselves as men," or "let's give some thought to things in our lives we're thankful for as men," was not just to state a reason for being there. It was to emphasize, at the same time, that those gathered were indeed men.

The frequent affirmation at gatherings that, yes, we here are all men (even if we don't meet certain traditional ideals) was an essential part of the identity work the men did. To get the full therapeutic value out of 'man' as a remade identity, the men had to reassure each other that this identity was truly theirs. It was better to do this indirectly—by restricting meetings to men only and by using terms such as "men's work" and "as men"—because this made it seem like a plain and simple fact that all present were men. In this way the men gave each other the affirmation they sought, without doing it so strenuously as to raise doubts about its validity.

The harder task was to reinvest 'man' with positive meaning. Another way the men did this was by giving accounts of what they had learned by doing men's work. These accounts were sometimes woven into personal statements; sometimes they came up in small group discussions. For the most part, these accounts echoed the claims made in the article "It's Good To Be A Man!" discussed earlier. Men thus said, for example, "One of the things I've learned through my involvement with the men's center is that men really can be nurturers," or "Men's work has helped me to see that men can be trusted," or "I've discovered that as a man there's a lot of good in me trying to get out." In each case the men were not just making claims about themselves, but were helping with the collective identity work—redefining *men* as good—being done by the group as a whole.

I noted in chapter 4 the men's use of the disclaimer "for me" when saying anything faintly contestable. I interpreted this as a way to avoid arguments that would have impeded communitas. One case in which the "for me" rule did not apply, however, was in offering opinions about the goodness of men. Never did I hear a man say, "For me, it seems that men are capable of nurturing," or "For me, it seems that men can be trusted." To use the qualifier "for me" when praising men would have weakened the identity work being done by implying that it was not unreasonble for others to see men as bad. Identity work was thus done by leaving some things unsaid.

Identity work was also done nonverbally. Here I include many of the acts that were commonplace at mythopoetic gatherings: hugging; touching or holding a man if he began to cry while telling a painful personal story; uninhibited dancing. By calling these acts instances of identity work, I don't mean to suggest that they were insincere. I mean that they were interpreted, within the mythopoetic frame of reference, as signifying the goodness of men. As one man said, "People think men are always closed-up and competitive, but if you go to one of these meetings you see men caring for each other, expressing their feelings, and not being competitive at all." These acts, which were uncommon elsewhere and thus so notable at mythopoetic gatherings, served to reinforce the identity work done in print and through poetry, story telling, and other forms of talk. The hugs, touching, and dancing were taken to show that what was said, in words, about men's capacities to be affectionate, nurturing, empathic, and wild were true.

One more example of nonverbal, or perhaps quasi-verbal, identity work is

worth noting. It was customary for men in the Local Group to end their meetings standing in a circle, drawn closely together, arms over each other's shoulders. In this closing circle the men would often say how much they had enjoyed
the meeting and thank the leaders; sometimes a poem would be recited or the
men would chant. But then, almost always, someone would say, "Let's end
with a growl." The men would then begin with a low guttural sound and slowly
bring it up to an ear-splitting leonine roar. When I once asked two ardent
growlers what this was all about, one said, "It's a way to feel your zest as a man."
The other added, "It's a way to exude male spirit and feel it being amplified by
the other men." As I saw it, it was a form of collective identity work—a way to
signify the power and wildness in men who otherwise appeared quite tame.

Reestablishing Men as the Defining Community

Feminist criticism did not just attack men's innate goodness; it challenged men
for control of the meanings of men, 'man', masculinity, and patriarchy.[27] It
was as if feminists, in theorizing about such matters, had usurped men's prerogatives to define themselves. It seemed wrong to the men that women—
not knowing what it was like to be a man—should be allowed to define the
meaning of 'man'. Thus in addition to redefining 'man' as a positive moral
identity, the men also had to reassert their right to have the authoritative say
about the meaning of this identity. It was as if to say, "Not only do *we* know
what men are, but no one else, certainly not women, can claim to know better."

Some of the mythopoetic men felt strongly about this. These were men who
believed that women had had too much power to define them as men.
Mythopoetic theory and practice gave these men the chance to overcome the
sour definitions of men and masculinity that had been implanted in them by
women in their lives. Finding a group of men who saw manhood and masculinity as good helped these men to, as several said, "break the spell" cast over
them by mothers or wives (usually ex-wives) who had denigrated men and
masculinity. Others saw it as a way to counter women's "bitching about men."
In either case, what the men found was a community that not only defined
men as good, but largely denied women any right to define men at all.

But because the men did not want to look like chauvinists, they couldn't
simply deny that women had anything intelligent to say about such matters.
They needed a gentler rhetorical tack. This they borrowed from the cultural
and spiritual feminists. Just as these groups of women had claimed a special
right, as women, to articulate women's experiences, strengths, perceptions,
suffering, and so forth, so mythopoetic men claimed this right with regard
to men. It made sense that if women got to define women—because, it was

said, men couldn't understand women's experiences—then men ought to define men. After all, how could women know what it was like to be a man?[28]

One problem, however, was that unlike feminists who had a rich body of theory to draw on to guide their thinking about gender matters, the men had few such resources. Much of the theoretical writing by men on men and masculinity was profeminist.[29] This literature was by and large critical of men and masculinity; it carried few, if any, of the healing messages the mythopoetic men were looking for. Nor did it provide a rationale for men to assert a special right to define men, manhood, and masculinity. If anything, as the mythopoetic men saw it, this literature grew out of the willingness of some men to accept the guilt heaped on them by angry women.

What the men wanted was a nonfeminist rhetoric to license their claims to being the community with the right to define 'man'. They found it—or rather people like Bly and Meade found it—in "tradition." This was a rhetoric suited to the 1980s, when politically ascendant conservatives used it to legitimate all manner of traditional capitalist practices: greed, violence, lifeboat individualism. Even though the mythopoetic teachers and most of the men were at odds with the neo-conservative political climate of the 1980s, they still used the decade's powerful rhetorics for their own purposes. It was necessary, however, in keeping with the men's values, to invoke tradition that predated the industrial revolution. And so, reaching back to places sufficiently ancient and pure, the mythopoetic teachers (following Jung, Joseph Campbell, and others) found tribal peoples.

In these ancient cultures the mythopoetic teachers found what they said were great repositories of wisdom about gender. Supposedly, women and men in these cultures knew their roles and had their identities down pat; there was no angst or ennui generated by living without a clear sense of how you fit into the community as a man or a woman. This was because the women took responsibility for teaching girls to be women, and the men took responsibility for teaching boys to be men. Each gender knew its gender ground and, at the right time, initiated youngsters into it. Though this did not guarantee an existence free of conflict, it at least kept things from degenerating into chaos.[30]

Most of the mythopoetic harking back to the initiation rites of tribal cultures was a way to reestablish men as the community with the right to define manhood and bestow the identity 'man' on men. To invoke ancient cultures or tribal peoples as possessing great wisdom—about how to live in harmony with nature, how to live in touch with one's emotions, and how to live as spiritual and gendered beings—was mostly a way to set up a chain of useful implications. The implicit reasoning seemed to be: If these wise cultures practiced initiation, this must be a good thing; if initiation was done by women to girls and by men to boys, this must be the way to do it; if so, people who are wise today will see that it's best to let women and men define their respective gender ground and identities, rather than letting one gender do all the defining; thus women should stick to their own gender ground and let men reclaim theirs.

Jumping on the rhetorical bandwagon of "tradition," the men rode it back to preReagan, precapitalist, and prefeminist times. No recourse to psychoanalytic speculation about womb envy or unconscious seduction by "the primitive" is necessary to explain the ideological maneuvering going on here. The men wanted a way to put themselves back in control of the meaning of their shared identity 'man'. To do this, they had to find a way to legitimate the claim that it was men's prerogative, not women's, to say what it meant to be a man. It was the rhetoric of "traditional wisdom," uncorrupted by industrialism, capitalism, and ideological feminism, that did the trick.

One reason that invoking tribal cultures and their traditional wisdom worked was that these cultures, being at a vast remove from the lives of middle-class white men in the United States, were easily romanticized, even fictionalized, in the pseudo-anthropology of the mythopoetic teachers.[31] Elders in these old cultures thus could be conjured as avatars of ecological and spiritual wisdom. To attain to such wisdom, modern men, it was suggested, needed to reclaim the ancient practices of initiation, drumming, dancing, mask making, storytelling, and talking with spirits. Most importantly, men had to learn to do these things *for themselves*. Trying to shed the repressive psychic baggage of two hundred years of industrial culture was hard enough without women sticking their noses into it.

Another reason for the appeal of the rhetoric of ancient tradition was that it seemed egalitarian. It implied no less freedom for women to define themselves than for men. In fact, reaching back to ancient traditions paralleled what some spiritual feminists had done in reviving witchcraft, fertility cults, and goddess worship. The men believed they had the same right to search the past for ideas and practices to help them be what they wanted to be as men. Again, if the men were willing to leave women alone to do this, then women ought to return the favor.

Finally, Jungian psychology again provided a resource for doing this last piece of identity work. The Jungian view implied that only men could define 'man', because masculine psychic energies coursed through men with a force that women could not understand. What's more, only men could activate in other men the archetypes that gave masculine form to psychic energy; because of how the psyche worked, women could not do this for men. Thus, again, there was said to be a need for distinct gender communities in which men learned from other men what it meant to be a man, and women learned from other women what it meant to be a woman.[32]

In this view, it was foolish to trifle with either gender's right to define what it meant to be a man or a woman. To deny men the right to do this was to keep them from developing all their innate goodness as men—just as, the mythopoetics admitted, men had unfairly limited women for thousands of years. But now, if feminists didn't have enough sense to butt out as men were reclaiming a gender ground of higher moral elevation, they would restrict men's growth and, perversely, contribute to the production of the immature, violent men who hurt women.[33] So for the good of both men and women, the mythopoetics believed, men had to reclaim their rightful place as the definers and creators of men.

IDENTITY AND THE MYTHOPOETIC MYSTIQUE

Remaking 'man' as a moral identity did not meet all of the men's identity needs. The men also longed for an identity that would make them feel special. In our society many people who live otherwise ordinary lives are able to derive special identities based on dedication to a profession or craft, from hobbies or sports, or from religion. Few of the mythopoetic men, it seemed to me, were passionate about such things. For some of the men this produced a depressing sense of having been captured and defined by their mundane routines. What they were thus hungry for was an identity that marked them as extraordinary in some way.

Another way to put it is to say that some identity needs are met by belonging, while others are met by being unique and different. Inside mythopoetic activity the men could affirm their shared identity and commonality with other men, and thus meet one set of identity needs by feeling part of a group. Raising the moral value of 'man' was a way to derive even more benefit from this belonging. But even when revalued, 'man' *per se* was not an identity that did much to make the mythopoetic men feel special. As much as they wanted to be men, they wanted also to be something more.

The tug between these two kinds of identity needs was evident in the men's ambivalence about calling what they were doing a "movement." On the one hand, the men disliked the connotations of politicality and marching-in-step that attached to "movement." On the other, they liked feeling part of something larger than themselves. As one leader in the Local Group put it, "This [mythopoetic] stuff is important and powerful for men because it helps them to know they're part of something, part of a movement." At the same time it also helped them to know that they were different from many other men. At one daylong gathering another man, in the midst of some joking about how many men's groups he was involved with, said, "If I didn't do men's work I'd be just a regular guy."

Just participating in men's work helped some men to meet this other kind of identity need. Doing men's work, they felt, set them apart. By participating in men's work they were doing things—taking risks, resisting some of their socialization into traditional masculinity, pursuing spiritual growth—that the mass of men in the United States were not doing. Thus, over and above the identity benefits that came from reinvesting 'man' with moral value, the men also got the benefit of feeling special for partaking in an activity that most other men were not sufficiently aware to know they needed, or would enjoy.

Doing men's work was not, however, like belonging to a group of skilled hobbyists or an exclusive country club. The sense of specialness the men derived from doing men's work was not because of any exclusiveness, since the doors were always open to newcomers. Rather, the sense of specialness came from the mystique the men attached to mythopoetic men's work.[34]

By *mystique* I mean the sense cultivated by the men that the experience of men's work was so sublime as to be impossible to put into words. Men's work was not like flying model airplanes or collecting rocks—activities that could be explained to outsiders. To the men it was something that allowed them to see, feel, and do things that were not fully explainable to outsiders—nor even to themselves. Men's work, they believed, got them in touch with powers and insights that came from somewhere beyond the mundane world. Where this place was or how exactly men's work took them there were matters that were more satisfying as mysteries than as matters for explanation.

The mystique was cultivated in various ways. One was by discouraging men from talking to outsiders about what went on at gatherings. At the end of a gathering, mythopoetic teachers and informal leaders typically urged the men to hold on to their experience, keep its power, and retain its heat, by not talking to outsiders about it. Besides, it was said, outsiders just wouldn't understand. Even at a men-only discussion group meeting devoted to the topic of gatherings, the men spoke about their experiences in only general terms, one man noting, "we don't like to be too specific about what happens at gatherings." This was said despite the fact that most men present had been to one or more of the gatherings being referred to.

Another way the mystique was preserved was by invoking the separation between the head and the heart. As discussed earlier, the men wanted to focus on feelings, speak from the heart, and avoid being "too much in their heads."

At gatherings this was enforced by challenging men who spoke abstractly or who failed to make "I-statements" about how they were feeling. At other times, after a talking circle had gone on for a while, someone would suggest that it was time to get away from words and do some drumming and dancing. Keeping much of the experience in nondiscursive form—and not theorizing about it—meant that it remained ineffable and thus retained its aura of mystery.

Just as the men avoided serious talk about politics for fear of inhibiting communitas, they also avoided serious analyses of their gender predicaments for fear of destroying the mystique of men's work. Analyzing how their troubles stemmed from concrete realities in their everyday lives or in the surrounding society—with no recourse to metaphor, image, spirit or psyche—would have negated mystique. The men wanted to tap into a realm of mystery, enchantment, emotion, and intuition where all questions did not have answers known best to experts. For middle-class white men in late twentieth-century America this was exotic. No comparable sense of specialness would have come from connecting to a world of data, theory, and rational argument about gender and inequality. Those things were seen as part of the bureaucratized world from which the men sought relief.

Talking about poems and stories in the way the men did also helped to create a sense of mystery. Though poems and stories sometimes provoked long discussions, the talk was not aimed at deciding what the author meant to convey or how she or he did it. Instead, discussion focused on the feelings the stories and poems evoked. Mystery was enhanced, rather than resolved, by such discussions, since it seemed amazing that the same poem or story could arouse so many different feelings. The men marveled, on some occasions, at the power of a story or poem and the images it contained to call forth such diverse reactions. Sometimes men said they were surprised by their reactions to the stories and poems; sometimes they claimed bafflement at where these reactions came from. This was seen, through the Jungian lens, as pointing to the awesome mystery and power of the psyche.

The men further added to the mystique by occasionally telling stories about hearing voices, seeing visions, experiencing marvelous coincidences, having revelations in dreams, feeling in touch with the powers of an animal or a direction, or being hit by a wave of emotion that came out of nowhere. The men listened raptly to these stories. The ones they liked best were those in which a man arrived, via some mysterious path, at a valuable insight about himself or a problem he was facing. Such stories evoked breathless wows and mmmms. What the men liked, it seemed, was not just the idea that men's work was helping men find new channels to self-knowledge, but that men's work was putting them in touch with powers and mysteries that transcended mundane reality.

The Jungian/pantheistic mystique the men cultivated gave them a view of the world as an enchanted place. In this view, things in the world were seen as the faces of mysterious energies and powers, at least half of which were masculine. The men could thus identify things of special power or strength as manifestations of the same noble energies that were in them as men. In other words, the mystique allowed the men to see signs of positive masculine energy, or male strength and beauty, wherever it benefited them to do so. This created possibilities for doing identity work by symbolic identification, that is, by seeing things in the external world as signs of the goodness that was in things male and masculine, and hence in men, too. An instance of this occurred at a weekend retreat.

About ten men were hanging around the site where a sweat lodge was to be built when one man saw a small lizard sunning itself on a log. He snatched it up and brought it to the group, handing it to the retreat leader. "What kind is it?" the man asked. The leader seemed surprised at being expected to know. But he took the lizard and flipped it over, looking for any signs of maleness. Nothing was evident, though there were shimmering, emerald blue spots under the lizard's jaw. The men, baffled by the lack of obvious sex organs, nonetheless marveled at the coloring. One man said, "Look at that color! That's beautiful." Stroking its belly, the leader said, "Well then, it *must* be a male," at which the men laughed, feeling good about the thought, if not confident about taxonomy.

Cultivating mystery in these ways made mythopoetic men's work seem special because it gave access to a realm of experience that defied explanation within an everyday frame of reference. Being part of the activity of exploring this realm of experience made the men feel special, too. It set them apart from women, for sure, because mythopoetic men's work was for men. It opened them to a world of special insights and experiences that only men could understand and appreciate. Mythopoetic activity also set the men apart from those men who were stuck in the iron cage and didn't even realize it. In these ways mythopoetic activity helped the men meet other compelling identity needs. Without the mystique, mythopoetic activity still would have been unusual but not sufficiently extraordinary.

The cultivation of mystique and the remaking of 'man' as a moral identity gave the men two things they badly wanted: assurance of their moral worth as men and a sense of being bigger than, deeper than, their rational selves. Some of the interview excerpts presented earlier attest to this. Another man, in talking about how men's work had affected him, summed it up this way:

For me [men's work] is really a way of life now. Some years ago I began to notice how much more solid I felt. I really feel like I know what it means to be a
man, even though this is real hard to put into words. I feel like there's something in the marrow of my bones which was not there before, and I feel grateful
for that. So I got what I wanted. I feel like through the experiences with the
other men, and the experiences I've had, I have the sense now of something inside me that's good and healthy and whole, and male.

CHAPTER 6

FALSE PARITY, THE MEN'S HUT, AND ARCHETYPAL ILLUSIONS

When it came to gender politics the mythopoetic men were not all alike. A minority of the men were profeminist in their outlook, believing that society in general, and most men, were sexist and in need of change so as to end the oppression of women. On the other end of the spectrum, a minority embraced a "men's rights" perspective, believing that in many ways women had achieved advantages over men, and men now needed to tip the scales back into balance. Most of the men were somewhere in between, though closer to the men's rights view than the profeminist.

The gender politics of the men were evident in their beliefs about gender, women's power, feminism, and sexuality, as well as in their mythopoetic practices. In considering the gender politics of the men's ideas and practices, I emphasize consequences, not intentions. As I said, intentions matter less than what people make happen, or keep from happening, through their actions. The political nature of mythopoetic activity can thus be seen not only in its advocacy of men's interests, but also in its tendency to reproduce a sexist status quo, whether the men meant to or not.

The men had difficulty seeing their activities as political for several reasons. One reason was that to construe men's work as political would have suggested it was somehow a struggle against women. The mythopoetic men rejected any such view of their activity or beliefs. The men in the Local Group were, in fact, good liberal feminists, in the sense of believing that women deserved political and economic equality with men. Thus the men objected to interpretations of their activity as harmful to women or as reproducing sexism. Critics who thought otherwise were seen as misunderstanding the inner focus of men's work. As the men saw it, only "outer work," aimed at changing laws or the behavior of employers, was political.

A second reason the men didn't see their activities as political was that they had no political *intent*. They did not feel that they were seeking to give men as a group power over anyone else; they were merely trying to empower themselves as individuals, primarily by achieving self-acceptance and self-confidence. Thus there was no sense of striving for status or power. This was why much feminist criticism, which presupposed that gender itself was about power and was thus inherently political, never hit home with the mythopoetic men. They simply could not see what was at all political about being men or celebrating masculinity.

Another reason was that the men did not see our society as male supremacist. While the mythopoetic men granted that men still had some economic and political advantages over women, for the most part the men believed that gender equality had been nearly achieved. Thus, since the men did not see women as oppressed any longer, there was no impetus for thinking about how the celebration of manhood or masculinity might contribute to the continued oppression of women. Their belief was that women had fought for equality—in a truly political, outer-oriented social movement—and had largely won. Now it was men's turn to engage in what was defined as an inner-oriented journey of self, not social, change.

A related belief that also kept the men from seeing the political nature of mythopoetic activity was that power was primarily an interpersonal matter. The men did not think about power in terms of control over institutional resources, but in terms of the needs and dependencies that arose in relationships between individuals. Thus when the men thought of power struggles between women and men they thought of interpersonal relationships, not politics. In this view, the men's personal relationships with women provided proof of women's equality in society as a whole. Since the men felt they did not have power over the women in their lives, they inferred that men did not have power over women in general.

Finally, the men didn't want to see their activity as political because they didn't want to see themselves as captives of a doctrine, nor as followers of anyone else's political program. They wanted to see themselves as seekers on a personal journey, having found some ideas and practices that were helpful in pursuing their quests for inner peace, self-confidence, and self-knowledge. To call men's work political would have tainted it not only by suggesting it was anti-woman, but by suggesting that its practitioners were something less than rugged, spiritual explorers.

To examine the politics of men's work is not to expose it as a sham or to suggest that the men were foot soldiers in a misogynist campaign. Rather it is to examine how mythopoetic ideas and practices bear on the relative status and power of women and men in our society. "In our society" is a key phrase here. In a sexist society, such as ours, no beliefs or practices that affect our understandings of gender, or the meaning of gender identities, or relationships between women and men, are politically innocent. Every belief or practice will, through some chain of effects, either challenge or help reproduce an unjust status quo. Every belief or practice thus warrants scrutiny. This can be thought of as the sociological equivalent of facing one's shadow.

The main elements of the gender politics of the mythopoetic men can be seen in their beliefs about the balance of power and pain between women and men in our society; in their practice of holding all-male gatherings; in their use of Jungian psychology; in their understandings of feminism; in their androcentric thinking; and in how they dealt with contradictions around the issue of homophobia. I'll look at each of these in turn, in this chapter and the next. Then I'll consider the men's political values more generally (at the end of chapter 7), since these values not only underlay the men's gender politics, but gave mythopoetic men's work the potential to become externally political in a progressive way.

BELIEFS ABOUT THE BALANCE OF POWER AND PAIN

As in any subculture, the mythopoetic men were bound, if only loosely, by a set of shared ideas and values. There was no catechism to which the men had to subscribe, but in books and in talks at gatherings the teachers in the mythopoetic movement espoused many ideas about men, women, and the balance of power and pain between them. These ideas formed an ideological nucleus around which a consensus about gender politics took shape. One of the main themes of this consensus was that women and men have different, though roughly equal, kinds of problems and suffering to cope with because of their respective genders.

For every problem women face in our society, the argument goes, there is a corresponding problem faced by men. This kind of thinking is usually associated with the "men's rights" perspective, which sees both women and men as victims of confining sex roles, but also sees men's victimization as denied by society. Herb Goldberg (*The Hazards of Being Male*) and Warren Farrell (*Why Men are the Way They Are*) are the best known proponents of this view. In its more extreme versions, women are said to have *more* power than men, and to use this power to exploit men by keeping them in harness as providers and protectors.[1] In general, though, it was the less extreme version of men's rights thinking, *à la* Goldberg and Farrell, that appealed to the mythopoetic men.

This kind of thinking was evident in a number of beliefs the men held. The consistent theme was parity between women and men. Here, for example, are various beliefs expressed in mythopoetic writings, in statements made by teachers at gatherings, in small talk at gatherings, and in interviews:

- Both women and men suffer pain from their psychic wounds. Men's wounds and pain are no less serious or valid or deserving of attention than women's.

- If women can meet by themselves, then so can men. Men need such meetings to feel safe in talking about their feelings and other sensitive issues, just like women do. If it's okay for women to meet in all-women groups, then they ought not complain when men meet in such groups.

- If it's sexist for men to criticize women, then it's just as sexist for women to criticize men.

- For every woman who has lived in fear of a man's anger, there is a man who has lived in fear of a woman's scorn.

- If women feel vulnerable to sexual harassment in the workplace, men feel just as vulnerable to the power of women's nonverbal sexual cues in the workplace.

- Women had their movement, which was directed at doing outer work. Men are having their movement now, a movement that is directed at doing inner work.

- A man's contribution to making a baby is equal to a woman's. Thus he should have an equal say in deciding the fate of the fetus.

- If women are often treated as sex objects, it's just as true that men are often treated as success objects. In both cases, individuals are not appreciated for their inner qualities.

- If men have had more power in the political realm, women just as often have had more power in the domestic realm. Men may have controlled money and property, but women have controlled sex and nurturing.

- Gender role prescriptions can keep both women and men from expressing their truest desires and fully developing themselves. Both genders thus need to work on breaking free of these constraints.

Not all of the men embraced each of these ideas without qualification. But if these statements had been read at a mythopoetic gathering, I suspect they would have drawn near unanimous assent.

Each statement aspires to a pleasant symmetry. Women's problems are not denied, nor is the need for women to address their problems collectively. But at the same time the point is made that men too have their problems, which they must be free to work on in ways befitting their gender. It's only fair, then, that if men respect women's efforts to solve their own legitimate, gender-related problems, women should likewise respect men's efforts. Each gender, in this view, has to solve its own peculiar life problems, which are no more or less serious than the problems faced by the other gender.

The mythopoetic outlook was vague about the source of men's and women's problems. It was implied that women and men were hurt in equal measure by an impartial culture, and neither group was responsible for oppressing the other. As one writer in a mythopoetic publication put it:

> Are women responsible for men's oppression? No more than men are responsible for women's oppression. Over tens of thousands of years, women and men have co-created the narrowly defined roles we live in, and both must take responsibility for ending the oppression that affects us all.[2]

Men and women are thus in similar, if not exactly the same, boats when it comes to suffering from and perpetrating oppression. If there is a villain in the mythopoetic view it is industrialism, which destroyed the traditional cultures in which women and men were supposedly better equipped—with ritual and myth—to cope with life's inevitable problems.

The mythopoetic outlook was also blind to institutional power, the kind that comes from a position of authority, and thus control over resources, in a corporation or government agency. From the mythopoetic view it was thus hard to see how men's near monopoly on institutional power gives most men labor-market advantages (better job prospects, higher pay) that translate into leverage over wives and families.[3] It was also hard to see that it is mostly men—as CEOs, politicians, and top administrators—who make the policy decisions that affect the fate of women in millions of households. This blindness helped sustain the coherence of the mythopoetic outlook. If the distribution and use of institutional power had been carefully examined, the claim of parity between women and men would have been untenable. If men's institutional power was acknowledged at all, its significance was downplayed by suggesting that it was balanced by women's allegedly greater power in the home.

The mythopoetic men's beliefs in these matters constituted a way of thinking about the relative status, power, and well-being of women and men. These beliefs are thoroughly political, as is obvious from considering their main effect: If one embraces them, then any sense of urgency about ending the oppression or exploitation of women is dissipated—especially if one is a man. Women and men might still work together to end injustice; yet, when it comes to gender troubles, women and men face roughly the same degree of hurt and are best off trying to cope and heal separately. Men, in other words, are absolved of responsibility for perpetrating and for helping to end the oppression of women.[4]

While the specific beliefs the men held about gender inequality can be challenged, it might be more helpful to consider the *style* of thinking that sustained these beliefs. This style of thinking amounted to a kind of strategic anti-intellectualism. By this I mean that the men truncated their otherwise rational inquiry into gender issues at those points where men might come in for blame, or beyond which the illusion of parity would collapse. I call this strategic because it served the men's interests in feeling better about themselves as men. In response to analyses that put these good feelings in jeopardy, the men invoked the old head-versus-heart distinction, claiming that they were not doing men's work to analyze society but to get in touch with their feelings.

The beliefs noted above were results of strategic anti-intellectualism. In each case, instead of trying to see just how women and men might face different kinds of problems of greater or lesser seriousness, the response was a knee-jerk claim that men had an equivalent problem. This turned into a kind of rhetorical game. No matter what problem women might cite, the challenge for men—the countermove, so to speak—was to conjure a reply that implied parity. Serious thought or discussion about gender inequality was thus halted. Strategic anti-intellectualism was, in other words, a style of thinking that precluded serious thinking.

Another example of strategic anti-intellectualism was the listing of facts about the health and well-being of men. Lists such as the following appeared repeatedly in mythopoetic publications:

- Male infants suffer a 25 percent higher mortality rate than female infants.

- Men must register for the draft or face prison. Women are exempt.

- Men commit suicide four times as often as women.

- Men constitute 95 percent of all job fatalities, even though women are 50 percent of the workforce.

- Men are almost 100 percent of those assassinated for political reasons.

- Men are 75 percent of the homeless.

- Men die, on average, seven years earlier than women.

- Men are 95 percent of all prison inmates.

- Men are 80 percent of all homicide victims.

Sometimes these lists were offered without comment, as if the meaning of such facts was self-evident. At other times the purported meaning of these facts was made explicit: men really are not powerful or privileged, or else they would not suffer in these ways.

Strategic anti-intellectualism was evident in the failure to look more deeply into these facts about men's lives. For example, the seven-year mortality gap between women and men was often cited as proof that men are not privileged. Yet the reasons for this gap were not probed. Epidemiological studies attribute about half the gap to smoking. The rest is accounted for by men's delays in seeking medical help; men's lack of close friends in old age; exposure to workplace hazards (affecting mostly working-class men); accidents; and heavy drinking.[5] The mortality gap, in sum, is largely attributable to behaviors associated with a form of masculinity that emphasizes toughness, aloofness, risk-taking, and emotional repression. In other words, men die younger than women because men kill themselves trying to prove to each other that they are men.

It is tempting to say that using statistics in the way the mythopoetic men did—that is, without putting them in context—amounted to nonsense. While it's true that such facts make little sense out of context, the act of putting them forth without discussion of context was not senseless. It was a political act intended to deflect feminist criticism of men and to preclude serious consideration of how men as a group are privileged, vis-à-vis women, in U.S. society. It was also a way to elevate men from the moral status of oppressors, or at least co-conspirators, to the status of co-equal victims. This was ironic, in that some of the men said they were "sick and tired" of women "trading on their victimhood" to gain status.

The mythopoetic men could have used the facts they mustered in the same way they used images in stories: as doorways into more complex realities. For example, men are struck by lightning seven times more often than women. Without context, this seems like just another peculiar statistic. But it could be used to work toward understanding important things about men's lives, such as why men feel compelled to compete with each other or prove themselves in risky ways, even on golf courses and lakes—those places where men are struck by lightning. What do men feel is at stake for them, in terms of costs and benefits? To find answers, we would need to look at culture and economics and their relationships to gender.

The mythopoetic men chose not to do this kind of intellectual work. This was a strategic choice on their part. The men were smart and well educated, and thus capable of reading feminist and other sociological analyses of the causes of trouble in men's lives. But they didn't. Nor did they attempt to develop serious analyses themselves. The men examined only as many facts as made them feel better about being men. In the case of the mythopoetics, this tactic belied a stronger desire to refute feminism and to absolve men of guilt for perpetuating sexism than to think seriously about the real sources of pain in men's lives. In this respect the men let their hearts get far out of touch with their heads.

Another aspect of the men's thinking was a tendency to overgeneralize from personal experience. One result of this was an almost egocentric view of inequality between women and men. The men seemed to believe that if *they* didn't have power over women, if *they* didn't feel like powerful patriarchs, and if *they* didn't seem to have privileges relative to women, then all the feminist clamoring about men's power was wrong or exaggerated.[6] Some of the men also observed that their wives and women friends did not seem to be the victims of male oppression, and thus concluded that such a problem, if it existed at all, was less serious than strident feminists claimed.

This style of thinking accounted in part for the men's blindness to institutional power. Since most of the men had little power of this kind, and since they saw themselves as kind and decent, it was hard for them to imagine other men using institutional power to oppress or exploit women. Institutional power was also less visible to the men because they were educated, white, identified as heterosexual, and middle class. As such, the men did not experience the oppressive reality of institutional power in the forms of exclusion, dismissal, discrimination, or harassment. The men may not have wielded much institutional power themselves, but they swam safely in the waters of institutions where the big fish usually looked a lot like they did.

Difficulty in seeing institutional power paralleled the difficulty the men had in seeing class power. This was evident in an allegory the men used (I heard this several times) to illustrate men's lack of real power. The allegory was this:

"People look at the man in the driver's seat of the limousine. He wears a uniform and looks important. And because he's behind the wheel, people assume he has power. But he doesn't. He's just the driver. He goes where he's told." This was offered as an apt illustration of men's powerlessness. The point was that it only seems as if men have power, but in reality they don't, because, like the chauffeur, they don't have control over the direction of their own lives. Someone else is giving the orders.

Of course, the allegory works for the mythopoetic men's purposes only if it is not pushed a step farther. One ought to ask, Who gives the driver his orders? In real life the answer is likely to be: The man who owns the car (who may also own the car factory). What the men's use of this allegory reveals is the difficulty they had in coming to grips with social class and class inequalities. If they had, one thing they would have had to admit is that, to the extent they were dominated by anyone, it was most likely to be more powerful men.

The men avoided bringing class into their thinking about gender and power for several reasons. For one, thinking seriously about class might have forced a recognition that feminist criticism of capitalist patriarchy had to be taken seriously if one wanted to get to the roots of the pain in most men's lives.[7] Another reason was that a class analysis would have put the blame for all manner of social evils back on the shoulders of men, those who were truly ruling-class patriarchs. Class analysis would have also forced the mythopoetic men to think about their own privileges relative to working-class men and women, and might thus have induced guilt. And finally, a class analysis was avoided because it would have threatened the untroubled brotherhood the men were seeking. There was simply no way to broach this kind of analysis—in a society where the reality of class is generally denied—without provoking arguments.

In sum, the main problem was, when it came to thinking about gender and power, the men embraced a style of thinking that censored any ideas that might have kept them from feeling better about themselves as men. This was both a therapeutic and a political maneuver. In the short term it served the men's more pressing interests in mental health than in social analysis. But it also had potential consequences, and less healthy ones, for women, in that this kind of thinking posed no threat to the sexist status quo. So the real problem was that the mythopoetic style of thinking about gender and power short-circuited attempts to do the hard work of figuring out just how the whole range of gender, class, and race inequalities in our society hurt most people, while benefiting a relative few.

Most of the men, I want to reiterate, were not in the grip of the worst type of men's rights thinking; nor were they uncritical of capitalist industrialism;

nor did they endorse renegade individualism. Most of the men, at least in the Local Group, did not buy the preposterous notion that women ruled the world and used their alleged control over the household to invisibly dominate men. (The extreme men's rights ideas appealed primarily to those men who felt they had gotten bad divorce and child custody settlements.) What most of the men found appealing in the mythopoetic outlook on gender politics was not a denial of women's pain, but a validation of their own experiences of pain and powerlessness—experiences that feminism, such as the men knew it, did not take seriously.

In general, the men were sensitive to injustice, valued equality and community, and knew, at some level, that the greed of corporate managers and stockholders caused many people to suffer. Yet because the men were materially comfortable themselves, they had little impetus for engaging in serious analysis of the class structure of society. Without such an analysis, or even an analysis of institutional power, the men were stuck. They were caught between their progressive impulses and their desire to feel better about themselves as men. The latter won out.

INSIDE THE MYTHOPOETIC MEN'S HUT

At the end of the Big Remote Gathering one of the teachers announced that reporters were waiting outside the camp to interview us about the gathering. The teacher said that outsiders were curious because they assumed that when men got together without women, it was to scheme about how to get or hold on to power. The last thing people expected, the teacher said, was that men were gathering to tell poems and contemplate beauty. While it was true that the men were not scheming about how to dominate women, mythopoetic gatherings were not politically innocent, either. A great deal of sexism crept into mythopoetic gatherings. It was seldom challenged and sometimes reinforced.

Almost all mythopoetic gatherings were for men only. A few gatherings sponsored by the Local Group were open to women, but most were not. The rationale for excluding women was that men felt safer and could talk more openly and honestly about troubling personal issues if women were not around. In interviews a few men also said they enjoyed getting away from their wives for a while (men's center events, they said, were "boys'-night-out" activities of which their wives approved); some said that in men-only groups the talk was deeper and more intense than in mixed groups; and some noted that restricting meetings to men created more emotional energy in the group.

As I would put it, excluding women helped the men achieve communitas. In meetings where *men's* experiences and *men's* feelings were the main concerns, gender difference would have been distracting. In all-male groups the men could act as if there was a common outlook and thus more easily create a shared mood. Keeping women out also reduced the risk that the men's identity work would be disrupted, since women were not entirely trustworthy when it came to affirming the essential goodness of men. While men had a clear interest in remaking 'man' as a moral identity and could be counted on, usually, to get with the program, women could not; they might have an axe to grind and mess up the works. Many of the men also seemed grateful for relief from the burden of having to worry about women's sensitivities regarding gender matters.

As with their other practices, the men did not see the exclusion of women as political; it was, for them, merely practical, since the goal was to create a "safe space" where men could talk freely. Women were excluded because they might inhibit or challenge men. By having men-only meetings, the mythopoetic men both avoided conflict and denied that it existed. As the men saw it, they were gathering to deal with their own gender issues, as women often did, and there was nothing political about it. It was simply what members of each gender needed to do. Ironically, however, the practice of excluding women presupposed the potential for conflict, and thus implied that men's troubles were indeed entangled with gender politics.

The practice of excluding women was another reflection of the men's belief in gender parity. The men felt that if it was okay for women to have exclusive meetings, then it was okay for men to do the same. Of course, this denied the fact that women met by themselves because in mixed groups they were often silenced by sexist men. Against this history, women needed exclusive meetings to practice speaking up and experience being heard. Men, historically, have had no problems speaking up and being heard, at least not vis-à-vis women. To claim that men needed to meet by themselves for the same reasons women did was again to deny gender inequality.

Men-only meetings also signified that men didn't need women's help to solve their spiritual and emotional problems. Men needed only each other.[8] Women's analyses of men and masculinity were presumed to be ignorant of men's feelings or motivated by anger, and thus not worth heeding. Feminist ideas about gender and men were thus dismissed along with other knowledge about men created by women (see chapter 7). The men didn't deny that women could have useful insights into the psyche, spiritual matters, emotions, or relationships. But in general, the implicit message was that women's knowledge of men was inferior to men's knowledge of men.

Another message conveyed by the practice of excluding women was that nothing dangerous to women was going on at mythopoetic gatherings. It was as if to say, "Don't worry about what we're doing here; we're just reading poems and contemplating beauty; this is no threat to women." What this denied was the possibility, indeed likelihood, of sexism being unconsciously reinforced among men, even kind and decent men, who were nonetheless steeped in a sexist society. Two examples show how this happened. In the first example, Robert Bly subtly reinforced a sexist stereotype while telling the Iron John story to a group of 700 men.[9]

The Iron John story is about a boy meeting challenges on his way to manhood. In one part of the story the boy is outfitted with a stout war horse and armor by his magical mentor Iron John. The boy then saves the embattled kingdom in which he is living. His actions, however, have been anonymous; no one knows the identity of the mysterious knight whose heroic warriorship carried the day. But the princess suspects it was the boy, who has intrigued her with his golden hair. Both the Grimm brothers' version and Bly's recounting of the tale in his book *Iron John* agree up to this point. After the kingdom has been saved by the mysterious knight, the Grimms' version says:

> The King said to his daughter: "I will proclaim a great feast that will last for three days, and you shall throw a golden apple. Perhaps the unknown man will show himself."

Note that it is the *king* who decides to proclaim a great feast, with little fuss about the matter. This was the same way Bly told the story in *Iron John* (pp. 190–193). But as a troubador on stage Bly told it differently:

> [The princess] goes to her father. She wants to find out [who the mysterious knight is], because a certain part of the feminine likes that kind of a decisive man. So she goes to her father and she says, "Listen Daddy, let's have a festival! What do you say? We'll invite all the machos in the neighborhood and they'll all come and you know how it goes: you gotta stand up there and you sit up there and they all come by on their horses and I'm there and then I throw a golden ball and then one of them catches it, you know? You know how that goes, Daddy. And then, you know, I get married and we do that whole thing. C'mon Daddy, let's have a festival." He says, "Listen, you're talking *ten thousand dollars!*" She says, "Aw, c'mon Daddy." So they do [have a festival].

In this version the princess is portrayed as wheedling and cajoling her father into holding a festival so she can meet the mysterious knight. The line Bly put in the king's mouth, "Listen, you're talking *ten thousand dollars!*", drew big laughs. What Bly did was to portray the princess as manipulating her father into spending money against his wishes. This played on the stereotype of women as manipulators who use emotion to extract largesse from men.

Although Bly prefaced his telling of this segment of the story with the disclaimer that the princess wasn't a real woman but a figure from "the other world," he clearly exploited a real-world stereotype to play the all-male audience for laughs. Whether Bly intended to do this or not is irrelevant. By embellishing the story to appeal to men steeped in a sexist culture, Bly subtly reinforced a demeaning image of women. This is exactly the kind of thing that could happen and pass without notice at all-male gatherings.

This happened often at mythopoetic gatherings, especially when myths and fairy tales were told. Sexist imagery in the stories was seldom challenged. A second example, where the imagery was challenged, shows how dangerous attitudes could be reinforced at all-male gatherings. This example is from the Big Remote Gathering.

During the week, one of the teachers told the Grimms' story "Faithful John."[10] The story is about a young king who inherits a servant and mentor named Faithful John. In the story the young king finds in the basement of his dead father's castle the picture of a princess. Her beauty is such that it causes him to faint. He awakes in love with the princess and orders Faithful John to find out where she lives. John does so and learns also that she loves gold objects. One hitch is that the princess's father won't allow her to be courted. John's plan is thus for the young king and him to disguise themselves as merchants, and to use gold artifacts to lure the princess away from her father's castle.

So John and the young king sail to the realm where the princess lives and carry out the plan. The princess is lured out of the castle and onto the young king's ship. While she is below decks looking at gold wares, the ship quietly moves out to sea. When she finally realizes she has been abducted, she protests. But then the young king reveals himself, says he means her no harm, and professes his love for her. The princess is moved by what she hears and agrees to stay. She and the young king then go back below decks to frolic. There is more to the story, but this is the part that is pertinent here.

The story was told in segments during the week. After each segment the men talked about what the images in the story brought to mind and how the images made them feel. The discussion of the segment described above began with a few exegetical comments by the teacher who was telling the story. Then another teacher asked what "the feminists" would say about the young king's abduction of the princess. Because the ensuing discussion revealed so much about the gender politics of the mythopoetic teachers and men, it is reproduced below in its entirety.[11] About 120 men were in the audience. The five teachers (referred to as A, B, C, D, and E) were on a dais at the front of the room. Teacher A was the storyteller.

Teacher B: So you don't feel she was betrayed and tricked and cheated and he had no right to capture her and take her away?

Teacher A: No, I think all that's true. And I think it's all beside the point.

Teacher B: And you don't think the feminists' complaint that this is again the woman being taken and captured and seduced?

Teacher A: I think it's true. And it's beside the point. [*Laughter.*] You see, to me it's like you're talking about a dance, that the animals are referred to very specifically. You know how animals do it. The male has to come and do a dance. And they alter the feathers, they look bigger than they are, they look smaller than they are, they change in some way, they act out certain sequences in order to draw the female of the species. And I don't think that's an accident. I think it's the actual dance, the love dance. So I think that's part of it. Another part of it is that somehow, well, a trick is needed. It just is not an issue of sincerity. We talk about *falling* into love. We talk about seduction. All of those are aspects of being near the gold.

Man 1 (from audience): The princess wasn't raped, she was seduced. You can't be seduced unless you consent to it at some level.

Teacher A: Yeah, seduction is always mutual.

Teacher B: It wasn't her consent. She did not give verbal consent. [*Groans. Laughter.*]

Man 2: That's the only consent she *didn't* give.

Teacher A: Another way to look at is, to get to see her, remember that doorway thing—

Teacher B: This is a very important issue, actually.

Teacher A: —he had to transgress a whole setup at that doorway. Remember? His father said, "Don't do it." John said, "Don't do it." The door had been locked. There were warnings of danger. He had to transgress that just to *see* her. Now, in order to be with her, he has to transgress a whole bunch of other stuff, including putting aside who he thinks he is, in a sense. Having a disguise of some kind.

Man 3: On the princess's father's side, he's keeping a mature woman away from men, so it's not like she's in an ideal situation that she's being stolen from. She's been taken out of the frying pan and put into something we don't know about yet.

Teacher A: I'm not sure about the "mature woman" thing. I'm not sure what you mean. But what happens in the story—

Man 3: Sexually aware, let's say.

Teacher A: I don't know. Maybe you know her better than me. [*Laughter.*] No, I don't know if she's—I'm just poking at your language. I mean, for all we know, she may have *originated* sex, not just be aware of it.

Teacher C: But she *is* held by her father.

Teacher A: Yes. The story has now two kingdoms in it. And in this kingdom is the father who actually turns out to be a generous father in many ways, because he leaves all these resources for the son, including the connection to Faithful John. But, that father locks up that little room. He does want to keep the son out of something. Then you have this other kingdom where the princess is, and she's being kept away from things in general, it would appear. Although she has a lot of gold around her as well. So you have two kings and two aspects of the king, which is important. In other words, if you want to follow what [Teacher D] was saying, you have a shadow king kind of thing going on around all that gold. She's being held. Now, she may be complicit in that. We don't know.

Man 4: Where's her opportunity for choice? I think what [Teacher B] is pointing to is that this whole story robs her of any moment of choice.

Teacher A: Oh my god. Is *that* what you're pointing at, [Teacher B]?

Teacher B: That's the whole feminist position. That's the whole legal position. She doesn't give verbal—if you don't face this issue somewhere, you're going to be cut off from your capacity to engage in this kind of trickery and seduction because the whole system now as it is being established through language—"verbal consent" and so on and so forth—is to eliminate the trickster from the society, to eliminate Hermes from the work. So we have to face this. We have to talk about this.

Teacher A: Ok.

Man 5: That boat ride. They'd call it a rape.

Teacher B: Yes.

Teacher A: Yeah. Not only that, it's adbuction. It's date rape.

Teacher B: She was made drunk and abducted.

Several Men in Audience: Date rape.

Teacher A: Yeah. She was supposed to look at the gold, and he raped her.

Teacher B: And gave her a drink.

Teacher A: Gave her stuff to drink.

Teacher B: In *his* place. And so on.

Teacher A: And the word is choice. I agree with that.

Man 6: He did get laid, didn't he? I mean, they went downstairs, but we don't know what happened there. There was a presumption of sex there.

Teacher A: We're all presuming that. Someone there was presuming that as soon as they started down the stairs. [*Laughter.*] We know that it's not just getting laid, it's the mutual giving of everything to each other that we're talking about.

Teacher D: I just want to underline what [Teacher B] is saying. This is an area of discussion that is increasingly, increasingly hot and engaged and there are a lot of nuances here. There is an enormous amount of rape, which is not seduction. And we need to be up front about that. But there's a whole morass of issues here that do have to be addressed. And they're very complicated. The other thing I'd like to just raise at this point, two things about the story. We have to think about what is being imaged in this story. Is this sort of human or is this an image of nature? My take on this type of thing is that because of the asymmetry in male and female, we're really seeing an image of nature, the nature of gender here, especially young gender.

Teacher A: But how do we know in the story that it's not rape? Let's stay with the rape part. How do we know it's not rape?

Man 7: Part of her choice was, she was seduced by the gold at first. She was so enamored of the gold—

Teacher A: So she's going for something.

Man 7: —that she was oblivious to the other sensations, the ship moving and things like that.

Man 8: I've got this dialogue going on in my head. There's like a woman talking in my head right now and I say, "Yeah, she wanted that gold." And she says to me, "Fuck you! I wanted the gold. I didn't want to get *fucked!*" And that's the dialogue today—

Teacher B: That's exactly the dialogue today.

Man 8: —you know, like, "You asked for it," and, "Fuck you, I didn't ask to get laid, I just asked to dance."

Teacher A: The implication right away is that the sexual loving is not gold. That's one of the first implications. That this is gold which weighs—

Teacher B: Good answer.

Teacher A: —so much carets per pound, or whatever the fuck it is, and making love to a man is not gold. That's implied.

Man 8: It's a damn fairy tale to begin with. So to bring in a concrete argument to bear upon the imaginal realm is, as you said before, you know, kind of fucking the whole thing up. However—

Teacher A: We'll do it anyway! [*Laughter.*]

Man 8: Life is based on contradiction! However, there's a point in the fairy tale that is, as you were telling it, where their *eyes* meet. And there is that magical moment where they do find a mutual point of meeting and seeing one another. And dammit, there's consent in there! And anyway, if this is in the imaginal realm, this has to do with our psyches, and they should just keep the fuck out.

Teacher A (speaking to Man 4): Ok, now does that work for you, how does that affect your issue of choice?

Man 4: Well, what other options does she have in that moment? Choice presupposes she has options. She's out in the middle of the goddamn ocean, surrounded by water. It's a tough spot. She's alone. There's a whole crew. So what other options does she have?

Teacher B: What about that moment of their eyes meeting?

Man 9: Also, what about the moment where he discloses himself to her? I think that's the thing that keeps it from being rape. At some point the trickery stops and he discloses himself to her with the implication that if she denied him, he would return her.

Teacher A: Everybody hear that? He [the young king] says, "I mean you no harm. But rather I bring you love."

Man 4: Does she have a choice in that moment?

Several Men at Once: Sure! Yes!

Man 4: Where's it clear that if she doesn't like this game, she can bag it?

Teacher A: Why is that such a big issue?!

Man 4: Because that's the one I live with.

Teacher A: How's that?

Man 4: With my relationship to women.

Teacher A: Ok, but now we're back to you, in the bed, and your wife having the choice of rituals and *you* being the one with no choice.

Man 4: Well, I set it up so I don't have any choice. I'm looking for where my opportunity for choice is. Clearly she [my wife] has appropriated that territory completely. Sex is a function of me courting her and her saying yes or no. Her having choice all the time.

Teacher B: What about this meeting of the eyes? What happens to the question of choice when the meeting of the eyes occurs? Where does choice go? Is there still choice?

Man 4: I don't know if that's an issue at that moment.

Teacher B: It *isn't* an issue at that moment! Exactly. Choice disappears.

Teacher A: Thank god.

Teacher B: Because choice comes out of that part of the psyche that is called nowadays the ego. No one's ever seen one but we still believe they're around. [*Laughter.*] And it's out of there that choice comes. That's gone in the meeting of the souls. If we take the meeting of the eyes that way.

Man 4: So that courtship dance, that ritual moment, is by way of having that ego and the choice question collapse where there's an opportunity for souls to meet.

Teacher A: Yes. And then instead of choice, it's *being chosen*. It's the other thing altogether. It's being chosen.

Man 4: Except they spent a lot of time living in that, the asserting of their ego domains. But I do think she's open to that.

Teacher D: Well this is really the way that *any* relationship works. It's not just that one. It's like you don't start out to *choose* to be in a relationship. You *find* yourself in a relationship. You know, you wake up after the boat left. [*Laughter. Applause.*] And so, we are that princess, and it's already gone. And most of us probably wouldn't be in relationships if we had had that choice. [*Laughter.*]

Man 11: I talked to a woman a few years ago who was real clever and well defended and hard to get. And when she was eighteen I asked her how she met her husband. When she's eighteen she says, I'm in this bar, by myself. A nineteen-year-old man comes immediately over and sits down beside me. And he says, after we're talking about a minute, he says, "Well, aren't you going to ask me what kind of car I drive?" And she says, "What kind of car do you drive?" And he said, "I drive an '82 TransAm." And she said, I married him. And something happened right there and he just worked that deal.

Teacher D: Well, he had good taste in cars. [*Laughter.*] You got to understand that, see. Down here, a TransAm—shit, man. A TransAm—fuck, that's *Burt Reynolds's* car! [*Laughter.*]

Man 13: In the United States today we really worship choice, this sort of autonomy. I work in hospice where people are dying, and people regularly say, "Well, my choice is to be dead. Now doctor, give me a pill so I will die." And what I see in their faces is fear and I see that they hurt, and I know that they don't have to hurt. And that maybe around the corner it won't be like they fear. And it seems a lot of the time that the kindest and most helpful thing that I can do is to be a little bit paternal and to help them with the pain and the fear, because so often I've seen people come around and be glad that they weren't—that their choice wasn't honored. And I think we choose out of different parts. I think we choose out of our fear. And sometimes the kindest and most helpful thing is not to honor the choices made out of someone's fear.

Teacher A: Good. Thank you. Good point. Every time I hear the word "choice," I see one of those slabs of meat: "Grade A Choice." [*Laughter.*] You know, there's *choice* meat.

Teacher D: I'd feel a lot better about that example if the AMA was paying all these additional expenses for terminal patients.

Man 13: Close to the beginning of this century there was a film with Rudolf Valentino called *The Sheik*, I think it was, with roughly the same plot [as

"Faithful John"], and there was little outcry from the women in the country. As a matter of fact, Valentino was the heart throb of millions. I think
what women are saying now in complaints about choice and victimization
is that they don't believe in princes anymore—

Teacher B: That's nice.

Man 13: —because they haven't seen very many of them.

Man 14: Well, you've got to kiss a few frogs! [*Laughter.*]

Man 15: Maybe the men think that they show up with a ton of gold instead
of the ton of gold animals.

Teacher A: That's the TransAm story. The TransAm story is about *packaged*
gold. And again, one of the clues that it's not rape [in the Faithful John
story] is all of the art involved. Rape—well, [Teacher B] could say more
about this [*Laughter.*]—rape is very close to the word rapture. There are
rapacious birds; they're called raptors. The eagles and the hawks and the
falcons and so on. So there's this real close connection between rape and
rapture. The choice that I think that's involved, for both parties is, Is this
rape in the sense of the beak coming in and tearing? Or is this a rapturous
letting go? The story says when the eyes meet that there's a rapture that
happens. But the unfortunate thing is that the rape is always a potential,
it's always nearby.

Teacher B: [Teacher E], you got anything on this?

Man 15: If he's a prince it's rapture, if he's a merchant it's rape. So how do
you know yourself whether you are a prince or a merchant?

Teacher A: Yeah, that's a good turn. You see—

Man 16: But that's not true. He could have been a prince and, I mean, he
wasn't a king and a prince but she still might not have given herself to him
with her eyes. Or she still could have been pissed off and revolted against
him even though he was a king.

Teacher C: He sent the servant in first. He sends in the servant first. *He* doesn't
go into the castle and abduct. There's something about that, I mean, because, when you said the rape/rapture one, I went, if you said that any-
place in a mixed group you would be *beat*. You know, get out twenty-five
shields and get ready!

Teacher A: I know. That's why I'm saying it here. [*Laughter.*]

Teacher D: I don't personally want to be a part of trivializing this issue of
rape. I mean, I have had to deal with too many rape victims. And frankly,
I think we'd have a lot less rape if more women carried Ladysmith .38's
and shot the fuckers who were trying to rape her. So, I want to go on record
real clear that I don't see any real easy move between rape and rapture.

Teacher C: I don't either.

Teacher D: So I just wanted to let it be real clear where I am on that.

Teacher A: Well, I'd like you to be then clear about how you deal with the rape other than with a .38.

Teacher D: Aikido is good, too. [*Laughter.*] That is to say, I work a lot very closely with people that work with battered women and rape victims. And it ain't funny at all to me.

Teacher B: But you're on the level of the first level now. We're trying—

Teacher D: Now wait a minute—

Teacher B: —to understand this thing in terms of something else that is both the psychological and the mythological. And if we don't make moves in the culture towards that we will all be shooting each other with .38's or .45's. Do you see—

Teacher D: Well, I'm not real sure I'm operating on the first level here. I think I'm dealing with imaginings. I've dealt a lot with people's, with what has happened to their imagination because of violence against women. And so—

Teacher B: And what's happened to *women's* imaginations?

Teacher D: Yeah, that's right. That's what I'm talking about: women's imaginations. And I think we have to in all fairness here, at least I'm on record, that we have to be a little careful about too quick moves here.

Teacher B: But look what happens to the discussion when you make that move.

Teacher D: What has happened to the discussion?

Teacher B: The discussion freezes on the literal level about rape.

Teacher D: Well now wait a fucking minute. [*Laughter.*]

Man 15: That's exactly the point that [Teacher D] is saying. What it's getting to is that when you literalize a myth a couple things happen. One is, you begin imposing value judgments, really narrow value judgments, from a society, on a myth that's before our society ever existed. We don't have the right to do that. This is a story about something else, and for us to take a literal view, we begin to take all the things that are happening in our society outside of us, when that's really not what it's all about. What it's all about is what's been happening inside of us for thousands and thousands of years, independent of the particular culture or society or nation that we were born in.

Man 16: But the opposite is just as dangerous. That's to mythologize something that's concrete and is violent. And to try to make a story out of something that is really oppressive to at least part of our planet.

Man 17: I have a problem with the rapture/rape thing. And I want to bring it up a couple levels, because I see the rapture thing as, especially if you go to the raptor as the lover, and I guess, and I can understand that. But the *rape* thing—broken ribs, broken jaws—that ain't the lover, man. That's fucked-up warrior shit.

Teacher B: Absolutely.

Teacher A: That's right.

Man 17: That's boundary shit. That's fucked up. Rapture. Rape. I don't like the fact that those two words are so close together.

Teacher A: No one does.

Man 17: I just think they're two *separate* energies.

Man 18: They can be both at the same time, because in the movie *The Accused* Jody Foster is enticing a group of guys and they rape her; they gang rape her, and *they* think they're in rapture, and they're cheering, and they're not even the guy doing the raping. They're standing on the side, and those guys end up going to jail because they were in *rapture* in viewing what to them wasn't a personal experience in the contact. But they are in rapture and she's in rape.

Teacher E: I don't think that's right.

Teacher C: No, it's not right.

Teacher A: Don't confuse excitement with rapture.

Teacher E: The word rape and rapture comes from being caught up. And you can be physically caught up or you can be caught by seeing your soul mirrored in somebody else. And that wonderful male/female thing is the most delicious point in our lives when that happens. That's a catching up, too. And that can be ecstatic catching up. That's what the story is about.

Teacher A: Yes, and it comes from the imaginative—we can do the concrete part of it, too. But just to get clear what I'm talking about with rapture—when the bird becomes an image—and remember, this is the country that lives under the eagle. It's the eagle that swoops down and grabs one and takes them up into the heights where things are seen completely different. And the one being taken, you know, let's go into it.

Man 19: The one being taken also gets *devoured* too by the eagle. An eagle doesn't sweep up a mate and take it up there. An eagle sweeps up an animal to eat it and devour it. So you have to be careful with that image, too. It *mates* with another eagle up there. But it *rips apart* anything that it comes down and gets.

Teacher A: Has anybody ever been in love and not been ripped apart?

Man 20: Yes. I think there might be a ripping apart to some extent, but it does not have to be a violent ripping apart. And I think with maturity you certainly don't get torn as apart as I think the myth that you want to create says. Okay? I think to be in love is a wonderful thing. It doesn't always have to be a ripping thing. There are points that it rips but it also goes through pathways that are more gentle.

Teacher A: No one is denying that.

Teacher D: See, when we talk about these stories a lot we say more sometimes in getting into it about how these are aspects of our own inner world. This princess is me. And so, in working with that kind of thing, then we can have a lot of fun talking about the part of *me* that if somebody doesn't come in and take me out in a boat—now there's a big part of me that's like that princess. If you don't get me out in a boat before I know you got me out there, I might not be out there.

Teacher A: That's a good point.

Teacher D: So there's a lot in this story that reveals me and my relationship to relationship, my difficulties with eros. All that sort of thing. And I *love* that. But we just have to—there's another end of this stick over here we need to keep up in the air.

Man 21: But I think this is the same conflict that's going on about why people are attacking men's movements and making fun and ridiculing them. Because as we move from the literal level, that's the women—the women are going to take us at the literal level because we've been literal all along.

Teacher B: Exactly.

Man 21 (continuing): The world *is* full of men who brutally rape, because they live at the literal level. And their fear is they can't see the second or third level. They only see the first level. So they [women] do feel like, "Goddamn it, I didn't choose this. You *are* raping me." And it's the same thing as that—when you talked about yesterday the first, second, and third level I thought about like an entropy gradient. And it's like there's a lot of resistance to moving from one level to the next. There's the whole fear of change and the fear of the unknown. And women only see men, I think, today as very concrete and very literal, and don't see that potential any more. As this gentleman over here said, there hasn't been many princes around in a long time.

Teacher B: The difficulty is always to realize what happens when the imaginal is made psychological or when it is made literal. And that's what we were doing. That's what I was trying to press towards. That's why I started to raise those questions: What about what feminists would say? "Was that fair? She's being abducted." In order to meet that problem that you will always meet when the world of story is being taken, it's being moved from one—we're talking in the mythological level and then it's reduced to the literal or put into the literal level. And that's the thing we have to see. And when we begin to use the word *choice* we're right on the edge between the literal and psychological.

Man 4: What is the glue that holds that together, that creates the possibility for the princess? It seems to me there's the extension of trust.

Teacher B: It's the *eyes* meeting!

Man 4: But *before* that. Before you can even get to that point.

Teacher C: You have to send in what serves you. You have to see that part. You don't come in. You have to send in what serves. And then she's already made a choice there. She's gotten some clue that there's art, that there's beauty, available.

Teacher B: That's important. That there's art and beauty.

Teacher A: To go back to where [Teacher D] was talking from this morning. If the king—if there's an awareness of the king, then the whole situation, the whole possibilities of rape is changed and removed. You see how that goes? In other words, this story says that this is a young king who also is connected to a faithful servant who knows an awful lot of stuff.

Man 4: What she can trust is in the structure of her culture, that it has a king, and everybody kind of—there are definitions that aren't going to be radically violated.

Teacher A: Well that may be the case. And many cultures and, most cultures, when a part of the initiation of girls that brings them to women is the girls come before the entire tribe, men and women, and they're brought out and they're dressed in—they've been gone for a while—and they're brought back dressed in usually some kind of beautiful garments, painted, and they're given gifts by the elders of the tribe. And they're shown to both the men and the women and the children of the tribe, saying, "This is a woman." And they're respected and honored before everyone. And there's different things that are said to make it clear that you have to honor this person as a human, but also for the divinity they carry. Now that's how a lot of cultures have taken care of it.

Man 22: We don't have that.

Teacher A: No. We don't have that. But wait a minute. If we don't start to *imagine* this stuff, then we're going to *be* solving it with weapons.

Teacher B: That's the whole point of being here.

Teacher A: I want to ask you, [Teacher D], What has happened to the imagination of the rapist?

Teacher D: Well, a lot of things. But in this thing, we just need to be aware that—this is not speculative—there is enormous and growing violence between men and women around these issues, if you look at some of the figures lately on this stuff. Are you talking about the studies that have been done on what these men are thinking and feeling and imagining?

Teacher A: I'm thinking about two sides. Generally the fantasy, or the theory, is that a man who rapes cannot tolerate much feminine energy at all.

Teacher D: That's right.

Teacher A: He's afraid of being completely overwhelmed by it, so he tries to dominate and subdue it.

Teacher D: That's right.

Teacher A: So his own feminine, to use your term, has not been blessed—

Teacher D: That's right.

Teacher A: —has not been honored and has not been pulled up. That's one thing. The second thing is that the man does not feel like he's a king. He feels like he has to pillage and rob and rape in someone else's kingdom. He doesn't feel, as the one in this story says, "I am not a merchant, I am a king, and the son of a king, and a king in my own right and realm." So the rapist doesn't have either of those capacities: an awareness of his own femininity and the beauty of the feminine, or an awareness of his own kingliness. And I think that's what the story is saying.

Teacher D: That's true. That's right.

MS (Michael Schwalbe): I think that one of the possible connections there is that rapists treat women as objects. They don't recognize a woman's subjectivity or appreciate her pain. And if you read studies of rapists, this is what a lot of them say: "She was nothing to me." Now, to take the story on the literal level, you see the same thing going on. The prince treats the princess as an object to be acquired. Now, later in the story—

Teacher A: I completely disagree with you! How do we know in the story that he's not treating her as an object? How do we know that he knows something about her subjectivity?

MS: Only a man could write and tell a story like this, where you would imagine that, after being abducted, "their eyes meet" and then some magical transformation occurs. [*Moans.*]

Man in Audience (to MS): Ah, that's horseshit.

Teacher B: Let him go on. Push it all the way. Go on.

MS: I intend to push it. You see, because I think you're trivializing the feminist objection to this. I'll make that point in two ways. One is that women could listen to this story and say, "Geez, only a man could imagine that after a woman were abducted like this, under false pretenses, that then this meeting of the eyes would occur and a legitimate seduction would go on."

Teacher B: I don't agree. Definitely not.

MS: Now that's one objection. But then, look at this group. We've got a lot of people here who have a lot of experience thinking on a mythological level, and then look at all the confusion we have. When we started telling this story, there was a lot of literal interpretation—mapping this back on to the concrete world, and mapping concrete stuff into this mythological realm. I think that's a potential danger with this. Even men who are *experienced* in thinking this way, who are trying to cultivate the use of these stories to expand the imaginal realm, have problems keeping them separate.

Teacher B: Of course.

Teacher A: Of course. There's no *solutions* in the mythological realm. It's an *expansion*. It's a *complication* that happens. There is no, there is—god, you're blowing my mind! [*Laughter.*] The reason everybody disagrees is because everybody's seeing a different aspect of the symbol and the movement in the story. It's *supposed* to be that way!

MS: There's no changing the fact that the story is written from the prince's perspective—

Teacher B: No.

Teacher A: You're absolutely wrong! You're just making that up! You don't know who wrote the story!

Teacher B: No.

Teacher A: Jesus Christ!

Teacher B: That is already a perspective, when you say that.

MS: No. The story begins with the prince, it begins with the king—he's the one talking to Faithful John, they're the ones who are organizing this, they're the key characters—

Teacher A: That's sociology, not mythology!

Man 22 (to MS): You need to read more Gothic romances. They're written *by* women and *for* women and—

MS (to A and B): I'm astounded that you don't think this is written from a man's point of view!

Teacher A: No, no, no! These stories—

Teacher B: These stories are told for thousands of years. They're not written by a person.

Teacher A: By men *and* women! In other words, the women would be involved too, saying, "Wait a minute, the last time the story was told, it went a little bit that way. How about this?" I mean these stories are not—

Teacher B: I have an answer for that. You [MS] are understanding the mythical, which is the story, from the psychological, that there's a human writer—

Teacher A: And a motive.

Teacher B: A motive, and an angle, and a perspective. That's the dominance of the psychological over the mythological. We're taking the perspective, or at least I am, that the story dominates the psychological. And you can take different places in the story, and different moves with the story. You can say the princess is in me. And you can do all sorts of things. But from the mythological point of view the story comes first. There *is* no author. And there is no *intention* of the author.

MS: As [Teacher D] said yesterday, he made a wonderful point: it's not the *image* that makes us weak, it's *reifying* the image. And I think there's a real danger here, when you say that the story doesn't have an author, that it's not told from a perspective. I think that's reifying it and not looking at what perspective it was told from, and the kind of power relationships that are implicit in it.

Teacher B: So it's a patriarchal story, so to speak?

MS: Of course. Who has the resources? Who does the abducting?

Teacher B: That's the sociological.

Teacher A: Wait a minute! Wait a minute! Wait a minute! Wait a fucking minute!!! [*Laughter. Hoots. Applause.*] What resources does the story describe the princess as having?

MS: I said the prince.

Teacher A: I know. You said *she* [the princess] has no resources.

MS: What resources does she have?

Teacher A: You tell *me* what resources she has! I already told you. [*Laughter.*]

MS: In the story she has what? The wealth of her kingdom to purchase art objects but she remains cloistered in her room.

Man 23: She's got beauty!

Teacher A: C'mon. You're diminishing the princess.

Man 24: And the story.

MS: Isn't that a patriarchal notion, that the most valuable resource a woman has is her beauty?

Teacher A: Well, I don't know. I'll ask some women about it.

MS: She doesn't have a ship, she doesn't even have a Faithful John.

Teacher A: How do you know she doesn't have a ship? Wait a minute. She has her maid servant, with two *golden* buckets, dipping water from the well.

Teacher B: She's got a well.

Teacher A: She has a well, the implication is.

Teacher B: How deep's your well this morning?

MS: Well, she can't even seem to afford decent bodyguards to go with her on the ship. [*Laughter.*]

Teacher B: Your sympathy is misplaced!

MS: Well, I heard a lot of confusion as you were talking before—

Teacher A: The confusion is fine. I just have to defend the story. In this story, she has *tremendous* resources. And everybody knows about it.

Several Men in Audience: And nobody can get near her. Nobody can get near her. She's the most desirable woman in the world.

Teacher A: And everything around her is gold. Her plates, and the goblets, and the curtains that hang, so that when the sun's not out the curtains remember the sun and reflect it to her.

Man 24: She's blessed.

Man 25: Even more than that, she's so powerful that she was able to knock him [the prince] out, just from a picture.

Teacher A: Just the single sight of her knocked him to the ground and drove his consciousness away. Is *that* patriarchal? [*Laughter.*] I thought patriarchal held on to consciousness no matter what!

MS: She's a princess. In the story she's being held captive [by her father]. Someone else made this point—

Man 26: She's *already* captive, incidentally—

MS: Right.

Man 27: Her *father* won't let anybody marry her.

MS: That doesn't sound patriarchal?

Man 27: She has a need. Imagine a woman wrote this story. And she has a need to be free from that connection, that man, that image of the king. But she can't have it—

MS: But she's not the one going on a quest.

Man 27: If she's the most beautiful woman in the world, she is not a woman! [*Laughter.*] She's *beauty*. It's about beauty. It's about how do you capture beauty. It's not about a woman. She's the most beautiful woman in the world.

Teacher B: If you're on the psychological level it's always about a woman or a man. That's the great difficulty.

Man 27: You can't go get beauty by asking for it. You've got do something—

Teacher B: This is a demonstration of a point of view that's very useful to listen to, you just don't have to believe it. [*Laughter.*]

Teacher D: It's the psychological interpretation.

Teacher B: Exactly.

Teacher D: There is no right interpretation of this story. It's the conflict of interpretations which we tried to foment.

Teacher A: And one of the good things that's happening is the clarifying of if it's psychological or concrete or mythological.

Teacher B: We've had all three.

Teacher A: We started out saying that all are incredibly important. If the concrete is not dealt with, then survival is not going to occur, right? There will be no psychological, because everybody will shoot each other with the .38's.

Teacher D: That's right.

Teacher A: So the concrete has to be dealt with. I agree with that.

Teacher B: Exactly.

Teacher A: I agree with that. But at the same time, I don't know how the concrete ever gets healed *except* through the psychological and the mythological. Or you wind up with *only* concrete solutions. And the jails are already overcrowded. So there is this issue. Another issue I would say, rather than only the Aikido approach, is psychological or mythological Aikido on the part of a woman. A woman before she gets in the TransAm should try to find out whether this guy has an image of feminine beauty or not. That can happen at the bar, too. Instead of saying, when he says, "You know what kind of car I've got?" And she says, "No, what is it?" And he says, "A TransAm." She could come back and say, "Well, what's the most beautiful thing in the world? Your TransAm?" I mean, she could move right into moving the image. She doesn't have to accept his image of the TransAm. And the story, I think, implies that a princess, or a woman, or the feminine, with resources, knows something about that. She's not caught by him and his patriarchal power. She's caught by the beauty of the objects presented.

Teacher B: Good point.

Man 28: It takes incredible craft to make those objects. And to get past her father.

Man 29: And it was in the *recent* past, that I can remember in *my* life, when women would have *loved* to have a man come and steal her away. To want her so much. But the man has to be worthy of that.

Man 30: Which is why it's so hard for us as men to get in synch with trying to have any of that feminine in us because we're always in a conflicting kind of place with women with whom we're trying to communicate. And this man [the young king] had his feminine fully attached, to put the art forward first. Then he brings the woman and communicates with her on a want/desire basis, and she goes with it. But she *was* abducted. And that was the trickster that you find hard to eliminate when you're dealing in life.

Man 31: I want to say something about a violation that I've been feeling—it feels like to my soul. It's been going on in my life the last couple of years, since I got up and tried to do something. Got off my ass, out from in front of the TV. And in the story, you know, the king which—my perception is that he seemed like a pretty good fuck. He sees something, something larger than him comes in, okay? He becomes blissful. He goes after his bliss. Maybe he has an ideal. He goes for it, you know? He gets there, something plays in. He's got her kind of, you know, kind of. He can parallel it with an ideal. You know, I have an ideal. I go in to someone with that ideal. I'm out where I'm at with my heart. I feel good. I'm a man. I go in and I want to talk to someone about maybe working with some children. And all of a sudden all these things come in. You know? All these things: "Well, you're a man. Maybe you shouldn't work with them. Maybe you can't be trusted. Maybe we need to look at these thousand different things before you do a fucking thing." Now that hurts.

Teacher B: Yes.

Man 31: And rape is a violation, but there's many violations. And I think that, you know, I need to know where these are coming from. And a lot of them come from me and from other men. And I do it to other men. And my own distrust, that my heart can leave me. And then other things can come into play. Sometimes I need to really respect and look at what I'm doing and saying.

Teacher A: I want to say one other thing. That made me think of it. If a man is so afraid of being raped himself, if he cannot give himself up to something bigger, then he's going to rape. You get what I'm saying? One of the functions of initiation was to rip the boy and the ego, the persona of the boy, apart and to introduce it to something greater. And if a man himself has not allowed himself to be in the circumstances to be torn, then the fear of it happening becomes greater and greater as one gets older—

Teacher D: That's right.

Teacher A: —and then the possibility of doing it to someone else becomes greater also. One of the things about initiation was to put boys into rapture. And it always has a wound and a cut in it. It always has to rip open like the eagle's beak the body, to remind him that things can get torn and broken and ripped open. So I mean there's a cultural reason why it's such a problem and it stays concrete. It's because many, and most maybe, of the men in the culture don't have conscious experience of being ripped open themselves.

Man 31: But the wound heals.

Teacher A: And the wound *stays*.

Teacher D: The *scar* stays. How much more time do we have to work with the story?

Teacher A: We've gone way past what we were ever going to do.

Teacher B: We've already entered conflict hour. [*Laughter.*]

Teacher D: The one thing that I was really interested in on this thing that we didn't get to really look at, which is related to this whole thing about showing your gold that [Bly] talks about a lot, is that taking his [the young king's] kingly robes off before he goes into this stuff. And I wondered what folks thought of what is going on there, the taking those clothes off. Because I think that's a really powerful image in the story. And we haven't really said much about that. And I'd like before we leave to—

Teacher A: Well, I want to say something really quickly back to the men who were saying there about power and patriarchy. He [the young king] takes off the patriarchal—you know, patrius, father, king—he takes off the patriarchal robes when he goes on this thing [quest for the princess]. That's the advice of [Faithful] John. We have to go as merchants, as people who are trading and into exchange, not as the patriarch of your realm. So the story actually deals with that patriarchal issue.

Teacher D: What is that anyway?

Man 32: It made me think of the garden work and the kitchen work the boy did in "Iron John."

Teacher D: That's what I'm thinking.

Man 32: He [the boy in the Iron John story] doesn't show his gold. He covered up his head, his golden hair. You don't use your tools and your gold until you're ready, 'til you've had the experience in the world, and 'til you're ready to make your move, so to speak.

Man 27: That was the mentor doing it.

Man 32: Well, Iron John helped the boy but—

Teacher D: But what about this story?

Teacher E: The king takes off his robes to become a lover? Why can't the king be a lover?

Teacher D: I think the sacred king is.

Teacher E: Can he go on courtship?

Teacher D: Say that again?

Teacher E: Can he go courting?

Teacher D: Oh yes. I think so.

Teacher E: Why does this man take off his robes?

Teacher D: What I was thinking, wondering about, that is, how much one needs to, if you're going to get in a relationship, be sensitive about how much brilliance and radiance you're showing all the time. [*Laughter.*] If you show too much radiance it's kind of hard to see you. That's kind of what my take on that is. There's a concept in Christian mythology called kenosis, and it's also related to Kabbalistic traditions—about how the divine sort of reduces some of its radiance so that—

Teacher E: He's taking off in an archetype.

Teacher D: Yeah, it's sort of making room for the other person. That's what I kind of think is going on there. And I think [Faithful] John understood that and the young man [the young king] didn't.

Man 33: Also, a king going into that situation would be subject to her father checking him out real close, whereas a merchant can kind of slip on in there.

Teacher A: That's a nice turn. See, if he came in as a king, then it would be the two kings struggling over the disempowered daughter. He [the young king] is actually coming in at the level of the woman, not at the king. Nice turn.

Man 8: And I see that as one of the things that's really attracting her. What hit me was that this princess not only sees gold that she values, it's the most *beautiful* gold; it's not just *any* gold. *And* he's a handsome king. But he also managed to figure a way to get her beyond her father's control. I would think that she would say, "Hey, this dude's wealthy, and he's a king, and he's good looking, and not only that, but he's *smart*."

Teacher B: Hold on to that "wealthy." Hold on. It's *art* he brings.

Teacher D: And a nice bottle of wine. [*Laughter.*]

Teacher B: Let's end right on that.

Teacher A: Let's go out and do the dance break. Just take all the energy out there.

This discussion unfolded as it did largely because of Teacher B's early invocation of "what feminists would say" about the princess being abducted. Teacher B said that he raised the question about what feminists would say to help clarify the differences between concrete, psychological, and mythological thinking. The discussion certainly revealed confusion about these matters. So Teacher B's gambit to provoke a discussion aimed at clarification might seem reasonable.

But such a discussion could have been pursued in other ways. Teacher B's approach delegitimated feminist objections to the imagery in the story. He implied that if feminists thought the imagery in the story was sexist or patriarchal, then they were hung up on a moot issue, because they were failing to think mythologically. Judging by their reactions, most of the men relished this debunking of feminist concerns. Thus it seemed to me that antipathy to feminism, rather than a desire to clarify thinking, was the impetus that launched the conversation from this starting point. A more strictly Jungian treatment of the story might have focused on the princess as an image of feminine beauty in men.[12] While this point was briefly touched upon in the discussion (by Teacher D), it was not the point to which the men's attention was drawn.

If Teacher B's reference to feminist objections was a setup to provoke contention and reveal confusion in the men's thinking, then most of the men in the room, including some of the other teachers, fell into the trap. Various statements suggested that many of the men saw the princess not as an archetypal image but as a representation of women in the concrete world. Recall the statements about women being attracted to Valentino; about women wanting to be swept up, enraptured, by princely men; about women loving Gothic romance novels; about women's imaginations; and about the woman falling for the man with a TransAm. These were not references to feminine energies in the psyche, but to what *women* thought, felt, or did in the concrete world.

When I spoke from the audience one of my concerns was that the men were taking the imagery of the story literally, that they were seeing the princess as a representation of women. I tried to say that it was dangerous to map the story back onto the concrete world, because in the story the princess was the object of a man's quest—a prize to be obtained. To map this back onto the concrete world would imply that men, to be good kings, must obsessively pursue women, not be put off by initial resistance, and, if necessary, use trickery to get what they want. The idea also seemed to be afloat that women liked this sort of thing. My concern, in other words, was with the sexist implications of men failing to think mythologically enough, to keep the imagery of the story out of concrete reality.

Yet when I raised my objections, Teachers A and B, and many of the men, were incensed. They felt I had interpreted the story psychologically or sociologically, hence incorrectly. But the strong reaction of the teachers and the men suggested that something else was going on. Other men who made statements indicating a genuine confusion of the concrete and the mythological did not elicit such hostile responses. My statements angered the men because I was mucking up the mythopoetic works by raising issues of gender politics (which were deemed not to exist in the mythological realm), and because my remarks threatened the moral identity the men were trying to construct.

The men did not want to see themselves as sexist, nor did they want to see mythopoetic activity as in any way contributing to the oppression of women. My interpretation of what was encoded in the story, and of what was going on in the *discussion* of the story, threatened this view of themselves. I was suggesting not only that the men were confused about the concrete and the mythological, but that this confusion, combined with the uncritical use of a story that was redolent with sexist imagery, implicated the men in the reproduction of sexism. This was the last thing they had come to a mythopoetic gathering to hear.

I got angry because I thought the discussion was pursued in such a way as to delegitimate any concern with the possible harmful effects of sexist imagery in the story. Inasmuch as I saw the men mapping the imagery of the story back on to concrete reality, such effects seemed to be taking root even as the discussion was happening. And though in retrospect I do not think that the men were denying the seriousness of rape, my sense at the time was that date rape was being spoken of as if it were a feminist fantasy.[13] I'm sure this was the view of at least some of the men in the room, judging by their keen response to Teacher B's remarks. I thought this too was dangerous.

The danger was more apparent during a later session at this gathering. In his preface to a lecture, Teacher B said, alluding to the discussion of the Faithful John story, "I'm going to harangue you—without your explicit verbal consent. It's a form of date rape." This drew laughs from the men in the audience, some of whom joined in the joke by calling back: "Can I like it anyway?" and "Our eyes have to at least meet!" and "I'm feeling disempowered without choice!" This kind of joking did not strike me as harmless musing about the mythological. Date rape was clearly being trivialized on this occasion.

The discussion of the Faithful John story also showed the men's reluctance to think sociologically about what they were doing. Recall the statement by Man 15: "This is a story about something else, and for us to take a literal view, we begin to take all the things that are happening in our society, outside of us, when that's not really what it's all about. What it's all about is what's been happening inside of us for thousands and thousands of years, independent of the particular culture or society or nation that we're born into." This man knew the difference between the concrete and the mythological. Yet his statement implied an impossible separation of self and society. What this man and many of the others wanted was an escape from the irritation of gender politics. The Jungian/archetypal perspective offered this in allowing the men to imagine that myth transcended culture and that by moving to the "mythological level" they could leave gender politics behind.

There was tension among the mythopoetic men over these matters; not all thought that gender politics could or should be left behind. I was not the only man who challenged the portrayal of the princess as a prize, seemingly with little control over her fate. Several men also spoke strongly against any implied trivialization of rape, recognizing the danger of doing so in a society where violence against women is rampant. So it was not as if all the men were so focused on the mythological that they lost all grip on the concrete reality of gender inequality. That was not the case, even though the majority of the men probably did not want to dwell much on these matters at a mythopoetic gathering.

The aftermath of the discussion was also revealing. As we walked outside for our dance break, two men whom I had not met before told me that they agreed with what I had said but were themselves afraid to speak up. They praised my willingness to challenge the teachers and to take a position at odds with the dominant view of the group. From this I learned that the range of political views present in the room was wider than it seemed. The dominant view of the group was exactly that: a dominating view rather than a universal one. I also learned from witnessing and participating in the discussion how an all-male gathering of this kind could inhibit critical self-examination and the expression of divergent views about gender politics.

Several men from the Local Group witnessed my exchange with the teachers during the discussion. I worried that by taking the stand I had, I had ruined my chances of doing more interviews. My fears were alleviated somewhat when a third man told me, as we were still moving outside for the dance break, that while he disagreed with what I had said, he thought I had "a lot of balls" for standing up for my views. After the dance break I spoke with one of the men from the Local Group, a man whom I had already interviewed. I said that I thought I'd blown it during the discussion. He said, "No, actually, you've probably got the respect of every man in the room for standing up to [Teacher A]." Then he hugged me. What I learned from this was that, for many of the men, being supportive of other men was more important than arguing over gender politics.

This valuing of support was part of the gender politics *created* in the mythopoetic men's hut. In these settings, emotional solidarity between men was more important than political solidarity between men and women concerned with gender justice in the outside world. The genuinely warm and rare feelings so often evoked at gatherings made it hard for men to dissent when something— perhaps sexist imagery in a story—bothered them. So the problem with all-male gatherings was not just that men brought in sexist baggage that often went unchallenged. It was also that the men created a feeling that such things were less important than the communitas and self-acceptance they wanted for themselves. To maintain this feeling the men had to push from their minds the feminist voices that might have urged them to dissent.

After the dance break that followed the discussion, and after the remainder of the morning's activities, as we were going to lunch I overheard one man make a point to another about all-male meetings. He said, "I read somewhere that in tribal cultures when the men have their meetings there's always one woman present. And when the women have their meetings, there's always one man present. I guess they do that to keep an eye on each other. Maybe we should do that kind of thing." To which the other man replied, "Well, that might be a good idea. But it's hard to imagine a woman being comfortable in this kind of situation."

JUNGIAN THINKING

The discussion reproduced in the preceding section showed how Jungian ideas influenced the men's thinking about gender politics. Jungian psychology posits that men and women tend to think, feel, and act differently because they have different archetypal endowments. Masculine archetypes tend to predominate in men, while feminine archetypes tend to predominate in women. In the Jungian view, gender is thus an innate, essential quality of males and females. When Man 15 said that the issues being discussed were about what's been going on *inside us* for thousands of years independent of external social arrangements, he was taking a Jungian view, one in which gender and gender troubles were seen as transhistorical, as rooted in human nature rather than social organization and culture.

One implication of this view is that to understand gender and gender inequality we need not study unjust social arrangements, harmful socialization practices, or oppressive belief systems. What matters, really, is what's going on inside us—it's the state of our psyches, not society, that accounts for our troubles. A further implication, then, is that solutions to people's gender troubles are to be found in the realms of myth and ritual rather than politics. Such a notion is likely to appeal to those who are least hurt materially by the workings of a capitalist, racist, or sexist society. It is in the interest of those who are materially privileged by the status quo to look for internal dragons to slay.

The inward turn inspired by Jungian psychology kept the mythopoetic men from trying to understand how their gender troubles stemmed from the organization of the society to which they belonged. Jungian psychology thus had a conservative effect in that it did not inspire serious social criticism or activism. Because of this, Jungian thinking posed little threat to either the taken-for-granted beliefs, social policies, and everyday practices that hurt women, or to the economic conditions that cause men to compete destructively and stifle their feelings.

The Jungian notion that myths transcend politics also had a conservative effect, because it inhibited thinking about how the imagery in stories reinforced presumptions of male superiority. Teachers A and B tried to derail this kind of thinking when they claimed that the Faithful John story had neither an author nor a perspective.[14] They wanted to treat the story as if it had been spun out by the collective unconscious, with no political intent or content. To treat the story this way meant there was no need to consider how its imagery—of men in dominant social roles and women in subordinate ones—encoded messages that might affect men's thinking, if only by subtly reinforcing beliefs about the propriety of male supremacy. To worry about such things was, as the teachers saw it, to lose the value of the story for exploring the depths of men's psyches. Exposing the sexism of the ego was not considered important.

Imagery in stories like "Faithful John" naturalized inequality between women and men. Such stories thus of course had a point of view, one in which women were seen as inferior to men. Even if a storyteller does not consciously adopt this point of view, the imagery in a story can still affect people's thinking about what is right and natural with regard to the balance of status and power between women and men. The point I tried to make in the discussion of the Faithful John story was that we needed to guard against the political content of the imagery creeping back into the concrete realm. Because of their commitment to Jungian thinking, the teachers dismissed my concern.

Several times when I asked mythopoetic men about the possible effects of sexist imagery in myths and fairy tales, I was told that my fears were unfounded. One man assured me that these stories had been around for ages and hadn't caused any harm. Another told me that "studies had shown" that even the most violent movies did not incite viewers to commit violence themselves. Fairy tales, being mild by comparison, were therefore harmless. I was struck by how these responses denied the Jungian premise that images are powerful shapers of psychic energies. It seemed that when the suggestion was made that some images might shape psychic energies in ways that reinforced sexism, those images were conveniently deemed to be powerless.

Of course, the effects of imagery in a story (or film) are not straightforward and automatic. Much depends on how a story is told, to whom, and how it is handled. If sexist imagery in a story is handled in a way that makes inequality problematic, the effect will be different than if it is handled in a way that makes inequality seem natural. The latter kind of handling often takes the form of no comment at all. As shown in the discussion of the Faithful John story, the mythopoetic teachers and most of the men did not want to examine the imagery in their myths and fairy tales in ways that made an issue of gender inequality. By not making an issue of it, they signified that gender inequality was less important than making therapeutic use of the stories for themselves.

A key way in which gender inequality is maintained is by making it appear natural. Jungian essentialism, even the loose essentialism embraced by the mythopoetic men, helped to sustain this appearance. If the masculine archetypes that naturally predominate in men incline them to be aggressive and rational, while the feminine archetypes that naturally predominate in women incline them to be nurturing and emotional, then it is likely that our biology will bring us to a state where men dominate women. This tendency is verified in many people's minds by the observation that male supremacy is nearly universal. Jungian psychology, like some religious belief systems, provided an explanation for this. If it wasn't God who ordained male supremacy, it was Nature or Evolution that formed in us the archetypes that predispose men to rule.[15]

Most of the mythopoetic men did not see in Jungian psychology any explicit endorsement of male supremacy. Nor would they have accepted such an endorsement if had been explicit. Yet perhaps they felt it, since the implications were there. If the masculine archetypes that predominated in men gave them an edge when it came to competition, and if archetypes were transcultural and transhistorical, then, well, perhaps male supremacy should be tempered rather than resisted. Occasionally this was said by mythopoetic writers, but then only in the gentlest of terms:

> Tremendous conflict ensues, from men trying to be more like women, and vice versa. Harmony will result when we begin to honor our differences, instead of trying to make one another the same. One of the major areas of conflict in our relationships right now, seems to be the balance of power in both romantic and occupational situations. By understanding our nature, we can achieve an equilibrium that's not based on sameness, but on diversity—embracing and supporting our unique and natural contrast as men and women.[16]

Although this writer, the author of a popular mythopoetic book, was not explicit about the precise nature of "our unique and natural contrast as men and women," it is clear that his idea of harmony can be realized only if women stop trying to be like men. A plausible interpretation of this would be that women should stop challenging men for power.

Construed as an archetypal reality, gender comes to be seen, in the Jungian view, as a part of the natural order of the universe, even taking on a sacred quality. Jungians thus see in men not just king and warrior archetypes, but the *sacred* king and the *sacred* warrior. Such language elevates alleged behavioral predispositions to the status of "gods within us." To achieve harmony and equilibrium, as the writer quoted above desires, we must honor these gods. It's not just disruptive, in this view, for men to act more like women or women to act more like men. By implication, it is sacrilege.

There was another way in which Jungian thinking allowed the men to distance themselves from the reality of gender inequality. This was evident in the men's occasional use of the term "the feminine" as a substitute for talking about women. So, for example, when I asked in interviews whether mythopoetic men's work posed any threat to women or was opposed to feminism, the men said no. Because they valued "the feminine," they said, their work posed no threat to women. As one man said in an interview:

There is a lot of femininity in these [mythopoetic] conferences. The story Bly told, about Medusa and Andromeda, was a very feminine story. The leader of men—the feminine was the leader of men in that story. And even [at the Big Remote Gathering] there was a great deal of regard for the feminine side. Even some of the little chants were about the mother seed. There's no repudiation of the feminine at all at the conferences I have seen. In the way the men treat each other there is something very affectionate. I guess that would be traditionally feminine. The very fact that you have men's groups is in some ways a kind of feminine thing. I think in some ways men's work helps empower the feminine. It makes it stronger, in a way. It allows it to come out because men can feel more secure in their own maleness, so then they don't have to feel threatened by it. They don't have to feel ashamed and defensive about it.

This man spoke of "the feminine" as an aspect of the psyche and as a label for nurturing. An impression of respect for women was thus created. But women were really irrelevant in this view. Men were not seen as learning from women the value or skills of nurturing. Men were accomplishing these things on their own. Jungian thinking thus not only masked conflict by replacing women with "the feminine," it also made women disappear as men discovered, all by themselves, the value of womanly ways of being.

Note, too, the effect of male supremacy evident in the last few lines of this man's statement. Even though the men were supposedly valuing and empowering "the feminine," they also felt insecure and defensive about possessing feminine qualities. These qualities made them feel insecure in their "maleness," which was the more important quality to embrace and affirm. So one reason for doing men's work was to feel less *ashamed* of possessing "the feminine." Why a feeling of shame? Because in a male-supremacist society qualities associated with women are devalued. A man's claim to the privileged identity 'man' is weakened if he finds, or others find, too much of "the feminine" in him. But if feminine qualities are seen as worth keeping, or too deeply ingrained to be purged, then a solution is to redefine them as aspects of the "deep masculine." Jungian psychology offered this solution, and by accepting it the men implicitly reaffirmed the greater value of things masculine and male. Which is to say, they reinforced male supremacy.

Jungian psychology gave the men "the feminine" to think about instead of women. One danger of this was that it kept the men from considering how women might be hurt, through some chain of effects, by mythopoetic men's work. Thus the men avoided thinking about how the valorisation of maleness and deep masculinity could hurt women by aiding, if only indirectly, the reproduction of male supremacy. Another danger arose because some of the men used the Jungian notion of the feminine to think about how women ought to be. For example, as one mythopoetic writer explained, the reason "ideological feminists" were opposed to men's work was that they were out of touch with the *true* feminine.[17] If these women were in touch with the true feminine, he suggested, they would know that the true masculine, such as mythopoetic men sought to develop, posed no threat to women.

Perhaps the most pernicious use to which Jungian psychology was put was to delegitimate feminist criticism of men. This was done by turning feminist anger into a symptom of neurosis. Bly was notorious for this. As he said in *Iron John* (p. 97): "A father's remoteness may severely damage the daughter's ability to participate good-heartedly in later relationships with men. Much of the rage that some women direct to the patriarchy stems from a vast disappointment over this lack of teaching from their own fathers." Feminist complaints about men's behavior or about sexist social arrangements were thus the results of psychic trauma in childhood rather than sane analysis in adulthood. Bly's claim here doesn't grow specifically out of a Jungian view, but it does reflect the same tendency to reduce social problems to psychological ones, and to deflect criticism by attributing it to a problem inside the critic.

Not all the men subscribed to this kind of reductionism. While most of the men claimed to know some genuinely irascible feminists, they also knew feminist women who could not be dismissed as neurotically angry. Still, many of the men found comfort in the idea that harsh feminist criticism of men was not truly credible because it grew out of psychic injury, and was thus out of proportion to any harm men actually did to women.

This was confirmed for some of the men by their reading of Gloria Steinem's book *Revolution from Within.*[18] At a small retreat several of the men talked about Steinem's book. They said they liked it because, as they interpreted it, Steinem admitted that feminist anger came from childhood wounds, and that anger-motivated feminist politics had to be replaced with something more spiritual. This suited the men just fine. It confirmed their suspicions that many feminists, due to their own unresolved *individual* problems, condemned men unfairly. Steinem's advocacy of an inner, spiritual turn also seemed to validate what the men were doing in their own mythopoetic work.

One thing the mythopoetic teachers were often criticized for was their seeming tendency to blame women for men's troubles. Jungian psychology also played a part in encouraging this kind of women-blaming. In the Jungian view, to become men boys must break away from the warmth and protection of their mothers. This is one of the themes of the Iron John story. To release the wild man from the cage, the boy must steal the key from under his mother's pillow. Until he does so, he can't begin the arduous journey toward manhood.

Women can come in for blame, in this view, because mothers are seen as tending to cling to their sons.[19] The problem is that some mothers want their nice little boys to remain nice boys forever. Mothers supposedly do this to meet their own needs for power and love. But of course this messes up their male children, who then have difficulty becoming confident, self-accepting adult men. Other women may also keep men from growing up when they insist that men be soft and passive and repress their masculine energies.

According to some mythopoetic writers, many of the ills of the world stemmed from men failing to break away from their mothers and to find a community of men to help them get in touch with their masculine energies. This view is summed up in the following passage:

> Our gravest problems—rape, domestic violence, child abuse, environmental devastation—are due in part, not to a lack of Mother relatedness, but to an over-abundance of it. Men are drowning in the Mother! With ritual male initiation virtually nonexistent, men stay entangled in mother-dependency long into adult-hood. Many never escape. They either marry a powerful woman who, as Bly has noticed, radiates all the energy in the relationship, while the man himself has little vitality to offer, or remain Don Juans who, entranced by the siren call of the femme fatale, move from one relationship to another in search of feminine perfection. Other men attempt a violent separation. What are rape and wife beating if not the desperate thrashings of a boy-man to escape the Mother's grasp? Let's not be deluded. Men may control the world of politics and money, but the negative Mother and her siren daughters dominate the realms of emotion and sexuality. Violence against women, never to be tolerated or condoned, must nevertheless be understood for what it is before it can be stopped: a mother-dependent man's attempt to gain a sense of power in the face of what he experiences as all-powerful.[20]

In other words, men sometimes act badly, to the point of raping and plundering, because their mothers refused to let them become men. If these men could just be initiated into mature manhood, they would stop struggling against an image of women as smothering and all powerful, and would thus stop hurting others in the process. Note that the blame here does not fall solely on the mother or on women. Older men have failed to do the necessary initiating.

Some of the men in the Local Group believed they fit this pattern. They felt that their mothers had—by being domineering, over-protective, manipu-lative, excessively critical of men, or sexually abusive—kept them from grow-ing up and becoming self-confident men. And in some cases these men felt that they had reproduced, in later relationships with women, the same infanti-lizing patterns that had existed in their relationships with their mothers. As one man said in a small group discussion, "I went from having a mother until I was eighteen to having a wife when I was twenty. I never had a chance to grow up. When I got divorced fifteen years later, I was lost. I'd never learned how to take care of myself or how to socialize with others as an independent person."

Though some of the men harbored feelings of anger toward mothers, ex-wives, and other women who had hurt them, when it came to assigning blame for psychic wounds it was *fathers* who got the lion's share. In the Jungian view, the boy or young man who breaks away from his mother must have a place to go. There must be a community of older men, or at least one older man, to help activate a young man's masculine archetypes. The mythopoetic teachers and men did not spare older men blame for dropping the ball. Older men, especially fathers, were blamed for being absent, for not providing tutelage in the enactment of responsible masculinity, and, in many cases, for being abusive. The strongest feelings of anger toward parents I heard any men express were directed at fathers, not mothers.

This matter of apportioning blame for men's troubles is an important piece of the men's gender politics. As I said, the men did not simply lay the blame for their troubles on their mothers. The pattern, rather, was for the men first to blame their fathers, then to come to see things as more complex. For example, in an interview one man said that for most of his life he blamed his abusive, alcoholic father for causing all the family's troubles. "I wanted to be completely different from him," this man said. But then, he said, he began to see that for all the problems his father had, he was still a hard worker, consistent provider, and a forthright, honest man. And so, owing to his men's-work experiences, this man had arrived at a different view of his parents:

> Now when [my siblings and I] see that there were some positive aspects in him, we are beginning to see that there were some not so positive things that my mother did. She put up with his bullshit for so many years. She could have gotten us out of that stuff. So my father, being the bad guy in the family, is starting to get more positive stuff coming at him and more warmth and more closeness. And my mother, having been the warm, cuddly, easygoing one, is starting to get a lot of anger from me and from my sister and from my brother too, really, which I think was unexpected for her. It was unexpected for us to start seeing this come out because she always seemed like she was the good one. But I think that when we began to see that *he* had two sides, we began to see that *she* had two sides, and we stopped looking at him through her eyes more, and started seeing him for ourselves through our eyes. And we could see her with our eyes, too. And so we've dealt with some of that and some of that's been tough. [My mother's] been doing some growing and some struggling with that, too. So those relationships are still growing and getting better.

Another man similarly described his father as an alcoholic who was physically and emotionally absent, though still a reasonably good provider. The same tendency toward blaming the father was apparent: "I was totally my mother's ally growing up and somehow really demonized him," this man said. But then this man too had arrived at a new view of his father:

> It's true he wasn't a very good father. I really did demonize him in many ways. But now I'm doing a bit of revisionist history of my family. It's interesting how that history has changed and how I see my father in a much more human sort of way. I mean, [I see him as] being terrified of having five children. My mother had cancer, had a series of surgeries, was in pain all the time, was constantly bitching and critical and very unpleasant to be around. He would come home and she would yell at him almost all the time he was there. I'm sure that the only sense of solace and community he got was with his buddies in the tavern. But the amazing thing was that he stayed married and continued bringing home some paychecks and honored his responsibilities to the family to the degree he did. And I realize that I totally accepted her view of him and saw him as just an absolutely terrible person and her as a small, suffering martyr who somehow managed to put up with him. And I just realize now that things are never that simple, that black and white. I can see many of the ways she mixed in with [my father's troubles]. It's valuable for me to reinterpret my father—and not to whitewash him at all—but to, I guess, have some forgiveness for him.

The common pattern in these and other men's accounts of their family lives was a realization that, as the man above said, "things are never that simple." What the men came to see was that both of their parents had good and bad qualities, and that neither parent could be solely blamed for the wounds family life had inflicted. Jungian thinking did not help the mythopoetic men see the economic constraints under which their mothers and fathers struggled, but it did help them see their parents more realistically, as neither all good nor all bad. In this way, Jungian thinking worked against a simplistic assignment of blame to either the mother or the father.

In chapter 5, I said that the men's identity work—their efforts to revalue 'man' as a moral identity—was in part a response to feminist criticism of men. This implied that women, or at least some feminist women, were indeed to blame for men feeling bad about themselves as men. Some of the men in the Local Group would have readily laid blame for this particular trouble, as they had experienced it, on the shoulders of certain women in their lives. While this sometimes came out in personal statements at gatherings—wherein the men might talk about how their mothers and other women had bewitched them and made them feel small—there was rarely any talk that could be construed as woman-bashing.

On the sole occasion when I heard a man begin to disparage women as a group, he was quickly cut off. The man who stopped him said, "We're not here to talk about what's wrong with women. We can't change women; we can only change ourselves. That's what we need to stay focused on." In this way the Jungian emphasis on inner life curtailed woman-bashing. But so did the men's desire for communitas, since griping about women was likely to produce a mood tinged with bitterness rather than one of pure brotherly love. Bashing women was also no way to signify the essential goodness of men.

CHAPTER 7

FEMINISM, ANDROCENTRISM, AND HOMOPHOBIA

No one understanding of feminism was shared by all the mythopoetic men. Some views, however, held sway more than others. Perhaps the most common view was of feminism as an ideology that sees all men as bad, or at least sees men and masculinity as responsible for most of the world's problems. Feminists who subscribed to this view were called ideological feminists, infantile feminists, separatist feminists, pop feminists, angry feminists, anti-male feminists, or radical feminists. Most often when the men had such folks in mind, they referred to them simply as "the feminists." The pejorative tone with which this was said conveyed a sense that "the feminists" were a cabal of muddleheaded man-haters who had nothing to say worth listening to.

The kind of feminism the men disdained was that which, as they saw it, issued a blanket indictment of all men for possessing that inherent evil, masculinity; which saw all men as equally powerful oppressors of women; and which said that for men to be decent human beings they had to become more like women. Feminism of this kind was, as the men saw it, an ideological bludgeon used by angry women who wanted to shame men as a way of salving their own wounds, or as a way to turn the tables and dominate men.

Other versions of feminism had less ominous meanings. Feminism could also mean exaltation or celebration of the feminine, militant pursuit of civil rights, or women getting together without men to deal with their issues. In these cases feminism was okay, because it was mostly about helping women and not about attacking men.

By and large the men approved of liberal feminism (though they did not call it that). This was feminism that argued for better job opportunities and political equality for women—without arguing that men were evil or had to give up power. The men also approved of spiritual feminism. It was okay for women to form groups to explore feminine spirituality, provided that they did not treat masculine spirituality as inferior. Feminism that critiqued sex roles, as opposed to blaming men for women's problems, was also acceptable. Some of the men in their 40s even cited encounters with this kind of feminism (ca. 1970–75) as helping them see the harmful effects of traditional masculinity.

Real feminists, some of the men felt, respected men's needs to gather by themselves to work on their own healing. *Real* feminists, in this view, were women who appreciated spiritual matters and the need to do inner work; who valued women's feminine ways of being; and who were secure enough to feel no need to denigrate men. In an interview, a man from the Local Group cited an instance of what he saw as bogus feminist criticism of mythopoetic men's work:

> I guess it was the *USA Today* article a couple weeks ago. It was about men's work. It was quoting the editor of *Ms.* as saying that all this drumming is a bunch of silliness. "Silliness" is the word she used. But in general, the women that I've known, the more radical feminist they are, the more they like this [men's work]. If they're just kind of playing around with feminism, pretending they're feminists, then [they won't like it]. Strong women, the real feminists, *they* went out by themselves. That was one of *their* big things, and still is. You know, it's like it's *their* thing, that sisterhood. So women who have done that are, I think, very understanding [of men's work]. So I don't know what's going on with the editor of *Ms.*

This man did not use the term "radical feminist" in a disparaging way, though his definition of a radical feminist excluded women who were critical of men's work. Women who were just "playing around with feminism," like the quoted editor of *Ms.*, Robin Morgan, were false feminists who criticized men's work out of ignorance.[1]

It was hard to tell how much feminist writing the men had actually read. Some men in the Local Group claimed to have read quite a bit of feminist writing, even if they couldn't remember exactly whose. A few men recalled reading Betty Freidan, Marilyn French, Susan Brownmiller, or Gloria Steinem. One article in a mythopoetic publication cited, disdainfully, Mary Daly, Andrea Dworkin, Sonia Johnson, and Catherine MacKinnon. In the Ritual Group, several men drew upon the work of the feminist spiritualist Starhawk. So at least some of the mythopoetic men had read feminist work and could name names. It seemed, however, that most of the men took their impressions of feminism from newspapers, magazines, and television.

This left the men, like many people, with an image of feminism that was largely a media-created caricature of a few radical feminist ideas.[2] So even if the men saw feminism as once having usefully defied constricting sex roles, they now saw it as offering little hope for men wanting to heal themselves, and even less hope for building bridges between women and men. As one man explained to me, the chance for "constructive dialogue" between [mythopoetic] men and feminists depended on feminists being willing to do two things: drop the critique of men and patriarchy, and admit that men are oppressed by sexism. This was akin to saying that no dialogue was possible unless feminists abandoned feminism.

At least two big things were missing from the understanding of feminism exhibited by even the most knowledgeable of the men. For one, the men did not grasp the feminist analysis of gender as a social construction. Feminist arguments that the bad aspects of masculinity, no less than the good aspects of femininity, were the results of socialization, not innate moral qualities, seemed to have escaped the mythopoetic men. This is one reason why the men took feminist criticism of men and masculinity so personally. The men did not understand the critique as aimed at the social arrangements that produced a lot of genuinely harmful behavior on the part of males trained to be men of a particular kind. Of course, not all feminist writers aimed so carefully, either.

As I argued in chapter 2, the men had an interest in not seeing the social constructionist premises of feminist critiques of men's behavior. The men, of course, disliked it when feminist arguments seemed to imply that all men were naturally inclined to rape and kill. But the men couldn't get beyond first appearances to consider the social-constructionist premises that rejected the idea of males and females as essentially good or bad. They did not want to do this because they needed to believe in essentialism for their own purposes.[3] To remake 'man' as a moral identity it was easiest to claim—in harmony with widely held notions about the biological bases of behavior—that there were good qualities *inherent* in males. The social-constructionist premises of much feminist thinking denied this (just as those premises, consistently applied, denied that females were any more inherently good than males) and gave the men one more reason to be wary of feminism.

Also missing from the men's understanding of feminism was a grasp of its critique of institutional power and class inequality. Feminism, as the men knew it, lumped all men together as powerful oppressors of women, with no appreciation for inequalities between men. One mythopoetic writer saw this as a fatal omission in feminist thinking:

> A lot of the violence that men perpetrate is not because we are, as some feminists allude, "testosterone poisoned"—or, as Mary Daly has said, "ontologically evil," which is an academic way of saying "rotten to the core"! Rather, men's lives are systematically and institutionally degraded. Boys are touched and talked to less. They receive much more physical punishment than girls. The battering and sexual molestation of males, young and old, is more acceptable than that of females—especially if the abuse is done by women. We send men to war, but not women. One in twenty men are in the justice system, and only 1 in 400 women. And as I've mentioned, men fill all the more hazardous occupations. Warren Farrell is doing some excellent work on this. His forthcoming book [*The Myth of Male Power*] elaborates on these inequities, providing compelling evidence that—regarding the well-being of our bodies and souls—American men are second-class citizens. One or two percent of the men in this country have a vastly disproportionate amount of wealth and power. But the other 98% of men—and this is something that feminism never addresses—are really left out of the power conduit. And they're struggling. So we need to, first, understand how our institutions, social services, and judicial system, are skewed against males, then have our educational system and social services respond to our gender concerns.[4]

Feminism was thus seen as offering no realistic account of power relations between men. This perception was not wholly wrong, in that liberal, cultural, spiritual, and separatist feminisms offer little, if any, analysis of class inequality. Only Marxist and socialist feminisms do, and it was clearly not this sort of feminist thinking to which the men were exposed via the popular media, nor even via such ostensibly feminist sources as the 1980s incarnation of *Ms.* magazine.[5]

The men knew that there was an older stream of the men's movement which took gender politics and feminism as its points of departure. This was the profeminist stream, or what some of the mythopoetic men called the "guilt wing" of the men's movement. The profeminist men were seen as buying into anti-male feminism and thus unable to appreciate their own "masculine energies" and "male modes of feeling." For these reasons the profeminist men's movement was anathema to many of the mythopoetic men, who sought to avoid any further feelings of guilt over being men. One editor of a mythopoetic anthology said that membership in the profeminist branch of the men's movement was declining, because its "critical attitude toward men alienates many potential supporters and newer branches offer more positive alternatives."[6]

Profeminist men were seen not only as accepting a guilt trip laid on them by wounded, angry women, but as in denial of their own problems. In other words, profeminist men, in the mythopoetic view, always wanted to worry about the pain of some other group—women, blacks, gays—instead of dealing with their own issues. One of the men in the Local Group offered a view of profeminist men that was typical:

> We have some profeminist guys in the men's center here. They're the kind of guys that if it isn't women, it's the gays. They sort of want to take care of other people. That's probably good. It reminds us that we're this middle-class, white, age-fortyish group. And see, this bothers [the profeminist men]. They say, "Where are the blacks? Where are the gays?" But anyway, the profeminist guys—Bly talks about this; he's got a tape on it; he talks about this fairy tale with the dwarfs and how you can't pick up on women's pain. You know all the stuff: the discrimination and all that stuff that's happened to them for thousands of years. We can't pick that up. We can't bear that pain of theirs. It doesn't mean we can't be sympathetic to women, and I *am*. I feel that strongly. And the more we get *ourselves* together and empowered as men—that's what I see in this mythopoetic stuff. It's a very inward, self-oriented thing.

Buying too deeply into feminism was thus seen as distracting men from the soul work they needed to do for themselves. It wasn't that feminism   in the form of belief in equality and justice for women—was seen as wrong for men to support. What was wrong, or harmful, was to embrace the feminist notions that men were to blame for all the world's ills and that now men should be motivated by guilt to fix the damage. This kept men from dealing with their own legitimate pain, which, many of the mythopoetic men believed, had to be dealt with before they could be effective political actors.

The inner/outer dichotomy evident in the preceding quotation was at the core of the men's thinking about gender politics. Whereas women had once struggled for "outer power," men were now struggling for "inner power." This simple inner/outer split kept the men from examining—as feminist women had done—connections between the personal and the political. Yet it would be wrong to say that the mythopoetic men had no sense of these connections. When I asked a man in the Local Group whether there was any *philosophical* conflict between mythopoetic men's work and feminism, his answer summed up a view shared by many of the men. The goals of men's work, he said, transcended such conflict:

> No [there's no conflict]. Well, it depends on who you listen to. We don't have a leader, but Bly tries to make it clear that it's not oppositional. It's also what men

bring back to their wives from it, because I could see where a lot of men can maybe do some stupid things. Maybe they get all pumped up but then they go back and become more abusive. But the real intent of it, if I hear Hillman and Meade and Bly and Moore and the others—I think the intent of it is that it's *human* liberation. I mean, it's about human connectedness that enhances growth. It's about affirming life. It's equality, fraternity, sorority—fraternity's the wrong word. So I don't think it opposes feminism in these respects.

Many of the mythopoetic men would have agreed that their concerns for "human connectedness" and for "affirming life" should have made them allies of feminists, especially cultural and spiritual feminists, who often touted these same values. Yet there remained differences with regard to other of women's and men's concerns. As this man further described the conflict:

> But are there a lot of women who attack [men's work]? Of course, because I don't think they get it. The women's movement to me is something that obviously— *everything* starts *internally*, because somebody has to feel it or think it before they act on it. But the women's movement to me was an *external* movement. It was political, socioeconomic liberation. It was, "I don't get paid what you get paid. I don't even get the opportunity to do the job you get to do. In fact, you even enslave me in the home by telling me this is women's work." That's an external thing, even though I certainly realize liberation has to come from within. But that was an external movement. And rightly so, because they did it within the confines of a patriarchal society—a male-dominated, women-being-submissive society.

This man thus recognized that there was a connection between oppression, feelings, and action for change. If the men's movement was focused on the internal, it was because men didn't face the same constraints women did. Men simply didn't have to struggle for job opportunities, fair pay, and political power. Men needed liberation from within. He went on:

> The men's thing is definitely an internal movement. It starts internal, as every- thing does, but it *stays* internal. Men—I don't care what some of these guys are saying about men not really having power in this culture because they have to go out and slave to work and to take care of their women. That's a lot of crap. Men love and have loved knowing that they control the political, social, and economic mechanisms. They just do. [Men's work] is inner because I think men have for- gotten what it's like to be *human*, never mind forgetting what it's like to be equal. They've lost sense of what it is to be human. So I think they're real different movements the ways they manifest.

Rejecting the men's rights notion that men are hurt by a lack of power, this man saw men as suffering a loss of humanity because of their power. A generous inference here would be that humanizing men will yield benefits for women, and thus women ought to support men's work. Even if men were focusing on "external stuff," in this man's view there was still much common ground:

> I don't know if the men's movement and the women's movement are going to meet. Maybe. Because a lot of women are doing a lot of inner work. Maybe they won't meet in the middle until the men do what Hillman says: get on with the inner work but then start realizing we've got to change the world out there. If that happens, if this becomes a true external political movement, I think the women would find more common ground with us, because I sense that the men I talk to who go to these weekends—if you talk to enough of them who've done this kind of work—we support the same things in terms of human liberation that a lot of progressive or radical women support—when we're dealing with external stuff.

But if there was one thing that remained an obstacle to mythopoetic men and feminist women standing together on their supposed common political ground, it was gender itself. As this same man put it:

> The problem is when we're dealing with internal stuff. I don't think men and women understand each other. I gave up expecting [my woman friend] to really understand deeply what goes on inside me as a male, although I think she wants to. She validates me in [men's work]. She doesn't expect me to be a carbon copy of her. Equality doesn't mean we become the same. It means more like, "I respect you for being a human, and I respect you for being a woman—who is obviously different from me as a male."

This man's comments illustrate some of the main lines of the men's thinking about gender politics: women and men struggle with many of the same generic human problems; for the most part, women and men are looking for similar, or at least parallel, solutions; right now men need to deal with their long-ignored inner troubles; these are different from women's and thus hard for women to understand and appreciate—in which case, women and men will have to carry on separate movements for a while longer.

Despite their disdain for profeminist men, the mythopoetic men saw themselves as caring about women and about women's issues. Some of the men felt that because they had had so many women friends, they understood women's issues fairly well—certainly no less well than profeminist men. The difference, again, was that profeminist men were seen as letting women dictate how men should be and act. Justice, as the mythopoetic men construed it, demanded that good men—and all men were essentially good—be free to define *for themselves* what was an appropriate "male way of being." Profeminist men and feminist women were of course wary, because the mythopoetics seemed to put no moral limits on what was an appropriate male way of being, especially vis-à-vis women.[7]

I've shown here and in the previous chapter how the men were not of one mind when it came to gender politics. Some men embraced the men's rights notion that men were not powerful and privileged. Others, such as the man quoted at length above, saw that, on the whole, men did have more institutional and political power and that women suffered because of this. This meant there was enough diversity in the men's views to put communitas at risk if gender politics became a topic of conversation. Communitas was fostered by sticking to the principle upon which the men agreed: for them, liberation had to come from within.

Another kind of tension arose because the men wanted to be sensitive to injustice, including that suffered by women, yet they also needed to legitimate their "inward, self-oriented" movement. It took some mental gymnastics to cope with these simultaneous tugs toward the inner and the outer. Men's rights notions and Jungian thinking did the trick. The men's rights perspective suggested that maybe women really had acquired all the power they needed to win whatever battles were left for them to fight. The Jungian perspective let the men believe that women and men were sufficiently different to need their own ways to deal with inner troubles, which were not seen, in the Jungian view, as caused by external injustices.

Many of the men, wanting to see themselves as men of conscience, also believed that they were headed toward political action but that they had to empower themselves first. Once they were healed and could work in community with others, then, supposedly, political action would follow. This claim of a need for prior self-empowerment put the men at odds with many feminist women and profeminist men, in whose views the idea of middle-class, college educated, heterosexual white men needing to band together to empower themselves was not only absurd, but offensive in its insensitivity to the realities of institutional power and to women's more pressing claims for justice. But as the mythopoetic men saw it, this rejection of their need to do inner work was one more example of feminists' ideological blindness to the pain and powerlessness felt by most men in this society.

ANDROCENTRISM

About many things having to do with women the mythopoetic men were silent. Saying little about women was a point of pride for some of the men, since they saw it as evidence that men's work was not sexist. After all, if men were not talking about women, this meant that no bashing or patriarchal plotting was going on. A relative silence about women was part of the gender politics the men created at their gatherings. The problem with this wasn't that the men denied the importance of so-called women's issues, at least not in principle. It was that by largely ignoring women's issues the men reinforced a narrow, androcentric worldview.

At one large gathering a mythopoetic teacher said that our society was "in denial" about various social problems. He cited destruction of the environment, overpopulation, racism, the resurgence of tribalism, violence among young males, and community decay. To solve these problems, he said, men had to face them squarely and stop pretending everything was fine. His list of problems did not include the feminization of poverty, restrictions on women's reproductive freedom, inadequate prenatal health care, the lack of affordable daycare, job discrimination against women, or violence against women. Thus there was another kind of denial going on: that these "women's problems" had anything to do with the behavior of men, or that such problems should be prime concerns of politically active men.

Women were left out in other ways. In most of the fairy tales told at gatherings the central characters were men; when the men were asked at gatherings to make a statement about their lineage, the usual instruction was to invoke the father (e.g., "I am Michael, son of Harry"); and while talk about fathers was common, there was relatively little talk about mothers. This focus on men and men's concerns—stemming from the desires to give each other support, foster self-acceptance, and deal with personal troubles—made it harder for the men to take women's perspectives seriously. This tendency to take men's realities as paramount and give lesser weight to women's realities is what I mean by androcentrism.

Androcentric thinking dulled the men's sensitivity to women's perspectives inasmuch as it kept them from asking, on certain occasions: How might women see this matter, this situation, this behavior? How might a particular woman see these things? What might her thoughts and feelings be? and Why? This problem is best illustrated with examples from my field notes. All of the following instances occurred at different gatherings:

> A man about 30 years old described an occasion on which he, his wife, and another couple had just had a "wonderful weekend." He said he was feeling great about this and everything seemed fine. But then his wife began to cry. He said he asked her why and she couldn't say. At this point the man shrugged as if to indicate exasperation, and said no more about why his wife had been upset. It wasn't clear to me what this story was supposed to mean, but I took the suggestion to be that women are emotionally unpredictable, inscrutable, and sometimes

a pain in the ass for mysterious reasons. This is how the other men in the circle took it. One guy said, "Jesus, talk about raining on your parade." Another man made a casting and reeling motion with his hands, as if to suggest that this guy's wife had reeled him back in from his high. The men were reacting as if the only possible problem in this man's story had to do with his crying wife. *He* was happy and *she* brought him down—end of story. I wondered what else might have happened during the "wonderful weekend," something he might have missed, to upset her. It also occurred to me that the men in the circle were quick to dismiss the wife's distress rather than trying to understand where it came from.

A man talked about breaking up with his wife. The other men in the circle laughed when he said, "She thinks I'm slimy because I'm attracted to other women. Maybe women aren't attracted to other men." He presented this as if she were unreasonably resentful of his perfectly normal male attraction to other women. But then later in the evening, when the talk turned to "unfinished business," this same guy said, "I have a tendency to overlap relationships. I'll get a new one started before the old one is finished." It wasn't apparent that he saw a connection between his wife's accusation of sliminess and his admitted tendency to "overlap relationships." I thought that if women had been present the connection might well have been served up to him. No man in the circle raised this issue.

During the afternoon, as several of us were sitting around the stove in the living room of the cabin, the topic of housework came up. The men talked about how women don't appreciate all that men do. Some of the men told stories about how their wives failed to appreciate the time and effort that went into mowing the lawn, tending the yard, maintaining the car, fixing the house, etc. One man even said that he once did a careful accounting of the amount of time he and his wife spent doing various household chores and it turned out he put in more time— and yet his wife refused to believe it. The other men sympathized. Then I told a story about how housework had been an issue in a relationship I'd been in. I said that for a while I argued the same point: That I was putting in an equal amount of time, all things considered, and that being harangued about who cleaned the bathroom was unfair. But then I said that what we'd finally figured out was that time was less of an issue than the meaning of the particular pieces of work involved. I said that what I'd learned was that cleaning a bathroom, besides not being as pleasant as working out in the yard, was for my partner a symbol of women's historical subservience, and that was what made it so onerous. Seeing this, I said, helped me get over arguing about time spent doing the work, which wasn't the point. It also helped get the housework issue resolved. The men seemed to get the point. One man said, "Yeah, I can see how the meaning would be different if you were a woman." A couple other men nodded their heads. I liked this conversation because I got to play professor and also because it showed that the men are movable on these matters.

At one point a guy said that his therapist, a woman, had advised him against joining a support group while he was still in therapy. He didn't say what his therapist's specific concerns were. He asked the men in the circle for their thoughts about being in therapy and in a support group at the same time. One guy said, "I heard you use the 'she word.'" Immediately another guy said, "Women don't like it when men get together by themselves." Another man, a therapist himself, said, "She's probably worried about losing you as a client." There were some more comments along these lines. No one asked if the therapist had said anything more specific; no one hinted that her concerns might be legitimate. It struck me how quickly the men keyed on the therapist's gender and used this to discount her concerns—whatever they might have been. The men were good enough perspective-takers to know that some women worried about men getting together by themselves. But they didn't want to invest much effort in trying to figure out why, at least not in this case.

The men got to talking about how women like to talk so much. It was said that talking is "women's way of connecting," whereas men do it differently, sometimes through just sitting together silently. A newcomer said, "My girlfriend won't just sit silently with me. My mother certainly won't." This drew laughs from the other men in the circle. The joke seemed to be that we men know how addicted women are to ceaseless chatter. The talk about how men enjoy "powerful silences" while women have to yak so much went on for a while, then one of the old-timers said, "Yeah, that's one reason men like [to receive] oral sex—it keeps women quiet." This drew some laughs, though it seemed that some men were uncomfortable with the remark.

The commonality in each instance can be seen as either a kind of sexism or, as I am calling it, an androcentric bias against taking women's perspectives seriously. In each instance it would have been reasonable to try to imagine how some women, or a particular woman, might have seen things differently, whether the matter was responding to a partner's tears, overlapping relationships, a prescription for therapy, or the importance of talk for creating intimacy. To try to imagine such things could have helped the men achieve their goal of self-knowledge by giving them another perspective from which to look at themselves, though such knowledge might not have been comforting. To the credit of the men who talked about housework, they were amenable to considering how women might see things differently. But on most occasions no one showed any interest in trying to adopt women's or a woman's point of view.

For the most part, the mythopoetic men were not crass sexists. As individuals they disavowed sexism. They were also commendably restrained, compared to many other groups of men, when it came to making sexist remarks or telling sexist jokes. Nonetheless, being steeped (like everyone else) in a sexist culture, the men unavoidably brought sexist baggage with them to their gatherings. But the problem was not simply that the men occasionally let slip a sexist remark or joke. The problem was that mythopoetic ideas and practices fostered androcentric thinking, which could have sexist consequences, despite the men's nobler intentions.

Mythopoetic ideas and practices encouraged the men to focus on their own pain, grief, wounds, and healing. The men were supposed to stop denying inner troubles out of misguided allegiance to a harmful notion of masculinity that said men must be stoics. At all-male gatherings and in support groups, the men encouraged each other to talk about their feelings. By being empathic and sympathetic the men helped each other achieve self-acceptance and, collectively, the joy of communitas. To achieve these goals it was not necessary to say much about women. In fact, as I've suggested, to achieve these goals it helped to say as little as possible about women.

But since many of the men's troubles were somehow linked to relationships with women, women inevitably appeared in personal statements and other kinds of talk. On these occasions the men's desires to stay focused on their feelings, to avoid hiding those feelings behind talk about other people, to find self-acceptance, and to build a mood of warm fellow-feeling kept them from pursuing distracting lines of thought—such as how women might see things differently, and why. And since some of the men felt that they had previously been *too sensitive* to women's perspectives, it was a now a relief to be licensed, by other men, to avoid that kind of risky, possibly guilt-inducing, imaginative work.

The mythopoetic men knew that good things could happen when they shared stories of grief or joy. But, to use the Jungian term, the men seemed to be in denial about the political shadow of their activities. Focused as they were on their own pain and desires for solidarity, they tended to reinforce an androcentric worldview that made it harder for them to take women's perspectives seriously. I count this as a bad result. Gentle though the men were as individuals, by making their all-male gatherings "safe places"—that is, safe from having to worry about how women might see things differently or challenge what was being said—they behaved collectively in a way that made them less sensitive to women's perspectives and thus less able to see the gender politics implicit in doing men's work.[8]

HOMOPHOBIA

Heterosexual ardor is one of the key signifiers of traditional masculinity. Competition among men for the best portrayal of traditional masculinity is thus

what leads to bragging about sexual conquests and to the concomitant objectification of women. Part of this same competition is denigration of some men
for showing insufficient interest in sex with women. And men who show any
sign of sexual interest in other men are even more severely shamed and abused
for their betrayal of traditional masculinity. Such men taint the category 'men'
by acting like women.

Homophobia (the intense fear or hatred of homosexuality) among men is
thus a part of reproducing male supremacy because it involves the devaluation of things defined as female, feminine, or womanly, such as the desire to
have sex with a man. Men who show such desires are seen as traitors to their
class because their deviance threatens the ideological belief that men are different from, and implicitly superior to, women. Men (and women) who are
fervent believers in rigidly defined gender roles tend to be the most
homophobic.[9]

It is impossible to grow up in a society where heterosexuality is the privileged norm and not be homophobic to some degree. The mythopoetic men
wrestled with this. They saw homophobia as a problem primarily because it
kept straight men from showing affection for each other, and secondarily because it hurt gay men. Homophobia was thus an obstacle to the kind of support and nurturing the men wanted to feel good about giving each other. Yet
the men were not always reflective about how their words and deeds reinforced
homophobia. This happened most often when the men talked about wanting
physical closeness with other men. When they talked about this, almost invariably they used the disclaimer "in a nonsexual way, of course," thus implying that showing affection in a sexual way was wrong.

The mythopoetic men were predominantly heterosexual and wanted others
to know it. One publicly unstated reason for refusing television coverage of a
retreat, as a man in the Local Group said in an interview, was fear that the
camera would show men dancing with each other and then "people would think
we're a bunch of gay guys or something." Other comments the men made
indicated an awareness and concern that outsiders might think they were gay.
Considering the homophobia of the society at large, the fear of being so labeled was not unfounded. Several times I was asked by outsiders whether a lot
of the men were gay. Clearly the practice of gathering to drum and dance and
talk about feelings made them suspect.

I don't know what percentage of the men in the Local Group were gay or
bisexual. Only two men identified themselves in interviews as bisexual. At
gatherings I heard only a few men, out of hundreds, identify themselves as
gay. On other occasions, in small group discussions, a few men who had been
married for years talked about having had, or having considered, homosexual
affairs. Don Shewey, a *Village Voice* reporter who wrote several articles about

men's gatherings, once estimated that—according to his "gaydar"—about one-third of the men he saw were "gay, bisexual, or undeclared."[10] That estimate seems high to me, though perhaps Shewey saw signs that I didn't (we never attended the same gathering, as far as I know). My own estimate is that about one-fourth of the men had some interest in erotic contact with other men.

More interesting than percentages is the way the men struggled with the contradiction between their desires for closeness with other men and the homophobia that was inherent in their notions of masculinity. Although the men rejected traditional, stoic masculinity as represented by the images of John Wayne, Clint Eastwood, and others, they still wanted to be *men* and to feel *masculine*. In the culture in which the men were steeped, manhood and masculinity were inexorably linked to heterosexuality.[11] The men resisted this, at least in principle, but could not escape it. As liberals they accepted individual diversity in sexual expression, including gay sexuality for men, but heterosexual procreativity remained an implicit aspect of their masculine ideal.

This contradiction haunted some of the men in the Local Group. One man talked in an interview about his desire for physical intimacy with other men and how this conflicted with his sense of what masculinity was about. When I asked what masculinity meant to him, he said:

> I still feel like I've made relatively little progress [figuring that out], because I'm still very insecure in my masculinity. I think that's partly because I still keep playing back these traditional tapes that a large part of masculinity is how you relate sexually to women, and I just don't relate that way to women. So I would say I'm still in bad shape in terms of self-image in terms of masculinity. But it's something I'm continuing to work on.

This man wanted to be secure in his masculinity, but his attraction to men made this difficult, since such an attraction was antithetical to his culturally inherited notions of masculinity. Thus he needed to work on creating a version of masculinity that didn't crumble at the first sign of homosexual desire. The contradiction remained, however, because this man also staked his sense of masculinity on maintaining a public identity as a heterosexual. This was implied earlier in the interview, when he said:

> I don't do anything [sexually with men] that I would feel uncomfortable telling my wife. And everything I do I tell my wife. So it's very open and I try to tell her that I love her a lot. And I reassured her that I don't walk out on a marriage. I don't. I'm not fooling either her or me. It's hard for me to imagine that I would ever find anybody with whom I was more compatible. I also like being married. I always wanted to be married. I guess being married was something very important to my sense of masculinity early on, and it's still very important.

Despite this man's belief that his primary sexual orientation was to men, he still needed his masculinity affirmed through attachment to a public identity as a heterosexual. The concern shown by other mythopoetic men for their public identities as heterosexual reflected a similar reluctance to give up the status conferred by traditional masculinity.

The bisexual men involved in mythopoetic men's work were different only in degree from the straight men. Both groups were looking for a way to satisfy their desires for closeness to other men without sacrificing their public identities as heterosexuals. Some further evidence for this came from an interview with another bisexual man. When I asked if men's work had changed his feelings toward men, he said:

> It's enabled me to have more closeness with men, including sexual touching. I've had affectionate relationships with some men in the men's center, but not real homosexual experiences. I've not actualized that side of myself, and I don't plan to. My marriage and my life means more to me than that. You can't have two primary relationships. My primary relationship is with my wife. Talking with my wife about [my sexual interest in men] has improved my sexual relationship with her. We've gotten much closer. So I wouldn't want to give up my hetero way of life.

At least some of the men in the Local Group knew of this man's erotic interests, so I asked if he had felt any hostility from them. He said:

> No. I feel fine. Nothing. I've given them ample opportunity to reject me, but I've found everything's the same or deeper. I do know of someone else who *doesn't* feel this way, but for me [telling the men about being sexually attracted to men] hasn't made any difference.

I then told him a story about a gay man who mentioned his male lover during a sweat lodge ceremony and got a bad reaction from the other men. In response to this story, he said:

> That's different. That's going a step beyond. All the references I make—I don't have gay sex. It's like, "what kind of a world do I live in?" All my references are to my children, my wife, my hetero side. It's like we all laugh in the [gay married men's] support group. There's not a real queer among us. We're all half-assed. We're not fully accepted in either world.

In fact, the bisexual men wanted to remain accepted in the straight world. Mythopoetic men's work let them have it both ways. At mythopoetic gatherings bisexual men could get close to other men, even express physical affection for them, without risking their public identities as heterosexuals.

The men also valued the acceptance they found in the mythopoetic community. Despite the undercurrents of homophobia and the tendency of mythopoetic leaders to keep homosexuality invisible, bisexual and some openly gay men found mythopoetic contexts attractive because of the prohibitions against judging each other and competing for manhood status.[12] The man quoted above, who said he was insecure in his masculinity, said also that he had found acceptance and affirmation at a mythopoetic gathering:

> [Before that gathering] it seemed so impossible, so out of the question, to be held and cradled in another man's arms. I can't say it didn't feel sexual, but it also had a very big component of just feeling nurturing in the way that a father feels toward a son. In my case, I was the son and the other men were the fathers. I would say to a large extent that a lot of the intensity of the sexual feelings that I had have diminished, and it now feels more like a nurturing relationship—like a brother/brother relationship. You idealize a brother/brother relationship rather than an intensive sexual one. But still there is no question in my mind that my orientation is towards men. I feel that not only because of what I feel towards men, but because of what I don't feel towards women.

For men whose sexual interests had made them feel like failed men, this uncritical acceptance was a relief. To be firmly ensconced in the category 'men' and to have their masculinity affirmed by other men gave them the security they longed for.

Ironically, the affirmations of heterosexual identity may have actually allowed straight and bisexual men to get closer to each other. By agreeing that "deep masculinity" included rather than precluded being nurturing and affectionate, and by using the "nonsexual, of course" disclaimer, the men felt safe enough—felt their heterosexual identities were safe enough—to hug and touch in ways that they might otherwise not have. Another benefit of this was that the enjoyment of physical closeness with other men forced homophobia into the open. On several occasions, after some activity involving touch, I heard men say that they were beginning to realize the damage caused by homophobia.

Along with the undercurrent of homophobia among the mythopoetic men, there was also a tendency to romanticize or take a mystical view of gay men. Gay men were sometimes said to be specially gifted because they had "a foot in both gender worlds"; or because in some mythologies or primitive cultures they were seen as being "gateways to the spirit world" or more in touch with the rhythms of the earth.

Although these references to the special gifts and perceptions of gay people were sometimes phrased as if meant to include lesbians, at other times teachers and men spoke as if lesbians were not included. Lesbians were certainly not romanticized; nor was the sexual preference of some women for other women given so much as the blessing of essentialism. As one mythopoetic teacher said at an all-male gathering, "Women become lesbians out of anger, not joy." These disparate views of gay men and lesbians revealed some old-fashioned misogyny. Perhaps another reason for the greater acceptability of gay men was that gay men at least still liked men.

Romanticizing gay men was a kind of penance the men did for their homophobia. This may indeed have helped some of the mythopoetic men feel more at ease with the gay men in their midst. But more importantly, romanticizing gay men always involved essentializing gayness. This is what truly put straight men at ease, since it was also a way to assure themselves that they were essentially straight.

The homophobia exhibited by some of the mythopoetic men was another reflection of their belief in parity between straight white males and every other group. For example, the profeminist branch of the men's movement was described in one mythopoetic book as the "profeminist/gay affirmative" branch, a not inaccurate label. The profeminist branch of the men's movement, as represented by the National Organization for Men Against Sexism (NOMAS), is explicitly gay affirmative, seeing homophobia as linked to male supremacy and the perpetuation of sexism. NOMAS also sees the affirmation of gay relationships as linked to its goal of enhancing men's lives.

But then in this same context, the profeminist men's movement was said to be one in which straight men were far outnumbered by "heterophobic gays and bisexuals." The term heterophobic—coined to mirror homophobic—is revealing. It implies political and moral equivalence between the disparagement and abuse of a gay minority by a straight majority, and the *resistance* offered by gay men to this disparagement and abuse. This is the same kind of thinking that led some of the mythopoetic men—those who leaned more toward the men's rights perspective—to label as "neo-sexist" any statements by women that were critical of men.[13] With these lexically conjured illusions of parity, vast differences in power between women and men and straights and gays were swept from consciousness.

Many of the men remained ambivalent about gay sexuality. In interviews, when I asked if men's work had changed their feelings about men, most of the men said yes, that men's work had helped them learn to trust men, to see men as good, and to desire closeness with them. In this context, several men said that this was hard for them, because they still had a lot of homophobia to overcome. To this, several men added that, even if they were intellectually accepting of gay men, they still were uneasy with "that lifestyle." Ambivalence was also evident when an editorialist in a mythopoetic publication used a disease metaphor to encourage straight men to accept and support gay men: "You will not become gay by hugging or touching a man."[14] Gay men were thus okay because straight men didn't have to worry about catching gayness from them.

The men did not see any connection between homophobia and sexism. Homophobia, such as the men cared about it, was a thing between men; sexism was something else entirely. But because the men weren't aware of a connection between homophobia and sexism, they unconsciously reproduced both sexism and homophobia whenever they defined heterosexuality as a key feature of masculinity. For example, during a discussion a man told a story about how his father had "shamed him" when he was 13 years old. He said:

> We were at the state fair and we stopped at the Bavarian food tent to get something to eat. The waitress who served us was wearing a low-cut top. When she leaned over to serve us her breasts almost popped out—and so did my eyes! My dad caught me looking and snapped at me, "Don't stare like that." It really hurt when he said that. I thought he should have been proud of me.

The other men showed sympathy by joking about the incident. One man said, "Maybe you should have said to your dad, 'Well, Dad, how *should* I stare?'" Several other men offered similar comments, all of which suggested that the father had erred in not affirming his son's burgeoning manhood. The implication was that being a man meant showing signs of heterosexual desire. Leering at a woman's body parts was not seen as a reproachable way to do this.

The mythopoetic men were conflicted about gender politics. It could hardly have been otherwise, considering the contradictions in which they were caught up. The men professed beliefs in justice and equality, yet wanted to identify themselves with the dominant social group. They wanted to escape the emotional strictures of traditional masculinity, yet didn't want to give up the privileges that derived from enacting it. They also wanted to overcome the homophobia that kept them apart from other men, yet were afraid to jeopardize their status as publicly identified heterosexuals, and thus acted in ways that reinforced homophobia. Some of the men saw, reflected on, and struggled with these dilemmas. Others wanted only to satisfy their therapeutic or spiritual needs, preferring to explore the depths of their psyches rather than the tangled gender politics implicit in their beliefs and practices.

POLITICS IN GENERAL

Though the men rarely talked at length about politics, their political beliefs were evident in small talk at gatherings, responses to comments made by mythopoetic teachers, articles in mythopoetic publications, and in interviews. Most of the men in the Local Group were solidly liberal. I heard men speak (if only briefly) in favor of government spending to create jobs and to provide housing, education, and health care for everyone—instead of wasting money on the military. I also heard men oppose the death penalty, racism, environmental destruction, and war. With one exception (see below), the most "conservative" statement I heard (that did not have to do with gender politics) amounted to a few words of appreciation for the freedoms guaranteed by the U.S. Constitution and Bill of Rights.

In general, the men were critical of government and corporate policies that put profits before the health of people and the planet. And while the men also generally favored the use of government to redress social inequities, they also believed in taking personal responsibility for doing what one could to solve social problems. To use two other 1990s benchmarks to locate the men: most of them were Clinton supporters and no big fans of Rush Limbaugh.

Many of the men were of the generation whose political consciousness was shaped by the civil rights, women's rights, anti-poverty, and anti-war movements of the 1960s. The men of this generation who became involved in the mythopoetic movement in the 1980s generally embraced the values espoused in the rhetoric of these earlier movements. Peace, justice, freedom, equality, respect for the earth, and the right to self-actualization were the features of a good society, as many of the men would have it. What the men believed these abstract values would look like if put into practice was another matter. One thing they did believe was that mythopoetic activity was consistent with, and even supportive of, these values, especially the right to self-actualization.

Because both the men and their critics saw mythopoetic men's work as therapeutic in purpose, and perhaps because of the contrast between the mythopoetic movement and the more public movements of the 1960s, the men were sometimes accused of being apolitical. This was not true. Such criticism mistakenly conflated the political lives of the men with their mythopoetic activities. In my observations, many of the men kept up on local, national, and international issues; most voted (or said they did); some joined in rallies for abortion rights and in protest of the Gulf War (I saw them); and some did volunteer community service work. Other studies of "awareness groups" have also found the apathetic, navel-gazing stereotype to be untrue. As Wendy Simonds noted in her study of women and self-help culture, "Though these groups may encourage self-involvement, it is not a self-involvement that necessarily encourages disinterest in everyone else."[15]

Some of the same kinds of tensions evident in the men's gender politics reappeared in their politics in general. Recognition of their own class privilege—if only in the sense of having the time and money to go to mythopoetic gatherings—clashed with a sense of justice that was offended by poverty. This same recognition of privilege was hard to reconcile with the men's rights notion that men were second-class citizens—a notion that was still seductive because it affirmed the men's feelings of powerlessness. Some of the men were also torn between their wishes to have no demands for political action put on them, and their belief that saving the environment, creating decent jobs, and making their communities better places to live would require such action undertaken collectively by people who cared about these matters.

To minimize these tensions the men tried to keep their politics separate from mythopoetic and other spiritual activities. One mythopoetic man put it plainly when he said (in response to a talk I gave at a conference on men and masculinity), "I don't go into the woods to be socially responsible. When I want to be socially responsible I march, write letters, and sign petitions."[16] As I've suggested, the problem with this convenient split was that it kept the men from thinking critically about the political aspects of mythopoetic beliefs and practices. As I argued in chapter 4, this separation of the spiritual and political had much to do with a desire to create and sustain communitas.

An example of this occurred on the night of January 17, 1991, when, near the outset of the Gulf War, Iraq bombed Tel Aviv. A Local Group meeting that night was supposed to be devoted to learning about guided imagery. But when news came of the bombing, the men agreed to put guided imagery aside and discuss their feelings about the war. During the discussion many of the men criticized what they saw as George Bush's eagerness for war and his macho posturing. Only one man, a newcomer that night, defended Bush. This man sat outside the tight circle into which the other men had pulled themselves. Despite his discordant views, he was urged several times to join the circle. Each time he refused. What struck me was that the men in the circle were more distressed by this man keeping his distance than by his views, which the men clearly found obnoxious. This was my first clue that communitas was more important to the men than politics.

I don't know what percentage of the men in the Local Group supported the Gulf War. Polls of the general public showed that about 90 percent of Americans supported the war, at least once "fighting" began. Among the mythopoetic men, support for the war was a minority position, it seemed. To the extent any men spoke in support of the war, their comments were on the order of "now that this is started, we need to pull together as a nation and try to finish it as quickly as possible." Several prominent mythopoetic teachers, most notably Robert Bly and Michael Meade, spoke against the war and participated in protest actions.[17] I heard that at gatherings in other parts of the country some men grumbled when Bly reviled Bush and the war. My guess is that this was not because the men disagreed with Bly, but because they feared that politics would spoil the emotional tone of the gathering.

The men's responses to the Gulf War revealed several things about their politics. They were, first of all, appalled by the prospect of thousands of U.S. soldiers, Iraqi soldiers, and Iraqi civilians being hurt in a war fought to serve the interests of powerful others, whether George Bush, Saddam Hussein, or faceless oil company stockholders. To the mythopoetic men this was one more example of people's control over their lives being wrested from them. And though the men may have valued the warrior archetype, some of the men argued that the Gulf War was not about men being *warriors* in defense of their families or communities, but about men being *soldiers*, mindlessly and heartlessly killing at a distance, at the behest of men—like Bush and Hussein—who were not kingly men but boys trying to prove their manhood.

This view of the Gulf War as a conflict between two men trying to out-macho each other was another reflection of the men's tendency to psychologize social problems. In this respect the men were at least consistent. It was not as if they had elaborate analyses of the institutional and systemic causes of war and then psychologized only gender-related social problems.[18] Whether the problem was international conflict, interracial conflict, or inter-gender conflict, the men tended to see its causes as rooted in some wounding of the psyche or sickness of the soul rather than in the routine operation of unjust social systems.

The men were not completely oblivious to social forces. Often they said that psyches were wounded, en masse, because "the culture" wasn't functioning properly. Because the culture didn't provide initiations to help young men feel secure in a valued kind of manhood, for example, most men grew up with a constant need to prove themselves, often in self-destructive ways. Exactly who was responsible for the culture going awry was not said. In their thinking the men were thus typical middle-class, American liberals. They knew something was wrong with a society that produced so much surplus misery. Yet they avoided blaming the ruling class for fear of being labeled shrill (and again because this would have put ruling-class *men* on the hotseat). Nor did they want to think that remedying social problems might require a radical overhaul of the economy that met their material needs quite well.

Even if ideas about class inequality were not central to the men's political thinking, the men were to some degree aware of their class privileges. They knew, for example, that many men could not afford to attend expensive

mythopoetic gatherings led by prominent teachers. Some of the men also recognized that education and time for reflection were important. As one man
said in an interview:

> There are few black men involved. Few minorities of any kind. Most of the men
> involved, including myself, are white, upper-middle class men who read, who
> are very literate and intelligent. And they've gone to college and maybe have
> M.A.'s or Ph.D.'s. That cuts out a lot of men. There wasn't one black man at
> that Bly day was there? No wait, there were two. That's right. But only two out
> of 120. And there's only one black man who ever comes to the drumming group
> meetings. You just don't find minorities and blue-collar types. I think that's
> hypocritical. I wish there was some way that could be rectified. But I don't know
> how to do that, because you have to have some awareness of a need for [men's
> work] before you can get involved. And many men who aren't educated, or who
> have to work 80 hours a week, don't know they need it. I think that recognition
> comes when you have the time and the education to understand, read, and ob-
> serve. It's a very leisure-class kind of thing.

Other men in the Local Group acknowledged the skewed class and race composition of the mythopoetic movement. This skewing was attributed partly to
the economic obstacles cited by the man quoted above. But it was also sometimes said that, if black men didn't want to come when they were invited, then
perhaps this meant that they just had to organize their own kind of gatherings
where they could "do their black-culture thing," as one man put it.

Another way that some of the men accounted for the class homogeneity of
mythopoetic gatherings was by noting that talking about feelings required
verbal skill, which, unfortunately, uneducated men often lacked. One man in
the Local Group also cited social distance as a problem. "In some ways it's easier
for me to talk to a middle-class black man than to a working-class white man,"
he said. While lip service was often paid to the desirability of class and race
diversity at gatherings, the men were stumped as to how to create it.[19] As one
man explained, "We've tried to reach out to other men but, for whatever reasons, they haven't wanted to come. So we just stopped feeling guilty about it.
We realized that middle-class white guys have a right to do their thing, too."

Because some of the men did not interact much outside their middle- or
upper-middle class circles, they developed a narrow view of the class structure
of U.S. society. This was evident on several occasions when men at gatherings
remarked on the diversity they saw among the men around them. These comments typically ignored racial homogeneity and confused occupation with social
class. For example, at a gathering where about 120 men were present, only
two of whom were black, a man spoke of how much he enjoyed the diversity

in his small discussion group: "My group is wonderful. It includes men from all walks of life. We've got a physician's assistant, an engineer, a therapist, a computer programmer, a restaurant owner, and a professor." These men were solidly middle class, and all white.

Sometimes the men came face to face with class inequality in their outside lives and then reported these experiences at gatherings. This too revealed something about the men's politics. At a gathering held not long after the Los Angeles uprising following the verdict in the Rodney King case, one man told this story:

> I needed two men to help me with a small landscaping job this week. So I went to the day labor station to see if I could find a couple guys. There were two black guys there ready to work, so I hired them. In my truck on the way to the site I asked them where they were from. One guy told me he'd left his wife and two kids in South Carolina to come here looking for work. The other guy said he'd like to have a family some day, but wasn't going to get married until he had a steady job. He said he'd been looking for three years and hadn't had any luck. He said if he didn't find anything here soon, he was going to try Boston. God, it just tore me up. First it made me think how lucky I am. But then I thought, What the fuck is wrong with this society that a man has to leave his wife and kids because he can't get a decent job?! What the fuck is going on?!!

Those last two sentences rose to the volume of a shout and were packed with outrage. The other men in the circle were stunned for a moment. Then several men belted out "Ho!" Then another man said, "What's going on *is* fucking insane. Anyone who can't understand the riots in L.A. after the cops who beat Rodney King were acquitted is out of touch with reality." This drew more loud Ho's. For a moment the men seemed ready to take up arms to fight racism.

As I saw it, this incident affirmed the sincerity of the men's beliefs in justice and equality. But it also showed the limits of their politics, for as soon as the impassioned moment had passed, another man said, "It's terrible that so many black boys are growing up without fathers. They're going to discover that they need to do this kind of [men's] work even more than we do. Unfortunately, they don't have the luxury of doing it." This statement threw guilt on the fire that had been sparked just a minute before. The next man said, "You're right, but I refuse to feel guilty about doing this kind of work, as if it's a luxury. I *need* to do it to maintain my sanity." Said another man, "I agree. I've discovered how important it is to be *centered* before I can respond to these kinds of injustices." After this exchange, the talk turned in a different direction.

The sentiments expressed on the occasion described above were not leading the men toward political action but back to themselves. The men still had
an ideology of individualism to use to deflect the moral obligations implicit in
the outraged demand to know what the fuck was going on. I saw this ideology used during another group meeting when a (white) man said it was in-
cumbent upon all good men to work to end racism. To this a man responded:
"I think if that's your issue you ought to work on it. I care about racism, too.
But I'd hate to think I'd have to feel guilty if I didn't work on it because it
wasn't my issue." Here an argument about the need for political struggle was
reduced to a matter of lifestyle choices. If working to end racism didn't reflect
a white man's true self, no one had a right to insist that he do it.

Many of the men nonetheless had strong communitarian impulses. Men's
work—with its ethics of community, stewardship, and kingly generosity—
revived some men's desires to be good citizens. Yet there remained a tension
between action guided by individualism and action guided by communi-
tarianism. Some of this tension and complexity were apparent in an account
given by a 42-year-old man who had been involved in a profeminist men's con-
sciousness-raising group in the early 70s, and who described himself as having been "pretty radical." In an interview I asked him if men's work had mod-
erated his political views, either with regard to women or in general. He said:

> No, I don't think so. I think some of my feelings about [women] have changed.
> I don't feel as responsible for women being oppressed. I mean, I don't feel *guilty*.
> You know, in the past there was always this burden of guilt. Just by being a white
> man you were guilty. You were part of the oppressing class—especially by being
> an educated white man. I mean, I was so ashamed of this that I put down my
> profession, grabbed a hammer, and [became a carpenter]. I couldn't change the
> color of my skin. I couldn't change my sex. But I didn't have to do what I was
> programmed to do. In retrospect I think this was in vain in a lot of ways. But it's
> probably the only way I could have gotten here. As for feminism, I do argue more
> with women about it. You know, when they come out with blanket indictments
> of men, and when they male bash. Now I try to stand up for what's good and
> true and noble in men, because a lot of that stuff no one is looking at nowadays.
> But no, I don't think [men's work] has changed my political views. If anything,
> it's pushed me back to where I was. I mean, I've sort of been a little too apoliti-
> cal, not caring as much politically as I used to. Now I think I'm coming back
> around to where I want to be more active. I feel I want to be more involved in
> the community. There are things to be addressed that no one is addressing.

This man was unusual in that he had a clearer view of class inequality than
most of the men. His response to the problem was typical, however, in being

an individual-level response. Rather than join a political organization, he tried to quit his social class.

One of the reasons the men, despite their progressive impulses, were generally not involved in political organizations was that they saw such organizations as places where men competed with each other for status and power. Many of the men felt that they had had enough of this kind of competition already, in school and the workplace, and wanted no more of it in any other setting. The men were also cynical about the leaders of political organizations, seeing them as often power hungry, self-serving, and eager to impose their views on others. Formal politics was thus shunned as another realm where men who enacted traditional masculinity exploited or devalued less aggressive men. This fear of collectivism and of political machinery was, as noted before, one of the reasons the men disliked calling mythopoetic men's work a movement.

Still, men's work was saturated with political values that the men expressed, reinforced, and sometimes challenged through their activities. Political values were evident in even the most spiritual parts of men's work. At a gathering devoted to "finding and nurturing the spirit to heal and grow," about two dozen men partook in a sweat lodge ceremony. During the final round in the lodge, the leader asked through the heat and darkness, "Brothers, what are you going to use the power of the spirit to do?" Men began calling out:

> To speak the truth!
> To be true to myself!
> To laugh!
> To love!
> To honor men!
> To honor women!
> To honor the inner woman!
> To be silly!
> To resist injustice!
> To refuse to live without beauty!
> To reclaim my life!

These statements reflected the liberal values that underlay the men's politics. Again, what was left out also told about the men. No one said he would use the power of the spirit to end male supremacy.

CHAPTER 8

A CRITICAL APPRECIATION

On a sunny Saturday in October of 1992, thirty-two men met at a rustic camp for an event called a "spirit gathering." The name of the event referred to both a gathering of men and their spirits, and a summoning of other spirits to aid self-discovery and healing. After a welcoming ritual that included 20 minutes of silent reflection, the men sat in a circle on the grass in the shade of tall oaks and pines. At the center of the circle was a pile of flat gray stones about two-feet high. On the stones were a candle, a tambourine, a water pitcher with stag-horn handles, a crow's feather, and a small, woven basket out of which hung thin strips of colored cloth. One of the day's leaders stood and said that we were now in sacred space.

To further mark our break from the mundane, two large bowls of water and two hand towels were passed around the circle. As the bowls and towels went around, each man washed and dried the hands of the man on his left—symbolizing a washing off of everyday concerns. After the hand washing, one of the leaders lit a stalk of sage and walked around the circle, wafting smoke over each man. Another leader then called upon the spirits of the elements—air, fire, rock, and water—to help us do the work we had gathered to do. The day's work included talk about wounds to the spirit, discussion of a fairy tale about four brothers on a quest for spiritual renewal, poetry reading, drumming, dancing, and a sweat lodge ceremony. The day ended in peaceful, warm fellow-feeling, with the men hugging and wishing each other safe journeys home.

On the same day, about 30 miles away, fifty thousand people gathered to partake in another kind of ritual. This one involved a metaphorical enactment of war by large men who battered and strove to dominate each other for close to three hours while scantily-clad women cheered them on and urged spectators to do likewise. At this event, people shouted and shrieked in excitement at the drama of masculine power being played out before them. A few enjoyed the feminine burlesque on the sidelines, though no one mistook this for the main action. Here, then, was a ritual that buttressed male supremacy by celebrating the grandeur of the male struggle for domination while keeping women in their place as decoration. That same Saturday on which thirty-two men held a spirit gathering, millions of other men across the country were enraptured by the violent, sexist ritual of football.

I draw this comparison to put the mythopoetic men and their work into perspective. Feminist critics of the men said that mythopoetic men's work reinforced patriarchy by celebrating regressive elements of traditional masculinity, by keeping the men from seeing how they were unfairly privileged as men in a male-supremacist society, and by keeping the men focused on their psychological troubles instead of moving them to work for social justice.[1] All this was true, to a degree, as the preceding chapters have shown. But the threat to women posed by mythopoetic men's work has been exaggerated, relative to other things. Misogynist rap lyrics, media stereotypes of feminists as angry man-haters, and, yes, football, are all likely to do greater harm.

My account of the men has stressed the ironies and contradictions in their beliefs and practices. It might thus seem that the men were so confused, or self-serving, as to deserve all the criticism they got. But again, to put the mythopoetic men in perspective, we should recognize that contradictions abound in the domain of gender politics. We can find self-styled feminist women who eagerly pursue status and power; gay men who resist heterosexism but still want the labor market advantages of being men; women who want easygoing men as partners but also want their partners to ambitiously seek higher incomes; feminist women who want their men friends to be gentle, empathic, and emotionally expressive, but want men who enact traditional masculinity for lovers; lesbians who have no feminist consciousness; and, of course, radical men of all colors who claim to want universal equality but resist challenges to their privileges as men. In dealing with gender issues, and in enacting gender, the mythopoetic men were hardly alone in being fraught with contradictions.

Some critics didn't take the mythopoetic men seriously enough to worry about contradictions in their beliefs and practices. Such critics dismissed the drumming, dancing, mask making, and so on as silly. In this view, the mythopoetic men threatened nothing but their dignity as they cavorted in the woods like overgrown boy scouts. The men and their activities were indeed fat targets for cynical journalists and academics. A deadpan description of men sobbing in each other's arms, or of men wearing masks, dancing wildly, or imitating animals was enough to make the men look like buffoons. The men knew they were vulnerable to this sort of mockery because it was hard for outsiders to see the sense in mythopoetic activity. As one man said in a conversation at a gathering, "If anyone had looked in on us drumming in the teepee last night, it would have seemed pretty ridiculous. But I suppose two people screwing would look ridiculous. On the other hand, if you tried it you might not think it was so bad." The same point can be made about any religious ceremony, sporting event, therapy session, or academic seminar. Any human activity can be made absurd and laughable by stripping away its frame of meaning.

It is true, however, that some of the men's activities had no clear frame of meaning. Some rituals, for example, were concocted on a whim, with no link to any deep or complex system of shared meanings. So, too, some of the chants used at gatherings meant nothing to the men. This is why even some long-term participants admitted that they were unsure of the meaning or purpose of certain mythopoetic activities. Nonetheless, one muddled or baffling activity did not obviate the value of everything else the men did; nor did the presence of a few men who were unserious about what was going on. In both regards there was diversity: some men worked hard to give meaning to, and take meaning from, as many mythopoetic activities as they could; others took it more lightly, simply enjoying the opportunities for fellowship afforded by mythopoetic gatherings. The same things would likely be true about any group engaged in similar attempts to create meaning and emotional communion.

Men gathering to enjoy the fellowship evoked by rituals was nothing new. The fact that this was an old practice associated with patriarchy made the mythopoetic men suspect. Critics thus saw the men as gathering to close ranks against the slings and arrows of feminist criticism, to put a blissful New Age face on masculinity, and thus to resist changing the patriarchal social order. My account of the men and their activities has shown, I hope, that matters were more complicated than this. Here I want to make the point, once more to put the men in perspective, that mythopoetic gatherings and rituals were not purely escapist or defensive, or hollow vehicles for male bonding.

Unlike members of nineteenth-century men's fraternal orders, the mytho-poetic men were not just playing games to distract themselves from the te-dium of work.[2] Many of the men were in fact looking for ways to face up to and deal with their troubles. Mythopoetic activities often brought these troubles painfully into the open rather than pushing them from mind. And while the men were indeed trying to repair the damage done to 'man' as a moral iden-tity, they were not trying to restore this identity to its former patriarchal glory. They wanted to create new options for themselves, new ways to be men and to feel good about it.

As for male bonding, what the men sought was not the easy camaraderie of the locker room, barroom, or golf course. They wanted deeper connections that arose out of honest sharing of feelings and mutual giving of support. And though any male bonding in a male-supremacist society bears watching, what the mythopoetic men were trying to do must be distinguished from male bond-ing through the objectification and abuse of women, through war-making or violent gaming, and through shared interests in exploiting others. Even con-sidering its potentially sexist consequences, mythopoetic activity deserves to be seen in a different light.

Not that this takes the men off the hook. As I have shown, if one cares to expose the roots of sexism, there is much about the men and their activities that warrants criticism. I have already put forth much of the criticism that I think is warranted, and am not trying here to level any final, devastating blows. My aim, rather, is to sum up, flesh out, and qualify my criticisms, and to bal-ance these against appreciation for what is good about mythopoetic men's work. I also want to urge its movement in a more progressive direction.

IDEOLOGICAL SHADOWS

Ideologies are belief systems that justify inequality, make it appear natural and immutable, keep people from seeing how they're exploited, or make the in-terests of a dominant group appear to be the interests of all. Jungian psychol-ogy served as an ideology for the mythopoetic men. It did so by offering ideas that helped the men feel better about themselves as members of a dominant group, by obscuring the link between masculinity and gender inequality, and by portraying gender as natural. This latter notion—that gender is an out-growth of innate differences between males and females—is a powerful piece of ideology in itself. The men embraced what I earlier called loose essential-ism, which held that males were inherently good because they naturally pos-sessed the noble qualities of deep masculinity. Yet this biological determinism had to stay "loose," leaving room for the influence of social life, so the men could feel good about being able, through their own efforts, to bring out the best in themselves as men.

Ideologies can also help manage contradictions. A nation that proclaims liberty and justice for all, yet denies those things to some people, needs ideological mortar to fill the gap between promise and reality. For the white male revolutionaries who founded the United States, this mortar was a belief that women and blacks, being nonproperty owners and thus "dependent classes," lacked the standing and wherewithal to warrant full participation as citizens of the republic. As my account has shown, the mythopoetic men had their own contradictions to manage. One of these was between their political awareness and their psychic needs.

On the one hand, they knew that men had more status and power than women, and that if existing gender arrangements cried out for anything, it was for justice for women. On the other hand, they found themselves trying to meet their psychic needs through involvement in a movement that largely ignored women in favor of giving intensive care to men. The men thus knew that mythopoetic activity could be construed as narcissistic and insensitive. Somehow they had to reconcile their politics, including their views of themselves as concerned with social justice, with their involvement in activities that focused on the distress of the privileged. A solution was drawn from a deep-running ideological current in American culture: individualism.

Therapeutic Individualism

American individualism is a hodgepodge of ideas. Its basic tenets are these: individuals freely choose their perspectives, values, attitudes, and paths through life; it is good and right for individuals to make such choices; the workings of society can be understood as arising from the choices made by individuals endowed with roughly equal amounts of information and other resources; social problems can be understood as the results of freely-made individual choices; and solving social problems is primarily a matter of convincing individuals to act more decently and responsibly.

The mythopoetic men obviously did not invent these ideas. Individualism has been evolving in American culture for over two centuries. How this came to be is another story.[3] Pertinent here is how the men used individualism to license their practices.

What the mythopoetic teachers and men did was to take the basic tenets of American individualism and create what I call therapeutic individualism. Again, they were not alone in this; similar ideas were developed in the self-help, recovery, and New Age spirituality movements, as well as in various schools of psychotherapy. This form of individualism holds that in every person there is a unique, true inner self which springs from a divine or mystical source; that every person has an inalienable, even sacred, right to express his or her true inner self; and that the true inner self—being untainted by the corruptions of culture—is a reliable intuitive guide to moral judgment. In distilled form, the propositions of therapeutic individualism can be put like so:

> Out of my true inner self comes feelings that are uniquely mine. I have a right to express these feelings, which make me who I am. No one has a right to tell me these feelings are bad or wrong. My feelings are my feelings, and I have both a right and an obligation to honor them. I should let no one shame me because of my feelings.

> I am responsible only for myself. I can't change other people. Just as I expect others to respect the feelings that come from my true inner self, I must grant their feelings the same respect. They have their feelings and I have mine.

> I don't need to change to please anyone else. My happiness depends on being in touch with and expressing what comes from my true inner self. When others insist that I behave like someone I'm not, it wounds me. If others don't like what comes from my true inner self, that is too bad.

> Knowledge of my true inner self comes from introspection. I find out what I am by looking deep inside. Others might help me find this place, but only I can see what is there and what I truly am. I must seek to define myself and not let others do this to or for me.

These ideas helped legitimate the mythopoetic movement and guide its practices. In light of therapeutic individualism it was okay for people to meet to tell personal stories, to go deep psyche-diving and report what they found, and to look for truth in their gut feelings—as long as this was what people chose to do as part of finding their paths through life. The problem, however, was that the mythopoetic men were not just people, they were men, and they were doing these things in a time when male bonding and the celebration of masculinity had been made morally problematic by feminism.

In this context therapeutic individualism helped the men make space for doing their version of men's work. It allowed the men to turn inward without feeling guilty about turning away from the harm done by men to women in the outer world. The rhetoric of therapeutic individualism let the men justify their activity and put off critics by saying, "As long as we're not hurting anyone, we have a right to attend to the compelling needs arising out of our true inner selves, even if we are middle-class white guys." Who indeed could object to a good-faith search for self-knowledge, self-acceptance, and authenticity?

The acceptability of this rhetoric rested on the premise that the men weren't hurting anyone. They certainly didn't *intend* to hurt anyone, so to them this claim seemed perfectly sound. Of course, individualism (as a more general ideology) also inclined the men to see their activity as harmless to women. It did so by emphasizing the intentions of individuals rather than the unintended consequences of collective action. Feminist critics emphasized the latter. It was thus hard for the men to understand this criticism. To take it seriously the men would have had to let down the shield provided by therapeutic individualism.

Recall the man who said (in chapter 7) that racism wasn't his issue, and he didn't want to be made to feel guilty for not working on it. This illustrates one of the dangers of therapeutic individualism: It can be used to justify whatever action or inaction makes people feel good.[4] While the mythopoetic men typically did not use therapeutic individualism to defend complacency in the face of racism, they did use it, when they felt threatened, to mitigate guilt and to avoid taking feminist criticism seriously. If critics attacked the men's use of stories rife with sexist imagery, or the men's celebration of masculinity, the men appealed to the genuineness of their feelings and the goodness of their intentions, and thus excused themselves from listening to any "shaming" criticism.

The problem with this defensive stance is that it leaves no opening for interrogating feelings, which can be genuine and pleasant, yet still grow out of adaptation to inequality and produce harmful results.[5] If dominating others makes men feel good about themselves, that feeling deserves uprooting, not honoring. Likewise, if whites find in their true inner selves no compelling desire to end racism, this lack of feeling is a problem. So, too, is the pride capitalists take in finding better ways to exploit workers. The point is that *feelings*, including numbness, shaped by life under conditions of inequality, must be as subject to criticism as the *ideas* that more obviously serve to legitimate inequality. Sometimes the head has to give the heart a hard time.

Therapeutic individualism was a problem too because it led the men to psychologize women's resistance to sexism. Recall the man (in chapter 7) who said that men needed to focus on their own troubles because men can't "pick up women's pain." The implication was that women's issues are about only psychic pain, and that there is nothing for men to do about these issues but empathize, though since this won't accomplish much, men might as well deal with their own issues. Therapeutic individualism thus deflected feminist demands for men to change more than their attitudes and intentions.[6] If men's true inner selves didn't dictate political action to change government or economic policies, or even to change their own behavior, then that was too bad. By the light of therapeutic individualism, it was unhealthy for men to suppress their true inner selves to meet the demands of women. Of course, in all fairness, as the mythopoetic men saw it they were not demanding that women change to please them, either.

Therapeutic individualism not only allowed the men to feel okay about focusing on themselves, it also discouraged them from adopting any discomfiting perspectives. According to therapeutic individualism, self-knowledge comes from introspection. Thus the men could look inside themselves without worrying about how what they found there might look to anyone else, especially feminist women. This approach limited what the men could learn about themselves as gendered beings, since self-knowledge comes from taking a variety of perspectives on one's self. We learn about ourselves, in other words, by imagining how we—as individuals and as members of groups— appear to people who think differently.[7] But this was not the kind of truly risky self-examination the men wanted to do in the safe spaces of their gatherings.

Because it opposed thinking about people in terms of the social categories to which they belonged, therapeutic individualism also exacerbated the false parity problem. Therapeutic individualism encouraged the men to think of women and men as "equally special individuals," rather than as members of groups that stood in unequal political and economic relations to each other. Focusing on individuals, and especially on feelings, obscured the advantages men enjoy as members of a dominant social group. This made it seem like everyone, man or woman, was struggling with life on an even footing and deserved exactly the same support, respect, and freedom from criticism.

Because they tended to think about gender troubles as psychological or interpersonal, it was hard for the men to see sexism and patriarchy as institutions that benefited men as a group relative to women as a group, even if some men didn't *feel* much benefit. This also made it hard for the men to see why radical feminist critiques of men and masculinity did not spare sensitive guys. Feminists were not pointing to psychological problems afflicting a few piggish men, but to institutional arrangements that benefited *most* men, and which nearly all men helped to reproduce, whether they realized it or not, by enacting almost any form of masculinity. The mythopoetic men, like most others, resented having any such insight forced on them. It was so much nicer to be appreciated as a kind and decent individual.

Therapeutic individualism also made the men resistant to seeing how the consequences of their joint actions could escape their intentions. Specifically, therapeutic individualism led the men to see their choice to "take care of themselves" through mythopoetic activity as a *personal* one, with no bad consequences for the relative status of women and men in the larger society. In contrast, the feminist critique, taking a more sociological view, said that mythopoetic activity helped to reproduce the gender categories—and the unequal valuation of these categories—that caused women and men distress in the first place. Therapeutic individualism kept this point from getting through.

Despite their implicit reliance on individualism to justify their inward turning, the men still valued community. Part of the mythopoetic philosophy was that for individuality (or individuation, in the Jungian sense) to flourish, there must be community to provide nurturance, tutoring in myth and poetry, and initiation rituals. Moreover, men were obligated to serve the community. An inward turning was thus said to be only *for a time*, because psychic healing was a prerequisite for men to act effectively on behalf of their communities.

Taking a larger view, the men can be seen not just as users of individualism but as its victims. While the men used individualism to deflect challenges to their activity, it was the practice of masculinist, American individualism that had left them isolated, distrustful of other men, and afraid to ask for help in coping. In these respects the mythopoetic men were not unusual. Like most American men they had learned that being a man meant being self-reliant, self-possessed, and self-directing. What many of the mythopoetic men also learned, by mid-life, was that striving to be men by developing these qualities—with no connection to a larger community or purpose—left them feeling not just individual, but alone, afraid, confused, and depressed.

Therapeutic individualism was good in that it encouraged the men to introspect, to pause from trudging forward in their ruts and ask how satisfied they were with their lives. Moreover, therapeutic individualism licensed the men to resist the routine squelching of their feelings and spirits. It gave them reason to believe it was good and right that they should live creative, zestful lives, and that attention to their inner states was a necessary part of this. In these ways therapeutic individualism reinforced a progressive impulse to resist the alienation induced by the bureaucratic machines and capitalist culture of which the men were a part.

Jungian Psychology and Essentialism

Jungian psychology was the theory behind the practice of mythopoetic activity. It provided an analysis of men's troubles and a prescription for dealing with them. While Jungian psychology was helpful in that it gave the men a language with which to talk about their inner lives, as a scheme for analyzing the gender troubles of women and men it was a dead end. The other problem with Jungian psychology was its essentialist premises—that is, its view of gender as a natural outgrowth of differences in the archetypal endowments of males and females. This kind of thinking is worse than a dead end. It is dangerous.

Essentialism, as I've said, takes strong and weak forms. In its strong form it discounts the role of culture and holds that biological differences cause males and females to think, feel, and act differently. Strong essentialism further implies that masculinity and femininity are not only inherited qualities, but that each person gets, by the luck of the genetic draw, a fixed amount of masculinity or femininity. This is like saying that gender and personality are inborn. A weaker form of essentialism says that males and females have innate propensities to think, feel, and act in somewhat different ways, but that culture also shapes gender and personality. It was the latter, loose form of essentialism that the mythopoetic men embraced.

At first glance, loose essentialism may seem harmless, perhaps because it is so familiar. But familiarity makes it neither correct nor benign. All essentialist thinking carries three principal dangers. One is that it keeps us from seeing how the social categories into which humans are placed—categories that largely determine how people are treated and what their life chances will be—are human creations. If the categories of race, ethnicity, gender, class, nationality, and so on are seen as corresponding to natural differences between human beings, then these categories and the social arrangements built on them will seem hard or impossible to change. This is precisely the perception that those who benefit from existing arrangements try to foster. If these arrangements produce injustice and suffering, elites (and their apologists) will admit that this is unfortunate, but it's just how nature/God has caused things to work out, and we'd be better off not tampering with its/his plan.

Essentialism also fosters divisiveness and ethnocentrism. Even if different social groups are not explicitly defined as superior and inferior to each other, to say that the people in these groups are naturally and essentially different implies that there are ineradicable obstacles to human understanding. It is as if to say, "We cannot fully know *them*, because they are, at the core of their being, different from *us*." There's also the tendency, if driven by nothing more than a desire for feelings of self-worth, to inflate one's own group, seeing it as the repository of all that is good in human nature. Even if this doesn't necessarily lead to denigration of other groups, chauvinism is still likely. If one believes in essential differences between groups of humans, it is tempting to believe that one's own group is better than the others in some way.

The third danger, as suggested above, is that essentialism lends itself to legitimating existing inequalities. This is clear in the case of essentialist thinking about gender in a male-supremacist society. In this case, differences in women's and men's thinking, feeling, and behavior that are caused by inequalities in power are attributed instead to biology. But it is not just innocuous differences that are accounted for this way; it is inequality itself. Why do men rule? Not because they have used violence or the threat of violence to coerce and intimidate women and to keep women trapped in exploitive relationships, but because males are naturally superior in the ways that count when it comes to succeeding in the struggle of life.

Such a notion deflects challenges to the morality of male supremacy by making nature or God responsible (presuming that nature and God do no wrong). Gender inequality is legitimated by implying that men's dominance is a natural result of their endowment with traits—aggressiveness, strength, competitiveness, rationality—conducive to ruling. While a few women, freaks of nature perhaps, possess these traits, the essential traits of normal women— meekness, servility, emotionality—simply make them less able to rule. Anyone who buys this line may conclude that male supremacy makes good sense and is more or less inevitable. At the same time, resistance to male supremacy may be seen as futile and foolish.

Claims about essential differences between groups of people have often been used to justify oppression and exploitation. European whites defined blacks as essentially less intelligent than whites and thus in need of whites to benevolently govern them and give them productive work to do, perhaps in a cotton field or diamond mine. Nazis defined Jews as essentially parasitic and conniving and thus deserving to be exterminated, lest they taint the purity of the Aryan gene pool. Examples of essentialist ideologies abound. The basic principle is the same: the supremacy of one group—the group that controls the symbolic and material resources necessary to propagate ideologies—finds it helpful to define as naturally inferior or evil the group it wishes to dominate or destroy.

It is not that the mythopoetic men embraced the worst kind of essentialist thinking, nor that they sought to justify male supremacy. They were, however, seduced by an idea that grew out of, resonated with, and helped to reproduce male supremacy. To claim that men's psychic energies were naturally manifested in the archetypal forms of king, warrior, and magician was to make at least an implicit claim—considering that king, warrior, and magician are powerful social roles (moreso than beggar, peasant, squire, or stable boy)— that men are well suited to dominate. And though contemporary Jungian psychology sees women as having the same basic psychic energies as men, women are still seen as archetypally challenged when it comes to ruling. No matter how firmly a woman's queen archetype might be constellated, she is no match for a king.

Jungian psychology contains essentialist premises, and so carries with it many of the dangers of essentialism. I have already discussed this in chapters 2 and 3. Here I want to comment on the limitations of Jungian psychology as a way to understand how society works, how women and men fit into it, and where gender troubles come from. The problem in these respects lies in the Jungian strategy of archetypalizing social roles. What this amounts to is labeling certain social roles either literally (e.g., king) or metaphorically (e.g., magician) and then supposing that these roles arise from archetypes naturally present in the human psyche. This strategy appears to offer an explanation for human behavior, but it is really an illusion created by the fallacy of reification.

Philosopher Kenneth Clatterbaugh refers to the Jungian style of thought as the "reification game." According to Clatterbaugh, Jungians "find a human behavior, label it, invent a psychic thing that is said to cause that behavior, name it or find a metaphor for it, and pretend [they] have an explanation."[8] In Jungian psychology the causal psychic thing is an archetype that supposedly gives form to psychic energy and, in turn, behavior. But since there is no independent evidence that archetypes exist—their existence being inferred from observed behaviors—a Jungian "explanation" of behavior is circular: patterned behavior is presumed to be caused by an invisible thing that is presumed to exist because a pattern of behavior is observed. We might as well say that people do what they do.

Applied to explaining the behavior of women and men, this kind of thinking gets us nowhere. If gender differences are observed, they are attributed to different archetypes; if similarities are observed, they are attributed to common archetypes; if traditional gender behaviors change, the changes are attributed to newly emergent archetypes. Whatever the behavior, whatever the situation, and with no regard for culture, power, or economics, a Jungian can expediently invoke an archetype to "explain" gendered behavior—no reference to any objectively documentable causes or influences is required. It should be obvious that this is less a matter of explaining anything than a matter of playing an entertaining language game.

As I noted previously, when Jungian psychology reifies culturally-specific social roles it sacralizes them as well. By linking these roles to transhistorical archetypes it endows them with an eternal, sacred quality, thus obscuring their nature as human creations. This truncates inquiry into how people create social roles to serve particular values and interests, often to the benefit of themselves and the expense of others. Because of this, a traditional Jungian approach to gender doesn't help us to see how "gender roles" have been shaped and enforced by men to benefit men at women's expense. Such an analysis is unlikely to occur to a Jungian.

This is not to say that one cannot be a Jungian and be concerned with gender equality, or that Jungian psychology cannot be adapted to serve feminist ends. The partial use of Jungian psychology doesn't preclude either possibility.[9] Even so, traditional Jungian thinking doesn't help to explain how people make culture, how culture and the organization of society shape the behavior of women and men, or how male supremacy is maintained through the use of

institutional power. And perhaps worse, because it offers the illusion of explanation, Jungian psychology may also, as Clatterbaugh says, block other,
more productive lines of thought.

Defenders of Jungian psychology might say that its proper use lies in gaining insight into the workings of the psyche, not in analyzing the workings of
whole societies. This can be granted, as it can be granted that Jungian psychology offers some people a useful language for describing their emotional
dynamics. This was true for many of the mythopoetic men. In Jungian-inspired
mythopoetic activity they found a language for talking about what was going
on inside them, and for creating emotional bonds with other men. That this
had therapeutic value for many of the men is undeniable.

But again, it's important to consider the consequences of how the men actually used Jungian psychology. They used it not only to explore their psyches,
but to find goodness in themselves as men. What Jungian psychology led them
to find was "goodness" in the form of inborn archetypes. These archetypes—
especially the noble and invigorating ones of the king, warrior, magician, and
wildman—constituted an innate masculinity of which the men could be proud.
Jungian psychology enabled this "discovery" (by definition, actually) of men's
archetypal goodness. It thus provided more than a set of concepts for exploring the psyche; it provided grounds for the men to celebrate their supposedly
distinct qualities and powers as men.

In doing these things the men were not only making themselves feel better.
They were reproducing gender in a society where gender is not simply a matter of differences between women and men, but a system for maintaining inequality. As I've said, the men didn't understand gender in these terms; nor
did they intend to reproduce inequality. Inasmuch as they were influenced by
individualism, the men could not see beyond their intentions; inasmuch as they
were bent on relieving their own psychic pain, they did not try to. The men
thus failed also to see that in celebrating a masculinity defined by archetypal
images of male power—images drawn from male-supremacist societies—they
were reproducing some of the same elements of traditional masculinity that
had hurt them, and which helped to sustain the oppression of women.

The mythopoetic men did not, however, celebrate everything that men did.
They knew that under the influence of "old models of masculinity" men often
behaved in ways that hurt others. Unfortunately, Jungian psychology provided
no tools for understanding how such behaviors grew out of the routine workings of political and economic systems and their supporting ideologies. If men
behaved badly, this was attributed to the dark side of an archetype rather than
to the position of men, or a class of men, in an economy that rewards selfish-
ness and greed. About all that a Jungian analysis could yield was a suggestion

that men who make wars, pollute the earth, and destroy the economic foundations of communities are out of touch with their nobler archetypes.

Though it obviously did not create capitalism or male supremacy, Jungian psychology did incorporate ideological presumptions of both. But these were presumptions in which the men were steeped long before they found the mythopoetic men's movement. Jungian psychology is thus best seen as a resonant, derivative ideology that helped the men deal with painful contradictions in their lives as nonelite men in a male-supremacist society. The danger of it was that it let the men feel better about being marginal members of a dominant social group, rather than challenging them to change the system that created unequal gender, class, and race groups.

What Jungian psychology did, in sum, was to give the men healing messages that helped them feel better about being members of a dominant social group, the morality of which had been impugned by critics of male supremacy. Jungian psychology, to put it another way, soothed the men's consciences and helped them repair their damaged identities. In these ways it served a therapeutic purpose, though one might say that in healing individual men it contributed to healing the wounds to patriarchy rightfully inflicted by feminism.

But the main ideological effect of Jungian psychology was to depoliticize gender. In a male-supremacist context this was of great benefit to men and great risk to women. Jungian psychology led the mythopoetic men to think of gender as being about nothing but complementary differences in modes of thinking, feeling, and acting. Differences in political and economic power between women and men, and the injustices and suffering caused by these inequalities, were thus obscured. Jungian psychology, ironically, kept the men from seeing and facing the shadow of patriarchy.

Sexist and Masculinist Imagery

The imagery in the fairy tales the men used was sexist in that women typically appeared in demeaning or subordinate roles—as prize princesses, cloying mothers, or ugly witches. Almost invariably the central figures in the stories were male, while in some there were no female characters at all. If the men had challenged the portrayals, or invisibility, of women in these stories; if the men had used the stories in a strictly Jungian manner, always treating female characters as representing impulses or archetypes instead of real women; if the men had been willing to see the political content of the stories rather than insisting that the stories were nonpolitical products of the psyche—if the men had approached the stories in these ways, critics could have rested easier.

The men saw the imagery in their fairy tales as helping *individuals* gain insight into their feelings and lives. What the men did not see was the cumulative social effect of thousands of men blithely imbibing imagery that subtly reinforced presumptions of male superiority. This cumulative effect was the reproduction of male supremacy, which is abetted by imagery that fosters complacency about it. Other images the men drew upon were *masculinist* in that they celebrated the link between masculinity and power. These too helped to reproduce male supremacy by making it appear to be a sensible outcome of evolution.

The two most popular pieces of masculinist imagery among the men were the warrior and the wildman. These images had special meanings. To the mythopoetic men, the wildman was not a rampaging rogue male, but an image of the unfettered, zestful, robust animal-like spirit found in everyone. This was the spirit, or psychic energy, that the men saw as having been quashed by bureaucracy and industrialism. The image of the wildman was a path to accessing this energy, per the notions of Jungian/archetypal psychology. So, too, with the warrior. This was an image to access the spirit that all humans could use to be assertive, resolute actors in service to a higher good. As noted earlier, the men distinguished the warrior, who retains his moral autonomy and nobly serves the community, from the soldier, who mindlessly serves whoever commands him.

Despite the supposed universality of these psychic energies, their associated imagery was undeniably gendered. The wildman was a wild *man*. And while warriors could be male or female, the weight of history gave a male body to this image as well. To critics, these images represented the worst aspects of masculinity, in particular the will to violence.[10] In their defense, the men said that these images simply inspired them to be more resolute, assertive, creative, and spontaneous—so they could be better husbands, fathers, citizens, and stewards of the earth. This was an honest reply, as far as it went. What the men were reticent to admit was that these images, and mythopoetic activity itself, would have been far less appealing without the connotative link to masculine power.

But this leaves the matter in abstract terms. It would be better to show how the men saw "warrior energy" being manifested in their lives based on what they had learned from mythopoetic activity. Here are four instances (from my field notes) where men spoke at gatherings about feeling and acting on their warrior energy:

> After the dancing some of the men hung around talking in the backyard. One man talked about an experience he'd had while moving. He said that he and his wife had been looking through the new house and thinking about where to put the furniture. He said, "We were going through the house and suddenly she

announces that the table will go here. I said, 'Wait a second. Time *out*! I'm not sure I *want* the table there. We need to figure something else out.' She thought about it and said okay." He beamed with pride as he told us this tale of his warrior spirit at work. Another man said, "I'll bet your wife liked it that you stood up to her."

One man said that he'd had a hard week because his wife was away and his kids had gotten rambunctious. He said that at one point he and his 11-year-old daughter had gotten into a shouting match, and that later she squirted him with something and that led to a water fight. For a while, he said, his daughter was getting the best of him. He said, "So, I thought to myself, what would a warrior do? So I got a bucket of water and snuck up on her and poured it over her head. She screamed she was drowning. I got her good but I felt a little bad about it." Another man said, "Yeah, eleven-year-old girls can be real monsters."

Six of us were sitting around the wood stove in the cabin talking about how old relationships can come back to haunt. During the conversation one man said, "I was talking on the phone this week to an old girlfriend. She asked me how I was doing, and I told her. But then before long she started up like she used to, telling me what I *should* be doing. I told her I didn't need her to tell me what I should be doing, and that if she couldn't find something else to talk about I'd hang up. She said, 'Well, you've really changed.' I was glad that she could see that. I think a lot of it has come from doing [men's work]."

After the drumming, men in the circle began to check in with their emotional weather reports. One man talked about an incident at work during the week that had upset him. He said that he had inadvertently slighted a co-worker by not giving her credit for an idea she came up with. He said, "She was pissed and said some nasty and unprofessional things about me on e-mail. But instead of responding right away and getting into a big fight about it, I took a day to cool off and then sent her a memo apologizing for hurting her feelings. But I also pointed out that I *had* given credit to the people who *originally* developed the idea. I felt better after this and she said she did, too. And it happened because I stood my ground and was *fierce*!" The other men gave him approving nods and Ho!'s.

These instances show how the men used their newfound warrior energies: not to be violent, but to be what most people would call mildly assertive. For these men it was a big deal to stand up to their wives, kids, lovers, and co-workers and not let themselves be pushed around. So the men were not reveling in warrior imagery to pump themselves up to be bullies, but to be more assertive in their relationships with others. This was all rather innocuous compared to the hyperbolic charges of barbarism leveled by some of the men's critics.

Still, this doesn't mean that the warrior and wildman imagery was benign. Use of this imagery might have led some men to think that problems in their lives could be solved simply by getting in touch with their inner warrior or wildman. In such cases, more assertiveness could lead to deeper trouble. Use of this imagery might also have led some men, who were already more assertive than they realized, to be abusive. Although I have no evidence of effects like these among men in the Local Group, one therapist told me he had worked elsewhere with several "post-mythopoetic" men who had experienced just such problems. There was, however, testimonial evidence (as shown above) that some men benefited from being inspired to be more assertive.

But again, the cumulative social effect was different. By celebrating warrior and wildman imagery the mythopoetic men helped keep alive ideas supportive of male supremacy. Celebrating king imagery did the same. Even the image of the magician—the master of esoteric skills and knowledge—linked manhood and masculinity to power.

The men treated these images not just as therapeutic tools for individuals, but as signifying essential qualities of men and masculinity. What these images signified was that a vital part of a man's nature was his capacity to act as forcibly as necessary to achieve his heart's desires. It was thus implied that when push came to shove, the strongest masculine energies would prevail—and ought to. The subtext leaking out of this celebration of masculine energies was, once again, that in a world naturally full of pushing and shoving, it was to be expected that men would be on top.

Quite reasonably the mythopoetic men wanted to be more confident and assertive. Warrior and wildman imagery helped inspire them to achieve these things. But this imagery was connotatively linked to the same ideological apparatus that had propped up male supremacy for ages. Men had dominated because they were naturally full of irrepressible passion, ferocity, and power— and now, for their own therapeutic purposes, the mythopoetic men wanted a piece of that psychic action. Unfortunately, by celebrating the imagery that did some of the ideological work of supporting male supremacy, the men inadvertently helped reproduce male supremacy themselves. Ruling-class men could argue, by the same logic the mythopoetic men used, that they were on top because they were the strongest warriors, wildest men, mightiest kings, and cleverest magicians of all.

Perhaps critics expected better of the mythopoetic men because the men had arrived at a rare awareness that gender could be a problem. Feminist critics hoped that this awareness would lead the men to see how existing gender arrangements were unjust and in need of radical change. The men, however, had different ideas. They wanted relief from the oppressive demands of traditional masculinity, yet they could not abandon the male-supremacist ideologies that made masculinity so valuable and attractive to them. But unlike advocates of so-called men's rights, the gentler and more sophisticated mytho-poetic men needed their ideology in disguise. This was what the imagery in the stories provided. These images encoded male supremacy, and allowed the men to celebrate the masculinity associated with it, while avoiding the stigma of being chauvinists.

DISTANT HEADS AND HEARTS

One time, in conversation with a small group of mythopoetic men, I said that I was bothered by the sloppiness of Bly's history and anthropology. Several of the men agreed that Bly's tendencies to simplify and exaggerate hurt the mythopoetic movement's credibility, especially among academics. But then another man, the staunchest Bly supporter in the group, said, "Well, you can't take Bly literally. He's not a historian or anthropologist. He's a poet. When he says stuff he's speaking poetic truth." In defending Bly against a critique by sociologist R. W. Connell, mythopoetic leader Shepherd Bliss said much the same:

> Sociology and poetry are distinct ways of knowing and communicating. Poets and sociologists tend to be different creatures. One uses metaphor, the other fact. R. W. Connell's article is a sociological critique of poet Robert Bly and the mythopoetic men's movement. . . . Does Bly "distort," as Connell claims, and engage in "excess"? Yes, he does. He is an artist; and artists do distort and en-gage in excess. Bly and other artists offer a certain kind of leadership, rather than the attention to details good sociologists have or the organizational acuity poli-ticians need. Bly would not make a good sociologist or politician. But he is a great poet.[11]

Many of the men knew that Bly's statements about history and about other cultures would not stand up to scrutiny, but pointing to Bly's factual errors didn't dent his credibility among the mythopoetic men.[12] Such errors didn't matter, as long as Bly was speaking "poetic truth."

One way to see the problem here is as a matter of men being misled by Bly's fanciful empirical claims. Another way to see the problem is as a matter of men refusing to think. The latter, rather than Bly's factual errors, was the more serious problem, because it meant that when it came to understanding the gender troubles of women and men, the mythopoetic men were less interested in facts and details than in poems. This was another example of what I've called strategic anti-intellectualism, or the self-serving disengagement of the mind. The examples I cited in chapter 6 included the men's disregard for inequalities in institutional power between women and men; their almost religious embrace of essentialism; their refusal to reflect on the implicit gender politics of mythopoetic activity; and their decontextualized citation of "facts about men" purportedly showing how men are oppressed. The men's inquiries into their gender troubles stopped, I said, at the point where those inquiries might induce guilt or bring other men in for blame.

While the men granted Bly wide artistic license, and there were matters of gender politics about which they didn't care to think too hard, they didn't want to think they were believing nonsense, either. The men were thus receptive to Bly's claim that gender is rooted in the DNA in every cell of the body, and to references by Hillman and Meade to unspecified studies that purportedly showed how men's ways of thinking, feeling, and acting are attributable to sex differences in testosterone levels and neurophysiology.[13] These claims had a scientific ring to them, giving the men's poetic truths a more credible scientific veneer. The boundary between the poetic and the literal was thus also blurred, as it was in the discussion of the Faithful John story recounted in chapter 6.

The problem was that the men did not want to think too critically about what they were being told. To do so would have been to stay in the head and stray too far from the heart. A retreat from analysis was helpful up to a point, in that it got the men to face their feelings and stop, at least briefly, hiding those feelings behind ideas. But it also left the men unable to connect their feelings to the real causes of trouble in their lives, or to see how the feelings of other groups of people, especially women, were affected by the different conditions of their lives.

Therapeutic individualism fostered this kind of psychological thinking about emotions, which supposedly issued from the unique, true inner selves of individuals. Men were thus advised not to spend too much time analyzing their feelings, lest this encourage the head to stifle the heart. The comments of a book reviewer, writing in a newsletter with a strong mythopoetic bent, illustrate this stance:

> [The editor of this collection of articles about men] wisely leaves it up to the reader to interpret the stories, and the emphasis here is clearly on experience, not analysis. Contributors from several different cultural and class systems are represented, including inner-city blacks, middle-class Americans, Native Americans, Chinese, and African. This kind of representation imparts the message that we all have our own personal experiences and pain, no matter where we are on the planet, and that dealing with them internally and effectively, is not best achieved by any one political, cultural or philosophical outlook.[14]

On the one hand, this is a nice allusion to the virtues of liberal multi-culturalism. It is hard to object to the recognition of others' pain and psychic struggles, or to the idea that such pain and struggles are best dealt with in ways suited to people's local circumstances. But what is missing here, typically, is any recognition of patterned differences in the kind or quantity of psychic pain experienced by people in these economically and politically unequal groups. Emphasizing experience, not analysis, also helped the white, middle-class mythopoetic men believe that their pain and psychic struggles were no less serious than those of young, unemployed black males in inner-city areas, Native Americans, people in less-developed countries, or women.

Despite the men's general concern for emotions, there were some emotions they didn't want to explore too deeply—for instance, women's anger. Strategic anti-intellectualism was evident in this case as well. Some men claimed to be baffled by women's angry responses to mythopoetic activity. Writing in the newsletter of the Local Group, a man said that an important issue for the men's movement to deal with was

> the jealousy, envy and hate as evidenced by the attacks on the Men's Movement. Robert Moore, Michael Meade and Robert Bly have experienced verbal attacks in open seminars or meetings from women who apparently had well rehearsed remarks. Where is all this anger coming from?[15]

While this question suggests concern for women's anger, the inquiry about this anger ends abruptly in puzzlement. What could women possibly be angry about? No suggestion followed that a good way to find out would be to listen to the substance of the "attacks," or to read and take seriously feminist criticism of mythopoetic activity. Nor was there any acknowledgment that if some women's criticisms seemed "well rehearsed," it was probably because they were drawing on decades of feminist writing about men and masculinity.

One thing the mythopoetic men did not see was that it was their refusal to listen seriously to criticism that angered their critics. The mythopoetic men claimed to be interested in understanding themselves as men, in dealing with their gender troubles as men, and in improving their relationships with women. Yet the men showed little interest in studying the work of feminist theorists, sociologists, profeminist men's studies scholars, or social critics who had written extensively on gender, masculinity, and men's lives—at least not if this work was the least bit critical of men or masculinity. In the parlance of therapeutic individualism, the men labeled such work "wounding" and avoided it.

To some feminists, the men's allergic reaction to criticism indicated that, no matter how real their pain, the men were frauds when they claimed to seek a kind of nonsexist manhood. If the mythopoetic men truly wanted more than balm for their aching egos, critics expected them to get their heads in gear and study the work of people who had been down these roads before. To ignore such work was seen as evidence of the men's narcissistic, short-term, and thus ultimately conservative orientation. In light of their education and all the information available to them, the men could not be forgiven as innocently mistaken believers that they were the first to discover something wrong with traditional masculinity.

Although not all mythopoetic men refused to consider feminist ideas, on the whole, mythopoetic theory and practice did not encourage men to give serious thought to analyses that were critical of men or masculinity.[16] For the most part, mythopoetic theory and practice discouraged men from thinking in any systematic way about how their feelings as middle-class, heterosexual, white men grew out of their social location in a white-supremacist, male-supremacist, heterosexist, capitalist society. It also thus discouraged the men from thinking about how the feelings of people in less privileged groups were linked to their social locations.

To point this out is not to say that the men would have, or should have, arrived at any particular conclusions if they had thought in these terms. It is to say that by not using their heads to interrogate their hearts in these ways, they failed to see how feelings are rooted in the cultural and economic conditions under which people live. This kind of analysis could have helped the men to see what sort of social change was necessary to solve the gender troubles that plagued them. Not taking time to develop an analysis of how the society as a whole operated, the men were left to attribute their troubles to "the culture" or to a mysterious, ungendered, powerful "they" who were said to want soft, pliable men. More careful thought might have given the men more sharply drawn targets at which to aim their warrior energy.

One sociological fact that the men did grasp was that social life bound men together emotionally. The men found that under the right conditions, they could achieve a deeper intimacy with each other than with women due to their similar experiences as men, the common criteria by which they judged themselves, and their shared social identity. Through mythopoetic activity the men found and used their commonalities to create the emotional connections they longed for, connections that traditional masculinity deprived them of. Even if gender itself caused some of the men's problems, it nonetheless enabled them to connect with each other in a way that gave at least temporary relief.

Having found a way to create emotional communion, the men didn't want to engage in social analysis that might have pushed them apart. The messages of mythopoetic philosophy—"stay with the feeling; don't kill it with an idea"—

and of therapeutic individualism— "no one can tell you your feelings are wrong or how you should feel"—repudiated the isolating and benumbing messages of traditional masculinity. Critics, it seemed to the men, wanted them to risk the fellowship and emotional vitality they'd found in mythopoetic activity for the sake of political correctness. The men refused, and when critics fired on the men, the men indeed stayed with their feelings—of hurt and anger, and of situational love for each other—rather than getting back into their heads and responding as intellectuals. Perhaps if masculinity itself had not created such distance between the men's heads and hearts in the first place, they would have known how to preserve what they'd created through mythopoetic activity while also dealing seriously with the contradictions inherent in their efforts to solve, as men, problems that came from being men.

THE REAL CAUSES OF TROUBLE IN MEN'S LIVES

Contrary to what Bly has said to thousands of mythopoetic men, the causes of grief in men are not mysterious.[17] The causes, if one traces them out, are usually the actions of other men. Sometimes this is a matter of injuries and insults inflicted as men compete with each other, more or less as equals. But more often it is a matter of the indignities, powerlessness, and despair men suffer as they are kept in place and used by other men with far greater economic and political power.

For reasons already discussed, the mythopoetic men were not interested in sociopolitical analyses that put any group of men, even ruling-class men, in the hotseat. While this aided communitas, it blocked insight into the real causes of trouble in most men's lives. It also kept the men from seeing how some of their beliefs and behaviors reproduced the conditions that caused them grief in the first place. In contrast, a sociological view of things can help expose the roots of the contradictions in which the mythopoetic men were caught. There's also no other way, I think, to see what needs to be changed to eliminate the surplus grief men suffer and so often spread to women.

Patriarchy as a Trap

One time in the Ritual Group (at the instruction of the day's ritual elder) each man pretended to be his own father. Instead of saying his own name during the welcoming ritual, each man pretended to be his own father and spoke, as father to son, to the next man in the circle. In speaking as our fathers, we were supposed to say whatever we wished our fathers had said to us. This was a revealing exercise. Most of the men in the group wanted to hear from their fathers a version of "I love you," or "I'm proud of you," or "You're okay, I see you as a success." Later in the day several men said that this was a powerful ritual for them, because it helped them to see how strongly they hungered for their fathers' blessing.

Another time a different group of men talked about what they wanted from other men. A word that kept coming up was "affirmation." When one man asked another what this meant, he said, "I'm not sure exactly. I guess I mean affirmation or validation of my feelings as a man. Or maybe affirmation that I can have the feelings I do and still be a man." The desire for affirmation was thus a desire not only to have the reality of one's feelings acknowledged, but also one's identity as a man—despite feelings of fear, vulnerability, compassion, or worse, affection for men. At this same meeting many of the men said that previously they had talked about their feelings only with women. They had been reluctant to do so with other men for fear that they would be rebuffed, lose an edge to a workplace competitor, or be perceived as gay.

The desire revealed on both of the above occasions (and numerous others) was to have other men affirm one's identity as a man. Of special importance was affirmation from *older* men: fathers, mentors, and nonspecific "elders." This is what the men got little of and seemed to long for most strongly. One mythopoetic teacher always struck a chord when he said that a man who wasn't being admired by an older man was being hurt.

This longing for the approval of older men is a product of patriarchy and a trap that keeps men recreating it—and hurting themselves in the process. The problem is that to impress older men, young men must distinguish themselves by outdoing others, usually at work. Competing for recognition makes it hard for young men to build intimate, trustful relationships with each other. This may intensify the need for recognition and approval from older, more powerful men, who remain the last audience with the authority to affirm one's worth as a man after everyone else has been left behind. Thus not only men's incomes but also their feelings of self-worth become dependent on the judgments of older men who can reward them for their abilities to get a job done, win, or make money. This is how patriarchy reaches into the hearts and minds of subordinate men and keeps them under control.

It is not that the mythopoetic men sought validation of their manhood from their bosses. Nor did they compete among themselves for blessings from their teachers or honorary elders at gatherings. But they did believe it was good and right for men to seek affirmation of their manhood from older men. They thus upheld an idea that is a cornerstone of patriarchy: *men are more important than women as judges of a man's worth.* Outside the container of a mythopoetic gathering, applied to the real world, this idea leads men to strive for approval in ways that cause them grief, because it fosters distrust and locks men into a game only a few can win.

The instilled and imposed need to compete with other men, and to be rewarded by the previous winners, is one of the real causes of trouble in men's lives. But this is not merely a psychological or cultural problem. Its roots are anchored in the structural arrangements that keep the power to affirm real manhood in the hands of men with power.

Capitalist Patriarchy and Masculinism

Patriarchy literally means "rule by the fathers." Sometimes this is romanticized as benevolent rule by the wise, elder men of a community. We face a rather different situation. Ours is a capitalist patriarchy run by "fathers" whose chief interests are in making profits. This kind of arrangement works smoothly only by keeping people out of touch with any archetypes that might make them intractable as workers, consumers, or citizens. In a society such as this, even men who are well-off materially may feel powerless and demoralized, especially if they find no purpose in the pursuit of money, status, and power.

Masculinism is the ideology that helps sustain capitalist patriarchy. This ideology holds that hierarchies in the authority, value, and worth of individuals and groups are legitimate; that competition (not excluding the use of violence) is a proper way to establish such hierarchies; and that doing and winning are more important than being and feeling. These beliefs serve capitalism well, for they encourage the subjugation of feelings, relationships, and spirituality to the pursuit of profit. Although often challenged, these beliefs still hold sway in American society. The capacity to dominate and control, through violence if necessary, is still widely admired (by women and men) and seen as a legitimate basis for hierarchy.

In a capitalist patriarchy only a few men get to be anything like the patriarchs of old. This is because, as Harry Brod points out, today "individual manhood is no longer the fundamental site of the exercise of male power."[18] Rather, male power is exercised through political and economic institutions. What this also means, again, is that few men (and even fewer women) ever obtain the positions that allow them to wield the enormous institutional power that can determine the fate of whole communities and the course of millions of lives. Because male power operates through institutions, it is understandable that most men feel powerless as individuals, despite the privileges that come from being male in a male-supremacist society. The inevitable concentration of wealth and power under capitalism tends also to make an empty promise of power through democratic politics.

In the version of capitalism we have inherited, a ruling-class of white men,

guided by an ideology of masculinism—which valorizes power, control, competition, and ruthless rationality—operates the levers of economic and political power in ways that devalue everything and everyone that is not dedicated
to profit making and not deferential to masculinism. These ruling-class men
are hard to identify, being faceless and nameless to most of us, but they do
exist in flesh and blood with real names and faces. Political scientists and political sociologists study them and their ways of exercising and preserving
power.[19] These men are not invisible, just distant and insulated.

The selfish actions of these powerful men, and the masculinist precepts on
which they operate, are prime sources of social problems in our society and
around the world. For nonelite men to deny this—in hopes of dodging any
splashed over criticism of men, in hopes of sharing in male privilege, or in hopes
of preserving feelings of brotherhood—is to ignore a real cause of trouble in
their lives. The mythopoetic men denied this because they wanted untroubled
brotherhood; because they were tired of being indicted along with men who
reaped much more benefit from capitalism and patriarchy; and because they
still desired male privileges.

Yet by rejecting traditional masculinity, the mythopoetic men rejected masculinism, at least in part. The capacity to dominate was not a principal feature
of the deep masculinity they sought for themselves. The value of the capacity
to *get things done* was indeed implied by celebration of king, warrior, and
magician imagery. But it was more worthy, in the mythopoetic view, to get
things done *with* and *for* others than to achieve glory for one's self. Mythopoetic
philosophy insisted on action tempered by empathy, love, care, and respect
for others. Heartless instrumentality in the pursuit of profit was antithetical
to the mythopoetic ethos and to the values of the men. The version of masculinity most valued by the men was thus subversive of the masculinism that
provided the ideological footings for capitalist patriarchy.

Lack of Community
A lack of community is another of the real causes of trouble in men's lives. This
problem is also linked to capitalism, in that relationships between people, and
between people and a place, will be smashed if profit-making demands it. The
dying communities of the so-called rust belt in the United States testify to this,
as do millions of defunct family farms. Countless other communities have been
destroyed to build factories, mines, power plants, waste dumps, and highways.
The men whose decisions produce these results act in accord with the imperatives of capitalism and with the blessings of masculinism, which allow them to
feel like real men—tough, nonsentimental, practical—who are willing to do
what they feel must be done, no matter how much it hurts other people.

Community is also undermined, less actively, because a capitalist economy makes it unnecessary. Most people can live quite well without being materially dependent on their family members, friends, and neighbors. In hunting-and-gathering and small-scale agrarian economies, people depend on each other, on a daily basis, to survive.

In industrial societies, most people leave home to earn money, as individuals, to buy what they need to maintain their separate households. To the extent that they live in a "community," it is one defined by arbitrary geographic and political boundaries, not relations of material interdependence. Neighbors are people who live nearby, not people with whom it is necessary to cooperate to survive, or with whom beliefs, history, and traditions are shared, or upon whom one can draw for moral support. Even if workplaces function for some people as small communities, such communities cannot serve the full range of human needs. Most people in industrial societies like the United States are thus bereft of the kind of community that could meet their needs for belonging, identity, and meaning. Clubs, fraternities, churches, and family networks are the substitutes.

The mythopoetic men knew that the lack of community was a problem. They believed that much of the distress men experienced came from not being connected to others emotionally or spiritually. For the mythopoetic men, the solution was to create temporary communities of men to do the things that communities used to do: affirm valued identities, attach purpose and meaning to those identities, and provide support based on mutual understanding of the experiences and emotions of those holding particular identities. But this was a palliative, not a cure. In the absence of real community, it was nearly impossible for the men to sustain the connections, feelings, and meanings they created at gatherings.

For example, at one gathering men were asked to make a list of actions they would try to take as kingly leaders. We were then to make a "contract" with another man to provide mutual help in carrying out these actions. I wrote in my field notes the problem that arose when the men in my clan tried to do this:

> We then shared our statements about what we wanted to do as leaders. One man said he wanted to be "willing to take risks." Another said he wanted to "empower others." Another said he wanted to "guide and influence others." I said I wanted to learn to "praise generously." But then when we were supposed to make contracts to help each other do these things, we sat looking at each other sheepishly. One man said what I think most of us were feeling: "I'm having trouble with this. This is too real. I was going to just close this notebook and put it away when I got home." About the best we could do, we agreed, was to remind each

other of our self-professed goals when we saw each other at monthly drumming
group meetings.

This exercise might have turned out differently had we not been men with
separate lives, overlapping only at mythopoetic gatherings. Without being
members of a real community, it was hard to imagine taking commitments
made at a gathering back into our daily lives. The separate and nonintersecting
ways in which we made our livings simply did not allow us to maintain our
temporary connections with enough force or frequency to change our behavior.

Some critics of the mythopoetic men decried their use of rituals taken from
Native American cultures. But it was precisely the lack of community in the
men's lives that made this borrowing necessary. Real communities depend on
rituals to affirm membership and values, to define and assign identities, to laud
valuable talents, to mark history, and to solidify relationships. Such rituals have
meaning because they are organic, that is, because they grow, in form and
purpose, out of the everyday struggles of the people who enact them. It is this
immediacy that keeps rituals alive. In industrial societies, which are held together by a complex division of labor rather than a common outlook, rituals
often become vestigial. The forms may survive long after their purpose and
vitality have evaporated.

Against this background, the mythopoetic men were trying to create rituals to give meaning to their life struggles. But unlike people in less-developed
societies, the mythopoetic men were not trying to meet basic needs for food,
clothing, and shelter. They were trying to meet needs for self-acceptance,
authenticity, emotional communion, and secure identity. It is no wonder, then,
that the men groped for rituals that had to do with affirming brotherhood,
celebrating masculine qualities, and bestowing the identity 'man'. But despite
their desire for initiation and the resurrection of rituals to attempt it, the men
were still left with no real community into which to initiate themselves or
anyone else.

Lack of Democracy and the Impossibility of Elderhood
Under these conditions it is hard for men, and even harder for women, to
become responsible elders. There are no real communities in which the skills
and wisdom of the middle-aged and older are valued. Nor are the communities in which most people in this society live democratically self-governed,
allowing the participation by all as equals. Rather, they are largely under the
indirect control of economic and political elites who try to maintain conditions conducive to profit-making. Moreover, the legal system that serves a
capitalist economy must value corporate property rights over any individual's

right to earn a decent living. As long as this is true, most people are vulnerable to having their security and dignity pulled from under them. If they get in touch with any unruly archetypes, they may become members of the reserve army of the unemployed.

But just as individual men can feel powerless because male power is exercised impersonally through institutions, it can also be hard to see any specific group of men as responsible for the political disempowerment, economic insecurity, enforced competition, and lack of community that create misery for so many men and women in our society. Indeed, these problems are historical products that have emerged from centuries of cooperation and conflict among millions of people. And so it is impossible to blame any one person or group, no matter how powerful, for what we have arrived at today. Yet in any capitalist society there is always a relatively tiny class that owns the means of production and uses its control over these resources to shape the law, politics, and culture to serve its interests. Such a system requires that democracy be limited; that economic insecurity be used to discipline workers; and that community and human relationships be subjugated to the imperatives of profit-making.

It was hard for the mythopoetic men to mount a critique of capitalism and patriarchy, because the ideology of individualism discouraged them from thinking about how men's troubles stemmed from inequalities and injustices built into the structure of society. As a result, their analyses of the causes of trouble in men's lives never got to the root of things. While sometimes blaming industrialism for separating fathers and sons, or "the culture" for not providing initiations, they did not try to see through these illusory culprits to the powerful men and social forces at work behind them. Lacking a good structural analysis of their troubles, the men were thus also susceptible to notions that women, feminism, sex roles, and lack of initiation caused their problems.

Because the men did not see their problems as structural in origin, they did not see how some of their beliefs and practices helped to reproduce the political and economic structures that hurt them in the first place. In seeking the blessings of older men, the mythopoetic men reinforced the ideology of male superiority that supported the patriarchal system within which competition for the approval of older, more powerful men left them feeling chronically insecure. The men also did not give up masculinism entirely. They celebrated men's alleged special powers in a way that implicitly vaunted the superiority of men when it came to running the world. In so doing they reinforced a basic premise of patriarchy: that powerful men—the best kings, warriors, and magicians—are entitled to dominate others.[20]

One thing men must do is recognize that women and feminism are not the real causes of trouble in their lives. In fact, feminism points more clearly and honestly to the causes of trouble in men's lives than the mythopoetic men gave it credit for. Twenty years ago feminists exhorted men of conscience to get their warrior and lover energies on line and pointed in the right directions. As Carol Hanisch put it:

> Women want men to be bold—boldly honest, aggressive in their human pursuits. Boldly passionate, sexual and sensual. And women want this for themselves. It's time men became boldly radical. Daring to go to the root of their own exploitation and seeing that it is not women or "sex roles" or "society" causing their unhappiness, but capitalists and capitalism. It's time men dare to name and fight these, their real exploiters.[21]

Sadly, and self-defeatingly, the mythopoetic men took the easy way out, discrediting radical feminism because it felt like an unfair personal attack, because it challenged their middle-class comforts, and because it would have cost them the approval of some older, more powerful men. If they had steeled themselves to listen to the whole message, if they had let the big picture come into focus, they might have found in socialist feminism the key they were mistakenly looking for under the pillows of their mothers.

PROGRESSIVE POTENTIAL

Looking at the men sociologically, as a group, and personally, as individuals, I can't blame them for not being radical social critics or activists. For half of their lives these men did what men were supposed to do: kept their heads together well enough to earn a living and support their families. To their further credit, most of the men eschewed the selfish pursuit of power and status. For the most part, they were ordinary middle-class men of liberal politics trying to be responsible earners, husbands, fathers, and citizens. For the structural reasons I've pointed to, they came to experience crises of meaning having to do with their identities as men, and spiritual crises having to do with their isolation from other men. Mythopoetic activity seemed like an effective, fun, and harmless way to deal with these problems. It seems unfair to expect these men to have critically deconstructed the gender apparatus of society and become the vanguard of the revolution.

According to Bly and many of the mythopoetic men, prescribing a radical overhaul of society as a way to uproot the causes of men's troubles is unrealistic.[22] Of course, what is realistic is a matter of what people are willing to try to do. Not long ago, tearing down the Berlin Wall or abolishing apartheid in South Africa would have seemed unrealistic. But what people have wrought, they can change.

The mythopoetic men may have suffered psychic pain, but their material needs were by and large well met. So it is not surprising that they did not want to challenge the system that provided them a comfortable place from which to launch their spiritual journeys. But as I've said, the mythopoetic movement is a palliative, not a cure for what ails men. To attack the causes of men's troubles, rather than just relieve their symptoms, would indeed be a risky and daunting project. But this strikes me as more realistic, in the long run, than resurrecting ancient fairy tales and myths to help individual men feel better about being members of the dominant social group.

Earlier I said that because of a lack of community it was hard for the men to help each other make big changes in their lives. This needs to be qualified. Mythopoetic activity did change some men's lives. It got them out of their isolation and into fellowship with other men. It raised their awareness of themselves as emotional beings. It helped them find self-acceptance. It brought on bursts of creativity. Some men were even inspired to quit their corporate jobs (four men in the Local Group did so). Mythopoetic activity did change some men's lives by opening their eyes to what they had missed by living in the iron cage of masculinist, bureaucratic rationality.

One place they found some of what they'd missed was in small (four- to eight-member) support groups that met on a weekly or biweekly basis. About ten of these support groups were affiliated with the Local Group. Although these groups were not explicitly mythopoetic, because many of the men in the support groups were also involved in mythopoetic activities (or read the same literature), there was overlap in beliefs and practices. Some of the men in the Local Group even thought of the support groups as the "backbone of men's work." In these groups the men did things that were unusual for men in our society: they talked about their feelings, gave each other near to unconditional support, and jointly sought insights into their emotions. For men to meet regularly in such groups *was* a significant change in their lives.

In these support groups, as in the larger gatherings, the men overcame some of their isolation and learned how to deal with their feelings in nondestructive ways. The fact that men were taking their own feelings seriously represented a potentially progressive break from traditional masculinity. As Victor Seidler argues, traditional masculinity insists on men repressing their feelings—this being part of what allows men to dominate others—for if men don't appreciate their own feelings, they are unlikely to appreciate the pain and sadness of the others whom they oppress.[23] I thus see progressive potential in the men learning to take their own feelings, and the feelings of other men, more seriously. This could even redound to the benefit of women.

Some evidence for this appears in a statement one man made in an interview. I asked him if men's work had changed his feelings about other men. He said:

> I think I trust other men a lot more than I used to. Clearly my friendship system has shifted a good bit. Up til the last five or six years I probably had more female friends than male friends. My co-workers were mostly female and my friendships were more with women. That's not true now. I'm not sure how else my feelings toward men have changed. One thing I'm sure of is that I know men better. I know me better. But again, in terms of other men, I think I know the range of other men's experiences better. Listening to friends and acquaintances sort of talk about their experiences somehow has broadened my appreciation for men—appreciation for the depth of men's feelings and men's experiences of life in a way that I just didn't have any notion of. I'd pretty well bought the feminist notion that men were basically walking testosterone bombs. But I found that that was simply not true. I think all this has helped me to appreciate women a lot more, too.

I asked him how the changes in his feelings about other men had helped him "appreciate women a lot more." He went on:

> I just see that people are more complicated. And I think that I've learned this by getting closer to men, by listening and really hearing what they're saying, and by feeling what I'm feeling when they're speaking. I think this has somehow helped me to really listen to what women are saying rather than tuning off and thinking that I understand them when I really don't have any notion of what is going on with them. So I think it's like I got into seeing the more complicated side of myself and of humans through men. It might have happened with women had I been ready to do that. But it didn't.

This sort of testimony is not evidence of behavioral change. But it is an account that suggests a change in consciousness. This man, and I think quite a few others, learned through men's work to appreciate the depth and complexity of their own emotions, as well as the emotions of other men. If this appreciation generalizes, then these men may indeed lose some of the capacity for domination instilled in them by traditional masculinity and the repression of emotion it teaches. Just how much *weight* men will give to others' feelings relative to their own, especially in times of conflict is of course another matter. Even so, just to recognize the existence and importance of one's own and others' emotions could open the door to farther reaching changes.

The mythopoetic men also deplored the absentee fathering that fits so well with traditional masculinity's discounting of emotion and nurturing. Many of the men knew from their own lives the pain and sadness caused by absent or abusive fathers. The men were thus determined to be more loving and involved fathers themselves. At least they often expressed desires to this effect. If they can live this out—and take equal responsibility for the dirty as well as the fun parts of child rearing—it would mark a significant change in men's behavior, a change that would benefit women.

But here again the limits of personal change become apparent. Without changing the economic system that gives labor market advantages to men, there will remain strong incentives for men to put more energy into their jobs and careers than into child rearing. To be the fully-involved fathers that the mythopoetic men claimed to want to be will require both economic sacrifice and, in the longer run, political action to change the economic policies that make it so costly for men to give priority to their partners and children.

Also necessary is a radical change in the dominant culture of masculinity, such that men no longer feel compelled to stake their self-worth on earnings, job prestige, and power in the workplace. The mythopoetic men recognized that these measures of a man's worth caused problems. They also tried to re-sist this culture of masculinity by valuing men's abilities to imagine, to love, to nurture, to feel, and to respond aesthetically and spiritually to the large and small wonders of life. In this way, too, the mythopoetic movement marked a progressive break from the soulless culture of capitalism. Perhaps the mytho-poetic critique of traditional masculinity will inspire more men to question what they have taken to be the goals of a worthy life and to reject the poisonous criteria of self-worth that a capitalist culture instills in us.

Even therapeutic individualism can help if it forces men to face the distress arising from contradictions between their actions and ideals. One mythopoetic teacher who was much respected by the men in the Local Group always ex-horted them to "walk their talk"—to put their values and ideals into practice. The men wanted to do this and expressed admiration for men whose lives exemplified their values.[24] Therapeutic individualism was part of the motiva-tion for this. Even if it didn't lead to political action, therapeutic individual-ism at least made the men feel responsible for making efforts toward personal change in the direction of their best values. A philosophy that encouraged nothing but intellectualizing would not yield even this benefit.

Though it in part reproduced patriarchy and did not challenge capitalism, mythopoetic men's work was still a form of resistance to domination. It was not just therapeutic identity repair, group lamentation, or retrograde male bonding. Their class and race privileges notwithstanding, the mythopoetic men were responding to the powerlessness, demoralization, and isolation caused by political and economic structures that served the interests of far more powerful men. Their goal of trying to awaken in men the human sensibilities that had been dulled by masculinism and by an exploitive economy was subversive. Unfortunately, the men's methods did not attack the roots of their problems. To do so would have required more than taking small risks in safe places. It would have required taking big risks in attacking the race, class, and gender hierarchies that damage us all.

The mythopoetic men do have something to teach activists and intellectuals: the importance of emotion. Cold analysis, no matter how on target, logically compelling, or factually supported, will motivate few people to do anything. Even to be *received*, social analysis has to be linked to what people are feeling.[25] Bly and the other mythopoetic teachers knew this and developed a compelling analysis of men's troubles. In contrast, few feminist or profeminist analysts acknowledged that many men felt frustrated and beleaguered in their struggles to be good men. Perhaps if these feelings had been taken more seriously, profeminist analyses of men's troubles would have had more effect.

The problem that remains, however, is how to take men's feelings into account, and even to respect those feelings, without treating them as sacrosanct. Men's feelings must be both acknowledged and interrogated. The latter runs counter to therapeutic individualism and is not likely to be comforting. Perhaps the Jungian injunction to face one's grief and shadow side is of value here. If men can learn to do this as part of mounting a sociological, as well as a mythological, analysis of their lives, they will not be deterred from seeking and seeing the truth about their own involvement in reproducing male supremacy and its damaging injustices.

APPRECIATION AND HOPE

The mythopoetic men did not want to engage in sociopolitical analysis, lest this impede their pursuit of self-acceptance, self-knowledge, emotional authenticity, and communitas. The men did not want to argue about whose account of social reality was correct. They wanted to feel better about themselves as men, to learn more about the feelings and psychic energies that churned within them, to live richer and more complex emotional lives, and to experience the rare pleasure and mysterious power of communitas. They also wanted untroubled brotherhood in which both their feelings and their identities as men were validated by other men. Mythopoetic men's work gave them all this, and in so doing helped heal some of the damage caused by masculinism, capitalist patriarchy, and misunderstood feminist criticism.

Though the men had difficulty acknowledging it, it was feminism that provided the intellectual basis and political impetus for the critique of traditional masculinity out of which the mythopoetic movement grew. What the men and their teachers nonetheless deserved credit for was devising a way for men to explore and express more of the emotions that made them human. Mythopoetic men's work also helped the men see how emotions could be the basis for connections to men they might otherwise have feared, mistrusted, or competed with. The men thus discovered that they didn't have to live out traditional masculinity, nor feel ashamed for refusing to do so. Instead they learned that they could cooperate with other men to create at least temporary communities where stoicism, dominance, and heterosexual prowess were not the measures of manhood. In this respect mythopoetic men's work constituted a progressive challenge to traditional masculinity.

Yet the progressive potential of mythopoetic men's work was stunted because it encouraged the men to think in psychological or, at best, cultural terms about gender and gender inequality. Mythopoetic men's work opened men to seeing things in themselves and helped them make connections with each other, but it did not illuminate connections between themselves, their practices, and society. One result was that the mythopoetic men did not see that in a male-supremacist society there could be no innocent celebration of masculinity. In such a context the celebration of manhood and masculinity implicitly reaffirmed the lesser value of women, whether this was intended or not. Nor did the therapeutic individualism that informed the men's outlook on their troubles help them see that many of their troubles came from being nonelite men trapped in the hierarchical structures of patriarchy and capitalism.

My own politics and biography leave me ambivalent about the mythopoetic men. Like many of them, I came from a working-class family, felt distant for many years from my father, grew up with both awe and distaste for traditional masculinity, and gravitated toward an upper middle-class occupation where a gentler form of masculinity was acceptable.[26] I also found that my ingrained attachment to traditional masculinity, albeit under a softer veneer, still made it hard to deal with emotions, to maintain intimate relationships with women, and to build close, noncompetitive friendships with other men. And in universities in the 1970s and 1980s I encountered all of the harshest criticism of men and masculinity that had tarnished 'man' as a moral identity for the mythopoetic men. So in many ways I could empathize with them, even if I disagreed with their gender politics and was irked by their anti-intellectualism.

I think this common background also helped me to appreciate and benefit from what the men were trying to do. As did many of them, I found the poetry and stories evocative and helpful for reflecting on my own feelings and on how those feelings were shaped by my experiences as a man. I found the camaraderie and accepting atmosphere of gatherings to be a relief from the competitive strains and superficial cordiality of academia. I found comfort and connection in hearing other men talk about relationships with their fathers; was moved by their expressions of sadness, grief, and joy; enjoyed the playfulness of drumming and dancing; and found inspiration in the willingness of many of the men to nurture and show affection for each other. I also learned a great deal about mentoring, friendship, and the power of ritual. These things that I gained—beyond a sociological analysis of what the men were doing and why—affirmed for me the value of mythopoetic men's work, or something like it.

Mythopoetic men's work helped me to see that in addition to democracy and justice, people need community and ritual. Communities that are good for people must create opportunities for emotional connection and support, for telling stories and sharing cultural wisdom, and for affirming the identities that give people a sense of security, worth, and place. Rituals are also needed to evoke the powerful emotions that help people bring forth parts of themselves they might otherwise never find. Reaffirming people's commitments to do the hard work that community entails is also best done with ritual. I do not mean that any ritual is better than none, for the moral content of a ritual makes all the difference. My point is that I have come to appreciate the need for organic rituals to keep communities healthy, growing, and nurturing of human potential.

Despite my criticisms of their beliefs and practices, my feelings toward the men in the Local Group remain positive. These men were gentle and decent, acting on good intentions, and trying to cope with life without hurting anyone. Considering the rarity of communitas in their lives, and knowing the joy they found at gatherings, I am reluctant to urge upon them a shift toward more sociopolitical analysis, because if this is not handled well it could ruin what they've achieved. Yet I also believe that the egregious inequalities that exist in the world make this shift a moral obligation. My hope is that the shift can be made while preserving the good things the mythopoetic men have learned to do.

There were times at gatherings when I felt that the men were creating a secular spiritual community that could be a model for a better world, if only it had been more inclusive. So I find it encouraging to see that the mythopoetic men are holding more multi-racial and mixed-gender gatherings. Even if the men succeed in only temporarily creating connections across race and gender lines, this is still a step in the right direction. Such connections, I believe, must be the basis for creating the kinds of communities into which we all might want to be initiated.

As a sociologist, I see a need for more. One thing we must do is abandon the false and harmful idea that any set of human virtues, talents, or powers is the special province of either sex. We must stop invoking genetics and physiology to rationalize differences in thinking, feeling, and behavior that arise out of inequalities in the status and power of women and men. Thinking about gender in these ways breeds chauvinism, fosters misunderstanding, perpetuates inequality, and keeps us from recognizing the full range of human capacities in everyone. A further danger of this kind of thinking is that under conditions of inequality it is likely that the dominant group—in this case men—will claim the best human qualities, or at least those most conducive to ruling, for its own members. In this respect the mythopoetic movement remains part of the problem, not the solution.

And so I challenge the mythopoetic men to think more critically about the dangers of archetypalizing social roles, embracing essentialism, celebrating masculinity, using stories that are full of sexist imagery, engaging in activities that encourage androcentrism, and insulating feelings from analysis. I challenge them, too, to pursue a serious study of institutional power and of the ways in which capitalist patriarchy, shaped by masculinism, affects their lives. Without more study and critical thinking about these matters, the mythopoetic men will never find a path to the self-actualization, real community, and social justice they claim to want. Walking that path will also require more direct challenges to the structural inequalities and injustices that are the root causes of trouble in men's and women's lives.

What matters now is what ordinary men do with their feelings of grief, of outrage, of affection for each other, and of longing for lives richer in meaning. My hope is that men will channel these feelings toward riskier social action and farther-reaching change. I wish this not just for the mythopoetic men, whose hearts lean in the right direction, but for everyone who cares about justice and equality. Part of this process is reflecting on the contradictions between what we'd like to see the world become and how we live in it today. Although we can never escape such contradictions once and for all, a sociological analysis can help us see where we're stuck. It can also help us see how to produce more of the consequences we desire and fewer of those we don't. But this is only a first step. The journey that follows must be a continuing collaboration of head, heart, and soul—and many hands.

NOTES

CHAPTER I   AN UNUSUAL MOVEMENT OF ORDINARY MEN

1. According to Chris Harding, editor of *Wingspan: Journal of the Male Spirit* (a mythopoetic periodical) and of *Wingspan: Inside the Men's Movement* (New York: St. Martin's, 1992), the 100,000 figure was often cited but was not based on any systematic study. The figure seems plausible, however, considering the hundreds of men's events, most with some mythopoetic content, held annually across the country from the mid-1980s onward.

2. In *Women Who Run With the Wolves: Myths and Stories of the Wild Woman Archetype* (New York: Ballantine, 1992) Jungian analyst Clarissa Pinkola Estes gave women much the same kind of inspiring mythological fare that Bly gave men in *Iron John*. Estes's book was also a bestseller, attesting to the popularity of a Jungian approach to gender, and to the strength of women's desires to resist the bureaucratization of the self. The women's spirituality movement, which is older than the mythopoetic, also ran on a parallel ideological track. As one illustration, the winter/spring 1986 issue of *Woman of Power: A Magazine of Feminism, Spirituality, and Politics* treats the theme of "woman as warrior" in a way that is hard to distinguish from the mythopoetic. For a sociological view of a women's spirituality group and illustration of other parallels, see Cynthia Eller, *Living in the Lap of the Goddess* (New York: Crossroad, 1993).

3. Shepherd Bliss, "Beyond Machismo: The New Men's Movement," *Yoga Journal* (Nov.-Dec. 1986): 36–40, 56–58. The term *mythopoetic* (or *mythopoeic*) has a longer history in literary criticism, referring to the writing of myths and fantasies. Literally the term means myth-making.

4. Nearly every introductory textbook in the sociology or anthropology of gender reviews the evidence for cross-cultural and historical variation in forms of gender enactment. Beyond the basics, see P. R. Sanday and R. G. Goodenough (eds.), *Beyond the Second Sex: New Directions in the Anthropology of Gender* (Philadelphia: University of Pennsylvania Press, 1990). Sources especially pertinent to men are David Gilmore's *Manhood in the Making* (New Haven, Conn.: Yale University Press, 1991) and Gilbert Herdt's *The Sambia: Ritual and Gender in New Guinea* (New York: Holt, Rinehart and Winston, 1987).

5. To say that gender arises out of social *experience* is not to say that it is a result of deliberate instruction. Children are of course taught how to behave as members the sex category to which they've been assigned based on anatomy. But they also learn from observation and experience, without direct instruction. What's more, much of this kind of learning occurs beneath conscious awareness; that is, kids learn about gender from what they see and from what happens to them, without realizing that they're learning how to be girls and boys, women and men. Adults don't always realize that they're teaching gender, either. The process is similar to language acquisition, which, like gender, seems to just happen. But without the instruction, constant subtle reinforcement, and experiences that are part of growing up in a gendered society, gender—as we know it—would not appear at all.

6. After decades of research showing how women in the United States and most of the world are disadvantaged relative to men, it is wearisome to think that some folks perversely deny that gender inequality exists. For a quick review of the facts, see pp. 1–20 in R. W. Connell's *Gender and Power* (Stanford, Calif.: Stanford University Press, 1987). For more details pertinent to women in the United States, see *The American Woman, 1994–95: Where We Stand* (Washington, D.C.: Women's Research and Education Institute [1700 18th Street, NW, Suite 400, 20009], 1994). For an analysis of how advocates of "men's rights" use tortured logic to turn the reality of male supremacy on its head, see Kenneth Clatterbaugh, *Contemporary Perspectives on Masculinity* (Boulder, Colo: Westview, 1990), pp. 61–83.

7. Robert Connell's term *hegemonic masculinity* comes closest to what I mean by traditional masculinity. To enact hegemonic masculinity a man must create the impression of being in control of himself and his surroundings, of being unshakeably self-confident based on supreme competence, and of being unfailingly rational in the face of tough problems. Creating such an impression is aided by a white skin, an Anglo surname, the right kind of body type, an adoring wife and children, and wealth. While this version of masculinity overlaps with traditional masculinity, the two are not the same. Hegemonic masculinity is the masculinity of elite WASP males. I prefer *traditional masculinity* because it evokes the working-class masculinity that many of the mythopoetic men, owing to their backgrounds, were still wrestling with. What the mythopoetic men in fact enacted was closest to what Connell calls "conventional masculinity." This is a gentler version of masculinity, one that appears to embody a critique of the hegemonic form. But according to Connell, conventional masculinity is hegemonic masculinity "in bad faith," because men who enact it take male supremacy for granted as a natural fact of social life, do not truly try to subvert male supremacy, and also deny responsibility for acting in ways that help to reproduce male supremacy (see R. W. Connell, *Gender and Power*, pp. 183–188, 215–217).

8. In nearly three years of fieldwork I saw only three different black men at gatherings sponsored by the Local Group. Two of these men I saw only once each. The local men

were aware of the racial imbalance of their gatherings and claimed to want more black men to participate. They also claimed to have made a number of fruitless outreach efforts. It remained largely a mystery to them as to why more black men didn't attend men's center events, although one man did say, "The black guys, like the gay guys, have got their own thing."

9. See Robert Bly, "Being a Lutheran Boy-God in Minnesota," in Chester Anderson (ed.), *Growing Up in Minnesota* (Minneapolis: University of Minnesota Press, 1976), pp. 205–219. Lance Morrow's profile of Bly, "The Child is the Father of the Man" (*Time*, 19 August 1991, pp. 52–54), offers a snapshot of Bly's family life and an interpretation of how it affected him.

10. Keith Thompson, "What Men Really Want," *New Age Journal*, May 1982, pp. 30–37, 50–51. Bly's comments in this interview struck a chord with many men and helped to launch the mythopoetic movement in a big way. In the early days of the men's center (ca. 1986), a man who had attended one of Bly's workshops in California gave copies of the interview to several men in the Local Group. This planted a seed of interest among key members of the men's center.

11. The references to female and male "energy" reflect the Jungian roots of the mythopoetic movement. The phrase, "overwhelmed by female [or feminine] energy," may also have echoed this passage from Robert Moore and Douglas Gillette's book *King, Warrior, Magician, Lover* (p. xviii): "What is missing [in the inner lives of many of the men who seek psychotherapy] is not, for the most part, what many depth psychologists assume is missing; that is, adequate connection with the inner *feminine*. In many cases, these men seeking help had been, and were continuing to be, *overwhelmed* by the feminine. What they were missing was an adequate connection to the deep and instinctual *masculine* energies, the potentials of mature masculinity" (emphasis in original). I heard this passage read aloud at two different gatherings. Both times it drew cheers and applause.

12. Findings regarding the prevalence of childhood sexual abuse can vary tremendously depending on the sample. Studies using random samples representative of the U.S. population have found rates of abuse ranging from 3 to 6 percent for men, and 12 to 15 percent for women (see Diane DePanfilis, "Literature Review of Sexual Abuse," U.S. Department of Health and Human Services, National Center on Child Abuse and Neglect, 1986, DHHS Publication number [OHDS] 87-30530). Studies using nonrandom, nonrepresentative samples have found rates ranging from 6 to 62 percent for females, and 3 to 31 percent for males (see S. D. Peters, G. E. Wyatt, and D. Finkelhor, "Prevalence: A Review of the Research," in D. Finkelhor [ed.], *A Sourcebook on Child Sexual Abuse* [Beverly Hills, Calif.: Sage, 1986]). The most careful study to date, using a random, representative sample of the U.S. population, found prevalence rates of 3.9 cases per 1000 for females, and 1.1 per 1000 for males (see *A Study of National Incidence and Prevalence of Child Abuse and Neglect*, USDHHS, National Center on Child Abuse and Neglect, 1988).

13. On the recovery movement, see Wendy Kaminer's *I'm OK, You're Dysfunctional* (Reading, Mass.: Addison-Wesley, 1992). For commentary on the victimhood mentality that helps feed the recovery industry, see David Rieff, "Victims All? Recovery, Co-Dependency, and the Art of Blaming Somebody Else," *Harper's*, October 1991, pp. 49–56.

14. One stereotype of the mythopoetic men held that they were all divorced and angry at their ex-wives. While some men fit this description, on the whole the mythopoetic men were remarkably average. About half of the men in the Local Group had been divorced or separated—which is approximately what would be found among a random sample of middle-aged men in the United States. Most of the rest of the men were in committed relationships. Only a few were never married or unattached.

15. Perhaps the greatest invisible privilege—something educated white men take for

granted and don't see as a privilege at all—is being recognized, listened to, and taken seriously. But actually there are many more such privileges enjoyed by men and by whites in this society. On this, see Peggy McIntosh, "White Privilege and Male Privilege: A Personal Account of Coming to See Correspondences Through Work in Women's Studies," working paper #189, Wellesley College Center for Research on Women, Wellesley, MA 02181. Part of what the mythopoetic movement was about was resisting the loss of these invisible privileges of white, middle-class manhood.

16. When the men talked about feeling compelled to please others and being unable to "defend their boundaries," I was reminded of Carol Gilligan's *In a Different Voice* (Cambridge, Mass.: Harvard University Press, 1982). Gilligan argues that because women are taught to invest so much of themselves in caring for others, they often fail to take their own needs seriously and to protect themselves from the excessive demands of others. Many of the mythopoetic men described themselves as having the same problems. This is another basis for my claim that the mythopoetic men were "womanly."

17. John Stoltenberg, *Refusing to be a Man: Essays on Sex and Justice* (New York: Meridian, 1989), and *The End of Manhood: A Book for Men of Conscience* (New York: Dutton, 1993).

18. These workplace experiences on the part of some of the mythopoetic men called to mind a passage from Michael Maccoby's *The Gamesman* (New York: Bantam, 1967, p. 186): "The most loving were not the ones who moved up the ladder rapidly. Corporate work stimulates and rewards qualities of the head and not of the heart. Those who were active and interested in the work moved ahead in the modern corporation, while those who were the most compassionate were more likely to suffer severe emotional conflicts."

19. Harry Brod argues ("Work Clothes and Leisure Suits: The Class Basis and Bias of the Men's Movement," in M. Kimmel and M. Messner [eds.], *Men's Lives* [New York: Macmillan, 1989, pp. 276–287]) that the values of the "new male"—the men's movement participant—accord with the nature of his work in a service-oriented economy. These values are those of cooperation, self-expression, and sensitivity. Middle-class men in service-oriented occupations thus feel less need to defend traditional masculinity. These men are also less likely, Brod says, to define themselves based on their occupational roles. Work, for these men, is primarily facilitating of a lifestyle rather than defining of who and what they are. Brod's analysis fits many of the men in the Local Group, though I would add that the men had a more ambivalent relationship with traditional masculinity than Brod suggests. It was something they both wanted and didn't want. Also, quite a few of the men *began* their careers very much staking themselves and their identities on work. Later that changed.

20. Robert S. Weiss, *Staying the Course: The Emotional and Social Lives of Men Who Do Well at Work* (New York: Fawcett Columbia, 1990). All of the 85 men Weiss studied were white and identified as heterosexual.

21. Michael McCallion, "The Satanism Scare or the Antisatanism Scare," *Symbolic Interaction* 15 (1992): 237–240.

CHAPTER 2   THE THEORY BEHIND THE PRACTICE

1. See Christopher Harding (ed.), *Wingspan: Inside the Men's Movement* (New York: St. Martin's, 1992), pp. xiii, 150–151. This volume of articles, mostly from the mythopoetic newspaper *Wingspan*, is unabashedly suffused with Jungian psychology. Not all Jungians have been pleased by how the mythopoetic men and teachers, especially Bly, have used

Jung's ideas. For a critique, see Andrew Samuels, "Men Under Scrutiny," *Psychological Perspectives* 26 (1992): 42–61.

2. My account of Jungian psychology draws on Jung's *Memories, Dreams, Reflections* (New York: Vintage, 1961); *Two Essays on Analytical Psychology* (New York: Meridian, 1956); *Collected Works, Vol. 11. Psychology and Religion: West and East* (Princeton, N.J.: Princeton University Press, 1958); *The Undiscovered Self* (New York: Mentor, 1959); and *Aspects of the Feminine* (Princeton, N.J.: Princeton University Press, 1982). The secondary literature I have used includes Calvin Hall and Vernon Nordby, *A Primer of Jungian Psychology* (New York: Mentor, 1973); Frieda Fordham, *An Introduction to Jung's Psychology* (New York: Penguin, 1966); and Edward Whitmont, *The Symbolic Quest: Basic Concepts of Analytical Psychology* (Princeton, N.J.: Princeton University Press, 1991).

3. Essentialism is the doctrine that sees differences in men's and women's thought, feeling, and behavior as resulting from biology. The opposing point of view is called social constructionism, which sees differences between women and men as resulting from differences in social experience. For reviews of the issues and research concerning essentialism and constructionism, see Anne Fausto-Sterling, *Myths of Gender* (New York: Basic, 1985); Cynthia Fuchs Epstein, *Deceptive Distinctions* (New York: Russell Sage Foundation, 1988); and Carmen Schifellite, "Beyond Tarzan and Jane Genes: Toward a Critique of Biological Determinism," in M. Kaufman (ed.), *Beyond Patriarchy: Essays by Men on Pleasure, Power, and Change* (New York: Oxford University Press, 1987), pp. 45–63.

4. For other Jungian perspectives on gender and archetypes, see Gareth S. Hill, *Masculine and Feminine: The Natural Flow of Opposites in the Psyche* (Boston: Shambhala, 1992); Helmut Barz, *For Men, Too: A Grateful Critique of Feminism* (Wilmette, IL: Chiron, 1991); J'nan Morse Sellery, "Gender: Crossing Mental Barriers and Cultural Boundaries," *Psychological Perspectives* 23 (1990): 6–15; Connie Zweig, "The Conscious Feminine: The Birth of a New Archetype," *Anima* 18 (1992): 5–12; Edward C. Whitmont, "Reassessing Femininity and Masculinity: A Restatement of Some Jungian Positions," *Anima* 7 (1981): 125–139; and Polly Young-Eisendrath, *Hags and Heroes: A Feminist Approach to Jungian Psychotherapy with Couples* (Toronto: Inner City Books, 1984).

5. The Jungian concept of the Self as an archetype is quite different from the concept of the self found in ego psychology or in interactionist social psychology. The latter schools see the self as a cognitive construct that emerges and takes shape as a result of social life. For Jungians, the Self is a wired-in archetype that is not subject to capture by paper-and-pencil tests.

6. Jungian theory has it that there is usually an archetype at the core of a complex (Whitmont, *Symbolic Quest*, 68–69). The archetype then is what gives the complex its power. An implication of this view is that complexes—say, a "mother complex"—must be dealt with archetypally, that is, by confronting images in which the mother archetype is manifested. This process might be aided by the use of fairy tales that call up such images. A further implication is that complexes, having archetypes at their cores, are not entirely personal. Tapping into complexes, with their archetypal roots, can thus also be a way of establishing connections with others in whom the same archetypes have been activated.

7. My account of archetypal psychology is based on these works by James Hillman: *Archetypal Psychology: A Brief Account* (Dallas: Spring, 1983); *Insearch: Psychology and Religion* (Dallas: Spring, 1967); *The Myth of Analysis: Three Essays in Archetypal Psychology* (New York: Harper & Row, 1972); *The Dream and the Underworld* (New York: Harper & Row, 1979); *Inter Views* (Dallas: Spring, 1983); *Anima: An Anatomy of a Personified Notion* (Dallas: Spring, 1985); *A Blue Fire: Selected Writings by James Hillman* (New York: Harper &

Row, 1989); and James Hillman and Michael Ventura, *We've Had a Hundred Years of Psychotherapy—And the World's Getting Worse* (New York: HarperCollins, 1992).

8. Hillman seems to argue that our grasp of what we take to be ordinary reality is always mediated by the mind working poetically on the stuff of the material world (*Archetypal Psychology*, 20–23). Thus the unusual perceptual stance required by archetypal psychology is really just an enhancement of the psyche's—not the ego's—natural mode of apprehending the world. It remains the case, however, that if we fail to cultivate the mind's poetic workings we will miss a great deal of the archetypal significance encoded in the world around us.

9. Hillman, *Archetypal Psychology*, 23.

10. Ibid., 26.

11. The trouble starts when one observes that these imagistic metaphors have political content. Many Jungians and archetypalists deny that such content is there, or that it matters. Concern for political content, the argument goes, amounts to confusing the mythological with the psychological or concrete. If myths and images are handled properly, then supposedly there is no danger of mistaking them for representations of real people. So, for example, a princess in a fairy tale can serve as an image of beauty without implying anything about women in the concrete world. Naomi Goldenberg, among others, has expressed feminist concern about these matters. See her "Archetypal Theory After Jung," *Spring: An Annual of Archetypal Psychology and Jungian Thought* (1975): 199–220; and "A Feminist Critique of Jung," *Signs: Journal of Women in Culture and Society* 2 (1976): 443–449.

12. Hillman, *Blue Fire*, 29.

13. See Hillman, *Inter Views*, 27–47. Here Hillman stakes out some of his differences with Jung and other of Jung's followers. In *Anima*, Hillman also develops some of the ideas about psyche, soul, and the anima that make his perspective distinct; see especially pp. 51–97. For an overview of various streams of Jungian thought, and some discussion of where Hillman fits in, see Andrew Samuels, *Jung and the Post-Jungians* (London: Routledge and Kegan Paul, 1985), 1–22, 241–248.

14. The connection between psychology, as they conceived it, and religion, is acknowledged by Jung and Hillman. Their respective psychologies both point to creative, mysterious powers greater than the individual—powers toward which an attitude of awe and respect is recommended. See Jung, *Collected Works, Vol. 11. Psychology and Religion: West and East*; and Hillman, *Insearch: Psychology and Religion*.

15. Hillman, *Archetypal Psychology*, 35.

16. Archetypal psychology uses myths and metaphors to tell stories about patterns of emotional experience in human life. Science uses mathematics to tell stories about patterns in data sets produced by strict adherence to rules of research procedure. Science is useful for giving literal and logically consistent accounts of the material world and its workings. But humans, being prone to contradiction, unruly emotions, wild imaginings, and crises of meaning, seem to need mythology and religion to manage their inevitable existential crises. Myths, in particular, are especially useful for generating a sense of resolution to what is fundamentally irresolvable; they let us believe in contradictory things at once. As Marilyn Robinson put it, ". . . myths [are] complex narratives in which human cultures stabilize and encode their deepest ambivalences. They give form to contradiction that has the appearance of resolution. . . . the attraction of the mind to myth comes from a sense that experience really is more complex than we can articulate by any ordinary means, or more than momentarily, emblematically. . . . the power of myth lies in the fact that it arrests ambivalence." See Marilyn Robinson, "Hearing Silence: Western Myth Reconsidered," in Kurt Brown (ed.), *The True Subject* (St. Paul, MN: Graywolf, 1993), pp. 135–151.

17. See Jung, *Collected Works, Vol. 11. Psychology and Religion: West and East*, and also Jung and Richard Wilhelm, *Secret of the Golden Flower* (New York: Harcourt, Brace and World, 1962). On the influence of the Gnostics on the Sufis, see R. A. Nicholson, *The Mystics of Islam* (New York: Arkana [1914] 1989). For discussion of how Sufi ideas have been diffused throughout the Eastern and Western worlds, see Idries Shah, *The Way of the Sufi* (New York: Arkana [1968] 1990). Shah (p. 41, n.26) also cites R. Landau's *The Philosophy of Ibn Arabi* (London: Allen & Unwin, 1959) as showing that the Sufis had the notion of archetypes long before Jung.

18. Hillman, *Archetypal Psychology*, 3.

19. Henry Corbin, *Creative Imagination in the Sufism of Ibn Arabi* (Princeton, N.J.: Princeton University Press, 1969). On the meaning of *ta'wil*, see especially pp. 242–243.

20. Shah, *Way of the Sufi*, 85.

21. Coleman Barks's translations of Rumi's poems were especially popular. See his *Delicious Laughter: Rambunctious Teaching Stories from the Mathnawi of Jelaluddin Rumi*, (Athens, Ga.: Maypop, 1990); and *Rumi: Like This* (Athens, Ga.: Maypop, 1990). For more on Rumi, see Annemarie Schimmel, *I Am Wind, You Are Fire: The Life and Work of Rumi* (Boston: Shambhala, 1992).

22. Shems Friedlander, *The Whirling Dervishes* (Albany, N.Y.: State University of New York Press, 1992).

23. Consider Coleman Barks's comment in introducing a volume of Rumi's story-poems: "But we should remember that these stories are not primarily about people. The characters here represent *impulses* within people, which can act and change, for the better or worse. . . . *Everything* is a metaphor for this poet." See *Delicious Laughter* (Athens, Ga.: Maypop, 1990), p. *x*.

24. Hillman, *Myth of Analysis*, 90.

25. For an account of the streams of ideas blending to form what I have called a New Age philosophy, see Mark Satin, *New Age Politics: Healing Self and Society* (New York: Dell, 1979).

26. Bly himself embodies this mishmash. In an interview with Joseph Shakarchi he said, "I believe in five or six different systems: the astrological system, the Jungian system, the Catholic, the leftist system, the Gurdjieff system, and the Bronze Age system Joseph Campbell is now teaching. Reality is so complicated that one needs about six more!" (see Joseph Shakarchi, "An Interview with Robert Bly," *Massachusetts Review* 23 [1982]: 226– 243). Other commentators on Bly's work have noted that his primary commitment is to Jungian ideas (see Richard P. Sugg, *Robert Bly* [Boston: Twayne, 1986]). Bly has also acknowledged his intellectual debts to the Jungians James Hillman, Alice Miller, and Marie-Louise von Franz. On the problem of father absence, Bly credits much of his thinking to Alexander Mitscherlich's *Society Without the Father* (New York: Harcourt, Brace & World, 1969).

27. For example, the mythopoetic movement also incorporated ideas from Native American religions. These were ideas about the sacredness of the earth and its ecology, and about human ties to nature. Such ideas accorded with the pantheism and notion of cosmic connection that were implicit in the Jungian core.

28. Some mythopoetic men might object to calling mythopoetic activity religious, since this seems to imply that it was driven by a dogma that all participants were required to embrace. That is not my claim, which is only that it fostered a religious *attitude* and, as a practice, had a definite religious flavor.

29. Demaris Wehr offers a similar analysis of the religious aspect and function of Jungian psychology. See D. Wehr, *Jung and Feminism: Liberating Archetypes* (Boston: Beacon, 1987).

30. Bly referred to "soft men" in his 1982 *New Age Journal* interview with Keith Thompson (reprinted in F. Abbott (ed.), *New Men, New Minds: Breaking Male Tradition*, Freedom, Calif.: Crossing Press, 1987, pp. 166–181). Softness, as Bly means it, isn't the problem, which is, rather, the one-sided development of men's psyches such that softness is not balanced by ferocity, pride, and radiant masculine energy. Bly also emphasizes that softness must be offset not with brutality but with compassionate resolve. Much of this is standard Jungian fare. The contentious part of the interview is Bly's blaming of women for men being nice-but-wimpish. Why are men this way? Bly says it's because possessive mothers and feminist women have led men to confuse their masculine energies with regressive machoism, thus shaming men into denying some of their best qualities as men.

CHAPTER 3   FEELING BETTER ABOUT BEING MEN

1. The men said that "shaming messages" came at them from all over: from women, from the media, from the culture. A shaming message was anything vaguely critical of men. For example, one man cited a *Time* magazine story on fathers who failed to make child support payments as a shaming message; another cited the portrayal of bumptious Homer Simpson on the cartoon show "The Simpson's"; another cited a greeting card that referred to men as scum. "The feminists" were another frequently cited source of shaming messages. This heightened sensitivity to criticism itself became an object of media attention. See David Gates, "White Male Paranoia," *Newsweek*, 29 March 1993, pp. 48–53.
2. These matters of masculine development, as seen from a Jungian perspective, are discussed at length in Eugene Monick, *Phallos: Sacred Image of the Masculine* (Toronto: Inner City Books, 1987).
3. Robert Moore and Douglas Gillette, *King, Warrior, Magician, Lover: Rediscovering the Archetypes of the Mature Masculine* (New York: HarperCollins, 1990).
4. Sam Keen, in another men's movement bestseller, *Fire in the Belly* (New York: Bantam, 1991), talks about WOMAN as the archetype, the image, that shapes so much of men's psychic energy (pp. 13–24). Keen emphasizes that WOMAN is different from the flesh-and-blood women in a man's life. In his workshops Bly makes the same distinction between archetypes and real women, saying that it is dangerous to confuse the two.
5. Initiation should be understood metaphorically. What the men wanted was to make transformative experiences out of wounding experiences in the past. They couldn't do this originally because, perhaps being unready or alone, they had to repress the pain, deny the wound, and keep getting the job done. In a mythopoetic gathering they could try to "rewrite the experience," go back to it, re-experience the emotion it induced, and let it change them. The men knew that this was not initiation as done to boys in tribal societies. It was a post-hoc attempt to help a man deal with a troubling experience, gain from it, feel changed, and have a community of men validate the experience and affirm the change.
6. In making this point I am thinking in what Hillman would call concrete or psychological terms. I indeed presume that the facts of people's lives—facts concerning their thoughts, feelings, behaviors, health, relationships, and material well-being—can be made sense of, literally, through sociological analysis. Theories that make sense of things in this way have what I am calling *analytic* power. Whether these theories have as much *therapeutic* power as poetry or mythology is another matter.
7. As Sandra Bem has shown, we often perceive gender differences where none exist. See S. Bem, "Gender Schema Theory: A Cognitive Account of Sex-Typing," *Psychological Review* 88 (1981): 354–364; and "Masculinity and Femininity Exist Only in the Mind

of the Perceiver," in M. Reinisch, L. A. Rosenblum, and S. A. Sanders (eds.), *Masculinity/ Femininity: Basic Perspectives* (New York: Oxford University Press, 1987). It's also worth noting that the most enduring finding of 50 years of research into gender differences in personality is that men and women are more alike than different. See K. Deaux, "Sex and Gender," *Annual Review of Psychology* 36 (1985): 49–81. For discussion of debates in this area, see D. L. Rhode, *Theoretical Perspectives on Sexual Difference* (New Haven, Conn.: Yale University Press, 1990). Carol Tavris also offers an accessible review of these issues in *The Mismeasure of Woman* (New York: Simon and Schuster, 1992).

8. The sociologist Lewis Killian writes about "stigma reversal" and the backlash that is likely to occur when members of a powerful group feel that their moral worth is being unfairly impugned by blanket condemnations. See Killian, "The Stigma of Race: Who Now Bears the Mark of Cain?" *Symbolic Interaction* 8 (1985): 1–14.

9. Enacting traditional masculinity has costs and benefits. If a man is unable or unwilling to enact traditional masculinity, he will be unable to realize all the usual material and symbolic benefits available to men who conform to the traditional ideal. There is by now a substantial literature in men's studies on how men experience the costs and benefits of enacting different verions of masculinity. Edited collections include Michael Kimmel and Michael Messner, *Men's Lives*, 2nd ed. (New York: Macmillan, 1992); Harry Brod, *The Making of Masculinities* (Boston: Allen & Unwin, 1987); and Michael Kaufman, *Beyond Patriarchy* (Toronto: Oxford University Press, 1987). Other works in this genre include David H. J. Morgan, *Discovering Men* (London: Routledge, 1992); Lynne Segal, *Slow Motion: Changing Masculinities, Changing Men* (New Brunswick, N.J.: Rutgers University Press, 1990); Victor Seidler, *Recreating Sexual Politics* (London: Routledge, 1991); Arthur Brittan, *Masculinity and Power* (New York: Basil Blackwell, 1989); and R. W. Connell, *Gender and Power* (Stanford, Calif.: Stanford University Press, 1987).

10. *Most* men don't meet the standards of traditional masculinity. At times we are all weak, emotional, dependent on others, tired, or afraid. In a sense, then, traditional masculinity, as a set of ideas about how men should be, functions to discipline men—to make us tractable workers and soldiers, always eager to prove ourselves by denying weakness, fear, and fatigue, and by getting the job done. But because the standards are so often impossible to meet, some men seek to alleviate their insecurity by invoking the standards to terrorize other men.

11. The same logic is often applied to sexual preference. The alleged determination of sexual preference by nature is felt to give it moral legitimacy because (a) nature has made the decision and nature is morally good or at least neutral; and (b) the bottom line is that the individual can't help being the way she or he is. The danger inherent in this sort of reductionist thinking is that it can be easily invoked to naturalize inequality. For example, in this view, male domination can be seen as good and right because nature ordained it by making men bigger, stronger, and more aggressive than women. Thus to resist male domination, the argument goes, is to perversely deny nature's wisdom, which is self-evident in our survival as a species.

12. Jungian psychology gains some credibility from its alleged affinities with modern physics. For example, it has been suggested that what Jungians call archetypes can be seen as analogous to the invisible ordering principles that give form to matter and energy. For thoughts in this vein, see Moore and Gillette, *King, Warrior, Magician, Lover,* pp. 102–104; G. Zukav, *The Dancing Wu Li Masters* (New York: Morrow, 1979); Ernest Lawrence Rossi, "What is Life? From Quantum Flux to the Self," *Psychological Perspectives* 26 (1992): 6–22; and Frederick D. Abraham, *A Visual Introduction to Dynamical Systems Theory for Psychology* (Santa Cruz, Calif.: Aerial Press, 1990).

13. Various psychiatric epidemiological studies have produced data suggesting that feelings of demoralization or spiritual malaise are widespread among men in the United States. See Bruce Dohrenwend, et al. (eds.), *Mental Health in the United States: Epidemiological Estimates* (New York: Praeger, 1980). For an overview of research on gender and mental health, see Janet R. Hankin, "Gender and Mental Illness," *Research in Community and Mental Health* 6 (1990): 183–201.

14. For an analysis of the power issues surrounding the "feeding of egos and the tending of wounds," see Sandra Bartky's *Femininity and Domination* (New York: Routledge, 1990), pp. 99–119.

15. Jung's essentialism and sexist biases are glaring in his 1927 essay, "Woman in Europe." See C. G. Jung, *Aspects of the Feminine* (Princeton, N.J.: Princeton University Press, 1982), pp. 55–75.

16. It is interesting to compare the success of Bly's 1990 *Iron John* to the obscurity of John Rowan's slightly earlier *The Horned God: Feminism and Men as Wounding and Healing* (London: Routledge, 1987). Rowan, who is British, offered a similar kind of mythological/spiritual program for men suffering from too much traditional masculinity and feminist criticism thereof. But instead of celebrating masculinity, Rowan urged men to get in touch with the goddess and embrace feminism. Few listened. Rowan's rejection of male supremacy undermined his appeal to most men. See also K. Clatterbaugh, "Wild Men and Horned Gods," in his *Contemporary Perspectives on Masculinity*, pp. 85–103.

17. See Max Weber, *The Protestant Ethic and the Spirit of Capitalism* (New York: Scribner's, 1930 [1904–1905]; trans. by T. Parsons). In the public realm, the "iron cage" metaphor refers to the total rationalization of everything, that is, the elimination of spontaneity in favor of formal rules and procedures to guide thought, feeling, and behavior. In Weber's private life, it seems his own psychic iron cage stemmed from his mother's ascetic, Calvinist work ethic and his father's patriarchal despotism. See Arthur Mitzman, *The Iron Cage: An Historical Interpretation of Max Weber* (New York: Knopf, 1970).

18. I am referring to Jungian psychology in principle, not to the political beliefs of the mythopoetic men. As a body of ideas, Jungian psychology was of little use for analyzing social inequality, and this suited the mythopoetic men just fine. My point is that the inward turn recommended by Jungian psychology made it more palatable than, say, the Marxist-Freudianism of Erich Fromm or, for that matter, any psychology that called for serious, critical examination of how social life shaped thought and feeling. To his credit, Hillman argued that men needed to engage the external world politically and not wait until they were healed before doing so. He made this argument in talks at gatherings and developed it in his book of conversations and letters with *L.A. Weekly* columnist Michael Ventura. See Hillman and Ventura, *We've Had a Hundred Years of Psychotherapy—And the World's Getting Worse* (New York: HarperCollins, 1992).

CHAPTER 4   THE SEARCH FOR COMMUNITAS

1. Victor Turner, *The Ritual Process* (Ithaca, N.Y.: Cornell University Press, 1969), pp. 131–132. On Buber's philosophy, see Martin Buber, *The Knowledge of Man: Selected Essays*, edited by Maurice Friedman (New York: Harper & Row, 1965).

2. Mark Carnes ascribes the popularity of late nineteenth- and early twentieth-century fraternal orders in America, such as the Odd Fellows, Masons, and Improved Order of Red Men, to their use of ritual to subvert the forms of social relations to which men were accustomed in their jobs. Carnes also proposes that the men who participated in these

orders sought relief from the discipline and circumscribed social relations of the capitalist workplace. In the fraternal lodge the men could be "recharged by an immersion in this undisciplined, unstructured, and emotionally expressive domain." See Carnes, *Secret Ritual and Manhood in Victorian America* (New Haven, Conn.: Yale University Press, 1989), pp. 32–33. Some of the mythopoetic men sought similar relief from the emotionally repressive social relations of the workplace. But unlike the men of the earlier fraternal orders, the mythopoetics were more therapeutically oriented, less escapist, less hierarchical, and more spontaneous in their rituals.

3. Turner, *Ritual Process*, p. 139.

4. Ibid., p. 138.

5. Ibid., p. 154.

6. A key piece of movement literature was Wayne Liebman's *Tending the Fire* (St. Paul, Minn.: Ally, 1991), which is an account of the formation of a ritual men's group and an explanation of its reason for being. Other expressions of the mythopoetic view of ritual can be found in "Men and Ritual Process: A Wingspan Interview (with Tom Daly)," *Wingspan* (April–June, 1992); and Michael Ventura, "Possibilities of Ritual: Walking with Michael Meade," *L.A. Weekly* (January 17–23, 1992), pp. 10–12.

7. Some of the men drew on the feminist spiritualist Starhawk as a source of instruction in the matter of how to create ritual or sacred space. See Starhawk, *The Spiral Dance: A Rebirth of the Ancient Religion of the Great Goddess* (New York: HarperCollins, 1979), pp. 69–89. For another sample of this New Age genre, see Renee Beck and Sydney Barbara Metrick, *The Art of Ritual: A Guide to Creating and Performing Your Own Ceremonies for Growth and Change* (Berkeley, Calif.: Celestial Arts, 1990).

8. Each direction was said to offer unique powers and spirits. The east, for example, because it is where the sun rises, was seen as offering the spirit of renewal. Sometimes the invocations of the spirits and powers of the directions were extemporaneous—the men individually called out whatever spirit they could think of to invoke from each direction. Other times the ritual elder led the invocation, using a prepared text. On one occasion the text was adapted from Starhawk's *The Spiral Dance* (pp. 69–71). Another source used was Elizabeth Roberts and Elias Amidon (eds.), *Earth Prayers from Around the World* (New York: HarperCollins, 1991); see pp. 134–136, 192–193.

9. Catherine Bell writes about how ritual "catches people up in its own terms" and provides a "resistant surface to casual disagreement." See Bell, *Ritual Theory, Ritual Practice* (New York: Oxford University Press, 1992), pp. 214–215. Other observers have noted how the improvised rituals at mythopoetic gatherings had this power to draw the men in. See Richard Gilbert, "Revisiting the Psychology of Men: Robert Bly and the Mytho-Poetic Movement," *Journal of Humanistic Psychology* 32 (1992): 41–67.

10. A description of the sweat lodge ritual can be found in Joseph Epes Brown (recorder and editor), *The Sacred Pipe: Black Elk's Account of the Seven Rites of the Oglala Sioux* (Norman, Okla.: University of Oklahoma Press, 1953), pp. 31–43. This account was a source of inspiration for some of the mythopoetic men. See also William K. Powers, *Oglala Religion* (Lincoln, Neb.: University of Nebraska Press, 1977).

11. The men were doing what Erving Goffman called "facework," which includes the talk and other tactics we use to maintain creditable images of ourselves in interaction. See Goffman, "On Face Work: An Analysis of Ritual Elements in Social Interaction," *Psychiatry* 18 (1955), pp. 213–231. According to Goffman, we do this work for ourselves, to protect our own "faces," and for others. We do it for ourselves to protect our own self-esteem; we do it for others partly out of respect for their feelings, but also because we need their support to maintain our chosen faces. The men thus played along most of the time

because to do otherwise would have threatened the serious and intelligent faces men presented at gatherings.

12. For analyses of how events can be scripted to evoke an organized flow of emotion in participants, see Louis A. Zurcher, "The Staging of Emotion: A Dramaturgical Analysis," *Symbolic Interaction* 5 (1982), pp. 1–22; and "The War Game: Organizational Scripting and the Expression of Emotion," *Symbolic Interaction* 8 (1985), pp. 191–206.

13. Turner, *Ritual Process*, p. 165.

14. Many of the poems frequently read at gatherings can be found in Robert Bly, James Hillman, and Michael Meade, *The Rag and Bone Shop of the Heart* (New York: Harper-Collins, 1992). Many of the fairy tales told at gatherings, including Bly's "Iron John" (aka "Iron Hans"), can be found in the Grimm brothers' collection.

15. John Plymale, "This Good Man." Reprinted by permission of the author.

16. Turner observes that the "concrete, personal, imagist mode of thinking is highly characteristic of those in love with existential [or spontaneous] communitas, with the direct relation between man and man, and man and nature. Abstractions appear as hostile to live contact" (*Ritual Process*, p. 141). The emphasis the men placed on specific images also grew out of Jungian psychology, according to which the psyche is best explored by use of evocative images.

17. For critical analyses of the sexism and other politics embedded in the Grimms' fairy tales, see Ruth G. Bottigheimer, *Grimms' Bad Girls and Bold Boys: The Moral and Social Vision of the Tales* (New Haven, Conn.: Yale University Press, 1987); and Maria Tatar, *The Hard Facts of the Grimms' Fairy Tales* (Princeton, N.J.: Princeton University Press, 1987).

18. In Jungian psychology this is called "synchronicity," which is an acausal connecting principle said to produce meaningful coincidences. Of course, whether or not a coincidence, such as a particular group of men ending up in a cabin together, was meaningful, depended on the meaning the men could create for it. Looking for a point of commonality among the men in each group was a way to create such meaning, which was then, posthoc, invested with spiritual significance. The men did similar things at other gatherings, looking for meaning in coincidental events. The idea was that invisible powers, spirits, or the objective psyche was at work in producing these coincidences, which held messages for those who could perceive them.

19. The names are pseudonyms.

20. Another man in the group later asked the chanter where he had learned this Native American chant. The man who chanted said that he hadn't learned it anywhere, as far as he knew. "It just came to me," he said.

21. This sort of vulgar verbal sparring is a common practice of working-class adolescent boys. In my old neighborhood and in high school we did a lot of it. We called it "cutting." It's better known as an African-American practice called "playing the dozens." See Harry G. Lefever, "Playing the Dozens: A Mechanism for Social Control," *Phylon* 42 (1981): 73–85.

CHAPTER 5 MEN'S WORK AS IDENTITY WORK

1. Identity, its formation, and its consequences for behavior are understood differently from various perspectives in psychology and social psychology. The perspective I use is called symbolic interactionism, which is rooted in the work of the American pragmatist philosophers John Dewey and George Herbert Mead. For an overview of the symbolic

interactionist treatment of identity, see A. Weigert, J. Smith Teitge, and Dennis W. Teitge, *Society and Identity: Toward a Sociological Psychology* (New York: Cambridge University Press, 1986). For a classic treatment of identity in this tradition, see Anselm Strauss, *Mirrors and Masks: The Search for Identity* (Glencoe, Ill.: The Free Press, 1959). For a recent exemplar, see John Hewitt, *Dilemmas of the American Self* (Philadelphia: Temple University Press, 1989).

2. For sociologists, Max Weber is the classic source on inequality in "social honor." Key pieces of theory and research, mostly in the Weberian tradition, can be found in the volume by R. Bendix and S. M. Lipset (eds.), *Class, Status, and Power* (New York: The Free Press, 1966). On the ubiquity of status hierarchies based on occupation, see Donald Treiman, *Occupational Prestige in Comparative Perspective* (New York: Academic Press, 1977).

3. On the average, all else being equal, the higher the status of the group to which a person belongs and the more material resources she or he can wield to make things happen, the more self-esteem and self-efficacy she or he will enjoy. For a review of the research evidence, see Viktor Gecas and Peter Burke, "Self and Identity," in K. Cook, G. A. Fine, and J. House (eds.), *Sociological Perspectives on Social Psychology* (Boston: Allyn and Bacon, 1994). Of course, I am referring to a general tendency that is found when studying large numbers of people, not to a rule that applies in all cases.

4. L. Richard Della Fave ("The Meek Shall Not Inherit the Earth: Self-Evaluation and the Legitimacy of Stratification," *American Sociological Review* 45 [1980]: 955–971) argues that people accept inequality as legitimate in large part because members of dominant groups are able to maintain an illusion of competence and morality. Members of subordinate groups, if they are conned into believing that rewards are commensurate with abilities in our society, may then also infer their own inferiority, based on their lesser power and status. Either way, inequality is reinforced. Della Fave's argument implies that challenging the morality and competence of members of dominant groups is a necessary part of abolishing hierarchies of status and power.

5. Sociologists and social psychologists have studied the process by which damning labels and deviant identities are imposed on people. Much of this work goes under the heading of what is called "labeling theory." A classic work in the area is Howard S. Becker, *Outsiders: Studies in the Sociology of Deviance* (New York: The Free Press, 1963). See also Thomas Scheff, *Being Mentally Ill: A Sociological Theory* (Chicago: Aldine, 1966). More recent documentation of the consequences of labeling can be found in Bruce Link, "Mental Patient Status, Work, and Income: An Examination of the Effects of a Psychiatric Label," *American Sociological Review* 47 (1982): 202–215.

6. This conception of identity work derives principally from Erving Goffman. My thinking on these matters has been influenced by Goffman's *The Presentation of Self in Everyday Life* (New York: Anchor, 1959), *Encounters: Two Studies in the Sociology of Interaction* (New York: Bobbs-Merrill, 1961), *Stigma: Notes on the Management of Spoiled Identity* (Englewood Cliffs, N.J.: Prentice-Hall, 1963), and his essays in *Interaction Ritual* (New York: Pantheon, 1967). For an example of another study of identity work, see David Snow and Leon Anderson, "Identity Work among the Homeless: The Verbal Construction and Avowal of Personal Identities," *American Journal of Sociology* 92 (1987): 1336–1371.

7. See Orrin Klapp, *Collective Search for Identity* (New York: Holt, Rinehart and Winston, 1969); Alberto Melucci, *Nomads of the Present: Social Movements and Individual Needs in Contemporary Society* (Philadelphia: Temple University Press, 1989); and William A. Gamson, "The Social Psychology of Collective Action," in A. Morris and C. M. Mueller (eds.), *Frontiers in Social Movement Theory* (New Haven, Conn.: Yale University Press, 1992), pp. 53–76.

8. The analysis of gender as an interactive accomplishment is developed in Suzanne Kessler and Wendy McKenna, *Gender: An Ethnomethodological Approach* (Chicago: University of Chicago Press, 1978); Candace West and Don Zimmerman, "Doing Gender," *Gender and Society* 1 (1987): 125–151; and Spencer Cahill, "Fashioning Males and Females: Appearance Management and the Reproduction of Gender," *Symbolic Interaction* 12 (1989): 281–298.

9. Just as the mythopoetic men were trying to reinvest 'man' with new moral value, some neo-traditional women and cultural feminists were trying to do the same thing with 'mother'. This was a backlash against earlier feminist analyses that had tarnished 'mother' by linking it to women's subvient role within the patriarchal institution of marriage. Some women bristled at this, taking the feminist critiques of marriage and of compulsory motherhood as personal attacks. As a general principle, it seems that a sure way for social critics to provoke a backlash is to target the social arrangements upon which are premised people's cherished moral identities.

10. This is documented in Martha McMahon's *Engendering Motherhood: Gender Identity and Self-Transformation in Women's Lives* (New York: Guilford, 1995).

11. Sam Mackintosh, "Rite of Initiation for a Male Adolescent," *Wingspan* (winter 1990), p. 14.

12. R. Moore and D. Gillette, *King, Warrior, Magician, Lover* (New York: Harper Collins, 1990), p. 155–156.

13. Not all of the men felt this sting with the same force or for exactly the same reasons. In some cases it stemmed from direct confrontation with feminist women in their lives, in other cases it stemmed from vaguely perceived "shaming messages" coming at men through various channels of popular culture. The experiences of the mythopoetic men were similar in many ways to those of the men with feminist sympathies described by Anthony Astrachan in *How Men Feel* (New York: Anchor, 1986), pp. 316–334.

14. The desire for affirmation from older men was also reflected in the amount of time the men gave to the topic of mentoring. When leading gatherings, Bly, Meade, Hillman, and Moore all spoke about the need for men to have their special talents recognized and nurtured by older, wiser men. Without this, it was said, a man might never learn to appreciate his own worth or acquire the real-world savvy needed to approach life and work with confidence. When the men discussed mentoring, they expressed a stronger desire for affirmation as competent and good men than for practical advice. In keeping with Jungian precepts, and the men's own feelings, it was generally agreed that this affirmation had to come from men.

15. Half a dozen or more men in the Local Group were therapists, for whom their professional work was an important source of identity and meaning. But for these men, the therapy they did for a living overlapped considerably with mythopoetic men's work. One therapist I interviewed said that he considered the therapy he did to be *part* of doing men's work. So even though these men could derive a moral identity from their professional work, this didn't conflict with or draw them away from involvement in mythopoetic activity; in fact, it drew them into it. Therapists thus got double benefit from men's work: they could sustain their own work-related moral identities while helping to remake 'man' as a moral identity. For an analysis of how the motivations of therapists influenced the development of a more profeminist stream of the men's movement, see Paul Lichterman, "Making a Politics of Masculinity," *Comparative Social Research* 11 (1989): 185–208.

16. The mythopoetic sources are William Anderson and Clive Hicks, *Green Man: The Archetype of Our Oneness with the Earth* (New York: HarperCollins, 1990); and Aaron Kipnis, "The Blessings of the Green Man," in C. Harding (ed.), *Wingspan: Inside the Men's Movement* (New York: St. Martin's, 1992), pp. 161–165.

17. David Tatman, "The Positive Attributes of Manhood," *Seattle M.E.N. newsletter,* July 1991, pp. 1–2; David Hartman, "Uniquely Masculine Qualities," *Seattle M.E.N. newsletter,* November 1991, pp. 10–11, 14.

18. Paul Boynton, "It's Good To Be A Man!", *Journeymen* (fall 1991), pp. 27–28. This article originally appeared in *Transitions* (May/June 1991), which is the newsletter of the National Coalition of Free Men. Excerpts are reprinted with permission of the National Coalition of Free Men (P.O. Box 129, Manhasset, N.Y. 11030).

19. Carl Sandburg, *Harvest Poems 1910–1960* (New York: Harcourt, Brace & World, 1960), pp. 47–48.

20. D. H. Lawrence, *The Complete Poems of D. H. Lawrence,* collected and edited with an introduction and notes by V. de Sola Pinto and W. Roberts (New York: Penguin, 1977), p. 501.

21. Rainer Maria Rilke, *Selected Poems of Rainer Maria Rilke,* translated by R. Bly (New York: Harper & Row, 1981), p. 13.

22. James Broughton, *Special Deliveries* (Seattle: Broken Moon Press, 1990), p. 104.

23. Nikki Giovanni, *The Women and the Men* (New York: William Morrow, 1975), unpaginated.

24. Jallaludin Rumi, *Open Secret,* versions of Rumi by John Moyne and Coleman Barks (Putney, Vt.: Threshold Books, 1984), p. 36.

25. Etheridge Knight, *The Essential Etheridge Knight* (Pittsburgh: University of Pittsburgh Press, 1986), p. 34.

26. Keeping television reporters out of gatherings was another way in which the men protected their identities as heterosexuals. When a network news crew wanted to film a retreat, the leaders of the Local Group refused. The main reason for this, the men said publicly, was that the presence of TV cameras would invade participants' privacy and ruin the experience for them. But in an interview, one of the Local Group leaders said that they also worried about people misinterpreting the story: "The TV would show us dancing or something and people might think we're a bunch of gay guys." In this case, identity work was done by keeping the media out and limiting the flow of information to the public. In a similar incident, Marvin Allen, organizer of the First International Men's Conference (Austin, Texas, October 1991), refused, according to *Village Voice* reporter Don Shewey, to admit two femininely-dressed young men to the conference because, "the press is always trying to make out like the men's movement is a gay thing or a weird thing. If you wear that, they're going to focus on you" (*Village Voice,* November 5, 1991, p. 43–44). Controlling the dress of participants could be seen as another form of identity work on behalf of the men as a group.

27. Some of the mythopoetic teachers rejected the view that U.S. society is a patriarchy. In their view, patriarchy meant rule by wise, benevolent fathers who take the best interests of the whole community into account. Most feminist theorists would probably agree that neither the United States nor any Western society is that sort of patriarchy. Of course, what the mythopoetic men were reacting to was the feminist use of "patriarchy" as a term implicating all men in the oppression of women. The men resented this implication and thus sought to redefine "patriarchy" in a way that neutralized its critical sting.

28. Women may know men better than men know themselves. The reason is that people in subordinate groups depend for their survival on knowing the minds and behaviors of the powerful. So it is women who, as a matter of survival, have had greater need to study and understand men, than men have had need to study and understand women. Power, in other words, is a large determinant of who must take whose perspective. See D. Thomas, D. Franks, and J. Calonico, "Role-Taking and Power in Social Psychology," *American Sociological Review* 37 (1972): 605–614; S. E. Snodgrass, "Women's Intuition: The Ef-

fect of Subordinate Status on Interpersonal Sensitivity," *Journal of Personality and Social Psychology* 49 (1985): 146–155; and M. Schwalbe, "Role Taking Reconsidered: Linking Competence and Performance to Social Structure," *Journal for the Theory of Social Behavior* 18 (1988): 413–436. For an application of this argument to the matter of men's moral behavior vis-à-vis women, see M. Schwalbe, "Male Supremacy and the Narrowing of the Moral Self," *Berkeley Journal of Sociology* 37 (1992): 29–54.

29. With the notable exception of Herb Goldberg's *The Hazards of Being Male* (New York: Penguin, 1976), the premythopoetic, mid-1970s literature on men and masculinity was predominantly profeminist. Although Warren Farrell has since moved to the Herb Goldberg camp (arguing that male power is a myth), his 1975 book *The Liberated Man* (New York: Random House) was highly sympathetic to feminism. Other books in this genre were even more avowedly feminist and critical of traditional masculinity and patriarchy. See, for example, Andrew Tolson, *The Limits of Masculinity: Male Identity and Women's Liberation* (New York: Harper & Row, 1977); Marc Feigen Fasteau, *The Male Machine* (New York: Dell, 1975); the essays in Joseph Pleck and Jack Sawyer (eds.), *Men and Masculinity* (Englewood Cliffs, N.J.: Prentice-Hall, 1974); and the essays in Jon Snodgrass (ed.), *For Men Against Sexism* (Albion, Calif.: Times Change Press, 1977).

30. In terms suggested by Hans Mol in *Identity and the Sacred* (New York: The Free Press, 1976), it could be said that the mythopoetic men were trying to "sacralize" the identity 'man'. According to Mol, sacralizing an identity means firming it up against symbolic threats by anchoring it in a system of meaning that endows it with special qualities of untouchability and awe. This typically involves objectifying the identity by linking it to a sacred or transcendent realm. For the mythopoetic men, romanticized "tribal cultures" and, to a larger extent, Jungian psychology, constituted these sacred realms. In these realms the meaning of 'man' was pure and good and stable, untainted by what men had become under capitalism or by what feminists had said about men. Seen in this way, Jungian psychology was the religion that the men used to sacralize the identity 'man'.

31. Bly's tendencies to give fanciful accounts of history and of tribal cultures are pointed out in R. W. Connell's critique, "Drumming Up the Wrong Tree," *Tikkun* 7 (1991): 31–36; in Fred Pelka, "Robert Bly and Iron John," *On the Issues* (summer 1991):17–19, 39; and in Gordon Murray, "Homophobia in Robert Bly's *Iron John*," *Masculinities* (summer 1993): 52–54. Other mythopoetic teachers were prone to taking the same sort of poetic license with the truth. No special knowledge of history or anthropology was needed to see this. Anyone's crap detector should have lit up when teachers referred to practices "in some cultures, such as Africa," or spoke of "what all primitive peoples knew."

32. The essentialism of Jungian psychology also served to indirectly protect the men's identities as heterosexual. Since one of the things men were supposedly archetypally wired for was attraction to women, the men could feel safe in knowing that, whatever affection they felt for other men at gatherings, they were still hard-wired heteros. During one discussion a man talked about how, whenever he interacted with women, some sexual tension was always present—"just like Jung wrote about." The other men concurred.

33. Robert Moore made this point. Feminists should not be critical of or impede men's work, he said, because it was through this work that men would become mature and responsible stewards of the community, rather than being stuck in a state of immaturity that led to abusive behavior toward women.

34. My thoughts in this section about identity and the mystique of mythopoetic men's work were influenced by Orrin Klapp's *Collective Search for Identity* (New York: Holt, Rinehart and Winston, 1969), especially pp. 138–210.

CHAPTER 6   FALSE PARITY, THE MEN'S HUT,
AND ARCHETYPAL ILLUSIONS

1. More extreme men's rights views can be found in the volume *Men Freeing Men* (Jersey City, N.J.: New Atlantis, 1985), edited by Francis Baumli. See especially the chapters by Fredric Hayward, Richard Haddad, and Richard Doyle. See also Richard Doyle's *The Rape of the Male* (St. Paul, Minn.: Poor Richard's Press, 1976).

2. Jon Pielemeier, "Man is the Fellow Victim, Not the Enemy," *Seattle M.E.N. newsletter*, February 1992, pp. 2–3.

3. A consistent finding of studies of household decision-making is that earning power translates into power within the home. Men's generally higher earnings and better jobs give them special leverage over *major* household decisions, even when women seem to have control over routine operations. See P. Blumstein and P. Schwartz, *American Couples* (New York: William Morrow, 1983); G. Allan, *Family Life* (New York: Basil Blackwell, 1985); and A. Hochschild, *The Second Shift* (New York: Viking, 1989). For a recent overview of the comparative labor-market status of women and men in the United States, see B. Reskin and I. Padavic, *Women and Men at Work* (Thousand Oaks, Calif.: Pine Forge, 1994).

4. During a conversation I had a with a man about men's obligations to help women overcome sexism, he said, "It's really an insult to women to think that men need to help them gain equality. That's like saying they don't have the capability to do it themselves. From what I can see, they're doing fine without us." This was exemplary of the general tendency to see sexism as a women's problem that was not linked to anything the mythopoetic men might do or not do. By exaggerating women's power (and seeming to praise them for their capability), this statement also rationalized a refusal to accept a moral obligation to help end sexism.

5. See J. Harrison, J. Chin, and T. Ficarrotto, "Warning: Masculinity May Be Dangerous to Your Health," in M. Kimmel & M. Messner (eds.), *Men's Lives* (New York: Macmillan, 1989), pp. 296–309; I. Waldron, "Sex Differences in Illness Incidence, Prognosis, and Mortality: Issues and Evidence," *Social Science and Medicine* 17 (1983): 1107–1123; and R. Retherford, "Tobacco Smoking and the Sex Mortality Differential," *Demography* 9 (1972): 203–216.

6. Some of the men spoke of being "overwhelmed by feminine [or female] energy" in their homes and workplaces—places where they as men were in the minority. In these situations it may indeed have seemed that women had achieved equality, or even superiority, since some of the men had women for bosses. As I said, the men overgeneralized from this experience of minority status. They did not see that it was possible for women to have more power than men in some families and a few workplaces, and for men still to have vastly more institutional power than women on both national and global scales.

7. In this view, our society is seen as not simply capitalist *and* patriarchal, but as a *capitalist patriarchy*. It is fundamentally patriarchal in that men have a near monopoly on institutional power, and that men at all class levels are able, to some degree, to exploit women for their physical, emotional, and reproductive labor. But this patriarchy is also distinctly *capitalist*, in that a relatively tiny group of extremely wealthy (male-headed) stockholding families and high-level managers (almost all male) are able to use their control over the means of production, and over government, to exploit the minds and bodies of nearly everyone else—including most men. Without taking these structural features of our society into account, it is indeed hard to see why so many men, supposedly the beneficiaries of patriarchy, are powerless, exploited, and alienated. Capitalism is of course only one system of domination. Feudal systems and rule by party bureaucrats are other possibilities.

8. Some of the men said that women who disliked mythopoetic activity felt this way because they stood to lose one of their traditional sources of power: men's dependence on women for nurturing and emotional support. Some men also thought that women tended to give support in ways that were not necessarily "male positive," or respectful of the "male mode of feeling." This was supposedly another way that women subverted men's confidence. So if some women objected to men's work, it was not, as these men saw it, because men's work encouraged men to dominate women, but just the opposite: it taught men how to free themselves from emotional dependence on and vulnerability to women.

9. This telling of "Iron John" was recorded at the Scottish Rite Temple in San Francisco in the late 1980s. The recording (1989) is available from Oral Traditions Archives, 1104 Lincoln Avenue, Pacific Grove, Calif., 93950.

10. A version of the Faithful John story can be found in *The Complete Grimm's Fairy Tales* (New York: Pantheon, [1944] 1972), pp. 43–51.

11. At larger mythopoetic gatherings, teachers' presentations and exchanges with audience members were often recorded. The tapes were then sold to participants on site or, sometimes, edited and sold through catalogs. Most of the large-group sessions at the Big Remote Gathering were recorded. The transcript that appears here is from my field notes and a purchased tape of the session. I chose to reproduce the discussion in its entirety because its content is political and conceptual rather than revealing of individuals. I think the discussion also gives readers a chance to see details and complexities that would be lost in a summary account of what was said.

12. The strictly Jungian approach to the stories would have us see characters in the stories as representative of archetypally-shaped psychic energies. Characters in fairy tales and myths are, in this view, "characters" in a drama being played out *inside* us. While Robert Bly emphasized this approach, the men themselves often had difficulty handling the stories in a Jungian fashion. What happened with the Faithful John story was typical. Characters in the story were not talked about as representing psychic energies in men, but as if they corresponded to the ways that men and women behaved in the concrete world. Although I heard a dozen different stories told and discussed at mythopoetic gatherings, only once—while discussing a Grimms' story called "Allerleirauh" (or "Thousandfurs")—did a man say that he was trying to understand what a female character could tell him about the feminine in himself. The other men present on that occasion did not pursue this line of thought.

13. For documentation of the seriousness of date rape, see M. Koss, C. Gidycz, and N. Wisniewski, "The Scope of Rape: Incidence and Prevalence of Sexual Aggression in a Sample of Higher Education Students," *Journal of Consulting and Clinical Psychology* 55 (1987): 162–170. On rapists' perceptions of the women they rape, see D. Scully and J. Marolla, "Convicted Rapists' Vocabulary of Motive: Excuses and Justifications," *Social Problems* 31 (1984): 530–544.

14. Bly was more likely to acknowledge that the stories had a point of view. At the start of the Iron John story, as Bly tells it, an eagle flies overhead, indicating, according to Bly, that it's a "male story." In prefacing a story about Gawain and King Arthur, Bly also acknowledged (before an audience of women and men) that the story was told "from a man's perspective."

15. Jungian psychology does not explicitly value the masculine over the feminine, or say that men should dominate women. However, if the world is a place of conflict and competition—such as our innate archetypes would seem to ensure—then those whose archetypes better suit them for competition will naturally end up in charge. Even women who run with the wolves are no match for kings, warriors, and magicians.

16. Aaron Kipnis, "Reclaiming Masculinity: Earth Fathers and the Next Century" (interview with Aaron Kipnis by Ed Schilling and Chad Mears), *Journeymen* 3, No. 2 (1993): 25–29. Kipnis was the author of *Knights Without Armor: A Practical Guide for Men in Quest of Masculine Soul* (New York: Jeremy Tarcher, 1991), a moderately popular mythopoetic book.

17. Paul Shippee, "Duped by Doubiago?" *Seattle M.E.N. newsletter,* March 1993, pp. 3, 21.

18. Gloria Steinem, *Revolution from Within: A Book of Self-Esteem* (Boston: Little, Brown & Co., 1992).

19. In reporting on a "multicultural" mythopoetic gathering attended by 50 black men and 50 white men, Don Shewey noted that some black men were dubious about the purported need to separate from the mother. For many black men who grew up without fathers, "Their mothers are often their only source of support and unconditional love; to take that away without offering anything in its place is totally unacceptable." See Shewey, "Stepbrothers: Gays and the Men's Movement," *The Sun,* May 1993, pp. 4–8.

20. Paul MacAdam, "Don't Shave Off the Wild Man's Hair," *Man!,* summer 1992, pp. 34–35, 40–41.

CHAPTER 7 FEMINISM, ANDROCENTRISM, AND HOMOPHOBIA

1. Robin Morgan was a poet and the author of a powerful feminist manifesto, "Goodbye to All That," which is reprinted in B. Roszak and T. Roszak, *Masculine/Feminine: Readings in Sexual Mythology and the Liberation of Women* (New York: Harper & Row, 1969), pp. 241–250. She also edited *Sisterhood Is Powerful* (New York: Random House, 1970), a classic volume of feminist writing.

2. The caricaturing, demonizing, and trivializing of feminism in the popular media is well documented in Susan Faludi's *Backlash: The Undeclared War Against American Women* (New York: Crown, 1991), pp. 75–168.

3. The belief in essential differences between men and women was, for some of the men, a belief held with almost religious conviction. As such, it was unassailable by argument or evidence. When confronted with arguments against essentialism, the usual response was simply an appeal to "deep and heartfelt experience" that testified to the biological basis of differences in men's and women's behavior. There was, in other words, no serious counter argument at all; the men found all the evidence and answers they needed by introspection and casual observation of a gendered society. The refusal to argue this matter more seriously was another example of strategic anti-intellectualism.

4. Aaron Kipnis, "Reclaiming Masculinity: Earth Fathers and the Next Century" (interview with Aaron Kipnis by Ed Schilling and Chad Mears), *Journeymen* 3, No. 2 (1993): 25–29.

5. Socialist-feminist perspectives are developed in Sheila Rowbotham, *Woman's Consciousness, Man's World* (Middlesex, England: Penguin, 1973); Ann Foreman, *Femininity as Alienation: Women and the Family in Marxism and Psychoanalysis* (London: Pluto, 1977); Nancy Hartsock, *Money, Sex, and Power: Toward a Feminist Historical Materialism* (Boston: Northeastern University Press, 1983); Andrew Tolson, *The Limits of Masculinity: Male Identity and Women's Liberation* (New York: Harper & Row, 1977); Zillah Eisenstein, *Capitalist Patriarchy and the Case for Socialist Feminism* (New York: Monthly Review Press, 1979); and Barbara Ehrenreich, *The Hearts of Men: American Dreams and the Flight From Commitment* (Garden City, N.Y.: Anchor, 1983).

6. Christopher Harding, "What's All This About a Men's Movement?" in C. Harding (ed.), *Wingspan: Inside the Men's Movement* (New York: St. Martin's Press, 1992), p. *xiv*.

7. For a criticism of the mythopoetics on this ground, see Jack Straton, "Where Are the Ethics in Men's Spirituality?" *Changing Men* 23 (fall/winter 1991): 10–12. Several of the contributions to the volume edited by Kay Leigh Hagan, *Women Respond to the Men's Movement* (San Francisco: HarperSanFrancisco, 1992), offer even harsher criticism of the implicit ethics of the mythopoetic movement. See chapter 8 for my evaluation of these criticisms and a partial defense of the men.

8. The men referred to their gatherings as "safe places." By this they meant more than safe from the inhibiting effect of women's real or imagined critical judgments. They also meant a place where all critical judgments of each other were to be suspended.

9. See L. Kurdek, "Correlates of Negative Attitudes Toward Homosexuals in Heterosexual College Students," *Sex Roles* 18 (1988): 727–738; G. Lehne, "Homophobia Among Men," in M. Kimmel and M. Messner (eds.), *Men's Lives* (New York: Macmillan, 1989), pp. 416–429; S. F. Morin and E. M. Garfinkle, "Male Homophobia," *Journal of Social Issues* 34 (1978): 29–47; and G. Herek, "Beyond 'Homophobia': A Social Psychological Perspective on Attitudes Toward Lesbians and Gay Men," *Journal of Homosexuality* 10 (1984): 1–21.

10. See Don Shewey, "Town Meeting in the Hearts of Men," *Village Voice*, 11 February 1992, pp. 36–42, 45–46. This article stands, in my judgment, as the best piece of reporting on mythopoetic men's work to appear in the mainstream or alternative press.

11. Trenchant analyses of the relationship between hegemonic masculinity and heterosexuality can be found in Lynne Segal, *Slow Motion: Changing Masculinities, Changing Men* (New Brunswick, N.J.: Rutgers University Press, 1990), pp. 134–167; R.W. Connell, *Gender and Power* (Stanford, Calif.: Stanford University Press, 1987), pp. 167–190; Arthur Brittan, *Masculinity and Power* (New York: Basil Blackwell, 1989), pp. 46–76; Victor Seidler, *Rediscovering Masculinity: Reason, Language and Sexuality* (London: Routledge, 1989), pp. 22–43; and R. W. Connell, "A Very Straight Gay: Masculinity, Homosexual Experience, and the Dynamics of Gender," *American Sociological Review* 57 (1992): 735–751. On how heterosexuality as a political institution affects women's lives, see Adrienne Rich, "Compulsory Heterosexuality and Lesbian Existence," *Signs* 5 (1980): 631–660.

12. While some gay men relished the noncompetitiveness and acceptance they experienced at mythopoetic gatherings [see, e.g., Ted Senecal, "Musings of a Man . . . (Gay)," Seattle M.E.N. newsletter, September 1993, pp. 3, 18–19], others found more homophobia and less acceptance. For accounts of the latter, see Gordon Murray, "Homophobia in Robert Bly's *Iron John*," *Masculinities* 1 (1993): 52–54; and Don Shewey, "Stepbrothers: Gays and the Men's Movement," *The Sun*, May 1993, pp. 4–8.

13. It was the men who leaned toward the men's rights perspective who used this kind of language. To them, any word of disparagement by members of one sex for another was an example of sexism. Women's joking about men's foibles or atrocious behavior was thus supposedly just as sexist, and just as unacceptable, as anything some men might do to demean or oppress women. Again there was blindness here to power differences. Women as a group do not have the institutional power to demean, oppress, or exploit men as a group. In the context of male supremacy, women's verbal criticism of men is an act of *resistance*, not sexism. Similarly, blacks may think of whites as evil, and may even be "prejudiced against" whites. But it is perverse to call this racism, since blacks as a group do not have the institutional power to hurt white people. In fact, when blacks do disparage whites, they must do it in the safety of their own communities, lest they become victims of truly racist retaliation.

14. Bert Hoff, "From the Editor," Seattle M.E.N. newsletter, September 1993, p. 2.

15. Wendy Simonds, *Women and Self-Help Culture* (New Brunswick, N.J.: Rutgers University Press, 1992), pp. 76–77. See also Donald Stone, "Social Consciousness in the Human Potential Movement," and Robert Wuthnow, "Political Aspects of the Quietistic Revival," both in T. Robbins and D. Anthony (eds.), *In Gods We Trust: New Patterns of Religious Pluralism in America* (New Brunswick, N.J.: Transaction, 1981).

16. For a version of this talk, see Michael Schwalbe, "Why Mythopoetic Men Don't Flock to NOMAS," *Masculinities* 1 (summer 1993): 68–72.

17. Bly's anti-war credentials were solid, extending back to his efforts in the 1960s to organize poets and writers to oppose the Vietnam War. Of the U.S. role in the Gulf War, Bly said it was "shameful" and "disgusting." He also invoked the image of My Lai to describe the mass killing of retreating Iraqi soldiers by U.S. pilots. Despite Bly's strong anti-war stance, a Seattle men's group reported (Seattle M.E.N. newsletter, September 1991) that in February 1991 the Seattle Coalition for Peace in the Middle East refused to endorse an anti-war "grief walk" to be led by Bly because some members of that group felt Bly was anti-feminist. To some men in the Seattle men's group (David Ault, "Understanding Feminist Objections to Robert Bly," Seattle M.E.N. newsletter, November 1991, p. 2), this was not only an unfair labeling of Bly, but a further example of the irrational, or at least counter-productive, behavior of overly "self-sensitive and angry feminists."

18. This kind of psychologizing was evident in Bly's PBS interview with Bill Moyers ("A Gathering of Men"), in which Bly described Ronald Reagan as having been "in denial" about the federal deficit, and then linked this to Reagan's living in denial about his father's alcoholism. During talk about the Gulf War other mythopoetic teachers and some of the men discussed its causes in terms of nations "projecting their shadows onto each other."

19. Although the Local Group did not sponsor any such events (between 1990 and 1993), elsewhere a few mythopoetic gatherings were organized to be "multicultural." For these events (the first of which was held in May, 1991, in Buffalo Gap, West Virginia) special efforts were made—reducing attendance fees, "affirmative action" recruiting—to bring together men of different racial and ethnic groups. Efforts were also made to include men of color in the pantheon of mythopoetic teachers. By 1992, the most visible of these was Malidoma Somé, who was said to be an initiated Dagara tribesman with Ph.D.'s from the Sorbonne and Brandeis University.

CHAPTER 8 A CRITICAL APPRECIATION

1. Major criticisms of the mythopoetic men can be found in Kay Leigh Hagan (ed.), *Women Respond to the Men's Movement* (San Francisco: HarperCollins, 1992); Kenneth Clatterbaugh, *Contemporary Perspectives on Masculinity* (Boulder, Colo.: Westview, 1990), pp. 85–103; Susan Faludi, *Backlash: The Undeclared War Against American Women* (New York: Crown, 1991), pp. 304–312; R. W. Connell, "Drumming Up the Wrong Tree," *Tikkun* 7, no. 1 (1992): 31–36; Sharon Doubiago, "Enemy of the Mother: A Feminist Response to the Men's Movement," *Ms.*, March/April 1992, pp. 82–85; Fred Pelka, "Robert Bly and Iron John," *On the Issues*, summer 1991, pp. 17–19, 39; Diane Johnson, "Something for the Boys," *New York Review of Books*, 16 January 1992, pp. 13–17; and Jill Johnston, "Why Iron John Is No Gift to Women," *New York Times Book Review*, 23 February 1992, pp. 1, 28–29, 31, 33. See also the special issue of the journal *Masculinities* (summer 1993), which was devoted to profeminist commentary on the mythopoetic men's movement.

2. See Mark Carnes, *Secret Ritual and Manhood in Victorian America* (New Haven, Conn.: Yale University Press, 1989), pp. 32–33. See also note 2 to chapter 4.

3. See Robert N. Bellah, Richard Madson, William M. Sullivan, Ann Swidler, and Steven M. Tipton, *Habits of the Heart: Individualism and Commitment in American Life* (Berkeley, Calif.: University of California Press, 1985); Richard L. Rapson, *Individualism and Conformity in the American Character* (Lexington, Mass.: Heath, 1967); David L. Miller, *Individualism: Personal Achievement and the Open Society* (Austin, Tex.: University of Texas Press, 1967); and Steven Lukes, *Individualism* (New York: Harper & Row, 1967).

4. My point is that therapeutic individualism makes feelings sacrosanct and protects them from interrogation as to their social origins. It is not that therapeutic individualism licenses any kind of behavior stemming from the "true inner self." Behavior that might injure the selves of others is implicitly proscribed It is considered wrong to "violate the [psychic] boundaries" of others. People are thus still expected to exercise judgment and control in *acting* on their feelings, no matter how genuine or powerful those feelings might be.

5. Victor Seidler offers a powerful analysis of how men's emotions are shaped by patriarchy and capitalism. See his *Recreating Sexual Politics* (London: Routledge, 1991), pp. 85–130. Sandra Bartky also examines the relationships between emotion, gender, and the reproduction of inequality in *Femininity and Domination* (New York: Routledge, 1990). For an example of a sociological study of gender and emotions, see Arlie Hochschild, *The Managed Heart* (Berkeley, Calif.: University of California Press, 1983).

6. It is quite possible for individual men to be nice, "sensitive," and nonsexist in interpersonal relations with women, yet do nothing to oppose institutionalized male supremacy and the privileges it bestows on men. On this see Michael Messner, "Changing Men and Feminist Politics in the United States," *Theory and Society* 22 (1993): 723–737.

7. Social psychologists say that self-knowledge comes from three main sources: others' reactions to us; observations of our own behavior and its results; and comparisons we make between ourselves and referent others. Of these sources, people tend to cite others' reactions as the most important (see M. L. Schwalbe and C. L. Staples, "Gender Differences in Sources of Self-Esteem," *Social Psychology Quarterly* [1991] 54: 158–168). The point in the text is that the more different perspectives from which we can reflect on ourselves, the more we can see about ourselves. I would add that self-knowledge also requires a sociological analysis of the *categories* to which we belong and which give us our public identities.

8. Kenneth Clatterbaugh, "Mythopoetic Foundations of New Age Patriarchy," *Masculinities*, summer 1993, pp. 2–12.

9. See the discussion by Demaris Wehr in her *Jung and Feminism: Liberating Archetypes* (Boston: Beacon, 1987), pp. 99–126.

10. See Jane Caputi and Gordene O. MacKenzie, "Pumping Iron John," in Kay Leigh Hagan (ed.), *Women Respond to the Men's Movement* (San Francisco: HarperSanFrancisco, 1992), pp. 69–81.

11. Shepherd Bliss, letter to the editor, *Tikkun* 7 (May/June, 1992): 5.

12. Some men in the Local Group joked about Bly's authority, referring to "the gospel according to Bly," and to things that "must be true, because Robert Bly wrote it." In doing this the men were poking fun both at Bly's pretensions and at those men who took Bly's empirical claims too literally and began to sound like True Believers. Nonetheless, the men still gave immense credibility to Bly's statements about gender and about men's emotional dynamics.

13. In *Iron John* (p. 234) Bly says, "Geneticists have discovered recently that the genetic difference in DNA between men and women amounts to just over three percent.

That isn't much. However the difference exists in every cell of the body." In talks at gatherings Michael Meade would sometimes allude to research that purportedly linked gender differences in psychological functioning to differences in brain structure or testosterone levels. In an essay on sports and the martial spirit, James Hillman also alludes to research linking testosterone to violence ("City, Sport and Violence," *Inroads* #7 [1991]: 10–18). Robert Moore, too, indulged in this, on one occasion claiming that there was "increasing scientific evidence" that males evolved to be less sensitive to pain because males had to defend against predators. These references to physiology and evolution show how the mythopoetic teachers wanted to have it both ways. They wanted license to mythologize or to speak "poetic truth" without being challenged for their dubious empirical claims, yet they also wanted to bolster the credibility of their poetic truths with an occasional glib reference to science.

14. *Dragonsmoke: Newsletter of the Ally Press Center*, November 1993, p. 6.

15. This issue was discussed at the Mendocino Men's Conference (a gathering of mythopoetic men and prominent teachers) held during the summer of 1993, according to one man in the Local Group who attended the conference. The other issues that were discussed, according to the account published in the Local Group newsletter, included "Getting more than one generation into the movement. . . . Enlarging the community so that it is less homogeneous [by] establishing links with women's organizations, working with prison inmates, providing space for gay and bisexual men, and seeking out men of many different races. Negative media treatment of the Men's Movement. . . . Tension between social outreach and inner work. The need for an individual man to be heard."

16. There was some overlap between the profeminist and the mythopoetic men's movements. As noted in chapter 6, some of the men drawn to mythopoetic activity were profeminist in their gender politics, if not overtly so at gatherings. And in the early 1990s, at annual meetings of the staunchly profeminist National Organization for Men Against Sexism (NOMAS), there were a few sessions organized around mythopoetic themes by men who were partisans of the movement and who felt there was no necessary conflict between profeminism and mythopoetic activity. At least one mythopoetic journal—*Mentor* ("about men and their journey of discovery"), published in Portland, Oregon—mixed mythopoetic articles with an occasional profeminist critique.

17. Bly makes this claim in *Iron John* (p. 229), and made it repeatedly in speaking about the "male mode of feeling." See (or rather hear) R. Bly, "The Male Mode of Feeling," audio tape, Oral Traditions Archives (1104 Lincoln Ave., Pacific Grove, Calif. 93950; (408) 373-1110), 1989.

18. Harry Brod, "The Mythopoetic Men's Movement: A Political Critique," in C. Harding (ed.), *Wingspan: Inside the Men's Movement* (New York: St. Martin's, 1992), pp. 232–236. See also H. Brod, "Introduction: Themes and Theses of Men's Studies," in H. Brod (ed.), *The Making of Masculinities* (Boston: Allen & Unwin, 1987), pp. 1–17.

19. Key contemporary works in this tradition of political sociology include G. William Domhoff, *Who Rules America Now?* (New York: Simon and Schuster, 1986); Thomas R. Dye, *Who's Running America?* (Englewood Cliffs, N.J.: Prentice-Hall, 1986); Michael Useem, *The Inner Circle* (New York: Oxford University Press, 1984); and Michael Patrick Allen, *The Founding Fortunes: A New Anatomy of the Super-Rich Families in America* (New York: E. P. Dutton, 1987). A few of the classics are C. W. Mills, *The Power Elite* (New York: Oxford University Press, 1956); E. Digby Baltzell, *Philadelphia Gentlemen: The Making of a National Upper Class* (New York: The Free Press, 1958); and Ferdinand Lundberg, *The Rich and the Super-Rich* (New York: L. Stuart, 1968). This body of research shows that it is entirely possible to identify members of the ruling class and the power

elite. While the gender composition of the ruling (capitalist) class is much the same as that of every other class, all but a few members of the power elite—which consists of those who occupy the highest echelons of the major political, economic, cultural, and military institutions of society—are white males.

20. While the mythopoetic men had democratic impulses and disliked it when teachers assumed too much authority, the men were not radically egalitarian, either. They believed in a need for hierarchy in the concrete world. This was evident in the leadership training programs that sprung up inside the mythopoetic movement. A brochure for one such program described it as intended for "CEO's, administrators, managers, consultants, ministers, politicians, decision-makers, entrepreneurs, heirs apparent, and those who want to expand their capacity for leadership." Part of the training included "techniques for transforming potentially divisive objections into a harmonious flow of directed work, converting that energy to our cause." Trainees would also learn how to "instruct and heal" those people who objected to managerial directives. Perhaps this heavy emphasis on business and on managing dissent was a result of market considerations. The price of these four- and five-day programs ranged from $1,260 to $1,675—affordable for CEO's, administrators, and managers, but somewhat steep (in 1992) for the average community activist.

21. Carol Hanisch, "Men's Liberation," in Kathie Sarachild (ed.), *Feminist Revolution—An Abridged Edition with Additional Writing* (New York: Random House, 1978), p. 76. I first saw this quotation in bell hooks's essay, "Men: Comrades in Struggle," which appears in her book *Feminist Theory: From Margin to Center* (Boston: South End Press, 1984).

22. In a brief response to Harry Brod's socialist-feminist critique of the mythopoetic movement (Brod, ibid.), Robert Bly says, "You say rightly that initiated men today are not and will not be in a position of power in this multinational airstream. I agree with you. To me that doesn't mean that one should abandon the study of initiation, nor abandon the effort to be initiated in our private lives. Your solution—that we should immediately join a political movement to overthrow the capitalistic patriarchal state—to me is highly naive. It belongs with the other habits of the naive male, such as the belief in Walt Disney game parks." This response appears in C. Harding (ed.), *Wingspan: Inside the Men's Movement* (New York: St. Martin's, 1992), p. 236.

23. See Victor Seidler, *Recreating Sexual Politics* (London: Routledge, 1991), especially his chapters on self-denial, morality, emotional life, and therapy.

24. In interviews I asked men in the Local Group to name men they admired. Most often mentioned was Michael Meade. Some men cited other men in the Local Group. Several cited the writer and farmer Wendell Berry.

25. Philip Wexler makes this point in discussing the inability of intellectuals to prevent the rise of fascism in Europe immediately prior to World War II. In this context Wexler quotes Wilhelm Reich: "While we presented the masses with superb historical analyses and economic treatises on the contradictions of imperialism, Hitler stirred the deepest roots of their emotional being." There is a lesson here for both intellectuals and for those who are inclined to be uncritical of emotionally stirring poetic truths. See Wexler, *Critical Social Psychology* (Boston: Routledge & Kegan Paul, 1983), pp. 57–58.

26. A longer autobiographical piece, "The Work of Professing (A Letter to Home)," appears in C.L.B. Dews and C. L. Law (eds.), *This Fine Place So Far From Home: Voices of Academics from the Working-Class* (Philadelphia: Temple University Press, 1995).

BIBLIOGRAPHY

Abbot, Franklin, ed. 1987. *New Men, New Minds: Breaking Male Tradition*. Freedom, Calif.: Crossing Press.

Abraham, Frederick. 1990. *A Visual Introduction to Dynamical Systems Theory for Psychology*. Santa Cruz, Calif.: Aerial Press.

Allan, G. 1985. *Family Life*. New York: Basil Blackwell.

Allen, Michael Patrick. 1987. *The Founding Fortunes: A New Anatomy of the Super-Rich Families in America*. New York: E. P. Dutton.

Astrachan, Anthony. 1986. *How Men Feel*. New York: Anchor.

Baltzell, E. Digby. 1958. *Philadelphia Gentlemen: The Making of a National Upper Class*. New York: The Free Press.

Barks, Coleman. 1990. "Scrimshaw." Introduction to *Delicious Laughter: Rambunctious Teaching Stories from the Mathnawi of Jelaluddin Rumi*, (versions by Coleman Barks), pp. x-xii.. Athens, Ga.: Maypop.

Bartky, Sandra. 1990. *Femininity and Domination*. New York: Routledge.

Barz, Helmut. 1991. *For Men, Too: A Grateful Critique of Feminism*. Wilmette, Ill.: Chiron.

Baumli, Francis, ed. 1985. *Men Freeing Men*. Jersey City, N.J.: New Atlantis.

Beck, Renee, and Metrick, Sydney Barbara. 1990. *The Art of Ritual: A Guide to Creating and Performing Your Own Ceremonies for Growth and Change*. Berkeley, Calif.: Celestial Arts.

Becker, Howard S. 1963. *Outsiders: Studies in the Sociology of Deviance.* New York: The Free Press.

Bell, Catherine. 1992. *Ritual Theory, Ritual Practice.* New York: Oxford University Press.

Bellah, Robert; Madson, Richard; Sullivan, William M.; Swidler, Ann; and Tipton, Steven M. 1985. *Habits of the Heart: Individualism and Commitment in American Life.* Berkeley, Calif.: University of California Press.

Bem, Sandra. 1981. "Gender Schema Theory: A Cognitive Account of Sex Typing." *Psychological Review* 88: 354–364.

———. 1987. "Masculinity and Femininity Exist Only in the Mind of the Perceiver." In *Masculinity/Femininity: Basic Perspectives*, pp. 304–311. Edited by M. Reinisch, L. A. Rosenblum, and S. A. Sanders. New York: Oxford University Press.

Bendix, Reinhard, and Lipset, S.M., eds. 1966. *Class, Status, and Power.* New York: The Free Press.

Bliss, Shepherd. 1986. "Beyond Machismo: The New Men's Movement." *Yoga Journal*, Nov.–Dec., pp. 36–40, 56–58.

Blumstein, Phil, and Schwartz, Pepper. 1983. *American Couples.* New York: William Morrow.

Bly, Robert. 1976. "Being a Lutheran Boy-God in Minnesota." *Growing Up in Minnesota*, pp. 205–219. Edited by Chester Anderson. Minneapolis, Minn.: University of Minnesota Press.

———. 1990. *Iron John: A Book About Men.* Reading, Mass.: Addison-Wesley.

Bly, Robert; Hillman, James; and Meade, Michael, eds. 1992. *The Rag and Bone Shop of the Heart.* New York: HarperCollins.

Bottigheimer, Ruth. 1987. *Grimms' Bad Girls and Bold Boys: The Moral and Social Vision of the Tales.* New Haven, Conn.: Yale University Press.

Brittan, Arthur. 1989. *Masculinity and Power.* New York: Basil Blackwell.

Brod, Harry. 1987. "Introduction: Themes and Theses of Men's Studies." In *The Making of Masculinities*, pp. 1–17. Edited by Harry Brod. Boston: Allen & Unwin.

———. 1989. "Work Clothes and Leisure Suits: The Class Basis and Bias of the Men's Movement." In *Men's Lives*, pp. 276–287. Edited by Michael Kimmel and Michael Messner. New York: Macmillan.

———. 1992. "The Mythopoetic Men's Movement: A Political Critique." In *Wingspan: Inside the Men's Movement*, pp. 232–236. Edited by Chris Harding. New York: St. Martin's.

———, ed. 1987. *The Making of Masculinities.* Boston: Allen & Unwin.

Brown, Joseph Epes, recorder and editor. 1953. *The Sacred Pipe: Black Elk's Account of the Seven Rites of the Oglala Sioux.* Norman, Okla.: University of Oklahoma Press.

Buber, Martin. 1965. *The Knowledge of Man: Selected Essays.* Edited by Maurice Freedman. New York: Harper & Row.

Cahill, Spencer. 1989. "Fashioning Males and Females: Appearance Management and the Reproduction of Gender." *Symbolic Interaction* 12: 281–298.

Caputi, Jane, and MacKenzie, Gordene O. 1992. "Pumping Iron John." In *Women Respond to the Men's Movement*, pp. 69–81. Edited by Kay Leigh Hagan. San Francisco: HarperSanFrancisco.

Carnes, Mark. 1989. *Secret Ritual and Manhood in Victorian America.* New Haven, Conn.: Yale University Press.

Clatterbaugh, Kenneth. 1990. *Contemporary Perspectives on Masculinity.* Boulder, Colo.: Westview.

————. 1993. "Mythopoetic Foundations of New Age Patriarchy." *Masculinities* 1 (summer): 2–12.

Connell, R. W. 1987. *Gender and Power.* Stanford, Calif.: Stanford University Press.

————. 1991. "Drumming Up the Wrong Tree." In *Tikkun* 7: 31–36.

————. 1992. "A Very Straight Gay: Masculinity, Homosexual Experience, and the Dynamics of Gender." *American Sociological Review* 57: 735–751.

Corbin, Henry. 1969. *Creative Imagination in the Sufism of Ibn Arabi.* Princeton, N.J.: Princeton University Press.

Deaux, K. 1985. "Sex and Gender." *Annual Review of Psychology* 36: 49–81.

Della Fave, L. Richard. 1980. "The Meek Shall Not Inherit the Earth: Self-Evaluation and the Legitimacy of Stratification." *American Sociological Review* 45: 955–971.

Dohrenwend, B., et al., eds. 1980. *Mental Health in the United States: Epidemiological Estimates.* New York: Praeger.

Domhoff, G. William. 1986. *Who Rules America Now?* New York: Simon and Schuster.

Doyle, Richard. 1976. *The Rape of the Male.* St. Paul, Minn.: Poor Richard's Press.

Dubiago, Sharon. 1992. "Enemy of the Mother: A Feminist Response to the Men's Movement." *Ms.*, March/April, pp. 82–85.

Dye, Thomas R. 1986. *Who's Running America?* Englewood Cliffs, N.J.: Prentice-Hall.

Ehrenreich, Barbara. 1983. *The Hearts of Men: American Dreams and the Flight From Commitment.* Garden City, N.Y.: Anchor.

Eisenstein, Zillah. 1979. *Capitalist Patriarchy and the Case for Socialist Feminism.* New York: Monthly Review Press.

Eller, Cynthia. 1993. *Living in the Lap of the Goddess.* New York: Crossroad.

Epstein, Cynthia Fuchs. 1988. *Deceptive Distinctions.* New York: Russell Sage.

Estes, Clarissa Pinkola. 1992. *Women Who Run With the Wolves: Myths and Stories of the Wild Woman Archetype.* New York: Ballantine.

Faludi, Susan. 1991. *Backlash: The Undeclared War Against Women.* New York: Crown.

Farrell, Warren. 1975. *The Liberated Man.* New York: Random House.

Fasteau, Marc Feigen. 1975. *The Male Machine.* New York: Dell.

Fausto-Sterling, Anne. 1985. *Myths of Gender.* New York: Basic.

Fordham, Frieda. 1966. *An Introduction to Jung's Psychology.* New York: Penguin.

Foreman, Ann. 1977. *Femininity as Alienation.* London: Pluto.

Gamson, William. 1992. "The Social Psychology of Collective Action." In *Frontiers in Social Movement Theory*, pp. 53–76. Edited by A. Morris and C. M. Mueller. New Haven, Conn.: Yale University Press.

Gates, David. 1993. "White Male Paranoia." *Newsweek* (March 29): 48–53.

Gecas, Viktor, and Burke, Peter. 1994. "Self and Identity." In *Sociological Perspectives on Psychology*, pp. 41–67. Edited by K. Cook, G. A. Fine, and J. House. Boston: Allyn and Bacon.

Gilbert, Richard. 1992. "Revisiting the Psychology of Men: Robert Bly and the Mytho-Poetic Movement." *Journal of Humanistic Psychology* 32: 41–67.

Gilligan, Carol. 1982. *In a Different Voice.* Cambridge, Mass.: Harvard University Press.

Gilmore, David. 1991. *Manhood in the Making.* New Haven, Conn.: Yale University Press.

Goffman, Erving. 1955. "Face Work: An Analysis of Ritual Elements in Social Interaction." *Psychiatry* 18: 213–231.

————. 1959. *The Presentation of Self in Everyday Life.* New York: Anchor.

————. 1961. *Encounters: Two Studies in the Sociology of Interaction.* New York: Bobbs-Merrill.

————. 1963. *Stigma: Notes on the Management of Spoiled Identity*. Englewood Cliffs, N.J.: Prentice-Hall.

————. 1967. *Interaction Ritual*. New York: Pantheon.

Goldberg, Herb. 1976. *The Hazards of Being Male*. New York: Penguin.

Goldenberg, Naomi. 1975. "Archetypal Theory After Jung." *Spring: An Annual of Archetypal Psychology and Jungian Thought* 199–220.

————. 1976. "A Feminist Critique of Jung." *Signs* 2: 443–449.

Hagan, Kay Leigh, ed. 1992. *Women Respond to the Men's Movement*. San Francisco: HarperSanFrancisco.

Hall, Calvin, and Nordby, Vernon. 1973. *A Primer of Jungian Psychology*. New York: Mentor.

Hanisch, Carol. 1978. "Men's Liberation." In *Feminist Revolution—An Abridged Edition with Additional Writing*, pp. 72–76. Edited by Kathie Sarachild. New York: Random House.

Hankin, Janet R. 1990. "Gender and Mental Illness." *Research in Community and Mental Health* 6: 183–201.

Harding, Chris, ed. 1992. *Wingspan:Inside the Men's Movement*. New York: St. Martin's.

Harrison, J.; Chin, J.; and Ficarrotto, T. 1989. "Warning: Masculinity May Be Dangerous to Your Health." In *Men's Lives*, pp. 296–309. Edited by Michael Kimmel and Michael Messner. New York: Macmillan.

Hartsock, Nancy. 1983. *Money, Sex, and Power: Toward a Feminist Historical Materialism*. Boston: Northeastern University Press.

Herdt, Gilbert. 1987. *The Sambia: Ritual and Gender in New Guinea*. New York: Holt, Rinehart and Winston.

Herek, G. 1984. "Beyond 'Homophobia': A Social Psychological Perspective on Attitudes Toward Lesbians and Gay Men." *Journal of Homosexuality* 10: 1–21.

Hewitt, John. 1989. *Dilemmas of the American Self*. Philadelphia: Temple University Press.

Hill, Gareth S. 1992. *Masculine and Feminine: The Natural Flow of Opposites in the Psyche*. Boston: Shambhala.

Hillman, James. 1967. *Insearch: Psychology and Religion*. Dallas: Spring.

————. 1972. *The Myth of Analysis: Three Essays in Archetypal Psychology*. New York: Harper & Row.

————. 1983. *Inter Views*. Dallas: Spring.

————. 1983. *Archetypal Psychology: A Brief Account*. Dallas: Spring.

————. 1985. *Anima: An Anatomy of a Personified Notion*. Dallas: Spring.

————. 1989. *A Blue Fire: Selected Writings by James Hillman*. New York: Harper & Row.

Hillman, James, and Ventura, Michael. 1992. *We've Had a Hundred Years of Psychotherapy—And the World's Getting Worse*. New York: HarperCollins.

Hochschild, Arlie. 1983. *The Managed Heart*. Berkeley, Calif.: University of California Press.

Hochschild, Arlie. 1989. *The Second Shift*. New York: Viking.

hooks, bell. 1984. *Feminist Theory: From Margin to Center*. Boston: South End Press.

Johnson, Diane. 1992. "Something for the Boys." *New York Review of Books* (January 16): 13–17.

Johnston, Jill. 1992. "Why Iron John Is No Gift to Women." *New York Times Book Review* (February 23): 1, 28–29, 31, 33.

Jung, Carl G. 1956. *Two Essays on Analytical Psychology*. New York: Meridian.

————. 1958. *Psychology and Religion: West and East*. Princeton, N.J.: Princeton University Press.

———. 1959. *The Undiscovered Self.* New York: Mentor.

———. 1961. *Memories, Dreams, Reflections.* New York: Vintage.

———. 1982. *Aspects of the Feminine.* Princeton, N.J.: Princeton University Press.

Jung, Carl G., and Wilhelm, Richard. 1962. *Secret of the Golden Flower.* New York: Harcourt, Brace and World.

Kaminer, Wendy. 1992. *I'm OK, You're Dysfunctional.* Reading, Mass.: Addison-Wesley.

Kaufman, Michael, ed. 1987. *Beyond Patriarchy.* Toronto: Oxford University Press.

Keen, Sam. 1991. *Fire in the Belly.* New York: Bantam.

Kessler, Suzanne, and McKenna, Wendy. 1978. *Gender: An Ethnomethodological Approach.* Chicago: University of Chicago Press.

Killian, Lewis. 1985. "The Stigma of Race: Who Now Bears the Mark of Cain?" *Symbolic Interaction* 8: 1–14.

Kimmel, Michael, and Messner, Michael, eds. 1992. *Men's Lives.* 2d ed. New York: Macmillan.

Kipnis, Aaron. 1991. *Knights Without Armor: A Practical Guide for Men in Quest of Masculine Soul.* New York: Jeremy Tarcher.

Klapp, Orrin. 1969. *Collective Search for Identity.* New York: Holt, Rinehart and Winston.

Koss, M., Gidycz, C., and Wisniewski, N. 1987. "The Scope of Rape: Incidence and Prevalence of Sexual Aggression in a Sample of Higher Education Students." *Journal of Consulting and Clinical Psychology* 55: 162–170.

Kupers, Terry A. 1993. *Revisioning Men's Lives: Gender, Intimacy and Power.* New York: Guilford.

Kurdek, L. 1988. "Correlates of Negative Attitudes Toward Homosexuals in Heterosexual College Students." *Sex Roles* 18: 727–738.

Landau, R. 1959. *The Philosophy of Ibn Arabi.* London: Allen & Unwin.

Lefever, Harry G. 1981. "Playing the Dozens: A Mechanism for Social Control." *Phylon* 42: 73–85.

Lehne, G. 1989. "Homophobia Among Men." In *Men's Lives*, pp. 416–429. Edited by Michael Kimmel and Michael Messner. New York: Macmillan.

Lichterman, Paul. 1989. "Making a Politics of Masculinity." *Comparative Social Research* 11: 185–208.

Liebman, Wayne. 1991. *Tending the Fire.* St. Paul, Minn.: Ally.

Link, Bruce. 1982. "Mental Patient Status, Work, and Income: An Examination of the Effects of a Psychiatric Label." *American Sociological Review* 47: 202–215.

Lukes, Steven. 1967. *Individualism.* New York: Harper and Row.

Lundberg, Ferdinand. 1968. *The Rich and the Super-Rich.* New York: L. Stuart.

Maccoby, Michael. 1967. *The Gamesman.* New York: Bantam.

McCallion, Michael. 1992. "The Satanism Scare or the Antisatanism Scare." *Symbolic Interaction* 15: 237–240.

McMahon, Martha. 1995. *Engendering Motherhood: Identity and Self-Transformation in Women's Lives.* New York: Guilford.

Melucci, Alberto. 1989. *Nomads of the Present: Social Movements and Individual Needs in Contemporary Society.* Philadelphia: Temple University Press.

Messner, Michael. 1993. "Changing Men and Feminist Politics in the United States." *Theory and Society* 22: 723–737.

Miller, David L. 1967. *Individualism: Personal Achievement and the Open Society.* Austin, Tex.: University of Texas Press.

Mills, C.W. 1956. *The Power Elite.* New York: Oxford University Press.

Mitscherlich, Alexander. 1969. *Society Without the Father*. New York: Harcourt, Brace and World.

Mitzman, Arthur. 1970. *The Iron Cage: An Historical Interpretation of Max Weber*. New York: Knopf.

Mol, Hans. 1976. *Identity and the Sacred*. New York: The Free Press.

Monick, Eugene. 1987. *Phallos: Sacred Image of the Masculine*. Toronto: Inner City Books.

Moore, Robert, and Gillette, Douglas. 1990. *King, Warrior, Magician, Lover: Rediscovering the Archetypes of the Mature Masculine*. New York: HarperCollins.

Morgan, David H. J. 1992. *Discovering Men*. London: Routledge.

Morgan, Robin. 1969. "Goodbye to All That." In *Masculine/Feminine: Readings in Sexual Mythology and the Liberation of Women*, edited by B. Roszak and T. Roszak, pp. 241–250. New York: Random House.

Morgan, Robin, ed. 1970. *Sisterhood Is Powerful*. New York: Random House.

Morin, S. F., and Garfinkle, E. M. 1978. "Male Homophobia." *Journal of Social Issues* 34: 29–47.

Morrow, Lance. 1991. "The Child is the Father of the Man." *Time* (August 19): 52–54.

Murray, Gordon. 1993. "Homophobia in Robert Bly's *Iron John*." *Masculinities* 1 (summer): 52–54.

Pelka, Fred. 1991. "Robert Bly and Iron John." *On the Issues* (summer): 17–19, 39.

Pleck, Joseph, and Sawyer, Jack, eds. 1974. *Men and Masculinity*. Englewood Cliffs, N.J.: Prentice-Hall.

Powers, William K. 1977. *Oglala Religion*. Lincoln, Neb.: University of Nebraska Press.

Rapson, Richard L. 1967. *Individualism and Conformity in the American Character*. Lexington, Mass.: Heath.

Reskin, B., and Padavic, I. 1994. *Women and Men at Work*. Thousand Oaks, Calif.: Pine Forge.

Retherford, R. 1972. "Tobacco Smoking and the Sex Mortality Differential." *Demography* 9: 203–216.

Rhode, D. L. 1990. *Theoretical Perspectives on Sexual Difference*. New Haven, Conn.: Yale University Press.

Rich, Adrienne. 1980. "Compulsory Heterosexuality and Lesbian Existence." *Signs* 5: 631–660.

Rieff, David. 1991. "Victims All? Recovery, Co-Dependency, and the Art of Blaming Somebody Else." *Harper's* (October): 49–56.

Robbins, T., and Anthony, D., eds. 1981. *In Gods We Trust: New Patterns of Religious Pluralism in America*. New Brunswick, N.J.: Transaction.

Roberts, Elizabeth, and Amidon, Elias, eds. 1991. *Earth Prayers from Around the World*. New York: HarperCollins.

Robinson, Marilyn. 1993. "Hearing Silence: Western Myth Reconsidered." In *The True Subject*, edited by Kurt Brown, pp. 135–151. St. Paul, Minn.: Graywolf.

Rossi, Ernest Lawrence. 1992. "What is Life? From Quantum Flux to the Self." *Psychological Perspectives* 26: 6–22.

Rowan, John. 1987. *The Horned God: Feminism and Men as Wounding and Healing*. London: Routledge.

Rowbotham, Sheila. 1973. *Woman's Consciousness, Man's World*. Middlesex, England: Penguin.

Samuels, Andrew. 1985. *Jung and the Post-Jungians*. London: Routledge and Kegan Paul.

———. 1992. "Men Under Scrutiny." *Psychological Perspectives* 26: 42–61.

Sanday, P. R., and Goodenough, R. G., eds. 1990. *Beyond the Second Sex: New Directions in the Anthropology of Gender.* Philadelphia: University of Pennsylvania Press.

Satin, Mark. 1979. *New Age Politics: Healing Self and Society.* New York: Dell.

Scheff, Thomas. 1966. *Being Mentally Ill: A Sociological Theory.* Chicago: Aldine.

Schifellite, Carmen. 1987. "Beyond Tarzan and Jane Genes: Toward a Critique of Biological Determinism." In *Beyond Patriarchy: Essays by Men on Pleasure, Power, and Change,* edited by Michael Kaufman, pp. 45–63. New York: Oxford University Press.

Schimmel, Annemarie. 1992. *I Am Wind, You Are Fire: The Life and Work of Rumi.* Boston: Shambhala.

Schwalbe, Michael. 1988. "Role Taking Reconsidered: Linking Competence and Performance to Social Structure." *Journal for the Theory of Social Behavior* 18: 413–436.

———. 1992. "Male Supremacy and the Narrowing of the Moral Self." *Berkeley Journal of Sociology* 37: 29–54.

———. 1993. "Why Mythopoetic Men Don't Flock to NOMAS." *Masculinities* 1 (summer): 68–72.

———. 1995. "The Work of Professing (A Letter to Home)." In *This Fine Place So Far From Home: Voices of Academics from the Working-Class,* edited by C. L. B. Dews and C. L. Law, pp. 309–331. Philadelphia: Temple University Press.

Schwalbe, M. L., and Staples, C. L. 1991. "Gender Differences in Sources of Self-Esteem." *Social Psychology Quarterly* 54: 158–168.

Scully, D., and Marolla, J. 1984. "Convicted Rapists' Vocabulary of Motive: Excuses and Justifications." *Social Problems* 31: 530–544.

Segal, Lynne. 1990. *Slow Motion: Changing Masculinities, Changing Men.* New Brunswick, N.J.: Rutgers.

Seidler, Victor. 1989. *Rediscovering Masculinity.* London: Routledge.

———. 1991. *Recreating Sexual Politics.* London: Routledge.

Sellery, J'nan Morse. 1990. "Gender: Crossing Mental Barriers and Cultural Boundaries." *Psychological Perspectives* 23: 6–15.

Shah, Idries. 1968. *The Way of the Sufi.* New York: Arkana.

Shakarchi, Joseph. 1982. "An Interview with Robert Bly." *Massachusetts Review* 23: 226–243.

Shewey, Don. 1992. "Town Meeting in the Hearts of Men." *Village Voice* (February 11): 36–42, 45–46.

———. 1993. "Stepbrothers: Gays and the Men's Movement." *The Sun* (May): 4–8.

Simonds, Wendy. 1992. *Women and Self-Help Culture.* New Brunswick, N.J.: Rutgers University Press.

Snodgrass, Jon, ed. 1977. *For Men Against Sexism.* Albion, Calif.: Times Change Press.

Snodgrass, S. E. 1985. "Women's Intuition: The Effect of Subordinate Status on Interpersonal Sensitivity." *Journal of Personality and Social Psychology* 49: 146–155.

Snow, David, and Anderson, Leon. 1987. "Identity Work among the Homeless: The Verbal Construction and Avowal of Personal Identities." *American Journal of Sociology* 92: 1336–1371.

Starhawk. 1979. *The Spiral Dance: A Rebirth of the Ancient Religion of the Great Goddess.* New York: HarperCollins.

Steinem, Gloria. 1992. *Revolution from Within: A Book of Self-Esteem.* Boston: Little, Brown & Company.

Stoltenberg, John. 1989. *Refusing to be a Man: Essays on Sex and Justice.* New York: Meridian.

———. 1993. *The End of Manhood: A Book for Men of Conscience.* New York: Dutton.

Straton, Jack. 1991. "Where Are the Ethics in Men's Spirituality?" *Changing Men* (fall/winter): 10–12.

Strauss, Anselm. 1959. *Mirrors and Masks: The Search for Identity.* Glencoe, Ill.: The Free Press.

Sugg, Richard P. 1986. *Robert Bly.* Boston: Twayne.

Tatar, Maria. 1987. *The Hard Facts of the Grimms' Fairy Tales.* Princeton, N.J.: Princeton University Press.

Tavris, Carol. 1992. *The Mismeasure of Woman.* New York: Simon and Schuster.

Thomas, D.; Franks, D.; and Calonico, J. 1972. "Role-Taking and Power in Social Psychology." *American Sociological Review* 37: 605–614.

Thompson, Keith. 1982. "What Men Really Want." *New Age Journal* (May): 30–37, 50–51.

Tolson, Andrew. 1977. *The Limits of Masculinity: Male Identity and Women's Liberation.* New York: Harper & Row.

Treiman, Dennis. 1977. *Occupational Prestige in Comparative Perspective.* New York: Academic Press.

Turner, Victor. 1969. *The Ritual Process.* Ithaca, N.Y.: Cornell University Press.

Ventura, Michael. 1992. "Possibilities of Ritual: Walking with Michael Meade." *L.A. Weekly* (Jan. 17–23): 10–12.

Waldron, I. 1983. "Sex Differences in Illness Incidence, Prognosis, and Mortality: Issues and Evidence." *Social Science and Medicine* 17: 1107–1123.

Weber, Max. [1904–05] 1930. *The Protestant Ethic and the Spirit of Capitalism.* New York: Scribners.

Wehr, Demaris. 1987. *Jung and Feminism: Liberating Archetypes.* Boston: Beacon.

Weigert, Andrew; Teitge, J. Smith; and Teitge, Dennis W. 1986. *Society and Identity: Toward a Sociological Psychology.* New York: Cambridge University Press.

Weiss, Robert. 1990. *Staying the Course: The Emotional and Social Lives of Men Who Do Well at Work.* New York: Fawcett Columbia.

West, Candace, and Zimmerman, Don. 1987. "Doing Gender." *Gender and Society* 1: 125–151.

Wexler, Philip. 1983. *Critical Social Psychology.* Boston: Routledge and Kegan Paul.

Whitmont, Edward. 1981. "Reassessing Femininity and Masculinity: A Restatement of Some Jungian Positions." *Anima* 7: 125–139.

———. 1991. *The Symbolic Quest: Basic Concepts of Analytical Psychology.* Princeton, N.J.: Princeton University Press.

Young-Eisendrath, Polly. 1984. *Hags and Heroes: A Feminist Approach to Jungian Psychotherapy with Couples.* Toronto: Inner City Books.

Zukav, G. 1979. *The Dancing Wu-Li Masters.* New York: Morrow.

Zurcher, Louis. 1982. "The Staging of Emotion: A Dramaturgical Analysis." *Symbolic Interaction* 5: 1–22.

———. 1985. "The War Game: Organizational Scripting and the Expression of Emotion." *Symbolic Interaction* 8: 191–206.

Zweig, Connie. 1992. "The Conscious Feminine: The Birth of a New Archetype." *Anima* 18: 5–12.

INDEX